WITHDRAWN FROM CLARK UNIVERSITY
LIBRARY

AMERICAN ANTI-NAZI RESISTANCE, 1933–1941

An Historical Analysis

AMERICAN ANTI-NAZI RESISTANCE, 1933–1941

An Historical Analysis

by

Moshe R. Gottlieb

KTAV PUBLISHING HOUSE, INC.
NEW YORK
1982

© Copyright 1982
Moshe R. Gottlieb

Library of Congress Cataloging in Publication Data

Gottlieb, Moshe R. (Moshe Raphael)
  American anti-Nazi resistance, 1933-1941.

  Bibliography: p.
  Includes index.
  1. Jews—United States—Politics and government.
2. Anti-Nazi movement—United States. 3. Jews—
Germany—History—1933-1945. 4. United States—
Ethnic relations. I. Title.
E184.J5G675   305.8'924'073   81-8144
ISBN 0-87068-889-8   AACR2

Manufactured in the United States of America

To
Ziporah A. Gottlieb

Contents

PREFACE	xi
ACKNOWLEDGMENTS	xv
KEY TO ABBREVIATIONS	xvii
INTRODUCTION: The Rise of American Jewish Defense Agencies	xix

PART I: 1933: REACTION IN GERMANY

CHAPTER 1: The Triumph of Nazism — 3
  The Rise of Adolf Hitler to Power
  Incipient Anti-Jewish Excesses
  The Post-Election Frenzy

CHAPTER 2: Nazi Roots — 9
  Teutomania and Antisemitism

CHAPTER 3: The First of April Boycott — 15
  A Day of National Affliction

PART II: 1933: THE REACTION OF THE AMERICAN JEWISH COMMUNITY

CHAPTER 4: The Policy of Public Protest — 27

CHAPTER 5: The Policies of Public Enlightenment and Diplomatic Representation — 35

CHAPTER 6: The Incipient Boycott — 45
  JWV Rumblings
  The Birth of the American League for the Defense of Jewish Rights
  European Liaison
  The Advent of Samuel Untermyer
  Press Reception

CHAPTER 7: The Committee and the Boycott — 59

CHAPTER 8: Congress Activities: Prelude to Boycott — 65
  The Giant Demonstration March
  The Washington Emergency Session

CHAPTER 9: The Jewish World Economic Conference 71
CHAPTER 10: Joining Battle 76
CHAPTER 11: Continued Committee Intransigence 83
CHAPTER 12: The Boycott in the Transnational Jewish Arena: 86
    The Eighteenth Zionist Congress
    The Transfer Agreement
    The World Jewish Conference

CHAPTER 13: The Last Months of ALDJR 97
    The National Boycott Conference
    Blueprint for Boycott
    First Major Engagement
    Three Personal Letters
    The Attitude of All Large New York Stores
    An Open Letter
    The Dissolution of the American League for the Defense of Jewish Rights

PART III: 1934–1937: CONSOLIDATION AND EXPANSION

CHAPTER 14: The Boycott Committee of the American Jewish Congress 125
    Preliminary Stage
    Macy's Surrender
    The Good-Will Fair

CHAPTER 15: At the World Jewish Conference 143
    Boycott Reaffirmation
    Conference Reverberations

CHAPTER 16: Legal Activities 153
    ANL Phase

CHAPTER 17: The Non-Sectarian World Conference 159

CHAPTER 18: The Phase of Decline 163

CHAPTER 19: Renewed Boycott Unity Quest 169

CHAPTER 20: The Birth of the Joint Boycott Council 176
    The Jewish Labor Committee

A.J.C.-JLC Relations
The Berlin Riots
BC-JLC Negotiations

CHAPTER 21: Last Major Boycott Unity Quest — 191

CHAPTER 22: Legal Activities — 197
JBC Phase

CHAPTER 23: The JBC and the U.S. Post Office — 204

CHAPTER 24: The Opening of the World Jewish Congress — 210

CHAPTER 25: Boycott Enforcement: Picketing — 213
Picketing
Pressure and Persuasion
Radio
Department Store Vigil
The Furriery Scandal
The 1936 Olympics Episode
Boxing

PART IV: 1938–1939: PRELUDE TO WAR
A. THE DRIVE FOR LEBENSRAUM

CHAPTER 26: Incipients of Nazi Expansion: From Vienna to Munich to Prague — 241

CHAPTER 27: The Worsening Jewish Plight — 245

CHAPTER 28: The Swelling Refugee Problem: From Departure to Flight — 250
The Evian Conference
Two Ransom Plans: Rublee vs. Schacht

B. THE RESPONSE IN AMERICA

CHAPTER 29: The Growing Resentment of American Public Opinion — 261
The Increase in Boycott Sentiment
The Founding of the Volunteer Christian Committee
The Coordinated Boycott Committee
League Aloofness

CHAPTER 30: Contra Ransom — 274

CHAPTER 31: Legal Activity and Department Store Vigil Bill HR 8099 Sears and Woolworth	285
PART V: 1939–1941: IN WAR	
CHAPTER 32: The Joint Boycott Council The Crisis of Obsolescence	293
CHAPTER 33: Boycott and Embargo Neutrality and Boycott The Moral Embargo Campaign Supplemental Arm	297
CHAPTER 34: The Jewelry Industry Vigil	307
CHAPTER 35: The Food Packages Issue: Racket and Controversy	313
CHAPTER 36: Latin American Activities First Phase Second Phase Third Phase	322
SUMMARY AND CONCLUSIONS	341
NOTES	350
DOCUMENTS	378
BIBLIOGRAPHY	415
INDEX	
I. Names, Organizations, and Places	417
II. Components of Boycott Organizations	425

Preface

i.

This book is an historical and ideological study of a resistance movement against the Nazis, their theoretical ideas, as well as their pernicious teachings and brutal practices. However, the general framework within which this study is presented is the anti-Nazi boycott movement conducted in America from 1933 to 1941. But this is not all.

The work also renders a descriptive account of the anti-Nazi protest movement which preceded the rise of organized boycott action. It stresses the anti-Hitlerian denunciations in the United States which resulted from increasing and intensifying anti-Jewish rumblings and actions in the newly emergent Nazi state. Emphasis is also placed on the more reserved policy of public enlightenment, as well as on the path of effective diplomatic representation. In short, various opposition media, other than the boycott, are delineated in order to help complete the picture of a growing *anti-Nazi resistance movement in the United States*.

The spark that ignited America's anti-Nazi boycott movement was Germany's nationwide boycott of its Jews on April 1, 1933. Jews reciprocated spontaneously in kind on a worldwide basis, the response being strongest in Poland, Great Britain, and America. In America, owing to its important commercial ties with Germany, and because it contained the largest and most powerful Jewish community on earth, the anti-Nazi boycott movement developed most auspiciously and proved most threatening and menacing.

The first established group in the United States to declare a boycott against the Nazis was the American Jewish War Veterans (JWV). It was followed by the American League for the Defense of Jewish Rights (ALDJR), an organization formed in May 1933 as a result of the unabating Nazi threat. The last and largest of America's Jewish defense organizations to adopt the budding boycott movement was the American Jewish Congress (A.J.C.). It joined battle in August 1933, followed by the creation of a Congress Boycott Committee.

The American League for the Defense of Jewish Rights was barely half a year old when its name was changed to the Non-Sectarian Anti-Nazi League to Champion Human Rights (NSANL or ANL). Some months later, also as an express result of the Nazi threat, the Jewish Labor Committee (JLC), claiming to represent around half a million American Jewish workers, was formed and immediately initiated a boycott program against Hitler Germany. Two years later—in 1936—that organization's central body for boycott activities combined with the Boycott Committee of the American Jewish Congress to form the Joint Boycott Council (JBC).

The League and the Council were America's two principal boycott organizations. The Jewish War Veterans and additional anti-Nazi groups that arose in the latter part of the 1930s cooperated with or actually joined these two boycott organizations. But various endeavors to unite the League and the Council proved unsuccessful. The two groups continued to maintain their separate existence and functions, successfully acting in unison at times, but never really uniting.

ii.

At least for the first two years of their rule, there is direct and indirect evidence that the Nazis feared that an air-tight boycott would actually cripple their economy.* However, Hitler's ensuing political victories, especially his "bloodless" conquests, made such an eventuality more and more remote. But after war broke out, the entry of each contentious country into hostilities against the Nazis replaced the use of economic pressures as means of attaining world supremacy.

In America, though a nonbelligerent until Japan's crippling attack on Pearl Harbor on December 7, 1941, the boycott was continued as a measure of self-defense and moral protest, as well as an instrument of economic and political pressure, until October 15 of that year. It was two years to the day from the time when the JBC office had first been scheduled for liquidation.

The author does not claim to possess the kind of knowledge required for making professional value judgments concerning an economic boycott as such. But wherever such assertions are actually made, they are ascribed to others. And to the extent that the anti-Nazi boycott was able to operate independently of the American Jewish Congress, the parent organization of the Boycott Committee, such an operation is delineated. Otherwise, particular emphasis and attention are given to the overall

---

*See, for example, pp. 344–46.

framework within which anti-Nazi boycott activities were structured and actually functioned. However, what is probably equally important to bear in mind is the ideological approach to this subject; namely, the search by the several boycott organizations for a legal but effective means for putting an end to the brutal and barbarous Nazi regime.

Reference is also made to the supposed effectiveness of the American anti-Nazi boycott movement. But the writer makes no claim whatsoever of being professionally qualified to assess and evaluate this medium of economic pressure. He does, however, depict such judgment insofar as the actual claims of the boycott leaders themselves are concerned. And occasionally, he reserves for himself the right to make critical judgments of events and people involved in the American anti-Nazi boycott movement.

The main leaders of this movement were Col. Morris J. Mendelson, erstwhile commander of the Jewish War Veterans; Dr. Abraham Coralnik, associate editor of the Yiddish daily, *Der Tog* (The Day), and first head of the American Anti-Nazi League's Provisional Boycott Committee; Samuel Untermyer, one-time vice-president of the American Jewish Congress, who soon became the main figure of the American League for the Defense of Jewish Rights, which name was, before long, changed to the Non-Sectarian Anti-Nazi League to Champion Human Rights; Dr. Joseph L. Tenenbaum, former chairman of the National Executive Committee of the American Jewish Congress; Baruch C. Vladeck, editor of the Yiddish daily, *Der Vorvertz*, (the Jewish Daily Forward) and chairman of the Jewish Labor Committee (JLC); William Green, president of the American Federation of Labor (A. F. of L.); Dr. William Jay Schieffelin, New York City civic leader and chairman of the Volunteer Christian Committee to Boycott Nazi Germany (VCC); Dr. Marie Emma Wooley, educator and past president of Mount Holyoke College. She headed the American Boycott Against Aggressor Nations (ABAAN), which pursued a policy of boycott against the three Axis powers. In 1939, VCC and ABAAN united with the JBC to form the Coordinated Boycott Committee (CBC), which was chaired by Dr. Schieffelin.

The main sources that were used in this work are: the general Anglo-Jewish and Yiddish press; the archives of the Non-Sectarian Anti-Nazi League to Champion Human Rights, records of the Joint Boycott Council, the Jewish Labor Committee, the American Jewish Committee (AJC) and the Yiddish Scientific Institute (YIVO); the American Jewish Congress (A.J.C.), the private papers of Stephen S. Wise and the periodicals of the principal boycott organizations. And save for the archives of Stephen S. Wise, which are located in the Brandeis University Library of Waltham, Massachusetts, all the other archival sources are located in New York City.

Acknowledgments

It need hardly be emphasized that the author feels the need to thank the people who helped him in the preparation of this book. They include, first and foremost, his wife, Ziporah Atarah Gottlieb, who did much more than words can express to help adapt this work for publication. He is also most grateful to his former teacher, Professor Ben Halpern of Brandeis University, who guided him during the first stage of this writing, namely, a Ph.D. dissertation entitled, *The Anti-Nazi Boycott Movement in the American Jewish Community: 1933–1941*, University Microfilms, Inc., Ann Arbor, Michigan, 1968.

Special thanks must be expressed as well to the following institutions which helped support the author during his doctoral and postdoctoral days: Brandeis University, Waltham, Massachusetts, which granted him a fellowship for 1960–61; the National Foundation for Jewish Culture, which granted him fellowships from 1962 to 1964; the Memorial Foundation for Jewish Culture, which granted him fellowships from 1962 to 1965, and 1978 to 1979; the Jewish Theological Seminary of America, which granted him a fellowship during 1978–79; and the Louis and Minna Epstein Fund of the American Academy for Jewish Research, 1980–1982.

Moshe Raphael Gottlieb

Binghamton, New York
February 15, 1980

Key to Abbreviations

AAU—Amateur Athletic Union
AFL—American Federation of Labor
AJC—American Jewish Committee
A.J.C.—American Jewish Congress
ALDJR—American League for the Defense of Jewish Rights
ANL—Anti-Nazi League
AOC—American Olympic Committee
BB—B'nai B'rith
BC—Boycott Committee
CBC—Coordinated Boycott Committee
CIAC—Committee for Inter-American Cooperation
F.B.I.—Federal Bureau of Investigation
FCC—Federal Communications Commission
GNP—German National Party
HIAS—Hebrew Immigrant Aid Society
IACW—Inter-American Cooperation Week
IGC—Inter-Governmental Committee
IOBA—Independent Order Brith Abraham
JBC—Joint Boycott Council
JDB—Jewish Daily Bulletin
JLC—Jewish Labor Committee
JTA—Jewish Telegraphic Agency
JWEC—Jewish World Economic Conference
JWV—Jewish War Veterans
NSANL—Non-Sectarian Anti-Nazi League
NSP—National Socialist Party
NYPL—New York Public Library
NYT—New York Times
RM—Reichmarks
SA—Sicherheits Abteilung (security division)
SS—Schutzstaffel (black boots)
VCC—Volunteer Christian Committee
WJEF—World Jewish Economic Federation
WZO—World Zionist Organization
YIVO—Yiddishe Vissenschaftliche Organizatzye-Yiddish Scientific Institute

Introduction: The Rise of American Jewish Defense Agencies

i.

After World War I, American Jewry assumed primary responsibility for aiding and defending Jews abroad. It had played a leading role in securing the Balfour Declaration of November 2, 1917, as well as the postwar national minorities treaties. American Jews were also the main support of the Jewish Agency for Palestine, which was building the Jewish National Home under the Palestine Mandate. Moreover, American Jewish organizations were the chief source of assistance in the postwar reconstruction of Europe's disrupted Jewries.

The need for an indigenous American Jewish organization dedicated to the protection of Jewish civil rights abroad came to be recognized following the Damascus Libel of 1840. The latter involved accusations of ritual murder lodged against the Jews of Damascus, Syria, as a result of which atrocities were perpetrated against them by Syrian rogues. And as such, the Damascus Libel proved to be the first case in which American Jewry requested its government to intercede in behalf of fellow Jews in another country; for, as yet, American Jews did not have a defense organization of their own.

In 1859, the Board of Delegates of American Israelites, a pioneer Jewish defense organization modeled after the Board of Deputies of British Jews, was formed in response to the Mortara Case. The latter event involved a Jewish child, Edgar Mortara, residing in Bologna, Italy, who was kidnapped by Papal guards after it was learned that he had been secretly baptized. But despite an upsurge of international protest, the Pope, Pius IX, refused to release the boy to his parents.

News of this scandalous behavior by a Pontiff greatly shocked and angered both European and American Jewry. The latter sponsored demonstrations of protest, the most impressive of which was held in New York, attended by a crowd of 2,000 people, a rather large number for those days. But the resolutions adopted by the sympathizers, calling for interventions by the American President, were ignored. For Lewis Cass, the Secretary of State, took the position that the American government had no right to meddle in a matter which did not involve or affect the rights of an American citizen.

Ultimately, as far as America was concerned, too much commotion had been aroused over an issue that had transpired in a distant Italian city. After all, were not American abolitionists kidnapping Negro slaves from their masters without really provoking the wrath of those who were so concerned about a little Bologna boy? In the final analysis, Mortara not only retained his Catholic faith, but even became a priest! His case was hardly forgotten, even if it was overtaken by the more eventful episode concerning the intercessional efforts of the famed English Jewish banker and philanthropist, Sir Moses Montefiore.

ii.

America's earliest civic Jewish agency, which is still in existence today, is the *International Order of the B'nai B'rith* (IOBB or BB), founded as the Bundes Brueder (League of Brothers) in 1843, by a dozen New York Jews of German origin.

In the first four decades of its existence, B'nai B'rith concentrated its efforts on philanthropic work. However, the pogroms in Tsarist Russia during 1881–1883 prompted the B'nai B'rith to charter a lodge in Berlin, thereby initiating a policy of protecting and aiding all Jews. The *Anti-Defamation League* (ADL), a special department that was to deal with this phase of its work, was created in 1913.

A second agency, the *American Jewish Committee* (AJC), was established in the wake of the dreadful Kishinev Pogrom of 1903. The capital of the province of Bessarabia, Kishinev, became the scene of a two-day attack of unprecedented brutality upon its Jews. In the wake of this disastrous flareup, a group of prominent Jewish leaders in New York and Philadelphia took the lead in raising funds for the support and protection of the victims of this attack. In 1906, this nucleus was expanded to a national committee of some sixty leading American Jews who undertook to act against the persecution of Jews in any part of the world.

But neither the B'nai B'rith nor the American Jewish Committee was representative of America's Jewish masses, overwhelmingly East European in origin. This fact, together with the fear that the older organizations would oppose the creation of a Jewish national homeland in Palestine, led to the founding, in 1916, of a third Jewish defense organization, the *American Jewish Congress* (A.J.C.). After a prolonged internecine struggle, the A.J.C. succeeded in uniting American Jewish organizations on a provisional basis to prepare proposals to the Peace Conference concerning Jewish rights. Thereafter, the desired unity strivings collapsed and A.J.C. remained a partisan Jewish organization which frequently clashed with the older agencies.

Having borne the major responsibility for the protection of Jews during World War I and for constructive aid in the years thereafter, American Jewry, constituting the largest and most powerful Jewish community in the world, was bound to react to such a brutal challenge as that of Nazism. The major organizations for the defense of Jewish rights were the natural channels for such a response. The challenge was one which would test the established methods for international and national action for the protection of Jews as developed by each organization. Actual confrontation developed at a relatively slow pace, but when it finally came to the fore, it was nefarious and unprecedented in its savagery and inhumanity.

In conclusion, one need definitely add two events of cataclysmic brutality associated with Hitler Germany: (1) the destruction of 15,000,000 Russians, 2,000,000 Poles, 2,000,000 Greeks and Yugoslavs, as well as responsibility for the deaths of several million of other people who perished as a result of famine and disease; (2) the systematic and deliberate extermination by the Nazis of 6,000,000 European Jews. These mark the most savage and cold-blooded record of murder in the annals of mankind!

Part I
1933: REACTION IN GERMANY

1

The Triumph of Nazism

The Rise of Adolf Hitler to Power

When, in the latter part of the summer of 1932, less than five months before Adolf Hitler became the *Reichskanzler* of Germany, the German Jewish delegates to the Preliminary Conference of the World Jewish Congress Movement being held in Geneva, Switzerland, learned that Dr. Joseph L. Tenenbaum, President of the National Executive Committee of the American Jewish Congress . . . , had revealed his intention of reading before the conferees a paper on the menace of Nazism to World Jewry, they tried by all means at their disposal to impede his intention. For Hitler, they declared, would never reach the steps of the German Chancellory; and even if he did, continued their impetuous argument, *Hitler the Chancellor* would radically differ from *Hitler the agitator*.[1]

For what the German Jewish delegates seemed to fear most intensely was that a German government under Nazi rule would definitely administer the restrictive laws and barbaric acts which the Fuehrer and his Party cronies had promised to carry out against the Jews once they were in power. The German people, it was thought, however, would just not let such things come to pass.

Not only the Preliminary Conference, but the world public, too, had divided views on the question: What kind of Germany would emerge under a Nazi Chancellor? In the words of one of the most influential newspapers in the world:

"It may be that we shall see the 'tamed Hitler' of whom some Germans are hopefully speaking. Always we may look for some such transformation when a radical or demagogue fights his way into responsible office."[2]

For it was well known that at the helm of the young Weimar Republic had been placed a man who had sworn to destroy it. However, it was expected that President Paul von Hindenburg, who still remained the supreme authority in the land under the constitution, would unseat Hitler should the young Austrian "upstart" dare to threaten the safety of parliamentary government and democratic rule. In fact, the aging President had even been led to believe by his confidant, Vice-Chancellor Franz von Papen, that with the help of their fellow Conservatives in the Cabinet, they would be able to control, if not to manipulate, the Nazi chieftain. It was, perhaps, the most tragic political blunder in modern times.

As Yet, Hitler had no majority in the Reichstag, and only two Nazis in the Cabinet, Wilhelm Goering and Wilhelm Frick. To overcome this hindrance, Hitler, after just one day in office, requested new elections, as well as dictatorial power for a four-year period. For under the constitution, the President was empowered to grant this to him in an emergency. In any event, on the night of February 27, 1933, several weeks after Hitler had been granted his first request, the Reichstag building went up mysteriously in flames, giving the new Nazi Chancellor a perfect pretext for the request of all-embracing powers. It was to prove the most decisive moment in Hitler's pertinacious struggle for power.

The following day Hitler secured an emergency decree, duly authorized and signed by Hindenburg, "for the protection of the People and the State" and "as a defensive measure against Communist acts of violence." As a result, all the constitutional articles guaranteeing personal freedom, including the freedom of speech and assembly, were suspended throughout the Reich. With calculated terror, Hitler had thereby weakened and demoralized all opposition; but he now also intensified his drive against the radical left, incarcerating hundreds of Communist leaders—including Reichstag deputies—and suppressing their private papers.

As the elections approached, barely a five-week interval from Hitler's appointment as Chancellor, some of Germany's politically powerful parties had been cowed, crushed, or silenced with apparent alacrity and their leaders either imprisoned or put to flight. In addition, practically every important administrative post—including the police force—had fallen into Hitler's hands. The Nazi tyranny, with its brutality and terror, was unleashed. Liberals abroad, and especially Jews, had every reason for the most serious apprehension and concern.

Incipient Anti-Jewish Excesses

The election news coming from Berlin on March 6, 1933, that the Nazis had actually won 44 percent of the national vote, was received with understandable forebodings in democratic capitals. France was particularly shocked by Hitler's victory, as she had hoped that the German people would disavow the Nazi chieftain. In any event, alert people were now convinced that effective parliamentary rule under a Hitler was unattainable.

Furthermore, for the first time, the Nazis—with the Nationalists—enjoyed a straight majority in the Reichstag. This hardly satisfied them, however, and they insisted that the Communists must not be permitted to be represented there. For without the Red delegates, the Nazis could enjoy a near two-thirds majority, and thus be in a position to make changes in or even scrap the country's constitution.

How democracy would fare under Nazi rule was well known. For fourteen years prior to his ascension to the German Chancellory, Hitler had vowed to extirpate it from his New Order. He did not even conceal this intent during the election campaign. Addressing a huge National Socialist mass meeting on February 10, 1933, in Berlin's Sportpalast, his first public appearance since his appointment, Hitler declared:

> We want to break with what a rotten brand of democracy has produced and realize that all that is great can be created only by the strength of individual personality and that all that is to be preserved must be entrusted again to ability and individual personality, while the parliamentary system must be fought.[3]

What of German Jews during this period? As early as February 2, the Berlin correspondent of the *Morgen Journal* (Morning Journal), a New York City Yiddish daily, was trying to ascertain what policy the Nazi regime would apply toward them. The German Foreign Office gave him the following encouraging but misleading reply:

> In order to reassure the Jews of New York City, who are anxious as to the fate of the Jews of Germany, we wish to state that the German government is earnest and determined in its desire to guarantee safety and order for all its citizens and it has no intention of making any unjustified experiments.[4]

The Central Union of German Citizens of the Jewish Faith, Germany's oldest and most effective Jewish defense organization,[5] expressed its deep concern on the very day of Hitler's appointment:

> We naturally view with the greatest distrust a cabinet in which the Nazis occupy the weightiest positions. We await its acts. We look upon the President of the Reich as a pillar of peace in changing occurrences. We place our trust in his sense of justice and his fidelity to the constitution. We are convinced that none will dare to infringe upon our constitutional rights. Any attempt to the contrary will meet with our most determined position for the defense of our constitutional rights. Our slogan today is: "We calmly wait."[6]

The period of "calm" endured a very short while, as on March 5 the Central Union issued another statement, reflecting this time the deteriorating position of Germany's Jews:

> In meetings and certain newspapers violence against the Jews is propagated. We believe the responsible governmental authorities are unaware of the full extent of this threatening situation. We have dutifully apprized them thereof and have pointed out the danger.
> The spirit of hatred now directed against the Jews will not halt there. It will spread and poison the soul of the German people.
> We do not believe that our German fellow-citizens will let themselves be carried away into committing excesses against the Jews. Such protection is the moral duty of the State. If it is not fulfilled, the fire will eat its way further, none knowing where it will end. For the sake of Germany, then, the government must act in time.[7]

A prophetic warning! However, as yet, the Nazi government was not propagating antisemitism openly. On the contrary, its official policy, as noted in the statement of the Foreign Office, was to conceal it. Moreover, Hitler, as we shall presently see, supported this policy, for he did not care to risk a showdown with the Jews in his first two months in office. His new government was still rather insecure and fully cognizant of its despised image abroad, especially in countries like France, England, and the United States. So when offices of the Central Union were invaded by Nazis on election day, Goering personally summoned the chiefs of the Jewish organization, apologized, and assured them he disapproved of such action. This led many to believe that, despite the tense atmosphere and the almost daily commission of political murders, Hitler would not really carry out his full antisemitic program.

At this stage, though, the Nazis were mainly interested in consolidating their power. The Jewish problem could wait until the "gigantic fight against Marxism, the spiritual crime of one Jew,"[8] was resolved. National Socialism would use one scapegoat at a time.

The Post-Election Frenzy

In the aftermath of the elections, while Hitler and his cohorts were scheming to obtain a two-thirds majority in the Reichstag, the first really concerted anti-Jewish riots took place. The outbreaks began on March 8, 1933, in Essen, where several Jewish stores were shut down "voluntarily" after swastika flags had been raised over their doors and windows by specially assigned S.S. (Schutz Staffeln—Elite Guard) squads. This done, the erstwhile brown-shirted street fighters proceeded to the second part of their mission, which called for the stationing of S.S. pickets in front of Jewish establishments and shouting to the passer-by the "patriotic" cry of "Buy in German shops."

This episode was repeated the following day in Magdeburg, Kassel, and Berlin. Bands of uniformed Nazi storm troopers, organized into agitating-shouting choruses, assembled in front of some of the larger department stores in these cities and coerced the gathering mobs to buy "in German, not Jewish stores." Some of these establishments, which included American chain stores, were able to admit and let out customers by back doors, while other concerns had to close down altogether because stench bombs had been set off in them.

Nazi officials, who were well aware of the feelings of shock and revulsion which such acts were arousing in the world, dismissed them as "temporary ebullitions of high spirits" which would soon be dissipated. Dissociating themselves from any responsibility for these acts, they asserted that the Nazi pickets had merely "volunteered" to preserve order and prevent the looting of shops. They then added:

> Apparently a large body of nationally minded persons is determined no longer to tolerate the existence of Jewish business houses and therefore demands their closing. Wherever such sentiment is asserting itself, the Nazis are gratefully willing to devote themselves to the preservation of public order so that the closing of objectionable shops may proceed without disturbance.[9]

These events brought a worried Central Union delegation to Goering's office, and again the Prussian Minister of the Interior sought to smooth matters over with assurances that the law would guarantee the life and property of all Jewish citizens loyal to the government. By now, however, more and more German Jews were beginning to believe that the antisemitic outbreaks, rather than Goering's guarantee, indicated the pattern of the future.

In view of Goering's other statements, this guarantee was, indeed, totally worthless. In Essen, for example, where he spoke in connection with the boycott manifestations, Goering declared on March 10, 1933: "When they say that the population is in great excitement because Jewish department stores were temporarily closed, is it not normal that we Germans at last declare: 'Do not buy from the Jews but from the Germans!'"[10] Almost a fortnight later, Herr Goering was quoted as having said: "They tell me that I must call out the police to protect them. Certainly, I shall employ the police, and without mercy, wherever German people are hurt, but I refuse to turn the police into a guard for Jewish stores."[11]

In the wake of Hitler's appointment, a relatively large number of wealthy Jews had left Germany until things returned to "normal." The alarming manifestation of the "temporary ebullitions" also convinced an ever-increasing number of Jews of other classes that they, too, had best pack their things and leave.

By early June, according to the report of the HIAS (Hebrew Immigrant Aid Society) European commissioner, the Jewish exodus from Nazi Germany totaled some 50,000 souls. It marked the first stage of a continuous and increasing trickle of Jews from Hitler Germany until unsparing immigration laws and the outbreak of hostilities on a worldwide scale put a complete end to the possibility of free immigration. Therewith, Hitler, Goering, and the Nazi power elite were also afforded the ruthless opportunity of undertaking the extermination of European Jewry.

2

Nazi Roots

Teutomania and Antisemitism

i.

The antisemitic ideas and programs which National Socialism propounded were based on a broad background of political views and politically-minded organizations in the generation that produced a Hitler. For nineteenth-century Germany not only gave rise to the ideas of nationalism and racism, as well as crystallizing the trends of Jewish emancipation and Jew-hatred; but Nazism, as such, also proved to be a vulgarization of the age in which such movements developed. However, because it came to be led by Hitler, who stood for the worst that the racialism of his day propounded, both Jewry and Judaism came to be consigned to a calamitous end which was one of the most disastrous cataclysms in history.

Hitler's anti-Jewish legislation was patterned after the nihilist doctrines underlying racism. His genocidal slaughter of the Jews was but a logical extension of these doctrines. But so dreadful and sadistic were the implications of such ideologies that both Jew and non-Jew alike regarded their actual implementation as impossibly absurd. Thus, *Mein Kampf* (My Struggle), which is filled with Hitler's pompous and personal ideas that rehashed many of these dogmas of hate, was dismissed by many as a dull, rambling propaganda treatise. Indeed, it was mistakenly thought that so responsible and important a position as the Chancellorship would tame even a Nazi Chancellor.

ii.

With the end of the Franco-Prussian War in 1871, German Jews were finally granted complete political emancipation. This new status was the product of the politics of the sixties, when the advocacy of equal rights and equal opportunity for all acted as a potent force in rallying Germans behind the banner of national unification. For as long as this principle remained the prime objective, the support and cooperation of German Jew and German Gentile alike were sought.

The seventies, on the other hand, which witnessed the consolidation of German unification, produced conditions more suitable for the disavowal of Jewish political equality. Thus, in 1873, when excessive speculative investing resulted in a sharp dip in stock market prices and ensuing losses to many buyers, the voices of discontent quickly seized upon this opportunity to vilify "Jewish speculators" to repudiate Jewish emancipation.

The Conservative Party press led the outcry, condemning the Jews for speculation and financial swindles, and branding them "an international of gold."[1] During the economic depression that ensued, similar attacks were made by other parts of the press. Such outbursts, increasing in intensity, set the stage for the debut of political antisemitism in Kaiser Germany.

Therewithal, in the late spring and summer of 1875, the leading newspapers of the Conservative and Catholic Parties, respectively, the *Kreuzzeitung* and the *Germania,* launched a press campaign directed against the government of Otto von Bismarck, Prussia's "Iron Chancellor." Using the Jews as a stick with which to beat the Chancellor, they blamed the pernicious policies of Bismarck's Jewish confidants for Germany's economic difficulties. Bismarck and the National Liberals were accused of aiding the hated Jews to usurp position and power as a result of their emancipation. Jewish support for the Liberal Party was also used as political ammunition by foes who sought to discredit the party by labeling it as "Jewish."

The *Germania,* the Catholic organ, in particular, used methods which set an example soon followed by the racists and subsequently perfected by the Nazis. Statistics were employed to attach a "scientific" appearance to the accusation that few Jews engaged in "productive" work. That most Jews entered business professions was presented as evidence that they were amassing fortunes at the expense of the general population. Advocating Christian economic unity in the face of the Jews' evergrowing economic power, the Catholic mouthpiece used boycott slogans like the simple, but objectionable: DON'T BUY FROM JEWS! Thus, the organ of a faith which taught the equality of all men before God embraced racialist antisemitism, arguing that Jew-hatred was not the result of religious intolerance, but German racial resentment of a "foreign" people's infiltration.

It was in a political atmosphere poisoned by such disastrous agitation that Adolf Stoecker, court chaplain to Kaiser Wilhelm II of Germany, and founder of the Christian Socialist Workers Party, as well as Wilhelm Marr, a hate-mongering and erratic journalist of Jewish stock, succeeded in attracting and influencing repugnant, albeit receptive, audiences. By 1880, the antisemitism that they stirred up was running amuck in Berlin. No longer was it unusual to find antisemitic hoodlums roaming the streets and cafes of the German capital in search of Jews to beat up. While such ruffians were doing the "dirty work," the hate ideologists were busily composing scurrilous antisemitic leaflets that demanded the political and economic exclusion of the Jews from the German nation. Their wives formed women's organizations for the boycott of Jewish goods. Underscoring this entire range of odious activities was the new catchword: DIE JUDEN SIND UNSER UNGLUECK! (The Jews are our misfortune!) It was a cry which, right into the years of the Third Reich, would haunt the Jews throughout the length and breadth of Germany.[2]

iii.

Racialist theorists like Joseph Arthur Gobineau and Ernest Renan, and racial philosophers like Friedrich Wilhelm Nietzsche, who believed in unabridgeable racial differences and in Aryan superiority, did not draw antisemitic consequences from these ideas or develop programs for political and economic war on the Jews. In Germany, however, such a development of racist notions was expounded by men of some intellectual pretensions, like the native, Eugen Duehring and the erstwhile Englishman, Houston Stuart Chamberlain. Compared to them, Theodor Fritsch, a prolific antisemite from Leipzig, was a mediocre mind at best, but he made up for this deficiency by unusual energy. An engineer by profession, he made antisemitism his life's work, since for almost half a century, this racist apostle peddled Jew-baiting with untiring devotion and assiduity.

Fritsch embarked upon his racialist career in the eighties, rising as a leader of the Leipzig branch of an antisemitic organization whose headquarters was in Saxony. The other branch was in Kassel, under the leadership of an antisemite named Otto Boeckel. Fritsch and Boeckel were, in turn, the lieutenants of one Alexander Pinkert, whose Deutsche Reformpartei was one of several racial organizations that had mushroomed outside Berlin (i.e., in Hesse and Westphalia). The party's adoption of racialism alienated it from the Christian Socials, albeit in its social pigmentation, it was comprised of the same elements that constituted Stoecker's party.

Neither party received a nationwide following, however. Nevertheless, Boeckel was voted into the Reichstag in 1887, becoming the first antisemite to ride into office independently of and in opposition to the Conservative Party. His support came mainly from the rural population which, through his propagandistic agitation, was duped into believing that Jews and Junkers had a vested interest in the peasant's exploitation.

With regard to the Jews, Boeckel's program barred them from election to and employment for legislative bodies, as well as state and municipal offices. It was a mild advocacy for a man who remained unflinching in his demand that the Jews' emancipation be rescinded and that they be placed under a permanent Aliens Law. As he put it, and subsequently the Nazis: Jews were to be Germany's "guests," not its "masters."

Boeckel organized in the Reichstag an antisemitic clique which, in one form or another, perpetuated itself until Hitler's rise to power. Boeckel's and Fritsch's efforts were strengthened with the election to the Reichstag in 1892 of Herman Ahlwardt, Germany's most celebrated antisemitic rabble-rouser in the period after Stoecker's decline. Ahlwardt outdid them both in foul-mouthed vulgarity, pathological lying, corruption, and perversity.

As to Fritsch, he pursued his career like a religion, even formulating an *Antisemiten Katechismus* (Antisemitic Catechism), into which he wove a Racist Decalogue.[3] Among other things, this cautioned the German to take cognizance that the Jew was his natural enemy and that he should not adulterate his unmixed blood by blending it with mixed Jewish blood. The sixth "commandment" of this fantastic concoction exhorted the German against having any business dealings with the Jews, enjoining complete economic ostracism. This came as a corollary to the fifth commandment, which called for a social quarantine of the Jews and, in itself, would certainly have assured their ultimate elimination.

Fritsch's hate activities continued well into the twentieth century, although World War I did interrupt them. Anticipating Hitler, who would ultimately put the blame for the start of both World Wars on the Jews, Fritsch, in 1919, produced a poster containing the following malicious and maligning charges:

> Who financed the World War, but didn't fight in the trenches? Who is the labor leader, but shuns all manual work? Who says we must curtail, but lives more luxuriously than ever? Who is against the death penalty for usurers and profiteers, but allows hundreds of workmen to be shot? Who preaches free love, but only for Christian girls? It is the Jew![4]

Until his identification with National Socialism, Fritsch failed to find a political party in the postwar era that actually satisfied his perverted racialist outlook. As a result, he decided to found the Deutsche Erneuerungsgemeinde (German Renewal Party), an organization that enabled him to express his cantankerous and perverse designs.

Fritsch's intractable and primitive ideas made their way, first into the Nazi Party Platform, then into the Nazi legal code. And following the merger in the 1924 elections of the Deutsch-Voelkische Freiheitspartei (German People's Freedom Party), the political party of General Erich von Ludendorff, Germany's Chief of Staff during World War I, with Hitler's National Sozialistische Deutsche Arbeiter Partei (National Socialist German Workers Party), Fritsch also became a Nazi deputy. He even lived to see the fulfillment of his racist dreams, dying in September 1933, about half a year after Hitler's rise to power.

iv.

Pan-Germanism was a natural manifestation in a general movement that rebelled against the Hapsburg Empire with its hodge-podge mixture of nationalities. But it was mainly the crosswinds of German racialism that actually fanned these militant elements into an antisemitic blaze.

By the time Hitler wandered into Vienna, the seat of Pan-Germanism, Georg von Schoenerer, founder of this nationalist-expansionist movement, had already dissolved his Pan-German League.[5] The latter step proved, however, a major influence on Hitler's rampant nationalism and extreme antisemitism, playing a comprehensive role in the subsequent Nazi program.

However, the national program of Pan-Germanism could not become effective until Hitler had actually attained power. Not so antisemitism; for nearly a third of the twenty-five-point program of the German Workers' Party, which Hitler proclaimed in Munich on February 24, 1920, consisted of planks calling for the relegation of Jews to an inferior social and legal status and for the restriction of their economic activities. In explanation of this program, wrote Gottfried Feder, a German economic eccentric: "Antisemitism is to a certain extent the underlying principle of the National Socialist movement."[6]

A literature purporting to interpret this program developed in the ensuing years. The consensus of opinion among leading Nazi commentators was that the antisemitic dicta were not only intended to exclude the Jews from governmental positions, such as teaching or judgeships, but also to disqualify them from serving as attorneys; nor would they be permitted to appear on the witness stand or act as jurors in a court of law. One could also expect the appointment of a special committee to investigate Jewish business enterprises, especially department stores and wholesale concerns, as well as factories and banks. Property confiscation was certain in the event that the owners were found to be "dangerous to the people."

Upon his release from the Landsberg Fortress on December 20, 1924, some fourteen months after an ill-fated, near comic putsch against the Bavarian government, Hitler, in a matter of a few years, succeeded in revamping his party into a powerful, efficient machine. And as the twenties drew to a close, Hitler had already set up the administrative apparatus for the coming of the Third Reich. Nazism was functioning as a state within the Weimar Republic.

It was also giving the Jews samples of what was in store for them once the Fuehrer became the supreme leader of the German people. As a direct result of Nazi agitation, a veritable antisemitic storm began raging in the public schools, the universities, the courts, and the various governmental departments. Not infrequently, Jews were beaten, their synagogue windows smashed, and their cemeteries desecrated.

In the latter twenties, the boycott of Jews became widespread in Germany's smaller towns and villages. Frequently, Jews were terrorized and ruined economically. The stock market crash of 1929 afforded Nazi propagandists an ideal opportunity for extending their boycott agitation into the cities. Thenceforward, an ever-growing audience was ready to accept the myth that the Jews had actually caused this debacle and were therefore also responsible for the worldwide economic ruin that followed. As a result, widespread signs in the cities and the countryside read: MEIDET DIE JUEDISCHEN WARENHAUSER! DEUTSCHER MANN UND DEUTSCHE FRAU, KAUFT NICHT BEI DER JUDENSAU! DER VON JUDEN ISST, STIRBT DAVON! (Avoid Jewish department stores! German men and women, don't buy from the Jew-pig! Food bought from a Jew will poison you!)[7]

So effective and serious did such boycott agitation become that the Jewish community of Berlin felt constrained to establish a Central Employment Bureau to assist discharged Jewish employees or the self-employed in finding new occupations. The Central Committee for Relief and Reconstruction, which was established shortly after Hitler rose to power, had to assume this function on a gigantic scale. And as is the custom among Jews when their brothers face uprooting, world Jewry, especially American Jews, stepped up aid; but to no real avail, for German Jewry had entered the preliminary stage of a travail from which there was no return!

3

The First of April Boycott

A Day of National Affliction

One can find no words to describe the fear and despair, the tragedy that envelops the German Jews. They are being beaten, terrorized, murdered, and to cap the climax, they are compelled to keep quiet. The Hitler regime flames up with anger because it has been compelled through fear of foreign public opinion to forego a mass slaughter of Jews. It threatens, however, to execute big pogroms if Jews in other countries make too much fuss about the latter pogroms it has hitherto indulged in.[1]

So wrote Mr. Jacob Leschinsky, the Berlin correspondent of the New York City Yiddish newspaper, *Jewish Daily Forward,* shortly after the German elections. It resulted in his arrest by the Hitler regime. Leschinsky obtained his release not long thereafter, but with an expulsion order out of the country.

Leschinsky's was but one of the many "atrocity tales" which, according to the Nazis, American and English Jews, with the aid of their "subjugated" liberal press, were attributing to the New German government.[2] The Nazis, as we shall see, were especially incensed at the rise of a spontaneous movement in England and the United States—as well as in other countries—to boycott German goods. They were also angered by mass protest rallies in these countries, at which they and their Fuehrer were publicly denounced. They therefore announced on the night of March 27, 1933—the very night that a giant protest meeting was being conducted under the auspices of the American Jewish Congress—that if American and English Jews did not cease their boycott and atrocity propaganda, the NSP (National Socialist Party) would conduct a counter-boycott against German Jews.

That such planned action met with Hitler's personal approval may be deduced from a long meeting that the Fuehrer had with Josef P. Goebbels, Nazi Minister of Propaganda, in which the main topic of conversation was how Germany could best counteract "the anti-German atrocity propaganda which interested Jews have started in England and the United States against the new nationalist regime."[3] A plan was obviously decided upon, since shortly afterwards, an NSP bulletin was released in which it was announced that instructions would on the morrow be issued "for the organization of a gigantic popular movement for the forming of committees to boycott the Jewish stores of Germany in response to the boycott threats of international Jewry."[4] The bulletin further stated that the German government would not do anything to oppose this National Socialist fight "so long as foreign governments do not take steps against the atrocity propaganda in their countries."[5] Officially, though, it was to appear that the Hitler government was not the perpetrator of or an accomplice to the planned nationwide boycott.

And as if to amplify the party bulletin, Josef Goebbels announced just after his conference with Hitler that his department would take "sharp" counter-measures against those responsible for the spread of the anti-Jewish atrocity reports:

> Drastic legal proceedings will be undertaken against the atrocity campaign which has been unloosed in America against the new German regime. A blow shall be struck at the intellectual movers and beneficiaries of these treasonable machinations, most of whom are Jews of German origin.[6]

An added announcement elaborated upon this declaration, stating that a nationwide agitation would follow to immediately restrict the admission of Jews to certain academic professions and public institutions. But in the Nazi code, the restrictive admission of Jews into the academic and business worlds was tantamount to their ouster; for even as this announcement was being prepared, Jewish professionals and Jewish public officials had already been ousted from office in various parts of Germany. Such ousters, like the rapid spread of anti-Jewish picketing and other forms of physical violence, had also been set in motion soon after the Nazi victory at the polls. They clearly showed that a decree in the "new" Germany, particularly where Jews were concerned, came only to legalize that which was already being done to them illegally.

The call for an all-out boycott was therefore a unique opportunity for exploiting this development thoroughly and unabashedly; that is to say, the anti-Jewish boycott was not to be restricted to business concerns only. It was in accordance with this broader application that the Nazis promptly formed special economic committees throughout Germany "for the practical and systematic execution of a boycott against Jewish business establishments, goods, physicians and lawyers."[7] And in line with Nazidom's restrictive policy toward the Jews, it was also the mission of the committees to create a social environment demanding that Jews be given employment on a "numerus clausus" basis.

The boycott was scheduled to commence on Saturday, April 1, at 10 o'clock in the morning, and to end at 7 o'clock that evening. If by that time anti-German agitation showed no signs of abatement, it was to be resumed the following Wednesday. Yet just the mere announcement of the forthcoming boycott sufficed to spur its implementation the next day in various parts of Germany. Thus, in some of the towns and cities of the Ruhr, the Rhineland, and Silesia, Jewish stores were compelled to close because of S.S. pickets warning the would-be shoppers not to enter them. In cities like Darmstadt, Mannheim, and Ludwigshafen, where similar demonstrations were loosed, store closings were actually enforced by the police. In Goettingen, this incredible spectacle assumed an uglier form still, as a number of stores, including that city's largest department store, had their windows smashed. And what is more, to prevent the likelihood of looting, the police department put a cordon around the shopping center.

Cities like Wiesbaden and Halle afforded a similar picture: picketing S.S. men, hostile as well as curious crowds, closing stores, a combination of stench-bomb throwing and window smashing, and some arrests. To pent-up German feelings, this was the second time in a month that relief was afforded through a "temporary ebullition of high spirits." Yet all this was only a rehearsal for the real holiday on April 1.

The broadcasted boycott proclamation was published in the press on March 28. The next day, various press organs circulated an eleven-point program for the conduct of the boycott.[8] Thereunto, the following statement was attached:

> The guilty ones are among us; they live among us and abuse day after day the right of hospitality which the German people have granted to them.... Responsible for these lies and slanders are the Jews among us. From them emanates this campaign of hatred and of lying agitation against Germany. In their hands lies the power to set right the liars in the rest of the world. Since they do not wish to do this, we will have to see to it that this campaign of hatred and lies against Germany is not directed against the innocent German people, but against the responsible inciters themselves.[9]

It was only fitting that Julius Streicher, notorious Jew-baiter and editor of *Der Stuermer* (The Stormy), who had been advocating a total boycott of the Jews, should at last be given his award by being appointed the chairman of the NSP's Central Boycott Committee. The following list of chimerical, vilifying charges, displayed in the form of huge posters, bespoke Streicher's perverted image of the Jew:

> On January 30, Adolph Hitler, the leader of the German movement of liberation, was appointed Chancellor of the Reich. On March 5, the German people in a miraculous uprising went on record for him and his task of liberation. The national revolution broke the old system to pieces; Marxism is smashed down and Germany advances towards new heights. This grand German fight for liberty fills the international Jew with hatred and fury. He realizes that his power in Germany is coming to an end. He realizes that he cannot make a Soviet Jewish colony of convicts out of this Germany.
>
> He now acts according to the program that the Zionist leader, Theodor Herzl, proclaimed in 1897, in Basle, at the big Jewish Congress:
>
> "As soon as a non-Jewish state dares to resist us Jews, we must be in a position to cause its neighbors to go to war against it. As a means to that end, we use public opinion by working on it through the so-called eighth great power (the press). With a few exceptions that do not figure at all, the entire press of the world is in our hands."
>
> According to this broadly conceived plan, the Jew these days excites the public opinion of the world against Germany. To this end he uses the press, through which he pours a tremendous flood of lies over the world. No crime is too base to accuse the Germans of it.
>
> The Jew lies: "In Germany members of the Jewish people are being killed through cruel tortures."
>
> The Jew lies: "The eyes of these Jews are being burned out, their hands chopped off, and alas! even their bodies are being cut to pieces."
>
> The Jew lies: "In Germany even Jewish women are being killed in a horrible way and Jewish girls are being assaulted in the presence of their parents."
>
> The Jews spread these lies in the same way and for the same purpose as they did during the war. They want to excite the world against Germany. Moreover, they agitate for a boycott of German goods. The Jew thus wants to increase the misery of unemployment in Germany and ruin the German export trade.
>
> German men and women! The instigators of this mad crime, this base atrocity and boycott agitation are the Jews of Germany. They have called those of their race abroad to fight against the German people. They have reported lies abroad.
>
> The leaders of the German movement of liberty have therefore

decided to decree, in defense against this criminal agitation, a boycott of all Jewish stores, offices, etc., to begin Saturday, April 1, at 10:00 A.M. We appeal to you German women and men, to join the boycott. Do not buy from Jewish stores or department stores! Do not consult Jewish attorneys! Avoid Jewish physicians!

Show the Jews that they cannot degrade us and throw dirt upon German honor without being punished!

Whoever acts against this appeal shows that he stands on the side of the Germans' enemies.

Long live the venerable Field Marshal of the great war, President Paul von Hindenburg!

Long live our leader, Chancellor Adolph Hitler!

Long live the German people and the sacred German Fatherland![10]

Still, it was Goebbels' invidious outpourings, which synthesized shrewd deception with unmitigated terrorism, that guided the preparations for the nationwide ostracism of the German Jew. On March 30, he noted in his diary: "The boycott is organized. We need only now press a button to set it going."[11]

And so it was. The following day, Goebbels announced:

> Tomorrow not a German man or a German woman shall enter a Jewish store. Jewish trade throughout Germany must remain paralyzed tomorrow. We shall then call a three-day pause in order to give the world a chance to recant its anti-German agitation. If it has not been abandoned at the end of that respite, the boycott will be resumed Wednesday, until German Jewry has been annihilated.[12]

It should also be pointed out that in its desire to avoid official responsibility for the boycott, the Hitler government did not see fit to go so far as to conceal its approval of it. Here, too, its mouthpiece was Goebbels, who, an hour prior to the aforesaid, declared:

> It is with satisfaction that the Government has noticed that the atrocity agitation abroad is abating. The Government sees in this fact a success of the boycott announcement of the National Socialist movement during the past days. But, furthermore, it sees also that the united Jewry in Germany has the possibility absolutely to restrict and to stop this atrocity agitation.
>
> It is convinced that the atrocity propaganda has passed its peak. Therefore, the National Socialist Party has resolved: Under these circumstances the boycott of tomorrow will be carried out with full power and the hardest discipline. It begins, as announced, at 10 o'clock and will be suspended tomorrow evening. The suspension will continue until Wednesday morning, 10 o'clock. If by Wednesday

morning, 10 o'clock, the atrocity agitation abroad will be absolutely stopped, the National Socialist Party declared its readiness to restore normal conditions.

If this, however, is not the case, the boycott will be resumed on Wednesday at 10 o'clock; but then with an impetus and vehemence hitherto unheard of, until the wirepullers of the foreign atrocity will have thought better of it. Fundamentally, the Government of the Reich expects the following results from the execution of the boycott tomorrow: the boycott will be carried out, by the organizations concerned, with a most rigid discipline and without the violation of any law. Nobody will be physically endangered by this boycott. The organizations which carry out the boycott have to assume the responsibility that by the boycott no innocent person will be affected.

No banks will be closed, because otherwise there could be a disturbance of financial transactions.[13]

Goebbels' conditional threat was a clear indication that there was no plan for the resumption of the boycott the following Wednesday; for it was in the best interests of a still insecure Nazi regime to prevent the complete ruination of its reputation abroad. It realized fully that the impending boycott would result, not in an abatement, but in an increase of the "atrocity agitation." Thus, only the credulous could actually believe that Goebbels' conditional threat was stated from a position of strength; for it was he who was empowered to decide whether or not "the atrocity agitation abroad" had been "absolutely stopped."

Details concerning Goebbels' retreat became known the day after the boycott. It was learned that the night preceding April 1, the non-Nazi majority in Hitler's Cabinet fought bitterly with the few Nazi ministers in a last-ditch effort to secure a cancellation of the imminent boycott. Foreign Minister Constantin von Neurath was particularly indignant, even threatening to resign if the projected boycott was not abandoned. Only von Papen's coaxing calmed him down enough to reconsider this move. Yet neither voiced his oppugnancy on humane grounds. It revolved, rather, on a sober-minded pragmatism, based on marks and pfennigs.

The Nazi ministers subdued the opposition only after pointing out that the order to boycott had already been received by their rank-and-file members and that an unexpected rescission would hardly prove effective. On the contrary, it would lead, they argued, to uncontrolled and widespread violence; whereas an organized boycott, Hitler himself asserted, would prevent the assumption of "undesirable forms." The stormy debate ended with the understanding that the strictest precautions would be taken against possible riotous outbreaks and that the government would never again resort to the use of a boycott.

The second half of this accord was carried out faithfully.[14] The boycott was well-organized, well-disciplined, and non-violent; and as prescribed in the proclamation, it was directed against the Jewish professional, as well as the Jewish businessman. Thus, Jewish judges and lawyers were barred entry to courthouses. Jewish physicians were denied entry to hospitals, and Jewish teachers to the public schools.[15] Similar misfortunes befell Jews in civil service and other areas. However, unlike the boycott impact on commerce, these manifestations did not turn out to be a one-day affair. Through a subsequent series of decrees, they became legal, permanent acts. The tendentious aims of Fritsch's decalogue (see p. 379), as refined by the NSP platform, thus made their debut in a nation gone berserk.

Perhaps even more harmful than the boycott itself were the multitudinous meetings held in almost every German city and hamlet during the April 1 weekend. Their particularly noxious feature was the delivery of inflammatory speeches designed to elucidate the official explanation for the implementation of the boycott, but exploited to incite Jew-hatred. Typical of this was a notification that all Christian employees of Jewish establishments should assemble at central points in their respective municipalities to be briefed as to why a boycott was being conducted against the Jews. Among the libelous reasons offered was the myth that international Jewry's hate propaganda had sicked the world on Germany in 1914, and that the Jews of 1933 were planning to destroy a newly-constituted Reich.

Masterful examples of such noxious mythicizing spouted forth at the Lustgarten, where thousands of Berliners gathered to hear the ominous forebodings that Hitler had in store for Germany's Jews. "Hang them!" "Hang them!" was the crowd's oft-repeated refrain to the hate-filled speech of the Fuehrer's propaganda minister. These hysterical outcries were reiterated when Goebbels said: "We have not hurt one Jewish hair, but if New York and London carry out a boycott of our goods, we will take our gloves off."[16]

To be sure, there was nothing new in this sort of warning. But to Goebbels and his ilk it was worthwhile repeating, as long as they threatened but did not actually advocate physical violence. As a matter of fact, they carefully avoided taking recourse to the latter for fear this would only increase the elicitation of military intervention.[17] But having chosen the less provocative course, they would make the most of it. In a way, this even became a necessity; for Goebbels, who was making such a tumult over the "foreign atrocity propaganda," certainly had to balance it by intensifying and accentuating his anti-Jewish threats.

The effort was well worth it, for if successful, the tactic could attain for Germany badly-needed political capital. Thus, if the German people could become convinced that the Nazis had put an end to all the clamor abroad, their beloved dictator would have gained an immense personal triumph; for it would convey the impression that the Fuehrer's arms were long enough to strike at a foe across a vast ocean, a feat calculated to strengthen his prestige at home.

We must also examine the boycott promulgation in light of the inner machinations of the National Socialist Party. This was of prime significance, as Hitler had to find a quick way of rewarding en masse his enthusiastic supporters, many of whom filled the ranks of the unemployed. By having the NSP declare a nationwide boycott, and thus confront German Jewry with collective ruin, he could set at ease the worries of the jobless who would presently fill the places of economically dislodged Jews. It was Hitler's way of sharing the spoils of his political victory with the economically ruined and hungry middle class that backed him so passionately.

Short of emigration, what could German Jewry do under such frightening circumstances and overwhelming odds? The thought of violence, if it was entertained at all, was tantamount to collective suicide. If common sense alone did not dictate this, the Nazis, on a number of occasions, had gone on record with warnings of a bloodbath in reprisal. This would follow, stated their menacing threats, if a major Nazi were slain by Jews. As for Hitler, murder or even an attempt to injure him, from whatever source, would suffice for a Jewish massacre in Saint Bartholomew's Day (massacre of French Protestants, Paris, August 24, 1572) fashion. The following is one of a number of such auguries:

> At the slightest attempt to harm our leader, we shall take bloody revenge on those whom we Nazis must consider to be the cause of our suffering and misery.
> Should a shot be fired at our beloved leader, all Jews in Germany would immediately be put against the wall, and bloodshed would result which in its ghastliness will exceed anything the world has ever seen![18]

For Jews to have a personal discussion with Hitler about anything was out of the question. He had expressly stated that he had no interest in meeting with them. Jews, therefore, did what appeared best in this dire exigency. On March 29, a representative board that included the stewards of Berlin's Jewish congregations joined in addressing a moving appeal to Hindenburg.

> German Jewry is deeply convulsed by the boycott proclamation of the National Socialist Party. Because of the misdeeds of a few, for which we are not responsible, it is now proposed to expose to

economic ruin those German Jews who with all their hearts feel themselves bound up with the Fatherland.

The reproach that we have injured the interests of the German people deeply wounds our honor. We solemnly enter a protest against this charge and trust that the President and the government of the Reich will take such steps as will further insure to us our right to a livelihood in our German Fatherland.[19]

To all appearances, this impassioned statement was ignored. Less apologetic objections were registered by some Jews on boycott day in the form of signs posted outside their shops: I SERVED FOUR YEARS AT THE FRONT: THIS IS MY REWARD and WE ARE JEWS BUT WE HELP TO PAY FOR THE UNEMPLOYED.[20]

One can venture a guess that a good percentage of the general population opposed the boycott idea, if only by reason of the possible harm it would do Germany's vested business interests and the equally damaging consequences to the Reich's reputation abroad. Frantic appeals from industrialists, bankers, steamship-company owners, and moderates of various kinds did come pouring into Berlin, pleading to have the boycott called off at all costs. How these were represented by von Papen and Neurath has already been described (p. 20). However, whether such groups were also prompted by humanitarian considerations cannot be ascertained with any degree of accuracy. Suffice it to say that what might have disturbed them privately, they cared not or dared not express publicly.

Be that as it may, it is clear that the Nazis and many cooperative citizens were interested in continuing the effects of the boycott without imparting to it the demonstrative character of April 1. They achieved this by announcing several days after the conclusion of the boycott that hereafter, all non-Jewish shops were to bear an identifying placard reading: GERMAN SHOP. Thus, all would-be purchasers could easily infer that shops not displaying such placards were to be avoided.

The world was still waiting to hear from Hitler, who, as yet, had made no public pronouncement concerning Jews. His reply to a communication by the German-American paper, *Der New Yorker Staatszeitung*, merely restates the official Nazi line:

> The Chancellor of the Reich extends thanks for your cooperation in the fight against Jewish incitement. German Jews will be treated like all other nationals in accordance to their attitude to the national government. The defensive action of the National Socialist Party was provoked by the attitude of German Jews in foreign countries.[21]

However, on April 6, the Fuehrer's "Jewish" silence was definitely broken. Challenging the growing anti-Nazi protest movement in the United States, Hitler declared:

> America, which leads all other countries in the strong countermovement, has least of all had reason for the protest. The American people were the first to draw practical political consequences from the differentiation of races. Through its immigration law, America has inhibited the unwelcome influence of such races as it has been unable to tolerate within its midst.[22]

As this was a direct gibe against America's restrictive immigration ban on the black and yellow races, Hitler made certain to add: "Nor is America ready now to open its doors to Jews fleeing from Germany."[23]

In another part of his pronouncement, Hitler dashed the hopes of those who thought, especially during the tense days of the boycott commotion, that his silence on this issue in particular and other anti-Jewish manifestations in general, possibly denoted his disapprobation of them:

> We must meet the natural demand of Germany for intellectual leadership according to our own kind by the early elimination of the preponderance of Jewish intellectuals from our cultural and spiritual life. True intellectual achievements have never been made by racial aliens, but always by strictly Aryan Germanic spiritual forces.[24]

Thus, for the first time in modern history, did a head of state announce openly and unequivocally that he intended to make Judeophobia a government policy. In so doing, Hitler "refined" a precedent set by Tsarist Russia.[25] But in Germany, this manifested itself in the sanction of legality and an utter contempt for and defiance of world opinion.

The year 1933 was only the beginning. The Fuehrer was, as yet, biding his time; or to use Streicher's ascription in light of the boycott day background:

> I have a feeling that the battle will not be further taken up Wednesday. This will prove a disappointment to millions of Germans, but discipline must be observed in any event. It was not easy to yield, but Adolph Hitler can only proceed one step at a time.[26]

Part II
1933: THE REACTION OF THE AMERICAN JEWISH COMMUNITY

4

The Policy of Public Protest

i.

How should American Jewry, as well as America in general, have reacted to the cruel, even savage, policies of the Nazis? To be sure, politically and economically, it was pretty well known just what Hitler and his cohorts were scheming to do with the Jews. The big question was, however, whether or not the Nazis would, now that their Fuehrer had risen to power, actually carry out the inhuman anti-Jewish program which he had been propagating for so long with such viciousness and savagery. In essence, though, what the problem really boiled down to was the fundamental, even tormenting question intimated above (p. 3): Would Hitler as Chancellor "radically differ from Hitler the agitator"? It was an answer to this harassing question that America, and undoubtedly world Jewry too, was seeking.

A response to this vexing query would not be had until Hitler was actually guiding the destiny of the German people. What, then, should the American Jewish Congress, as well as the several other American Jewish defense organizations, do in the meantime? It was an arduous question to which to find a satisfactory and fulfilling reply.

The idea which had been considered by the Congress for some time was to hold public anti-Nazi protest meetings on a massive scale. This may be traced to a communication that Rabbi Stephen S. Wise, then the honorary president of the American Jewish Congress, sent Justice Julian W. Mack, a civic leader and first president of the American Jewish Congress, on September 13, 1932. The message mentions Rev. John H. Holmes, founder of the National Association for the Advancement of

Colored People (NAACP), as well as of the American Civil Liberties Union (ACLU). Rabbi Wise, who was a close friend of Reverend Holmes, said the following in this connection:

> The Nazis here are behaving scandalously. Deliberate incitement to pogroms, which I simply cannot understand the Jewish financial world in America allowing to continue without protest! By an intelligent campaign they could play hell with the Nazis, of course, not by attacks in Germany, but by bringing moral pressure to bear upon this element in the country. The Nazis are very sensitive to foreign comment. Holmes has this from a most acute and well-informed observer of conditions in Germany.[1]

Even more revealing is the fact that on February 7, 1933, about a fortnight prior to the A.J.C.–AJC–BB agreement not to resort to the use of public agitation regarding the German Jewish question, the following was entered into the minutes of the Congress' Administrative Committee: "The Committee expressed its alarm at the danger of the Jews in Germany, and suggested that a number of protest meetings be held so as to make the Germans conscious of the fact that the situation is being watched."[2]

But Stephen Wise, who, of course, determined Congress policy, urged a period of reflection and consideration. His power and prestige helped him overcome organizational and popular opposition to this prudent stand. However, as we shall soon see, his cautious position persisted for a short duration only.

ii.

Until the German elections on March 5 (1933), Jewish "atrocity propaganda" was rather mild in the United States. The reason was that Jews in this country were waiting to see whether or not the prize of the Chancellory would induce Hitler to moderate at least, if not to abolish, his brutal antisemitic program. However, the disturbing postelection reports convinced many American Jews, as well as Jews of other lands, that Hitler had no intention of altering his anti-Jewish plans.

Jewish defense organizations in the United States had long been analyzing the antisemitic agitation in Germany; and up to the Nazi victory at the polls, it appeared that there were no pronounced differences between them on this issue.

In January of 1932, the American Jewish Congress initiated a conference with the American Jewish Committee on methods of counteracting Nazi anti-Jewish propaganda. After a lengthy and earnest discussion, the two Jewish defense organizations agreed to be guided by the decision of their brethren in Germany. The decision rendered was that German Jews had full confidence in the civil rights clause of the Weimar Constitution and faith in the sense of justice and sobriety of their non-Jewish fellow Germans. They, therefore, viewed as unnecessary and unwise the idea that Jews of other countries take any action in their behalf.

However, Hitler's appointment as *Reichskanzler* (the following January, 1933) compelled America's Jewish defense organizations to radically reappraise their policies vis-à-vis German Jewry. At the suggestion, this time, of B'nai B'rith, it was agreed that the German situation be dealt with jointly by itself, the American Jewish Committee, and the American Jewish Congress. The "Big Three" met on February 22, and discussed the implications of a Hitler Germany to both Reich and American Jewry. It was agreed to establish a Joint Conference Committee, consisting of an equal number of representatives—six in all—from the respective defense organizations. The basic task of the Joint Committee was to keep a close watch on developments in the new Nazi state and report these to the parent organizations. However, apropos of the variety of methods that might be employed in response to offensive developments, there was unanimous agreement that, for the present, public agitation would be an unwise means of succoring German Jews.

The Joint Committee was barely three weeks old when the parting of the ways came. For in reaction to Germany's first anti-Jewish manifestations in the postelection period, the Congress embarked on a series of deliberative meetings, culminating in a three-hour session of its National Executive Committee at New York's Hotel Commodore on March 12. When it was over, agreement was reached for holding mass meetings and parades on a nationwide scale. The meeting also accepted a resolution introduced by Dr. Samuel Margoshes, one of the two Congress vice-presidents and the editor of the Yiddish daily, *Der Tog* (The Day), that Madison Square Garden should house a major protest rally.

In pursuit of these plans, the Congress convened on March 19 an Emergency Conference of national and local Jewish organizations. Over 1,500 representatives attended what turned out to be a turbulent four-hour session. The mood was set by Congress President Bernard S. Deutsch, in his opening words:

> The offices of the American Jewish Congress are being flooded with messages from all over the country demanding protest action. We are met here to translate this popular mandate into responsible, vigorous, orderly and effective action.[3]

More than likely, what Deutsch had in mind was the Margoshes resolution, which was now also introduced before the Conference. It called for a day of national protest against the mistreatment of Jews in Germany. It also expressed "the deep sense of pain and resentment of American Jewry," adding:

> This tragic hour in Jewish history calls imperatively for the solidarity of the Jewish people. And we American Jews are resolved to stand shoulder to shoulder with our brother Jews in Germany in defense of their rights, which are being greviously violated, and of their lives, which are imperilled. This in a Germany, a land for which they have lived and served, fought and died through many centuries in order to maintain the ideals and safeguard the well-being of the country and its people.
> As Americans who believe in the brotherhood of man, we invite (you) to join with us in a demonstration of American faith in the sacredness of human rights and the sanctity of human fellowship.[4]

The resolution did not, however, go far enough to satisfy the commander-in-chief of the Jewish War Veterans, J. George Fredman, who proposed an amendment calling for the boycott of German goods. This, in turn, strongly aroused Joseph M. Proskauer, a prominent judge and leading member of the American Jewish Committee. Proskauer deplored Margoshes' resolution, but was completely exasperated with Fredman's proposal, which he criticized severely. In terms which were obviously directed at the JWV commander, the AJC spokesman cautioned against a hasty move and warned against "causing more trouble for the Jews in Germany by unintelligent action." Fighting repeated interruptions characterized by hissing and booing, Proskauer also counseled against a public protest campaign of "marches" and "meetings." Proskauer's final argument came from a letter addressed to the conference by Judge Irving Lehman, older brother of the New York governor and one of the Committee's two vice-presidents. Its basic message was: "I feel that the meeting may add to the terrible dangers of the Jews in Germany. . . . I implore you in the name of humanity, don't let anger pass a resolution which will kill Jews in Germany."[5]

At this, Rabbi Wise demurred. He insisted that even if mass protests were officially disavowed by the American Jewish community, an announcement to this effect would have no influence on the Nazi government. He, thereupon, proposed a vote on the substance of the Margoshes resolution and suggested that a committee of two revise its wording. If this was a gesture of attempted fairness to Proskauer's dissenting views, it turned out to be somewhat of a farce; for it was Margoshes and Wise who were appointed for the task. It is not surprising, therefore, that the record does not show that the resolution was changed in any way. In any case, as the tentative date of March 27 had also been confirmed, the Congress now began making feverish preparations for the solemn event.

Dr. Wise's stand was further eludicated in a statement that he made on the occasion of his fifty-ninth birthday, which fell during these days:

> The time for caution and prudence is past. We must speak up like men. How can we ask our Christian friends to lift their voices in protest against the wrongs suffered by Jews if we keep silent? . . . What is happening in Germany today may happen tomorrow in any other land on earth unless it is challenged and rebuked. It is not the German Jews who are being attacked. It is the Jews. We must speak out. If that is unavailing, at least we shall have spoken.[6]

The Congress planned to announce at the Garden four basic demands that it would make on Nazi Germany. They were to be officially presented to the German ambassador right after the meeting. Dr. Wise previewed them a day before the meeting in an address before his congregation at Carnegie Hall:

> There must be an immediate cessation of all anti-Semitic activities and propaganda in Germany; The abandonment of the policy of racial discrimination against and of economic exclusion of Jews from the life of Germany; The protection of Jewish life and property; There shall be no expulsion of "Ost-Juden."[7]

"If these demands be granted, as God knows they ought to be," Wise added, "there will be an end of every plan and undertaking of protest."[8]

Dr. Wise further revealed that he had received a telegram from Ernest Wallach, vice-president of the Central Union of German Citizens of the Jewish Faith, urging that the Garden rally be called off; and if that were not possible, that the speakers "refrain from stirring the emotions of the audience against Germany."[9] Wallach had assured Dr. Wise that the German government was interested in guaranteeing peace and order for all citizens without any discrimination.

A parallel note was struck in the first half of a statement that the Reich Federation of Jewish ex-Combatants sent on March 25 to the U.S. Embassy in Berlin. The statement was indignant and condemnatory, reflecting, apparently, a considerable degree of credulity.

> Maltreatment and excesses have occurred which it is certainly far from us to extenuate, but such excesses are unavoidable in any overturn. We want to emphasize that in all cases known to us the authorities have proceeded vigorously against excesses wherever this has been possible. The excesses have always been committed by

> irresponsible elements working in the dark, and we know that the government and all persons in authoritative positions condemn the acts of violence that have happened.
>
> According to our judgment, it is time to have done with the inexcusable and inflammatory propaganda initiated by so-called intellectuals abroad against Germany.
>
> These men, who for the most part have never avowed themselves Germans and at the most critical moment have abandoned their coreligionists at home, whose protagonists they have professed to be, have forfeited their right to speak on the German Jewish cause. Their arrows, discharged from a safe retreat, hurt Germany, indeed, and the German Jews, but do no honor to the archers. Their accounts burst with exaggerations.[10]

Wallach, on what was explained as a special business trip, arrived in New York a day or so prior to the Madison Square Garden rally and repeated his government's claim of pursuing a policy of nondiscrimination. His arrival was preceded by a March 24 release by the Central Union, denying the charges of German atrocity as "pure inventions" and "inexcusable distortions." The Central Union did, however, admit grave concern over the antisemitic situation; but it opposed attempts by the foreign press to pressure the German government to adopt a different course of action, arguing that this was a German domestic affair.

This was certainly a far cry from the viewpoint expressed by the Central Union only a month before,[11] indicating the swiftness with which the position of German Jewry had deteriorated. The Central Union's present attitude in its statement of denial made it seem the result of Goebbels' or Goering's coaching.

"Pitifully unconvincing," was Mr. Deutsch's reaction two days later. He then went on to say:

> The denial does not deny, as, indeed, it would be futile to deny in the teeth of the overwhelming evidence, the circumstantial tales of persecution and horror which the thousands of Jews are telling—tales which have justly shocked the whole of civilized mankind. It does not deny and cannot deny that the persecution, suppression and even the total expulsion of the Jews from Germany has been for years the avowed policy of the Nazis so soon as they attained power, that the Nazi Cabinet Minister in charge of the police[12] only last week announced derisively in a public speech that the police under his charge could not concern themselves with the protection of Jewish property, and that Hitler himself, in his speech in Potsdam at the opening of the Reichstag intimated that the Jews of Germany were outlaws and criminals. With the heads of state making public announcements of this character, what bloody excesses may one not expect from their frenzied followers! ...

However, most significant of all are the admissions contained in the denial of the Central Union. The denials admit that there have been "acts of political revenge, also reprisals against Jews"; and it admits further that "the antisemitic aims in the various domains of life and business which are manifesting themselves fill us, indeed, with grave concern." The Central Union goes on to say, however, that that is "a German domestic affair." This we, in turn, deny, and deny most vehemently. It is not alone "a German domestic affair" that antisemitism in the various domains of life and business is the official policy and program of the German Government. Antisemitism in Germany is a challenge to civilization itself; and all civilized people and peoples have a right and a duty to protest against it. Whether the plan is to crush out the 600,000 members of the Jewish race in Germany by economic repression and a denial of civil rights or by bloodshed is equally a crime alike against God and humanity which calls for the condemnation of mankind and for the exertion of every possible means by the outside world to prevent it.[13]

The American Jewish Congress was not going to cancel its Madison Square Garden rally in New York; nor would it reject its announced plan of similar and simultaneous rallies in about eighty other cities throughout the length and breadth of the United States. These included such large metropolitan areas as Chicago, Philadelphia, Boston, Baltimore, and Cleveland. In New York, from which the rally was broadcasted to Europe, as well as to the rest of the United States, Deutsch, as Congress president, delivered the opening address. Disclaiming that this protest rally had been decided upon with "any feeling of unfriendliness or ill-will towards the German nation," Deutsch declared:

> The time has come when the civilized nations of the world should be concerned not only for the safety and protection of their nationals abroad, but should be keenly interested in the preservation of human rights of all minorities wherever they may be. This day of protest throughout this country and in other countries[14] is also a day of mourning.[15] We are overwhelmed with grief as we behold a situation, which if permitted to continue, would result in the descent of a great nation from a high state of enlightenment to a position of barbaric medievalism.[16]

Dr. Wise's words, which were mainly directed against Germany's Jewish leaders, questioned whether they knew what was really best for their co-religionists.

> We have no quarrel with our Jewish brothers in Germany and their leaders, but their policy of uncomplaining assent and of super-cautious silence has borne evil fruit. They who have virtually been

silent through the years of anti-Jewish propaganda cannot be followed by us as the wisest of counsellors.[17]

William Green, president of the American Federation of Labor, was among the prominent non-Jews at the Garden who added his voice to the chorus of dismayed and protesting speakers. He made it clear that Americans had no intention of interfering in Germany's political affairs, adding, however:

> But when any nation violates the laws of humanity, shocks international conscience, engages in persecution of minorities and follows a primitive, barbarian course toward helpless men and women who have committed no crime and who become the victims of racial hate, then the voice of the American Federation of Labor will be heard in solemn protest. We will not remain passive and unconcerned when the relatives, families and brethren of the Jewish members of our great economic organization are being persecuted and oppressed.[18]

Other non-Jewish speakers of national acclaim included such figures as New York's Senator Robert F. Wagner and Alfred E. Smith, former governor of New York and presidential aspirant. Wagner's main point was that human tolerance, not Judaism, was the issue in Germany. More outspoken, Smith denounced Hitler for failing to condemn and curb his Nazi rowdies. New York City's Mayor John Patrick O'Brien, completing the term of Jimmy Walker (p. 139), paid tribute to the Jewish contribution to German culture. Noted Christian clergymen also addressed the aroused crowd, which was estimated at some 55,000 people.

New York's Governor Herbert H. Lehman had also planned to address the mass rally, but was prevented from doing so by a pressing Albany meeting. At this meeting, he made an earnest appeal to the German people, calling on them to restore religious equality. But this was one of the lesser worries of the Jew in a country where legal and economic disabilities, and, indeed, the guarantee of life and limb, were in a process of steady and rapid decline.

5

The Policies of Public Enlightenment and Diplomatic Representation

i.

The Congress' March 12 decision to call mass protest meetings all over the United States was greatly resented by a surprised AJC-BB. Not only did they resent it because it was contrary to the mutual accord for joint cooperation on the German situation, but also because this was in direct violation of a unanimous decision to forbear the recourse to public agitation insofar as defensive action against the Nazis was concerned.

But resentful or no, the AJC-BB now also felt constrained to reexamine their position on the German Jewish question. So on March 16, without Congress participation, they conducted a joint meeting with the view of trying to determine what course of action to follow for the amelioration of German Jewry's degenerative status. Appreciation and understanding were shown regarding the natural impulse to express the indignation that the reports from Germany were arousing. However, it was felt that any such utterance should be characterized by restraint in order not to make still more difficult the already desperate situation of the German Jews.

The Committee's annual report for 1933, upon which the aforesaid is based, tells of a Paris meeting that was called for March 19 by Jewish organizations of "several European countries." The Committee was also invited to attend, but undisclosed "practical difficulties" made this impossible. However, at its executive meeting, held likewise on the nineteenth, the AJC phoned Paris and learned that the issue of public protest demonstrations had also engaged the attention of the Jewish conferees in the French capital. In addition, the Committee learned that the conference had unanimously agreed that public agitation by Jews at present was "not only premature, but likely to be useless and even harmful."[1]

The AJC-BB, which decided to be governed by this advice, immediately communicated their information to the leaders of the American Jewish Congress. But the Congress, which had scheduled its emergency conference for that very evening, was hardly impressed.

In view of the imminent Congress action and the mounting crisis in Germany, the Committee and the B'nai B'rith met again on March 20 and issued the following statement:

> The American Jewish Committee and the B'nai B'rith express their horror at anti-Jewish action in Germany which is denying to German Jews the fundamental rights of every human being in a spirit contrary to the traditions of American freedom and conscience, religion and liberty. The events of the past few weeks in Germany have filled with indignation not only American Jews, but also Americans of every other faith. The conscience of the civilized world is aroused against this reversion to medival barbarism. . . . The American Jewish Committee and the B'nai B'rith have for months past addressed themselves actively to those serious problems which have now reached a crisis; they have requested the American government to make proper representations to the government of Germany, and we pledge ourselves to continued and unremitting efforts in behalf of the Jews of Germany. We confidently hope that the enlightened opinion of the German people can be made aware of the gross injustice of these anti-Jewish actions and that they will demand the restoration of civilized standards in their own great nation. We hope that the conscience of the world will not be further shocked by conduct unworthy of the traditions and ideals of the German people. . . . We shall take every possible measure to discharge the solemn responsibility which rests on our organizations to marshal the forces of public opinion among Americans of every faith to right the wrongs of the Jews of Germany and for the vindication of the fundamental principles of human liberty.[2]

The Committee also drew up a concurrent policy statement which depicted the basic complaint registered against the Congress at the meeting of March 16:

> Though in this bewildering situation it is only natural for decent and liberal-minded men and women to feel outraged at these occurrences and to desire to give public expression to their indignation and abhorrence, the American Jewish Committee and the B'nai B'rith are convinced that the wisest and most effective policy for the Jews of America to pursue is to exercise the same fine patience, fortitude and exemplary conduct that have been shown by the Jews of Germany.

This is not a time further to inflame already overwrought feelings, but to act wisely, judiciously and deliberately.[3]

Like the A.J.C., the AJC-BB claimed that their stand was influenced by numerous cablegrams from responsible organizations and private letters from respected individuals in Germany. These implored them to forestall the use of mass demonstrations and other forms of public agitation. However, the rather cautious defense organizations admitted that some of these messages might have been sent under duress, but this did not cause them to modify their conviction that others expressed unequivocally the views of responsible German Jewish leaders.

It was, of course, the AJC-BB that decided who was a "responsible" German Jewish leader. Moreover, one should not lose sight of the fact that these organizations were "predisposed" to adopt their present position by policies of long standing. For example, in the review of the year 1933, contained in its annual reports series, the Committee admits that the adoption of its "attitude" on the German-Jewish question was based on a "policy laid down in the original constitution of the organization":

> The purpose of this Committee is to prevent infringement of the civil and religious rights of Jews, and to alleviate the consequences of persecution. In the event of a threatened or actual denial or invasion of such rights, or when conditions calling for relief from calamities affecting Jews, exist anywhere, correspondence may be entered into with those familiar with the situation, and if the persons on the spot feel themselves able to cope with the situation, no action need be taken; if, on the other hand, they request aid, steps shall be taken to furnish it![4]

On this basis, the Committee could and did argue that the aid it was furnishing German Jews was in harmony with the desired requests.

But the Committee's "attitude" was not as unsentimental or as "objective" as the foregoing might have us believe; for it and the B'nai B'rith consisted of members who were, for the greater part, of German extraction. Many of them had relatives in Germany and feared that the initiation of mass protest meetings and protest marches, let alone boycott declarations, would greatly offend the Nazis, and, therefore, worsen, rather than improve, the lot of German Jewry. Moreover, Germany's Order of B'nai B'rith had considerable wealth and real estate in the Reich, and its U.S. counterpart feared sequestration if it took a militant stand against Nazism.

Not so the American Jewish Congress, which, for the most part, comprised an East European immigrant strain that was traditionalist and nationalist in outlook. This "East Side" element scoffed at the quiescent methods employed in behalf of German Jewry by the "assimilationist" and "escapist" Jews of the AJC-BB. It felt that, in the present emergency, vociferous and bellicose methods, but certainly not the dainty and overly cautious approach of "marginal Jews," should prove effective in stemming the antisemitic tide that was beginning to overwhelm German Jewry.

Nor was the Congress opposed, in principle, to the idea of an anti-Nazi boycott. For the present, it merely disapproved of it as a useful weapon. And since the Congress was still not absolutely sure of Hitler's intentions regarding "his" Jews, it simply tried keeping the door open for a possible compromise with him.

ii.

Diplomatic intercession in behalf of German Jewry remained, therefore, the one basic area of approach on which the American Jewish Congress found itself in agreement with the AJC-BB. But due to the ever-growing differences between the Congress and the AJC-BB over the adoption of other anti-Nazi measures, a cooperative modus operandi could not be arranged on this score either.

March was then the inaugural month of an incoming U.S. President. The American Jewish Congress and the AJC-BB, therefore, sought appointments with key figures of the new administration, as well as other important political leaders. Thus, on the twenty-first of that month, somewhat over a fortnight after the inauguration of President Franklin Delano Roosevelt, Dr. Wise and Mr. Deutsch headed a delegation of the American Jewish Congress, which appeared before the House Immigration Committee and urged the liberalization of immigration restrictions so that relatives of American Jews might be given immediate refuge in the United States. Testifying to the urgency of widening America's gates of entry, Dr. Wise appealed for the revocation of a 1930 Executive Order that had provided for so strict an enforcement of the immigration law as to bar the admission of potential dependents. This law, which particularly affected the young, aged, and infirm, now bore down hard on German Jews and their naturalized American Jewish relatives.

The A.J.C mission also paid a visit to the State Department, where Dr. Wise presented Undersecretary of State William Phillips with a detailed account of the anti-Jewish savageries perpetrated by the Hitler regime. In their discussion, Dr. Wise expressed the view that these outrages warranted diplomatic representation, but that he was withholding the recommendation of such action, pending a verification of his report by the department. More than his personal pleas, America's own ascertainment of the "facts," believed Dr. Wise, would convince her of the dire need for diplomatic representation.

The State Department agreed to Dr. Wise's proposal, which it embodied in this release:

> Following the visit of Rabbi Stephen S. Wise, the Department has informed the American Embassy at Berlin of the press reports of mistreatment of Jews in Germany.
> The Department also informed the embassy of the deep concern these reports are causing in this country.
> The Department has instructed the embassy to make, in collaboration with the consuls, a complete report on the situation.[5]

Following through an earlier request of the outgoing administration, the AJC-BB, at the March 19 meeting mentioned above, also sought to confer with the State Department. In compliance with their request, Secretary of State Cordell Hull met with Committee and B'nai B'rith representatives on the twenty-third; and like the A.J.C. delegation, they, too, requested that representations be made on behalf of German Jewry.

But while the A.J.C. and the AJC-BB thus sought to pave the way for American diplomatic representation, the Nazis prepared "representations" of their own in response to the "Anti-German agitation in the United States." On March 22, a day after the A.J.C.'s talks on Capitol Hill, the German ambassador called at the State Department and declared that law and order would be maintained in Germany and that outrages against Jews would be punished. His assurance was based on the following cable that the Foreign Office in Berlin sent to the German Consulate General in New York the day before:

> Part of the press in foreign countries is at present publishing most exaggerated reports originating from alleged fugitives from Germany, according to which persons arrested in Germany have been subjected to brutal mistreatments and many foreign visitors to the country assaulted.
> Such rumors emanate primarily from opponents of the present national government and are being spread with malicious intent in order that, other means being not available, a well-organized atrocity propaganda may undermine the reputation and authority of the national government . . .[6]

The statement ended by citing a declaration by Hitler that the undisciplined acts of individuals would be prevented in the future with the most stringent measures.

On March 26, upon the receipt of the same information from the U.S. Embassy in Berlin, Hull dispatched the following telegram to the respective presidents[7] of the three leading Jewish defense organizations in the United States:

> You will remember that at the time of your recent call at the Department I informed you that, in view of numerous press statements indicating widespread mistreatment of the Jews in Germany, I would request the American Embassy at Berlin in consultation with the principal consulates in Germany to investigate the situation and submit a report.
>
> A reply has now been received indicating that whereas there was for a short time considerable physical mistreatment of Jews, this phase may be considered virtually terminated. There was also some picketing of Jewish merchandising stores and instances of professional discrimination. These manifestations were viewed with serious concern by the German Government.
>
> Hitler, in his capacity as leader of the Nazi party, issued an order calling upon his followers to maintain law and order to avoid molesting foreigners, disrupting trade, and to avoid the creation of possibly embarassing international incidents.
>
> Later, von Papen delivered a speech at Breslau in which he not only reiterated Hitler's appeals for discipline, but abjured the victors of the last election not to spoil their triumph by unworthy acts of revenge and violence which could only bring discredit upon the new regime in foreign countries. As a result, the embassy reports that the authority of the regular police has been reinforced.
>
> The feeling has been widespread in Germany that following so far-reaching a political readjustment as has recently taken place, some time must elapse before a state of equilibrium could be re-established. In the opinion of the embassy, such a stabilization appears to have been reached in the field of personal mistreatment, and there are indications that in other phases the situation is improving.
>
> I feel hopeful, in view of the reported attitude of high German officials and the evidences of amelioration already indicated, that the situation which has caused such widespread concern throughout this country, will soon revert to normal. Meanwhile, I shall continue to watch the situation closely, with a sympathetic interest and with a desire to be helpful in whatever way possible.[8]

The record shows that only Dr. Wise and Mr. Deutsch prepared a reply, which was dispatched on the night of the twenty-sixth:

> In the name of the American Jewish Congress we wish to thank you for your prompt report on the situation in Germany, which confirms our fears that there has been "considerable mistreatment of Jews,

picketing of merchandising stores and instances of professional discrimination."

The American Jewish Congress notes your statement that Hitler "has issued an order calling upon his followers to maintain law and order, to avoid molesting foreigners, disrupting trade and to avoid the creation of possibly embarrassing international incidents."

We are deeply grateful for your assurances that you will continue to watch the situation closely with a sympathetic interest. For we feel that, in view of the official program of the Nazi party and its record of thirteen years of disseminating hatred against the Jewish people, the Jews in Germany are in great and immediate jeopardy of life and property, of civil rights and religious liberty. Until the status of the Jewish citizens of Germany is safeguarded and the position of the non-national Jews is secured, the enlightened opinion of America must watch with profoundest anxiety the development of events in Germany.

May we repeat what we emphasized in the course of our visit to the State Department, namely, that we are moved by no feeling of ill-will to the German nation. Our concern is for the security of the Jews of Germany and the safeguarding of their human and political rights.[9]

iii.

One had only to read the reports of reputable correspondents to realize that the Nazis were feeding Hull the kind of information he actually wanted to receive. But the true character of Nazi intentions was revealed in a matter of twenty-four hours, when it was announced that an anti-Jewish boycott would take place.

The disclosure caused an alarmed Jewish Congress to immediately raise an emergency fund for German Jewish victims, in addition to trying to stave off an already blistering antisemitic campaign by the Nazis. Moral support was promptly given by New York City's Board of Aldermen, of which Bernard Deutsch was a member. Without dissent, it resolved on March 28 to earnestly request the U.S. government to make "vigorous and proper representation" to the German government against the persecution of Jews.

The sudden crisis occasioned a renewed visit to Washington by an A.J.C. delegation; and in pursuance of its mandate to request the State Department to make representations to the German government, the impending boycott became the subject of a March 30 discussion between Undersecretary of State Phillips, Rabbi Wise, Mr. Deutsch, and a legal adviser of the two prominent Jewish leaders. Neither the contents of this discussion nor any statements pertaining thereto were announced to the public. The press, however, in line with Hull's recently declared position, stated that the U.S. government would make no formal protest, but use its influence quietly. For it was thought that a formal protest at this time would give the appearance of pressure against the Hitler regime. The April 1 minutes of the Congress' Administrative Committee confirm this opinion.

The announced boycott obviously had to have its reverberations in the Committee, too. Thus, on March 29, Eric Warburg of Hamburg, scion of a noted banking and philanthropic family, cabled his U.S. cousin, Frederick Warburg, as follows:

> Today's boycott threats against Jewish firms in Germany will be carried out if atrocities news and unfriendly propaganda in foreign press mass meetings, etc., does not stop immediately. Repeat, therefore, urgent request to use all your influence so that all that ceases. Utmost speed necessary as boycott otherwise starting Saturday morning.[10]

Frederick Warburg, who was a personal friend of Cyrus Adler, president of the American Jewish Committee, apprized the AJC chief of this telegram and the reply he intended to send his German cousin:

> Will do and have done my best but recent government boycott announcement viewed here as confirmation previous reports of discrimination. Resentment so widespread no individual efforts to stem it likely avail unless government changes attitude. Will continue to discourage mass meetings and unfounded atrocity stories. No responsible groups here urging boycott German goods merely excited individuals.[11]

Adler relayed this information to Morris D. Waldman, the Committee's executive secretary, commenting: "I also advised him to add that no responsible body in this country had proposed a boycott against Germany and the statements to that effect that had been made were purely sporadic."[12]

This was then inserted in the following statement that Adler suggested that Waldman issue:

> The American Jewish Committee declares that to its knowledge most of these so-called atrocity stories which were reported from Germany to have appeared in the American press did not so appear—in fact there were accounts of mishandling and threats of a boycott against all Jews in Germany. No threats of boycott in America have been made by any responsible Jewish body. They were irresponsible sporadic outbursts. It is impossible to tell, however, what will happen if the threat of boycott against all Jews in Germany is carried out on April 1st.[13]

Had Adler waited just one day before including in his statement a reference to the boycott of German goods—which was not mentioned in Eric Warburg's telegram—he could have pointed to a similar communication that did speak of this subject. It came from Oscar Wasserman, director of the Deutsche Bank, and a non-Zionist supporter of Palestine:

> There is no doubt that threatened boycott against Jews will be carried through with full severity if somewhere protest meetings would be held or boycott against German goods would be started by Jews or with Jewish assistance. As German Jews are faced with utmost poverty and distress if Jews in foreign countries continue to interfere, I request your help as far as you can and should be thankful for your reply.[14]

Adler's reply was:

> The American Jewish Committee, of which I am president, has taken no part in protest meetings. No responsible body in America has suggested boycott. We have been and are doing all in our power to allay agitation.[15]

What of the position of the American Jewish Congress in this regard? Revealing information is contained in the following May 1, 1933 minutes of a May 15, 1933 minutes document.

> In the report of the Conference with Secretary Hull, Mr. Deutsch stated he learned from reliable sources that the Nazi Government agreed to call off the official boycott in Germany if the State Department of the United States would issue a friendly statement to that Government. The proposed statement did not reach Germany in time to get the boycott called off entirely. This accounts for the fact that the boycott lasted only one day.[16]

On April 2, Hull spoke long-distance with the American chargé d'affaires in Berlin, and was informed that the situation was not distressing; that, generally, the boycott had gone off quietly, and that there did not appear to be serious signs of trouble. This was probably the reply Hull gave the AJC-BB presidents, who, on April 6, again communicated with him to inquire if he had taken further steps to help ameliorate the conditions of German Jewry. However, the Jewish Congress did not share the optimism expressed in the report Hull had received. The same day in which Cyrus Adler (p. 42) and Alfred Cohen, the president of the American Order of the B'nai B'rith, communicated with the American Secretary of State, Wise and Deutsch, in a signed statement, denounced as follows the NSP proclamation not to renew the boycott:

> Announcement was made today by the German Government that the organized anti-Jewish boycott will not be resumed. This announcement will not deceive anybody interested in the actual plight of the Jews in Germany. The attitude of the German Government is more truthfully reflected in the brutality which accompanied the organized execution of the boycott and its humiliating violations of human rights and dignity. Although the period of spectacular intimidation and terror may now be over, and despite official pronouncements to the contrary, the anti-Jewish policy of repression and cruel harassments is being systematically and authoritatively continued under the direction of the Hitler Government.
>
> It is apparent that the dominant forces in the present German Government willfully misunderstand and intend to persist in misunderstanding the meaning of the world-wide protest against its inhuman anti-Jewish policy. The indignation of the world has been expressed not merely against excesses and outrages, against one-day boycotts, against the irresponsible conduct of the political masters of Germany, but against that policy which these masters officially declare to be the program of the German nation. This program means the degradation of the Jews of Germany, by cutting them off from all civil pursuits and professions, by isolating them from the general life of the German people and accomplishing their ultimate economic extermination. These rights are basic and inalienable. The public opinion of the world demands that they shall be secured.[17]

The concluding section expressed the hope that Germany would come to realize that it was in her own interests that anti-Jewish propaganda should cease and that an end should be put to the economic persecution of the Jews.

6

The Incipient Boycott

JWV Rumblings

Fredman's proposal at the Congress' Emergency Conference of March 19, to tack on to the Margoshes resolution an amendment calling for the boycott of German goods, may have sounded to many like a cry in the wilderness; but not to the Jewish War Veterans, who, purportedly, voted for a boycott early that very day, in what appears to have been part of a series of meetings to deliberate the German-Jewish problem. Accordingly, Fredman presided over these meetings, while one Benjamin Sperling, commander of Brooklyn's East Post, advanced the boycott proposal at a March 18–19 session. Those opposed feared reprisals against Germany's Jews by the Nazis. Others, however, were quick to point out that the Nazis would continue their anti-Jewish policy irrespective of JWV action. Sperling's proposal was passed, in any event, and Col. Morris J. Mendelson, himself a four-time commander of the Jewish War Veterans, who, at first, opposed the motion, agreed to become chairman of the JWV Boycott Committee.[1]

Mendelson's first move was to schedule a veterans parade for March 23 to demonstrate JWV's indignation at the persecution of German Jewry. Thereto, he invited William W. Cohen, the other vice-president of the American Jewish Congress and erstwhile U.S. congressman, to act as marshal of the parade. On the evening of March 20, shortly following an announcement to this effect, W. W. Cohen was the honored guest of another JWV meeting. At this time, Cohen was, perhaps, the only senior Congress officer who favored the boycott. He evinced his approval of the

JWV's recent decision by saying: "Any Jew buying one penny's worth of merchandise made in Germany is a traitor to his people. I doubt that the American Government can officially take any notice of what the German Government is doing to its own citizens. Our only line of resistance is to touch German pocketbooks."[2]

On the day of the parade, approximately 2,000 non-Jewish veterans marched together with about the same number of Jewish veterans to the delight of civilian onlookers many times that number. The exservicemen were reviewed by Mayor O'Brien (p. 34), who was presented with resolutions calling for diplomatic protest to and an economic boycott of Nazi Germany. Regarding the latter, JWV claimed that, only several days following its decision to boycott, about $2,000,000 worth of orders placed in Germany had been canceled. The sundry number of JWV's boycott activities helps in the appreciation of this claim.

First and foremost, JWV activities centered in and around the various posts; and as such, each post was instructed to initiate "its own particular boycott movement." Often heading the list of such programming was a "campaign to picket with boycott placards all department stores selling German goods."[3] To offset the dependence of importers on German-made products, JWV boycott committees prepared fliers informing such businessmen that they could be furnished with the names and addresses of non-German manufacturers who could supply the same articles with just as attractive terms.

Striking slogans were often used by the Jewish Veterans in order to dramatize and vivify the boycott. One of them appeared on seals issued in May (1933), bearing the legend: FOR HUMANITY'S SAKE, DON'T BUY GERMAN GOODS. Another device was to circulate fliers listing catchphrases intended to drum into the recipient the boycott message:

DON'T BUY GERMAN GOODS
DON'T SELL GERMAN GOODS
DON'T SHIP AMERICAN MERCHANDISE IN GERMAN SHIPS
DON'T PATRONIZE GERMAN MOVING PICTURES
DO IT YOURSELF. TELL YOUR FAMILY AND FRIENDS TO DO IT, BUT BY ALL MEANS, BOYCOTT, BOYCOTT, BOYCOTT![4]

But as a strictly military organization, JWV lacked the prestige and recognition of civilian bodies like the A.J.C. and the AJC-BB. On March 30, J. George Fredman (p. 30), in the company of a JWV delegation, had managed to present President Roosevelt with a resolution condemning the mistreatment of Jews in Germany; however, this was little more than a symbolic act.

For nearly two months the Jewish War Veterans stood virtually alone in their declared boycott war against the Nazis. And there can be little doubt that it was the JWV that the Congress had in mind when it stated on March 21 that it looked askance, at least for the present, at a sporadic movement begun in some Jewish circles for a trade boycott on Germany. Such a boycott, the Congress maintained, was untimely. Nevertheless, it was indicated that the boycott might be resorted to if German propaganda and anti-Nazi activities did not cease.

The JWV must also have been intended when, a week later, the Committee declared in a public statement that "no threats of boycott in America have been made by any responsible Jewish body"; and that "they were irresponsible sporadic outbursts" (p. 42, item 13).

However, several anti-Nazi defense organizations were soon to learn, if they, indeed, believed their own statements, just how "sporadic" or "irresponsible" a movement the boycott really was.

The Birth of the American League for the Defense of Jewish Rights

On April 22, 1933, a rather inconspicuous notice appeared in the two New York City Yiddish dailies, *Der Forverts* (The Forward) and *Der Tog* (The Day), summoning all who believed in the need of instituting a boycott against "the bloody Hitler" to contact the American League for the Defense of Jewish Rights (ALDJR). The notice bore the signatures of Dr. Abraham Coralnik, associate editor of *Der Tog* and head of the League's Provisional Boycott Committee, and Louis Mayer, a movie producer, who had, apparently, promised the infant organization financial backing.[5]

Information relating to Dr. Coralnik's private and public life is too sparse to make it possible to pinpoint his decision to form a boycott organization. Coralnik was not well known to Anglo-Jewish readers and played no major role in Jewish communal affairs. He was a rather introverted man of letters, who, impelled by the emotionally charged events of the day, became strongly aroused and burst into action.

According to a May 4 press release, Coralnik had from the very first advocated a Jewish boycott. But just why he decided to announce it when he did is a matter of conjecture. Thus, he may have found the boycott declaration of the Jewish War Veterans a source of inspiration. Certainly, as we shall presently see, the call to boycott on the part of European Jewry greatly influenced him. However, there is less guesswork in the assertion that his action resulted from the failure of American and Jewish defense organizations to declare a boycott. This may be inferred from another part of Dr. Coralnik's press statement, in which he said that he took it for granted that, unofficially, American Jews—whether their leadership did or did not recognize it—had already instituted a boycott. His League, Dr. Coralnik emphasized, intended to organize and coordinate it by serving those who wished to avoid buying German merchandise.

To get the League underway, Coralnik called a conference for May 14 of all organizations favoring the boycott. Each such organization was instructed to be represented by two delegates. To make doubly sure that no anti-boycott organizations attended, Coralnik underscored the point that the conference was not open to a debate on whether or not to boycott. Its purpose, he stated most emphatically, was to devise a system that would produce the best boycott possible.

In a press statement made in regard to the forthcoming boycott conference, Dr. Coralnik expounded on the compelling circumstances that prompted his calling it:

> The need for Jewish defense against Hitler ruthlessness grows more urgent from day to day. His "cold pogrom" is proceeding in all its cruelty, aimed at not less than the extermination of the Jews of Germany. This is no ordinary antisemitism, but an inexorable war against the Jewish race, unparalleled in the history of modern times.
>
> Hitler's Germany has chosen the Jews as the special victims of attack. Those in his power are stricken and helpless, but their fellow Jews in enlightened lands are determined to spare no efforts to crush Hitlerism, the world menace.[6]

In an article written on the eve of the conference,[7] Cornalnik gave a digest of the arguments of the boycott adversaries: (1) that a boycott would be uncultural, unethical, and un-Jewish; and since Jews were a moral people, they should not resort to so coarse and uncivilized a weapon; (2) that Jews were not cohesive or organized enough to conduct a boycott—witness the rift between the Committee and the Congress, as even the present emergency had failed to unite them; (3) that a boycott would be a two-edged sword, which, if wielded, could have a disastrous effect upon the Jewish people, for should World Jewry embark on a boycott against Germany, the latter could declare a counter-boycott against the German Jews or Jews of other countries. Moreover, by declaring an anti-Nazi boycott, Jewry would deprive itself of the moral position which was its only means of effecting a change in German policy; for one who boycotted others would have no moral right to protest being boycotted by others.

In reply to these arguments, Coralnik said that he regarded the boycott as a sacrificial act: men sacrificing their own interests—even themselves if need be—for the sake of others. As an illustration, he cited Mohandas Karamchand Gandhi's efforts in behalf of India. Gandhi, said Coralnik, explained to his people that only through England's help could they ever hope to become westernized. This in itself, believed the Indian leader, was a desirable goal. But because, in the process, India was suffering degradation at England's hands, she had to forgo westernization; at least to reject living in luxury, the concomitant of the introduction of modern industry and advanced technology. India had to do this if she expected to save herself from undue national and psychological harm, a cause that made sacrifice imperative; and interestingly enough, Dr. Coralnik pointed out, India made the necessary sacrifice.

Coralnik believed that the Indian experiment could be applied by Jews in a manner to suit their present exigency. Jewish merchants could be told that they would have no joy in the end from profits earned by dealing with their bloodiest enemy, Hitler Germany. Nor should it be difficult to make them understand that for only a few pennies they were placing in jeopardy their own future and that of their children. Or to put it more bluntly: Germany had obviously become the Jews' greatest enemy, and one does not engage in trade with an enemy.

As to the charge that the boycott was unethical, and meant fighting a barbarian with barbaric methods, Coralnik argued that such "Biblical morals" could not and would not solve the Jewish question. Hitler was trampling the Bible under foot, and he had eliminated all those to whom one could have turned on humanitarian and moral grounds. The entire situation, concluded the Yiddish journalist, reduced itself to the crude formula that when one lives among wolves, one has to act like one to survive.

What follows after the discussion of the theoretical and ideological arguments against boycott is a cold and practical appraisal of Germany. Germany was an industrial country; and more than any other European power, she depended on her exports. Should the gates of import be shut to her, she was certain to become impoverished. Then, and only then, would Germany come to realize the enormity of her crime.

Coralnik admitted that a boycott would hurt Germany's Jewish merchants. However, this was the sacrifice he believed they must make to the cause of defeating Hitler.[8]

European Liaison

At about the time that an organized boycott movement was beginning to make its appearance in the United States, a similar development had started taking place in Europe. It is important to refer to this development, since it stirred the interest of the soon-to-be boycott leaders in America.

It seems that Poland, which contained the densest Jewish population on the continent, was the first country in which the boycott made itself manifest. Thus, on March 20, 1933, at a mass meeting of Vilna Jews, World Jewry was called upon to form a united front to block German attempts to annex the Polish Corridor and was urged to advise all Jewish businesses to prepare for a trade boycott of German goods and services.

In Warsaw, six days later, Polish Jewry resolved to shut its shops and factories the following day in unanimous protest against the harassment of coreligionists in Germany. Along the lines of, and seemingly influenced by, the policy of the American Jewish Congress, a resolution was adopted to arrange for mass meetings throughout Poland. Of the many Jewish organizations represented in the Polish capital, some merchants' associations resolved not to hesitate to use the boycott if Nazi outrages against Jews did not cease.

This threat was made good right after the anti-Jewish boycott of April 1. By the end of that week, the boycott of German goods embraced virtually all of Poland. The movement was directed by the Central Boycott Committee,[9] which consisted of twenty-two members culled from all of that country's Jewish economic institutions. These included the Central Merchants Association, the Retailers Association, the Union of Jewish Artisans, the Association of Physicians, the Association of Engineers, and the Association of Commercial Agents. The rapidity with which the boycott spread apparently gave the Nazis much concern, as by mid-April they renewed a protest to the Polish government in this regard.

Sharp anti-Nazi manifestations also took place in Great Britain. These were particularly visible on March 24, when placards bearing the words BOYCOTT GERMAN GOODS appeared in front of the stores of the high-class shopping district of London's West End. Identical posters were placed atop automobiles that were slowly driven through the streets. True to the spirit of this exhortation, a majority of the Jewish store-owners in the East End of the English capital posted notices warning German salesmen not to call on them.

Actually, it was in the Jewish quarter of the East End that this campaign originated through the creation, by 2,000 Jews and non-Jews, of a British Anti-War Council. This act was accompanied by a resolution to send a delegation to the German embassy at the head of a column of marchers representing all East End workers. However, this step was soon overshadowed by the spectacle of a spontaneous boycott movement that rapidly gained in momentum and intensity. The effect of the boycott was most evident in the English-German fur business, which was virtually strangled as a result.

However, not all of Britain's Jews favored a boycott, official or unofficial. Like the American Jewish Committee and B'nai B'rith, the majority of the Board of Deputies of British Jews—recognized as the authoritative voice and defender of English Jewry—opposed the boycott out of fear of reprisals against German Jews. As a matter of fact, the leading members of the foregoing organizations were in constant contact with one another on this issue.

The boycott fever in France did not break out as early, and seemingly, as intensely, as it did in either Poland or England. Still, on March 31, French Jews, in sympathy with their persecuted brothers in Hitler Germany, prepared to counter-boycott German goods as soon as the all-day boycott in Germany went into effect. In a manner similar to the notices that appeared in London's East End stores, numerous Jewish shops in France displayed posters notifying representatives of German concerns that they would be denied entry. By thus joining the Jewries of England and the United States in a boycott of German goods, the Jews of the West's third great power were now also threatening Germany's trade position. Moreover, with boycott movements developing in Czechoslovakia, Holland, Belgium, Switzerland, Turkey, Egypt, and other countries, the threat to the Nazi economy seemed serious. How to avert it was therefore becoming a major Nazi anxiety; for as the Nazis grew more secure about their political position both at home and abroad, the boycott loomed ahead as a distinct menace to their regime.

The Advent of Samuel Untermyer

i.

Mounting Nazi fury against the Jews also brought into public view Samuel Untermyer, former vice-president of the American Jewish Congress, a supporter of Palestine, a well-known political figure in the city of New York, and one of America's foremost attorneys. Untermyer appears to have been provoked into action by the April 1 boycott and the lack of a concrete sign that the Nazis had any intention of altering their decidedly anti-Jewish policy. These two basic considerations, more than likely, influenced his decision to voice his support in favor of an anti-Nazi boycott.

On April 13, Untermyer seized the occasion of the presentation of a memorial gift to the Hebrew University, to say:

> Our people would be justified in seeing to it that nowhere in the world and under no circumstances should a Jew, from this day forth, buy or use merchandise manufactured in Germany or support German industry in any form. The action taken in that respect by the

Jewish shopkeepers in London might well be followed the world over. It was not only a wanton and gratuitous insult to our pride, but one that had no reason or excuse in any social or economic situation, since the Jews constitute but one percent of the population of Germany.[10]

In another speech, a radio address delivered on April 16, Untermyer criticized the U.S. Congress for its failure to speak out against German antisemitism. Comparing this with Britain's stand, he said:

> The striking and unpleasant contrast between Great Britain's spontaneous outburst of protest and indignation in the House of Commons[11] and the British press[12] and the ominous silence of our Congress by way of reaction to this reign of terror, indicates the difference between a country steeped in the true love of racial and religious liberty that sees in such action an affront to civilization, regardless of race and creed, and a country that chooses to treat it with silence as a mere "racial question."[13]

Appearing in Boston at a Palestine campaign meeting held at Symphony Hall on May 7, Untermyer again availed himself of a speaking engagement to urge the American people to adopt an all-out boycott against Nazi Germany. Describing it as the "obvious remedy," and Hitler's political platform as the "most stirring call to arms in Jewish history," Untermyer said:

> I am an ardent champion of an effective boycott that will teach the German people that we Jews have not lost our self-respect. It is our only effective weapon against this brutal onslaught upon our people.
>
> I am, however, aware that there is a very large and respectable element among our people, for whose opinion I have the highest respect, that advises against this course, but fails to suggest, any other remedy. Their argument is based upon the fear that if the boycott proves effective, Hitler and his fellow-ruffians in office will carry out their implied threats and let loose their hatred by indulging and encouraging bloody pogroms against their unfortunate victims, which they would not otherwise dare.
>
> That is what they started to do and what I fear they will do, in any event, unless restrained by some remaining shred of fear of the opinion of the civilized world.[14]

ii.

Unknown, as yet, to Samuel Untermyer, his outspoken pro-boycott statements were being followed with great interest by Ezekiel Rabinowitz, the executive secretary of the American League for the

Defense of Jewish Rights and a member of its Provisional Boycott Committee. Rabinowitz was keenly aware that the infant League was barely known outside of a closely-knit Yiddish-speaking circle, lacked funds, and, perhaps, worst of all, had no nationally recognized member. He, therefore, felt that the League could greatly profit from an association with so prominent and wealthy a figure as Samuel Untermyer.

On May 11, Rabinowitz invited Untermyer to address the League's founding conference, which was scheduled to take place three days later. Untermyer sent a letter of acceptance the following day, and added:

> My conclusion in favor of the boycott was reached only after the most serious consideration and a full realization of all the risks it involves. We must either sit by and allow those fanatics to wreak their will upon our brethren in Germany or try to make the German Government understand that we have at least one effective method of registering our protest.[15]

ALDJR's opening conference, which was held in New York's Hotel Astor, proved a stirring affair. It was attended by nearly 600 delegates representing some 288 fraternal, professional, religious, and merchant groups. And in keeping with the scope and range of so ambitious an undertaking, an impressive roster of guest speakers, Jews and non-Jews, highlighted the eventful meeting: among them, (in addition to Mr. Untermyer) Congressman and soon-to-be Mayor Fiorello H. LaGuardia, James W. Gerard, former U.S. ambassador to Germany, Jacob De Haas, famed American Zionist leader, and Samuel Margoshes (see p. 29).

LaGuardia accounted for his presence as follows: "I am here not as a Jew, not as a Gentile, but as an American to join in a world movement for the purpose of putting Adolf Hitler out of power. The American people can by their action protest against this menace to world peace."[16]

LaGuardia was greeted with a burst of applause when he stated that an economic boycott against Hiterlism on a national and international scale would "render a great world service." He added that he welcomed the boycott as the first manifestation in history in which the peoples of the world themselves, acting in the spirit of the Covenant of the League of Nations, would apply economic pressure to bring to terms a nation menacing world peace. He pointedly stressed that:

> There is but one way we can get the people of Germany to realize that we are willing to help them rid themselves of the menace of Hitlerism. While the civilized governments of the world are making up their minds as to what to do about this menace, we are here today to launch a boycott against all German goods. I am sure if this boycott is successful in the United States, it will be followed in other countries.

This is the first opportunity the peoples of the world themselves have had to smash a menace to world peace. You are fighting for a just cause, for every mother who does not want to see her sons die in another war.[17]

LaGuardia concluded by urging an indefatigable boycott until German importations into the United States, which had been showing a decline since 1929, were reduced to zero.

Gerard, a non-Jew, urged that Jews seek to attain unity on the boycott issue: "We are with you in this fight for humanity, but first of all, you people have to hang together. You have to show your power and you have to do it in an economic way."[18] He added the following message of comfort and advice: "The Gentiles in this country are for you: they are with you in this. We see today the nations of Europe again arraying themselves against the new barbarism in Europe. It will not last long. In order to shorten the reign, it is up to you to do what you can."[19]

De Haas, a Herzlian disciple, who, in 1902, had replaced Stephen Wise as secretary of the Federation of American Zionists, urged public agitation to induce Jews not to purchase German goods and pressure to persuade merchants to display signs reading: WE DO NOT BUY GERMAN GOODS AND WE DO NOT SELL GERMAN SUPPLIES. He also urged that farmers be prevailed upon not to buy German potash, and that physicians, dentists, and pharmacists be persuaded to ban German-made medicinal products and drugs.

Margoshes, who had in the meantime come around to believe in the necessity of a boycott, stated that this meant commercial war with Germany; that "there will be no quarter given nor received." He then went on to say: "We must force into the open those who should be with us in this movement. Where are the Jewish governors? Where are the Jewish Congressmen? This is no time for pussyfooting. Whoever is not for us is against us, be he Jew or Gentile, or member of the American Jewish Committee."[20]

Untermyer criticized those businessmen who minimized the significance of events in Nazi Germany, describing the Hitler Cabinet as "the most astounding assemblage of irresponsible semi-savages ever gathered together."[21] He went into the mechanics of a boycott, so conducted as to affect all branches of German industry, trade, and shipping. In contrast to his previous statement of May 7, 1933, Untermyer now directly attacked the AJC and all "timid" elements that opposed an active fight against Hitlerism. He addressed himself to them as follows:

> To the few timid, credulous, well-intentioned souls among the

American Jews who have no defensive plan whatever to offer, but who are unwilling to commit themselves to a boycott, what are you going to do? Are you going to sit idly by while your brethren in Germany are humiliated, degraded, deprived of their rights of citizenship and kicked out of their professions and employment and left to starve by this Austrian upstart and his band of ruffians?

That is not my conception of your right and duty. You are no more peace-loving than the rest of us. The only difference between us is that you lack the will and courage to fight. It is so easy to counsel "peace" when there is no peace. What you recommend is virtually a counsel of despair and surrender to the most inhuman forces that have dominated government in centuries.

This boycott can and must be made so effective that it will strike at the very foundations of the campaign that is being waged against the Jews in Germany.[22]

Untermyer also pointed out that, in anticipation of the boycott, a number of stores had removed from their German-made goods labels stating the country of origin. This, he said, was in violation of the law, and he recommended action in Washington to secure statutory enforcement.

The conference gave unanimous approval to a boycott resolution.[23] It was not only aimed at enlisting the support of American Jews, but all American non-Jews sympathetic to the boycott movement. The movement, it was announced, would be patterned after the model of English Jewry. Thus, district trade committees were to be organized and enlightenment diffused among, or pressure applied against, merchants and consumers. It was explained that this objective was in keeping with an overall plan to give the boycott an international character.

The next day (May 12), Dr. Coralnik made the following announcement:

> It is our basic policy to divide the struggle against Hitlerism into two distinct parts—political and economic. The political side we are leaving to be conducted by the properly constituted authorities of the government and by Jewish official bodies in cooperation with such non-Jewish organizations as are in sympathy with our cause. The economic side must be confined to traders and industrialists, of whom as many as possible must be mobilized by the League, and must be a purely commercial movement. Hitler must be given to understand that decent businessmen will refuse to trade with a country in which racial discrimination prevails.[24]

It now remained to be seen to what extent the boycott struggle unleashed against Hitler Germany would prevail and what effect, if any, this would have on the antagonistic policy of the new and sinister Nazi regime.

Press Reception

When the JWV announced its boycott, the matter was given slight attention in the general press; certainly, no editorial comment. Understandably, coverage by the Yiddish press was more generous. Still, it did not elicit editorial comment. The same—with some exceptions closely linked to JWV—appears to have been the case with regard to the Anglo-Jewish press.

In the main, this kind of response was due to the fact that JWV did not represent American Jewry at large; and also, because it did not have or enjoy the support of newsmaking personalities. In addition, "militant" action was expected from a militant organization. But in itself, this did not necessarily signify the unfolding of a counter-boycott response.

However, the very opposite almost happened upon the close of the League's founding conference. The event was given extensive coverage in the Yiddish, Anglo-Jewish, and general press. Editorial comment was also available. The Yiddish press, represented by such dailies as the *Day,* the *Forward,* and the *Morning Journal,* wholeheartedly supported the boycott. The Anglo-Jewish press accorded it a mixed response. In the general press, however, only the *New York Evening Post* saw fit to react editorially.

The May 14 editorial of the *Day,* commenting on the scheduled ALDJR conference, concurred that the time for mere discussions and protests was over. It was time to act, it stated, for it was either Hitler or the Jews. If he succeeded, Jews the world over would be doomed. They, therefore, had not only the right to boycott him for the sake of self-preservation, but the moral duty to do so. For unlike Spanish Jewry in 1492, contemporary Jews had ways and means to wage a defensive war against their adversary. The editorial was also encouraged by the fact that the world's conscience and heart were with the Jews, and that they needed only to unite and remain strong.

The *Forward* reacted on May 16. It explained that it supported the boycott because, in the face of the present persecution, it saw no other way out for the German Jews. Having lost everything already, they stood to lose nothing from a boycott. If they were opposed to the anti-Hitler campaign, it was only because they were frightened and terror-stricken. Obviously, they could not and dared not protest or resist. It, therefore, fell upon non-German Jews to choose the means of righting the wrong of their German Jewish brethren. "Our choice is BOYCOTT" was the inevitable response.

The *Morning Journal* also reacted on the sixteenth. While expressing support of the boycott, it was critical of one of the suggestions made at the conference; namely, that no financial aid should be sent to German Jewry. "No cent for Relief" was the slogan of the proponents of this view, who held that this kind of support would only encourage further anti-Jewish legislation; for if the Nazis saw that World Jewry was willing to maintain Jews in Germany, German Jews might very well be robbed of all their savings.

However, the editorial denied that boycott and relief were mutually exclusive. On the contrary, such a view would merely enable wealthy Jews to default on their charitable obligations toward the German Jewish community and yet maintain an air of respectability by rejecting German goods and services. Many could be persuaded not to buy certain items or to buy substitutes instead; but only the philanthropy of the few could give succor to the jobless and homeless German Jews. Such victims would be unable to endure until the boycott produced the desired effect.

Derisive notions of this kind were not conductive to a united front, so important for boycott efficacy, the paper added. It doubted that sympathetic Christians would be amenable to the complete repudiation of the idea of relief for a Hitler Germany. The declassed German Jews must be helped in every way possible, however. For one thing, the breach between proponents and opponents of relief must be healed. With relief and boycott complementing one another, both would be assured a greater measure of success.

Of the general press, one popular city daily printed an editorial on May 15, 1933, entitled, "A Bad Weapon":

> We well appreciate the spirit of protest which animated last night's meeting of the American League for the Defense of Jewish Rights. We can even stand with Mr. Untermyer in calling the Hitler Cabinet, as revealed by their doctrines, "the most astounding assemblage of irresponsible semi-savages ever gathered together." And we can understand the purpose of the proposed all-Jewish boycott of German goods to be the only "effective weapon" against Hitler's tyrannous antisemitism. But we cannot approve the weapon. A boycott is a double—or triple—edged sword. No man can tell which way it may finally cut. Furthermore, in this juncture, when for the good of all of us we are trying to have a new barrier set up. All boycotts "hurt business." Finally, this action by American Jews may well tend to drag America into a form of opposition to Germany that it might not care to take. That matter should be left for Government determination in

some such manner as the announcement of the establishment of the French-British-American bloc.[25]

The paper also printed Dr. Coralnik's reply to the editor:

Sir, we appreciate highly the fine thoughts and sincere sentiment underlying your editorial of May 15, *A Bad Weapon,* concerning the economic boycott proclaimed by the American League for the Defense of Jewish Rights.

We fully appreciate the great responsibility which we took upon ourselves in announcing this boycott and the consequences it may entail.

Where I disagree with you, however, is that this weapon is a "bad weapon." What is a boycott? It is the only civilized weapon used against a warring nation. It is a method of isolation—the most effective means in a case of spreading pestilence. It wasn't the Jews but Hitler and his cohorts, who called first a boycott on Jews in Germany as a reprisal for the demonstration of protest and indignation against the atrocious treatment and the disenfranchisement of German Jews. The Nazi boycott on Jews, although officially suspended, is practically and to all effect carried on relentlessly in all ramifications of life. Against this governmental, officially recognized strangling of Jewish life and activities, against this degradation of Jewish men and women in every walk of life, our fight is intended.

It was with a heavy heart and in a sacrificial sprit that we adopted the last resource of our fight—the boycott. We are sure that the American public will appreciate the spirit of a people which is ready to undergo hardships in order to defend its honor and dignity and to help by this sacrificial act to re-establish peace and liberty in the world.

As far as the business interests are concerned, we are more than sure that by diverting temporarily—until Germany changes its course and re-establishes civil rights of the Jews to a full extent into other channels, in the main toward the industry and the markets of America, we are helping to revive in this country prosperity and affluence. By this policy of boycott adopted by us, we are doing a patriotic service as Americans without embarrassing in any way our National Administration and are fulfilling our moral functions in the society of free men.[26]

7

The Committee and the Boycott

i.

With the initiation of an organized anti-Nazi boycott movement, the Committee prepared to fight on "two fronts." For the time being, though, it still tended to treat the boycott as just another form of public agitation. For up to now, only the April 1 boycott of the Nazis had pressured it to issue some statements in which the growing anti-Nazi boycott movement was singled out for condemnation. At the time, it seemed an easy thing to dismiss this boycott as "sporadic" and "irresponsible." And in so doing, the Committee, which was obviously aiming its adjectival arrows at the JWV, did not care to dignify this organization by referring to it by name.

For a few months, as we shall presently see, such a position did not seem very much at odds with the rest of the American Jewish community. The Jewish War Veterans, even accepting their claim that they represented 250,000 men, did not, as already stated (p. 46), represent the Jewish masses. Coralnik's League was just getting under way; and the Congress, the Committee's most serious "competitor," still hesitated to proclaim a boycott, concentrating its energies, instead, on rallies and parades. As long as this was the predominant situation, the Committee did not see fit to actively resist the idea of an organized boycott movement.

But organized or not, in the circumstances produced by the Nazi victory at the polls, demands for boycott filled the air; and the Committee, like the Congress, received many inquiries and suggestions on the subject. One such communication was addressed by Cyrus Adler as early as March 22, by Ralph Friedman, a Wall Street businessman. It recommended the use of a boycott, rather than the mass protest, as the least dangerous anti-German weapon:

> Mass protests and denunciations are at times very satisfying emotionally to the framers of the resolutions, but we must keep in mind that they also carry in them an inherent danger of provoking further bitterness on the other side of the water, and consequently further retaliation against the Jews of Germany, who are already surely beset. Quieter action, involving an unrelenting boycott by Americans and American department stores of the German shipping lines, and as far as possible of German goods, is pregnant with less danger to the oppressed minorities in Germany, and also has more promise of speedy success than merely an outburst of emotion, however correct its motivation.[1]

The Committee's reply, dispatched on April 17 by Executive Secretary Morris Waldman, probably represents the earliest official document outlining specifically its boycott policy:

> We also believe that quieter and more realistic methods of dealing with the situation than mass agitation can be found and we are working on this principle. We are, however, not in agreement with you regarding the wisdom of a boycott against German goods. A boycott is a two-edged sword which hurts innocent people, including Jews, both in Germany and in countries where boycotting is practiced.[2]

But Friedman was not satisfied with Waldman's argument. On April 27, he sent him a reply, the most forceful part of which read:

> To sit back and do nothing on the theory that the boycott as an instrumentality of persuasion is a "two-edged sword," which may hurt the innocent as well as the guilty, to my view is a defeatist and completely untenable attitude to assume. The ruination of the innocent victims of Nazi intolerance, is proceeding apace, just as rapidly as if the measures taken by the German government were in the nature of reprisal for imagined acts abroad. Apparently, the only effective method left of calling a halt to this intolerant barbarism, is the long arm of world ecnomonic and intellectual pressure, and while it is true that this may coincidentally hurt German Jews as well as German Christians, the German Jews have little further to lose, as they have been already degraded into a servile status, with little or no prospect of relief from within. Their only hopes are: immigration, tantamount to starvation in the world today; or the pressure of the world revulsion as expressed through a rejection of German goods and ships. This latter course may well bring the National Socialists of Germany to their

senses, and as there is almost nothing left to lose and practically everything to gain, I do not see your objection.³

The correspondence concluded with Waldman's suggestion to discuss the matter in person at the Committee office.

ii.

Of greater interest is an exchange of letters between Untermyer and Waldman, which took place during the first half of the month of May. The correspondence was initiated by Waldman, who felt that the private crusade that Untermyer was conducting in behalf of the boycott represented a dangerous move. Waldman, therefore, sent him a special circular report, to which he appended the following piece of advice:

> Above all, it is imperative that in this grave and highly delicate situation, no individual should speak or act for the Jewish people, but all should entrust the responsibility to recognized organizations like the American Jewish Committee and B'nai B'rith who have been dealing with these problems for many years.⁴

To this, the famous attorney responded:

> As I view the tragic predicament of our unfortunate brethren in Germany, whom it is our duty and our self-interest to protect, the report of your Committee offers no hope for relief and no alternative other than through the boycott.
> I have given considerable study to this subject and have gathered a mass of information, all leading to the conclusion that the Hitler party is bent upon the extermination of the Jews in Germany, or upon driving them out of the country. The men in control are bigoted fanatics to whom neither reason, justice nor humanity makes the slightest appeal. Their hatred is deep-seated and nothing but the fear of consequences will affect them. With all due respect I therefore differ from the policy that has been recommended and is being pursued by the American Jewish Committee and shall feel at liberty, but always on my own responsibility, and without assuming to act for the Jewish people, to make such recommendations as, in my judgment, will best conserve the interests of the Jews in Germany.
> I am fortified in my course of action by a large body of the Jewish people in this country—a body vastly larger, though less influential, than that represented by your Committee.⁵

Compared to the statements that were soon to be issued by Mr. Untermyer, this one was mild and restrained. But in challenging the

Committee's credentials, it was sufficient to provoke a May 9 reply censuring the outspoken lawyer more sharply for his continued "irresponsible" conduct.

> All that I should want to emphasize here is that our position has been governed not only by the wishes of all elements of the Jewish population in Germany, but by the unanimous advice of responsible organizations in England, France and other countries who are especially engaged in the work of protecting the civil and religious rights of Jews. We have also been persuaded in this course by the official authorities at Washington, who, we have been assured, are doing everything in their power.
>
> Reliable persons who have been in close touch with the German authorities have advised us that the situation, grave as it is, is not hopeless; that avenues of approach toward a mitigation of the terrible anti-Jewish measures are not closed but that it is imperative, if results are to be attained, that actions tending to further irritation be avoided...
>
> Strong as your convictions, which we respect, may be, I keenly regret, frankly, that a man of your outstanding position in the community whose utterances exert a great influence upon public opinion, did not consult with the American Jewish Committee to ascertain the reasons for their attitude, and what methods they have been following, before giving public utterance to views which, you must have known, would be widely published and profoundly influence public sentiment...
>
> You say you are fortified in your course of action by a large body of Jewish people. I venture to remind you such popular support does not necessarily make your course right. It is hardly necessary to remind a master of public affairs like yourself that the mass of people feel more strongly than they think. Many of the great creative figures of the world to whose genius human progress is due were in the minority, and usually only secured posthumous endorsement of their ideas.
>
> Permit me to remind you, too, that Hitler has a large body behind him in Germany, vastly larger than Stressemann or Bruening had.[6]

Addressing himself to Waldman's forceful and critical remarks, Untermyer rejoined on May 15 that he did

> not understand why you should scold me for not having consulted with your Committee before giving public utterance to my views. I might well say, by way of rejoinder, that I too regret that your organization did not consult with me and ascertain the reasons for my attitude.
>
> If, as you say, the authorities in Washington are doing everything in

their power to ameliorate this situation, there has yet been no evidence of it, either in Congress or by responsible officials.

Frankly, I think you are assuming a great deal when you say that the position of the American Jewish Committee "has been governed by the unanimous advice of responsible organizations in England, France and other countries who are especially engaged in the work of protecting the civil and religious rights of Jews," unless you take the view that no organizations of Jews are "responsible" that do not agree with you. My understanding is that there are responsible people and organizations in all these countries (who do not agree with your Committee) and that a very effective boycott is being organized by them in England and another in France. I may, of course, be mistaken as to this.[7]

Next, it was Judge Proskauer who addressed himself to Untermyer, apparently hoping to wean him away from the newly formed American League. The communication, written on June 26, outlined three reasons against an organized boycott:

The prime consideration for us must be the continuance and upbuilding of Christian sentiment in our favor. I find an overwhelming objection among my Christian friends to action by Jews which may adversely affect the interests of this country. It crystallizes in the thought that if there be a breaking up of endeavor to reach an international agreement, and that be accompanied by an organized Jewish boycott, the blame for it will inevitably be placed upon the Jews, whether justly or unjustly. The expressions of a few men like Jimmy Gerard to the contrary are in my view wholly exceptional. I can conceive of nothing that would more foment antisemitism here in this country than organized boycott. Nor is it any answer to suggest that this is a counsel of cowardice. It is not. I would gladly risk harm to myself by adding increase of antisemitism here if that would help the German Jews. However, that will not help them, but hurt them, because our only hope here—and I say this after long conferences in Washington with the Secretary of State and many Senators—is to consolidate our Christian opinion on its impact on Germany.

When we organize a boycott we are doing what Van Loon[8] properly characterized last night as fighting Hitlerism with Hitlerism and to no effect. We put ourselves in the position, by concerted action of endeavoring to inflict harm on thousands of people, including indeed *Jewish German manufacturers themselves,* who have no responsibility personally for this Nazi menace. I like to keep our fight on the plane of moral rectitude, not only because that is morally right, but I think it is good tactics.

Finally, we are today getting without organization and the evil of concerted action everything that we get through an organized boycott. You know perfectly well that there is a widespread disinclination to purchase German merchandise. Nobody can criticize the individual for this attitude. Thousands will criticize an organization of individuals to foment this attitude.[9]

Untermyer responded three days later, countering Proskauer's arguments:

> If you were to see the letters that come to me from non-Jews on the subject of the boycott you might be disposed to change your point of view. Most of them are in agreement that this is the only effective weapon, and are anxious to see it pressed.
> Nor do I share your opinion that it would foment antisemitism here. I feel, on the contrary, that evidence of something like a fighting spirit on the part of our people commands their respect and support far more than would a do-nothing policy.
> I may be obtuse, but by what deduction or reasoning you reach the conclusion that the boycott "may adversely affect the interests of this country," I fail to understand. I feel that, on the contrary, the pressing upon all Americans of the policy of buying "Made in America" merchandise would advance the interests of the country . . .
> If I felt that without organization and concerted action we are getting everything, or even a small part of what we could get through an organized boycott, I should not be expending my time or money in the present effort. I am unable to see it that way.[10]

It was becoming increasingly clear that Mr. Samuel Untermyer, the wealthy and influential American lawyer (p. 51), was becoming more and more estranged from the Committee's reserved and rather stationary stand concerning Hitler Germany. In fact, it was Jews of his kind that the AJC became keenly interested in weaning away from the expanding anti-Nazi boycott movement in America. This effort was successful in most cases involving rich American Jews of German origin. Such Jews were often not only very wealthy, but also very influential. Notwithstanding this, America's Jewish masses, who were generally of East European origin, were becoming increasingly pro-boycott minded. Untermyer, who would soon begin playing a leading role in the growing anti-Nazi boycott movement in America, could definitely count on mass support from them. And so it was, as we shall presently see.

8

Congress Activities: Prelude to Boycott

The Giant Demonstration March

i.

The Congress was to launch but one more big public spectacle before the maximum effectiveness of such action would be called into question by ALDJR's boycott conference of May 14, 1933. It was to be this time a gigantic protest march through the streets of New York that would "in a vivid and dramatic manner give expression to the sense of outrage and indignation which is felt by Jews and non-Jews alike against the 'cold pogrom' practiced upon the Jews in Germany."[1] The proposal of such a march, like the March 27 rally at Madison Square Garden, was made by Dr. Margoshes (p. 29). He introduced it at the April 12, 1933, meeting of the Congress' Administrative Committee. As recorded in the minutes of that meeting, this proposal reads:

> It was decided in the form of a motion that a conference of national and local organizations is to be called within a week, or not later than April 23rd.
> ... The purpose of the conference is to discuss the calling of a protest march.[2]

The conference was held on April 19, fixing the afternoon of May 10 as the day of protest. The reason for the choice of this date was that the Nazis had announced their intention of burning publicly all "un-

German" books on that day. The marchers, said the Congress a week later, would "register the unity of Israel in its condemnation of the program of discrimination and vilification" and would provide "the first opportunity to the masses to register their protest against the wholesale declassing of their fellow citizens in Germany."[3]

Prompted by the Congress' plan to enter upon another form of public protest, the AJC-BB issued on April 28 a joint statement reasserting the futility of this and other forms of agitation:

> The American Jewish Committee and the B'nai B'rith sought to discharge the solemn responsibility resting on them to do everything possible to prevent the persecution of our fellow-Jews in Germany and to mitigate the effects of such measures as have been taken. But, governed by our own judgment of the effect of certain activities, notwithstanding our own keen sense of outrage at the attacks upon the Jews as a people, we counselled against public agitation in the form of boycotts and mass demonstrations. Responsible Jewish organizations of other countries have been in agreement with our position that such forms of agitation would tend to inflame already highly wrought feelings. We have, however, sought every other honorable and legitimate means, through the Government of the United States and in other ways, to bring to the attention of the German authorities the amazement and condemnation of the people of America, regardless of race or creed, of the course still being followed in Germany, in the hope that, being made acquainted with these sentiments, the German authorities would realize that their actions constitute a betrayal of civilization and an infamous blow at the highest ideals of humanity.
>
> Dismayed as we are that no evidence has yet been given by the authorities of Germany of their intention to undo the incalculable injury inflicted upon an innocent part of their citizenry, and fully understanding and appreciating the natural desire of human beings to express sorrow and indignation, we nevertheless consider such forms of agitation as boycotts, parades, mass meetings and other similar demonstrations as futile. They serve only as an ineffectual channel for the release of emotion. They furnish the persecutors with a pretext to justify the wrongs they perpetrate and, on the other hand, distract those who desire to help with more constructive efforts.[4]

The Committee also telegraphed the Congress, asking for a joint conference of the two organizations "to discuss the situation." Mr. Deutsch declared himself in favor of conferring with the AJC, but not with the BB. At a May 1 meeting of the Congress' Steering Committee, he referred to several telephone conversations with Alfred Cohen (p. 43), who insisted that, in a joint conference of the three organizations, the group would have to "be bound by the decisions of the majority." Of course, Deutsch refused to accept such an arrangement, since the BB shared the same views as the AJC; and the Congress could not, he added most emphatically, agree to a program of "do nothing."

But the Steering Committee, whose purpose was the arrangement of organizational business, refused to agree to a joint meeting with the American Jewish Committee, claiming that, in view of the latter's recent statement, such a meeting would be "ineffectual." However, upon Dr. Wise's suggestion, it was decided that no Congress statement would be issued to counter the joint declaration of AJC-BB.

The meeting also heard a report by Dr. Margoshes on the progress of the planned demonstration march. He stated that labor, socialist, and youth groups "were all making preparations" to participate in it. But above all, Dr. Margoshes stressed the importance of securing distinguished Washington statesmen to address the throng.[5]

The following week, Margoshes announced that the Manufacturers Association had promised that all their factories and places of business would close at 2:30 P.M. to enable their employees to join in the mass protest march scheduled for 4:00 o'clock in the afternoon of May 10. In the meantime, Deutsch and Wise had conferred with Justice Louis D. Brandeis, known for both his judicial liberalism and leading Zionist appeal, who counseled them to continue the anti-Nazi fight without any abatement whatsoever. Also encouraged by the possibility of Senate support, the two Jewish Congress chiefs instructed the main office to urge constituent organizations throughout the country to wire their senators and congressmen and the Department of State demanding governmental action on behalf of German Jewry. However, they emphasized the advisability of holding a parade only, and no subsequent mass meeting. The latter, they thought, should be reserved for a future date.

ii.

Unlike the Congress' previous mass-protest manifestation, the approaching one was characterized by an increasing demand for boycott by officers and members alike. A cursory examination of the Congress mail for the month of April reveals the receipt of many letters demanding a boycott.[6] A. H. Cohen, a member of the Congress' Steering Committee, made this point on the twenty-eighth at a meeting whose main order of business was the forthcoming protest march.

Wise insisted, however, that, officially, the Congress should refrain from promulgating a boycott. To delegates who shouted for a boycott at the April 19 conference that voted for the protest march, he replied that the "time has not yet come for an official boycott—we still have other weapons."[7] From the boycott advocacy of the Congress' two vice-presidents, it was clear, though, that as long as one did not speak in the name of the Congress, one was free to agitate for a boycott. This freedom was also honored at events sponsored by the Congress.

Thus, it was in connection with the protest march that LaGuardia may have made his first pro-boycott statement; for in accepting an invitation to address the marchers, LaGuardia remarked: "When we speak of a 'boycott,' we should not mean boycott of Wagner's music or Goethe's literature.... We must hit at the Nazis where it will hurt most—the pocketbook."[8]

Abraham Cahan, editor of New York's *Jewish Daily Forward,* who was also among the speakers, cited the dwindling fur trade at Leipzig as an illustration of the potency of boycott, thundering: "We have no soldiers, we have no cannons, and no war ships to fight Hitler; but we are capable of making him feel our power. And this can be done solely through a boycott."[9]

At the march, some trucks, beginning with the Bible, exhibited the burning of the books by Jewish authors or their sympathizers. They also displayed a pictorial description of the degradation to which German Jews had been subjected. Otherwise, motor vehicles were not permitted in the route of the march.

From some sections of the crowd, estimated at 100,000 by the police, shouts of "Down with Hitler" and "Boycott German goods" filled the air. Only at about 10:00 P.M. did the giant multitude begin to disperse, ending the greatest marching spectacle New York City had ever seen.[10]

The Washington Emergency Session

Despite the Congress' official disavowal of the boycott, it had by now become a subject of debate at nearly every one of its major functions and meetings. However, all such discussions were characterized by indecision. The following illustrative example, taken from the Congress' May 15 minutes, typifies this vacillation: "After considerable discussion as to whether the Congress should officially sanction the boycott movement, it was decided to refer the matter to the Administrative Committee at its next meeting."[11]

But before the Administrative Committee would meet again, the Congress found itself arguing this issue on May 20–21 at an emergency session held in Washington, D.C. The special session, which was called in order to take up the Nazis' persecution of the Jews, considered the following to be the prime topics of importance: demonstrations against Hitlerism, the creation in 1934 of a World Jewish Congress, and

A.J.C.-AJC unity. All delegates agreed to support the first two points, but rejected the third, claiming that the Committee's basic policy revolved around the confined bounds of diplomatic intercession; a policy that, in Dr. Wise's opinion, weakened the protest movement.

This conviction was expressed more incisively in a joint statement that Dr. Wise and Mr. Deutsch issued preliminary to the opening of the distinctive session:

> This Congress may be expected to do two things: to sound a new challenge to the American people, irrespective of faith and creed and racial ancestry, to unite in solemn protest against the wrong which is being committed by Hitler's Germany in the sight of all the world against the Jews.
>
> The second purpose of the Congress will be to move Jews to bethink themselves before it is too late concerning the grave status of their brother Jews in Germany. They who favor the policy of silence, of acquiescence and of surrender will remain away from the Washington sessions of the American Jewish Congress.[12]

However, it was at the opening session that the Committee received its worst rebuke by the American Jewish Congress. It came from Mr. Deutsch, who sharply criticized the former for having urged in a May 3 letter that the Congress call off its scheduled demonstration march, since it was possible that the Nazis might yet moderate or somewhat relax their stormy anti-Jewish legislation. Therewith, he lashed out at the Committee, saying:

> Responsibility for the failure to act long ago to prevent a portion of the horrors to which German Jews are being subjected, must inevitably fall upon those of the so-called leaders upon whose deaf ears fall our repeated admonitions.
>
> Our charge is made with profound sorrow and bitterness. These so-called leaders have adopted a policy tantamount almost to betrayal of German Jewry.
>
> Further, they are guilty of sabotage against American Jewry. Not content with advocating their own viewpoint, they have played into the hands of our enemies by deliberately striving to create the impression through the public prints, that a controversy is dividing the ranks of American Israel.[13]

The failure of the Roosevelt administration to openly condemn hitherto Hitler's infamous crimes against the Jews also impelled the Congress president to say: "We will not desist until our government makes publicly known its attitude towards the policy of discrimination and intolerance against the Jews of Germany."[14]

He added that World Jewry must be organized; that events might make it necessary to convene a permanent World Jewish Congress in the summer of 1934.

As these were aims which were also opposed by the American Jewish Committee, it became increasingly clear "that a controversy" was, indeed, "dividing the ranks of American Israel." Rabbi Eliezer Silver, president of the Agudath Harabonim,[15] who also attended the emergency session, tried desperately to assuage this situation. Pointing to the importance of unity at home, he appealed that the Congress try to come to terms with the Committee. But by now it was too late. In explaining why, Dr. Wise and other Congress leaders repeated the claim that this could not be achieved without resulting in a weakening of the protest movement and a complete dependence upon the method of individual intercession and behind-the-scenes diplomacy.

Moreover, the session showed that many delegates, if not most, were in favor of swinging even further away from the Committee by having the Congress declare a boycott. Margoshes and Coralnik, who also attended, strove to draw the Congress into the new boycott movement by fighting for the passage of a boycott resolution; but to no avail. Stephen Wise insisted on a "silent" or "unorganized" boycott, killing the resolution during a stormy administrative session.

The failure of the Congress to adopt a boycott resolution at this time made many feel that the emergency session was bereft of drama and a real sense of achievement. In the eyes of such observers and participants, its decisions to raise one million dollars to fight Hitlerism and to call into being a World Jewish Congress the following year were of secondary importance.

9

The Jewish World Economic Conference

i.

The news of the creation of a popular, organized boycott in the United States delighted Europe's boycott leaders. The United Boycott Committee of Poland, which joined similar groups in sending the new League congratulatory cablegrams, included a message suggesting that an all-Jewish conference be held in June in Geneva in order to organize the boycott on an international scale. Of course, the League was most amenable to this idea. It differed, however, with respect to the site of the proposed conference, believing that the boycott could best be dramatized if, concurrently with the World Economic Conference scheduled to take place in London (also in June 1933), a Jewish World Economic Conference were held in that city. Its proposal was based upon the suggestion of the Anglo-Jewish Council of Trades and Industries, a boycott organization formed in early April, which was presided over by Lord Melchett (Sir Alfred Mond), noted English industrialist and Zionist. The proposal prevailed, inasmuch as it caught the fancy of the world's various boycott committees; and since it was but an academic issue, Poland's United Boycott Committee also acceded to the plan.

But this was not the main consideration. The basic reason for calling a Jewish World Economic Conference was a desire "to link up the different national organizations into one, which would offer a clearing-house for the exchange of experience and information with regard to the alternative sources of supply."[1] London, the seat of the Anglo-Jewish Council, was chosen to serve as this center.

It turned out that Untermyer's schedule did not permit him to attend a June conference, and so at the request of the American Jewish Defense League, the gathering was postponed to the following month.

Of this conference, the *Jewish Economic Forum*, the British Council's official organ, noted the following:

> The conference would have been worthwhile even for its own sake as the first Jewish economic conference in history, but in the present circumstances, the conference will have the most important task of coordination and direction of the world boycott of German goods. A centrally organized boycott of all trades for all countries will be a more powerful weapon than a boycott in each country.
>
> The immediate task of the conference will be to establish the necessary machinery for coordination and direction with due regard to the special conditions prevailing in each country.
>
> The conference will consist entirely of Jewish businessmen.[2]

The agenda of the conference, scheduled to open on July 17, was made ready by a Preparatory Commission assisted by British, French, and Polish delegates. The Commission, which met from June 25 to June 27, requested that delegates from the attending countries be represented by chairmen, who should submit the following:

> The general attitude with regard to Hitler-land in the particular country; the boycott attitude of the consumer; the boycott attitude of the retail trade; the boycott attitude of the wholesale trade; to what extent are the trade and industry of the country bound with German imports; an outline of the organization of the commercial boycott; outline of applied propaganda methods, including specimens of posters, etc.[3]

The chairmen were also instructed to report the names and addresses "of the different boycott committees and exact information regarding their working methods." To help them judge the "effectiveness and results" of the boycott, the chairmen were further advised to bring a "detailed outline of the statistical situation" concerning German imports. However, it sufficed if such information "was to be carried out principally at first in the various trades."

In addition, the Preparatory Commission proposed the appointment of a number of Committees, including:

An Organizing Committee, which would formulate an organizational standard "along the lines of the English and Polish system" and "occupy itself with international organization and the establishment of the London Central Office." Further, this Committee "will recognize a single organization in each country as the centre of the boycott movement."

A "Committee for the opening up of new sources of supply and markets"; a "Transport, Shipping Committee—to see to it that the transit of goods through Germany is avoided." Furthermore, "the London Office would assist in finding new transportation routes, not via Germany."

A Propaganda Committee, which would adopt "an international poster with the same design and the same caption in the language of the individual country"; a Finance Committee, that "will have to decide on the methods to be taken for the maintenance of the London Central Bureau, as well as for the assistance that might be necessary to groups of Jewish merchants, who may be injured by reason of the boycott"; and lastly, an Economic Relief Committee, "to devise means of rendering assistance to German refugees desiring to re-establish their former businesses in non-German countries."[4]

But after the laying of some of this groundwork, the delegates began realizing that more time still was needed to complete preparations for a meaningful conference. Moreover, contemplated legal action against Nazi Germany through the League of Nations, and the need for considerable time to deliberate it, also made it wiser to postpone the conference once again. It was, therefore, agreed to convene in October.

The German Jews, for those benefit this entire effort was being made, repudiated the idea of a Jewish World Economic Conference. On July 14, in a joint protest cabled to Lord Melchett (p. 71) by the Reich representatives of German Jews and by the Jewish Community of Berlin, they stated: "We oppose very decidedly the renewed boycott movements which, according to press reports, are contemplated by the projected economic congress. We request—if the congress is not abandoned entirely—that demands and resolutions which damage Germany be eliminated."[5]

ii.

Many of the delegates in London were, nevertheless, convinced of the need to hold a pre-October parley, if only to pave the way for and broaden the scope of the fall conference. As if in defiance, the Netherlands, a country bordering Germany, was chosen as the place of meeting; but another reason for this choice was that Amsterdam, as the city where the delegates would assemble, had a very active anti-Nazi boycott committee. The conference, at any rate, was called for three days, July 19-21.

More than thirty Continental representatives gave the conference a thoroughly militant tone. This is reflected in the text of the adopted boycott resolution[6] and the demands proclaimed by Untermyer. Untermyer, the elected president[7] of this new world body, set them forth in a sort of keynote speech:

> The crisis which has been precipitated upon civilization by the cold and merciless campaign of persecution against 600,000 Jews in the country which was once Germany, but is now more appropriately dubbed Hitlerland, furnished the first supreme test of the League of Nations.
> To the supreme disappointment of its friends the League has not lifted its hand to stay this catastrophe that has been inflicted by one of its most important members upon a great army of its own defenseless citizens.
> Unless the League now moves quickly and before this world tragedy being enacted day by day before our horror-stricken eyes is complete, it might as well fold its tents and slink away, for its importance and uselessness to deal with great issues of humanity will have been demonstrated.
> Here are some of the things the League can and should at once do if it is to justify its existence:—Send a select committee into Hitlerland to investigate and report fully upon the facts and especially upon the pretexts whereon hundreds of thousands of unoffending German Jews have been imprisoned, tortured and lodged in hells on earth, called detention camps; provide Nansen passports[8] for those able to leave Germany, which would permit them to take their property with them as was done in the League in the cases of Russia, Greece and Rumania and thus open to them the gates of foreign lands; Enforce the labor union provisions of the Versailles Treaty,[9] which are being flagrantly violated by the expulsion and exclusion of all Jews from unions, and compel Hitlerland to reinstate them in their unions, or enforce and enlarge the provisions of the treaty for the protection of minorities by applying it to protection of disenfranchised German Jews. If Germany wants to modify the treaty by securing the rights to disarm defensively, there is no reason why it should not also be modified so as to make it plain beyond question that Germany definitely promised the League in writing that it would protect its minorities within its borders; Invoke and put into immediate operation the relief clause of the treaty to rescue these people from starvation.
> If the League takes these steps—and only then—it will be able to justify its existence in the sight of the civilized world, which has expected so much from it and thus far has received so little. If it fails to do so on its own motion, means must be found to enforce its jurisdiction and put its machinery into action if that is possible. It is, however, hoped this will not be necessary.
> The surrounding countries, suffering as they are from unemploy-

ment, cannot care for them even with the best of good-will. The only solution is for the League of Nations to revive for them the Nansen passport....

The first and most important duty of the League of Nations is to send a commission to Germany to uncover the despicable Hitlerite camouflage and find out what is really happening under cover of their lying propaganda. Or has the whole world been so callous that it can continue to look on without taking action?[10]

The conference backed these demands wholeheartedly and appointed Untermyer to introduce them before the world organization.

On the economic side, the conference dealt principally with the problem of supplying the boycotting businessmen with equally satisfactory substitutes—at no extra charge—for his liquidated German-made stocks. Finally, as a result of their satisfaction and encouragement with the conference, the delegates decided to form a World Jewish Economic Federation. They departed in anxious anticipation of the main conference scheduled for the fall.

10

Joining Battle

i.

In the three months following its emergency session of May 20–21, 1933, the American Jewish Congress continued dilly-dallying with regard to the boycott. Untermyer's charge on his return trip to the United States in early August, "that ninety-five per cent of their members are already with us and that they are being misrepresented by two or three men now abroad,"[1] was almost certainly true. His remaining remarks illustrate the typical Untermyer sting:

> Of them I ask that, prior to the meeting to be held this month in Prague by their executive committee, they instruct the false leaders in no uncertain terms as to the stand they must take on this all-important subject and demand that they shall either openly represent their views or resign their offices. One of them, generally recognized as the king-pin of mischief makers, is junketing around the Continent engaged in his favorite pastime of spreading discord, assenting at one time and place that he favors and supports the boycott and at another that he is opposed and indifferent to it, all dependent on the audience he is addressing; but always directly and indirectly delivering a stab in the dark.[2]

Untermyer's taunting gibe was obviously directed at Dr. Wise, who, on July 5, had left for Europe to confer with Continental Jewish leaders about setting up the projected World Jewish Congress in 1934, and to generally explore ways of alleviating the plight of his German coreligionists. Although it had been nearly six months since Hitler came to power, Wise still clung to his faith that President Roosevelt would try to sway the Nazi chieftain not to pursue his collision course with World Jewry. A boycott would certainly destroy the chances of such a move, thought the Congress' honorary president, while continued public protests and demonstrations could perhaps oblige Roosevelt and pressure Hitler to reexamine their respective positions regarding the Jewish question in Nazi Germany. Stephen Wise had suggested such an analysis on July 13, 1933, in St. Louis, whither he had gone in the belief that a woeful misunderstanding had been obtained regarding conditions in Germany. Speaking to a gathering of over 800 people, Wise said:

> I have no doubt that President Roosevelt has been as far from indifferent to the horror of the situation in Germany as you and I. But for reasons which must have seemed adequate to him, he has refrained from public utterance or public action excepting insofar as his non-appointment of an American ambassador to Berlin until just recently was a public act.
> I am not without hope that the President may yet, as I believe he ought to, see fit to choose some course of action which will make clear to the Hitler government the abhorrence of the American people for what Germany has done and is doing to one percent of its population.[3]

However, neither Roosevelt nor the Department of State lifted their voices in protest. With no signs of a let-up in Jewish suffering in Nazi Germany, Wise's anti-boycott stand began weakening. He broke his prolonged silence on this subject at long last on his arrival for the World Zionist Congress meetings in Prague: "As long as Germany declares the Jews to be an inferior race, poisoning and persecuting them, decent, self-respecting Jews cannot deal with Germany in any way, buy or sell or maintain any manner of commerce with Germany or travel on German boats."[4]

ii.

Officially, this brief statement marked Dr. Wise's first formal declaration favoring a boycott against Hitler Germany. It was to manifest a breakthrough in the enervating struggle against shocking Nazi barbarity against the Jews.

In the meantime, on the other side of the ocean, the Congress leadership was making a last-ditch effort, short of boycott, to save German Jewry. It manifested itself in a 5,000-word open letter that Deutsch, on August 15, addressed to Hindenburg, appealing to him to save Germany's 600,000 Jews from "certain extermination." The Congress president reminded the German President that while the dictatorial powers conferred upon Hitler permitted him to enact laws which "may deviate from the Constitution," the Weimar Constitution had still not been formally abrogated. Sixteen articles were then listed as having been violated by the Hitler government.

Deutsch also informed the senile German President that in conferring the aforesaid powers upon Herr Hitler, it had not at all been his intention to permit the Nazi Chancellor to "defy the foundations on which the German republic was built" or "to vanquish every principle of humanity in relation to the Jews." Citing instances of the maltreatment of Jews since the advent of the Nazi regime, Deutsch "innocently" added: "It could not have been your intention in signing over dictatorial powers to Chancellor Hitler to embroil the German people in fraternal strife, destroy the cultural prestige of the German nation and banish the confidence of the remainder of the world."[5]

To capture, however, the spirit of this pathetic letter, it suffices to quote its preamble:

> The American Jewish Congress, a central organization with which is affiliated the vast majority of American Jews, respectfully conveys to you its deep concern over the plight of its co-religionists in Germany and submits the urgent plea of its constituents that the great prerogatives of your office to be exercised to rescue from certain extermination the 600,000 Jews of Germany who look to you for succor.
>
> We recall the leading place which the German nation has attained among the civilized nations of the world; the esteem which the German people has won for themselves in the difficult days since the conclusion of the World War, and deeply regret that this hard-won respect and regard now have been destroyed by a cruel program unparalleled except by the barbarism of the Middle Ages which the government of Chancellor Adolf Hitler has chosen to launch against the Jewish people.
>
> Recollecting, as we do, your great devotion to the German people and your patriotic services to the German nation, we cannot believe that you associate yourself with acts and a policy, the avowed purpose of which is to destroy a section of the population which has made outstanding contributions to every phase of Germany's development in the 1,300 years the Jewish people have resided on German soil.
>
> Nor can we believe that the President of the German Reich, who has sworn "to consecrate all my energy to the welfare of the German people, to increase its advantages, to avert its injury, to preserve the constitution and the laws of the nation, to fulfill my duties conscientiously and to deal justly with all," is prepared now to permit the contravention of the oath of office.
>
> Yet, in the six-month period since Chancellor Adolf Hitler's ascension to power, the President of the Reich has given no indication of his

awareness of the assault upon the rights, the lives, and the property of an important section of the German population.[6]

In one section of this lengthy communication, the consequence of unabated Jewish persecution was hinted at: "The persecution of Jews has given rise to spontaneous reprisals in the form of boycotts in every country of the world on the part of liberals, irrespective of race or creed, in many instances tacitly sanctioned by the various governments themselves."[7] Deutsch's letter ended with a reminder that "the President of the Reich may yet offer redress to the Jews of Germany and save the German nation from degeneration and the ostracism of the civilized world."[8]

As could be expected, Deutsch's plea went unheeded; for the German embassy refused to forward his appeal to Hindenburg. The Congress president interpreted this to mean that the Reich President was being held incommunicado by the Nazis, so that, among other things, Hindenburg would remain ignorant about the fate of German Jewry. It was, of course, an unwarranted, if not a convenient viewpoint, to explain Hindenburg's absolute lack of reaction under the rather dire circumstances.

A little over a fortnight prior to Deutsch's desperate, albeit abortive appeal, Dr. Joseph L. Tenenbaum, (p. 3) sent a questionnaire to the various branches and affiliated organizations of the American Jewish Congress concerning the subject of an anti-Nazi boycott. Following this, Dr. Tenenbaum requested that his Committee meet in emergency session on August 6, to discuss, among other things, the question of an anti-Nazi boycott endorsement.

We have no details concerning either the response to the questionnaire or the talks at the emergency session. However, the following August 17 resolution, adopted by the Administrative Committee of the American Jewish Congress, clearly shows that this organization's boycott "patience" was at an end:

> It is the sense of this meeting of the Administrative Committee of the American Jewish Congress that the time has arrived for the active participation of the American Jewish Congress in this movement for the boycott of German goods and for whatever assistance the organization can give to the Jewish forces already engaged in the boycott of Nazi Germany.
> In this spirit we instruct our delegates to the World Conference[9] to vote in favor of a World Jewish boycott on German goods and shipping.
> To our Executive Committee meeting on Sunday, August 20, at the Hotel New Yorker, we recommend that it go on record as ready to promote the boycott and to cooperate with all Jewish agencies now

engaged in the furtherance of the boycott movement, to the end that a consolidated boycott organization may be affected to enlist the support of the Jewish as well as the non-Jewish population of America.[10]

A boycott declaration by the National Executive Committee would become Congress law; and since the element of "surprise" would enable the Congress to make the most of such an eventuality, no "scoop" was granted by its publicity department. As a matter of fact, Dr. Tenenbaum made no reference whatsoever to a boycott in announcing on the nineteenth to the press the reason for the August 20 meeting. Instead, he circuitously explained that its purpose was to plan a coordinated program of action for the defense and relief of Jews in Germany. But as we shall presently see, Dr. Tenenbaum's meaning was made quite clear at the meeting.

The meeting was chaired by Dr.Tenenbaum. It was tense and stormy. For the first time, at least at a meeting conducted under the auspices of the main office, American Jewish Congress leaders openly and sharply attacked their government. Thus, Dr. Tenenbaum expressed astonishment at Roosevelt's continued silence in the wake of Hitler's unabating persecution of Germany's Jews. In addition, he cited statistical figures to demonstrate the detrimental effect the boycott was already wreaking on Germany. Max Winkler, professor of economics at the City College of New York and soon-to-be director of the Congress' Boycott Department, also cited statistical figures showing that Germany's exports were falling from month to month. He, too, criticized his government, accusing it of failing to take a single step to protest against the mistreatment of the Jews by Hitler. Dr. Margoshes (p. 29), who had waited at least four months for this day, urged building an iron boycott wall around the murderous Nazi regime, as part of a common cooperative venture with like-minded organizations. And just returned from Germany, Ira A. Hirschman, vice-president of the Lord & Taylor department store, and later the director of the War Refugee Board, suggested various methods of prosecuting a boycott.[11]

Mr. Deutsch, who, together with Dr. Wise was criticized for having failed to adopt a tougher stand against the brutal Nazis, was particularly outspoken. He and Wise had traveled to Washington in a number of vain attempts to influence Roosevelt and Hull to denounce the Nazi outrages against the Jews. Frustrated and angered by their silence, Deutsch acridly condemned the administration on its entire range of policy toward Germany. He not only criticized the President and his Secretary of State for failing to protest against the maltreatment of Jews by the Hitler regime, but bitterly pointed out that American firms in Germany had been compelled to fire their Jewish employees. Meanwhile, Deutsch also charged, Nazi cells in the United States, organized by German-paid agents, were openly agitating for a boycott of American firms without any interference. Why were these Nazi agitators not deported, he asked shoutingly.

If Deutsch had heretofore attempted unsuccessfully to get the U.S. government to merely protest or denounce the Jewish persecutions by the Nazi government, he now also challenged the ethics of maintaining diplomatic relations with a regime that condoned and conducted so inhuman a policy: "American citizens have a right to ask why the American Government maintains its diplomatic relations with Germany, whose treatment of its citizens betrays every humanitarian concept."[12]

On the question of an anti-Nazi boycott, Deutsch referred to the well-known fact that the American Jewish Congress had repeatedly negotiated the settlement of the Jewish question in Germany through diplomatic channels. Claiming he was now in possession of fresh evidence that Hitler would not alter his anti-Jewish policy, the Congress president supported the idea of a boycott as the only possible course of action vis-à-vis a Hitler Germany.

In the boycott resolution[13] which was introduced by Dr. Tenenbaum, the Congress noted that it had refrained until now from endorsing such action in the hope that official American representations might bring the Nazi regime to its senses. As the American government had not acted, and Hitler's persecutions became progressively worse, the American Jewish Congress felt "compelled to take decisive action against Germany." The resolution further explained the course of action decided upon as only "a measure of self-defense against the barbarism of the Hitler persecutions."

Other policies adopted by this Executive Committee meeting included a resolution urging the U.S. government to admit at least 20,000 German Jewish children and permit their adoption in American homes. Immigration Committee Chairman Samuel Dickstein pledged his cooperation in efforts by the American Jewish Congress to secure the admission of German Jews into the United States within the framework of the immigration laws of this country. It was also resolved to appeal to the League of Nations to intervene on behalf of German Jews. A case was to be submitted on the ground that persecution by the Nazi regime constituted a violation of the clause guaranteeing the protection of minorities under the Treaty of Versailles.

iii.

It was fitting that Samuel Untermyer, the man who had come to personify the boycott in the United States, was a featured guest at the meeting that marked the Congress' official entry into this movement. The elderly attorney was heartily applauded as he was led in to speak, and applauded, in turn, the Congress' decision to initiate a boycott, predicting that "Germany will crack this winter,"[14] if it was conducted vigorously and energetically. Supporting the Congress resolve to work for the extension of the boycott among the non-Jewish population, Untermyer also appealed to the Christian world to make the ostracism of Germany a common human undertaking.

Untermyer was particularly concerned with forming a united American boycott front and probably agreed to speak at this emergency meeting in the hope of swaying the Congress to team up with ALDJR. Furthermore, he was anxious that the Jewish Congress not act independently of ALDJR, by also appealing to the League of Nations to deal with the painful German-Jewish question. However, the Congress did pursue an independent course, announcing in the August 20 issue of the Yiddish daily, *Der Morgen Journal*, that it intended to do just that. Untermyer, who was given ample notice regarding this statement, was afforded an opportunity to enter his reaction. In an open letter to Dr. Tenenbaum, also published in the *Morgen Journal* of August 20, Untermyer warned of the harm that disjointed American Jewish action could bring:

> ... From an interview which I had in my office with Mr. Deutsch and Dr. Margoshes, I understand that the American Jewish Congress will coordinate its activities with us who are the pioneers in this field. I hope this will be achieved, and that all attempts to compete will be terminated for the benefit of the cause in which we are all so deeply interested.
>
> Many weeks ago, I announced in public addresses and through other media that we are formulating an appeal to the League of Nations,[15] and I expressly stated the grounds for our proposed action. Sometime before this, I discussed this matter in London with our Secretary of State and at great length with the General Secretary of the League of Nations, Joseph Avenol. And further, there is a danger of fragmentizing our strength, something that must be avoided at all costs.[16]

Under separate cover, Untermyer sent Deutsch a copy of this letter. However, the following was appended: "As I understand it, the statement in the '*Morgen Journal*' was issued by the Publicity Department of the American Jewish Congress, of which you are president. The statement is at the very least, ungracious."[17]

11

Continued Committee Intransigence

In Untermyer's correspondence with the American Jewish Committee in May and June (1933), the Committee's continued opposition to the idea of an organized boycott was crystal clear. Nor did its stand on this issue change during the period when the Congress shifted from protest to boycott. The Committee was to remain unalterably opposed to both tactics throughout the Nazi era.

However, for any responsible boycott proponent, the Committee still remained too important an organization to be ignored in a concerted effort to expand the movement. Due to this, and, perhaps, to his exultation over, and personal success at, the Amsterdam Conference, Untermyer, in his return-trip speech (pp. 81–82), felt inspired to also address himself to the Committee:

> I appeal to the American Jewish Committee, whose public spirit and good intentions I do not for a moment question, but the wisdom of whose judgment I challenge, no longer to hold aloof but to rid themselves of their timid and ill-considered prejudices and join in actively pressing this boycott as our only weapon except the appeal to the League which I shall discuss at a later time.[1]

As far as we can tell, the Committee chose to ignore Untermyer's "appeal" together with his disparaging remarks. However, it did follow assiduously recent events in the Congress camp. Thus, in reaction to Wise's boycott declaration in Prague (p. 77), and information from Deutsch that the Congress' National Executive Committee would in all likelihood pass a boycott resolution at its forthcoming meeting, the Committee prepared to act.

On August 17, 1933, Waldman (p. 42) sent to all members of the Executive Committee of the AJC a confidential circular in which he asked them to state whether they thought their organization, in view of the latest developments, should issue a public statement. Adler, for one, who was out in California at this time to campaign against the boycott, expressed his disapproval. He cited the following reason in his reply on August 19:

> Now to come out immediately on the heels of Wise's statements and Deutsch's information is a little funny. Neither Wise nor Deutsch will get much noise out of this, for Untermyer has stolen their thunder. What the incident makes clear to me is the absolute insincerity of Wise and Deutsch and the impossibility of any real cooperation with them.[2]

The Committee president also took stock of the altered situation, in which the Congress would no longer have to be fought on the issue of mass meetings and parades, but on the less palatable subject of boycott. In light of this, added Adler, if a public statement is decided upon, it should run as follows:

> The American Jewish Committee, in agreement with responsible Jewish organizations in Europe declines to sanction a declaration of boycott against Germany. We will not make threats, but rather rely upon the moral forces of America and of other enlightened countries in the world. If these moral forces are dead, then civilized man will perish and brutes will rule. This is a question larger than Germany, even larger than the Jews. It should engage the attention of all men and of all nations who are still possessed of conscience.[3]

To Adler and other Committee members, the Congress' boycott declaration was also tantamount to the dissolution of the recently created Conjoint Consultative Council.[4] This new body, created officially on June 22, 1933, came to fill the void left by the demise of the Joint Conference Committee (see p. 29). Some information relevant to the background of the Conjoint Consultative Council is contained in the June 2, 1933, minutes of the Congress' Administrative Committee:

> Following upon an all-day conference in Washington D.C., May 26, 1933, announcement was made today by representatives of the American Jewish Committee, the American Jewish Congress and B'nai B'rith that recommendation would at once be made to these three organizations that there be established a Conjoint Consultative

Council to be made up of (three of five) representatives of each body, which Committee shall parallel the Conjoint Committee of the Anglo-Jewish Association of England.

This Conjoint Consultative Council is to meet regularly and have the power of making representation on behalf of the three bodies in dealing with the Government of the United States and with all official bodies.

This Committee, which, as its name implies, is to be a consultative body, shall be empowered to recommend joint action on the part of the organizations which it represents.[5]

The fundamental aim of the Consultative Council was the avoidance of a duplication of competing defense activities and the performance of common undertakings on the basis of mutual consultation. To overcome, though, the Congress' refusal to be bound by majority decisions, freedom of action was reserved for each group where complete accord proved impossible. The Congress' decision to declare a boycott without consulting beforehand the AJC-BB was a breach of faith; but it seems the A.J.C. saw little point in consulting them about a matter which they had repeatedly denounced.

Judging from the last point in the first of his two August 19 statements, Cyrus Adler hardly took the Congress' imminent boycott declaration in stride. Neither did the Honorable Horace Stern, chairman of AJC's Executive Committee, who noted this point in reply to Waldman's circular: "And if the Congress is going ahead on its own account, it not only shows a contemptuous indifference to our opinion, but makes a mockery of our recent cooperative alliance."[6]

When the American Jewish Congress joined the boycott movement, it obviously destroyed the last vestige of agreement with the AJC-BB regarding the methods of defending German Jewish interests. Thus, for the first time since the start of the Hitler crisis, the major Jewish defense organizations stood diametrically opposed to one another on the most agonizing problem of the day.

But in the beginning of August, when it was becoming apparent that the Congress was bent on a boycott course, the Committee had started drafting a policy statement summing up its major reasons for opposing this movement. However, unlike many of its previous statements, this one was not for publication. It was released, however, on the seventeenth of the month, and sent only to sustaining members, apparently, to reduce the impact of the impending Congress declaration. The Committee's statement remained final and irreversible.[7] Only the B'nai B'rith, for reasons to be discussed later, was to reverse itself four years hence.

12

The Boycott in the Transnational Jewish Arena

The Eighteenth Zionist Congress

i.

On August 21, the Eighteenth Zionist Congress convened in Prague; and by then, no responsible Jewish assembly could fail to confront the woeful realities of the Jewish situation in Nazi Germany. The anti-Nazi boycott was an obvious response, and Vladimir Jabotinsky, Zionist Revisionist Party leader, introduced a strongly-worded resolution proposing its adoption on a worldwide scale. Declaring that "we are conducting a war with murderers," Jabotinsky angrily cried out: "Not only should we harm our enemy, but destroy, destroy, destroy him; not only with the boycott, but politically, supporting all existing forces against him in order to isolate Germany from the civilized world."[1]

The Revisionist chieftain also demanded that the Zionist Congress strongly protest the anti-Jewish legislation imposed by the Nazis. However, he was equally emphatic in his readiness to sacrifice German Jewry for the overall preservation of World Jewry:

> The German threat to keep a half million German Jews hostages if World Jewry is not silent, should be ignored. We sympathize with our German brethren. Let them remain loyal to Germany. But Hitlerism presents a danger to sixteen million Jews and the fate of German Jews cannot influence us in fighting Germany. Our enemy must be destroyed.[2]

Jabotinsky made this statement to reporters after the Zionist Congress rejected his boycott resolution by a vote of 240 to 48. He further stated that, since the Zionist Congress had not seen fit to assume a position of boycott leadership, the less countenancing Revisionist Party would. This would manifest itself, Jabotinsky revealed, in the creation of a central world body of its own to guide and stimulate the boycott.

The Zionist Congress, for reasons that will soon be set forth, acted with greater restraint. Its resolution, passed on August 24, stated that the Zionist movement "will not remain silent until the deprival of rights and the indignity to German Jews comes to an end."[3] It also raised Zionism's voice in "solemn protest against the terrible injustice done to German Jews and the systematic policy of deprival of social and economic citizenship rights and the defamation of social and human rights and interference with religious rights through SCHECHITAH (ritual slaughter) prohibition."[4]

The Zionist Congress also appealed to the League of Nations, the Palestine Mandatory power, and other world nations to come to the aid of the Jewish people and to facilitate the creation of a Jewish National Home. Save for the Revisionist bloc, every Zionist faction approved the resolution. It was a determined position to retain under the dire circumstances.

ii.

The Zionist Congress delegates who voted down the boycott resolution were not of the AJC-BB variety; that is to say, they were not opposed to public agitation per se as an anti-Nazi tactic, nor to boycott, which they did not denounce, but felt should be left to continue in the course in which it was heading. What was it, then, that actuated them to defeat the proposed boycott resolution?

There were a variety of reasons. In the first place, as a Palestinocentric organization, it was not the main task of a World Zionist Congress to deal with questions relating to Diaspora defense. This, as shall presently be elaborated upon, was regarded as the principal function of the World Jewish Congress movement. And if the Hitler menace happened to be so all-encompassing and emotional an issue that discussion and action relating to it could not be ignored even by an organization that chiefly concerned itself with problems relating to the fostering of a Jewish National Home in Palestine, it did not mean that so "radical" a weapon as an international boycott had to be resorted to as the basic solution to the Jewish question in Germany.

Secondly, a pro-boycott vote entailed risks which the WZO (World Zionist Organization) did not think worth taking. Thus, only a week prior to the opening of this Congress, the *Juedische Rundschau*, Germany's Zionist organ, was closed down by the Nazis for a six-month period. No reason was offered for this protracted ban, but to the WZO it adumbrated trouble, especially since the Nazis could hold German Zionists responsible for all that was said and done against Germany at the Eighteenth Zionist Congress. One possible measure was particularly feared in the event of the passage of a boycott resolution: a prohibition of *Hechalutz* (i.e., Zionist) activities in Germany, thus stemming the flow to Palestine of valuable pioneering youth.

Thirdly, Revisionists opposed other Zionists on a wide front, and voting for a Revisionist boycott resolution meant strengthening the Revisionists on a number of other current and important issues, such as the latters' demand to have Jews settled in Trans-Jordan and the insistence that Palestine be immediately declared a Jewish state. Moreover, about two months earlier, Dr. Chaim Arlosoroff, brilliant Labor Zionist leader, had been purportedly assassinated by several Revisionist extremists. Rightly or wrongly—for the case has never really been solved—Jewish public opinion, both in Palestine and in the Diaspora, was furious with the Revisionists. Many Zionist delegates were therefore reluctant to be parties to a Revisionist proposal, no matter what its merits.

Fourthly, Jabotinsky was viewed by many as a Jewish Fascist. A slogan then in fashion ran somewhat as follows: Germany for Hitler; Italy for Mussolini; and Palestine for Jabotinsky. This catchword may have run through the minds of a lot of delegates when, a few minutes before the opening session of the Eighteenth Zionist Congress, Jabotinsky entered the auditorium with a retinue of uniformed men marching in military formation. Nor did Mussolini's official organ which, shortly prior to the Prague Congress, came out in support of a Jewish state in Palestine, help to remove the Fascist label with which Jabotinsky was being tagged.

Finally, because of its geographic contiguity with Germany, Czechoslovakia made an unofficial request that the WZO not be too outspoken against the Nazis. Nazi agents were lurking in Prague to observe and note all that would take place at the Congress; and so hostile a declaration as a boycott resolution could be used by the Nazis to accuse the Czechs of leasing the use of their capital to Germany's enemies.

The Transfer Agreement

i.

Samuel Untermyer could hardly have tried to obtain a more distinctive and powerful Jewish body than the WZO to help him realize his aim of making the boycott a mighty international force. But for reasons that lie in the realm of conjecture, Untermyer did not attend the Zionist Congress. He did the next best thing, though. On August 20, a day before the convening of the Congress, he cabled the following appeal to Louis Lipsky, veteran American Zionist, a leading member of the American Jewish Congress, and ardent boycott advocate:

> Kindly read the following message to the Zionist Congress: My best wishes for success. I need hardly remind you that I support, and I have always supported, every Palestinian movement and am strongly interested in the welfare of Palestine; and that I am a great admirer of Dr. Weizmann, whom I consider the greatest statesmanly Jewish leader of our generation.
>
> I hold that the present Congress is amongst the most important in Palestine's history. I hope that the Congress will not only declare itself in favor of the boycott movement, (against Germany) but will also join the World Jewish Federation, which was formed not too long ago in Amsterdam (and which has the main office in London, with Sir Alfred Mond[5] as chairman, and myself as president) in order to develop the world boycott, which is already being strongly led throughout the world, and which has great possibilities of success.
>
> Although the boycott is just at the first stage in certain countries and has not begun, as yet, in other countries; still, its effect is increasing rapidly and is likewise being supported by non-Jews the world over. They acknowledge that this problem strongly concerns the entire civilized world and all of humanity, irrespective of race or religion.
>
> Making compromises have proven themselves to be false. Germany is being kept uninformed about world opinion. The boycott is the only language that they understand. Only an economic collapse will open the eyes of the German people.
>
> I hope that the Congress will adopt resolutions that will lead to the complete coordination of the work through a common committee, or in another way. My investigations and the opinions of many international authorites have convinced me that one can obtain significant aid through the League of Nations. Our Federation is taking steps in this direction and we are seeking your cooperation and that of other organizations.
>
> The boycott logically goes hand in hand with the movement that I heartily support; to settle in Palestine as many Jews as the limited possibilities and the territory of the land can absorb, and that England will permit to enter. If World Jewry and the civilized world will in the meanwhile not stop and tolerate Germany's Medieval crusade, then global anti-Semitism will become encouraged. If you allow yourselves to be frightened by Hitler's and Alfred Rosenberg's threats from employing the only weapon of defense, then your only chance of helping your persecuted brothers will be lost.

What is, then, Hitler's cold, official program, if not the most horrible form of boycott that human devils have created? The entire world shakes in horror.[6]

The communication did not even have a remote chance of influencing the Zionist Congress to adopt a boycott resolution. This became painfully clear to boycott circles when, on August 23, the German Land Trade League announced that a barter agreement had been reached between Germany and Syria-Palestine. The agreement provided that Germany would import from 8 million to 10 million marks' worth of Jaffa oranges. In return, Palestine and Syria were to receive 20 million marks' worth of German industrial products. The goods were to be shipped on German vessels.

It was also reported that, under an agreement between the Anglo-Palestine Bank of Palestine and Germany's Ministry of Economics, the Hitler government would permit Jews desiring to emigrate from the Reich to take with them up to 6 million marks (about $2 million) worth in wares and machinery. Accordingly, such Jews would turn their monies over to a special Reichsbank fund for which they would be compensated in German-made goods to be taken with them upon embarkation.

This accord, known as the *Haavarah* (i.e., Transfer Agreement), was secretly reached with the Nazis by Dr. Chaim Arlosoroff[7] about two months prior to his assassination. It remained in effect until 1938. Modifications were added in the interim, but these always centered around the promotion of German-made goods.

Stormy protests broke out at the Prague Congress when the news about the Transfer Agreement became known. The Revisionists were first in demanding an explanation from the Zionist Executive Committee. They wanted to know what role the involved Zionists had played in the negotiations and whether the Eighteenth Zionist Congress would sanction the Agreement. Asserting that Nazi Germany was unworthy of human relationship, the Revisionists denounced as dishonorable the accord reached with the Hitler government. Jewish national honor, they insisted, had to be defended at all costs and sacrifices.

The Labor Zionists, as well as others, argued that *Haavarah* remained the only way for Jews to leave Nazi Germany with at least part of their possessions; that this was better than coming to Palestine empty-handed and becoming public charges. These Transfer proponents also claimed that such an Agreement would not interfere with the boycott, since Germany would receive no foreign currency for its merchandise. They, therefore, requested the Zionist Congress to sanction the Agreement.

This far the Zionist Congress was not prepared to go. It took a neutral stand, though, neither condemning nor denouncing the Agreement.

Therewithal, the hotly-fought issue was referred to the Congress' Actions Committee, where it eventually died.

ii.

To the Palestinian delegates at the Zionist Congress, the Transfer Agreement was probably the main factor in convincing them of the necessity of voting against the proposed boycott resolution. Certainly the news dispatch that described the accord was intended to dissuade the Congress from adopting it. Otherwise, why should it have been released a day before the voting?

Of course, to many of the delegates, the news came as a total surprise. Some were skeptical, believing it to be a piece of Nazi propaganda or mere rumor. Nor were their doubts dispelled when the Jewish Agency hurriedly denied that any deal had been made with the Nazi government. However, the Land Trade League, whose news release gave rise to this state of confusion, put an end to it on August 31 by revealing that it was George Halperin, Zionist leader and director of the Anglo-Palestinian Bank, who had conducted and would continue conducting the negotiations regarding German Jewry's transfer to Palestine.

Untermyer, as can be well imagined, was shocked and angered by the whole episode; and like many others, he, too, was skeptical at first. He did not, however, wait for absolute confirmation before denouncing the accord. Speaking on August 27 to a B'nai B'rith lodge in Youngstown, Ohio, Untermyer criticized the WZO, saying that the boycott would be far more effective in the struggle to help German Jewry than the terms of the Transfer Agreement. He expressed this along the lines of his prediction at the August 20 emergency session of the National Executive Committee of the American Jewish Congress; namely, that an effective boycott would topple the Hitler regime within a year. He, therefore, demanded that the Zionists sever their negotiations with the Reich.

Two days later, Untermyer sent the Zionist Congress another cablegram, demanding this time that its leaders immediately deny the authenticity of the report concerning the Transfer Agreement; if not, he threatened, a special convention would be called which would dissociate itself from the action of the Eighteenth Zionist Congress and recall all the American delegates. "World Jewry will tolerate no dealings with Germany," he stated forcefully. "We are loyal Palestinians," he added, "but the outcome of this struggle is vastly more important than selling oranges."[8]

"Why, the very idea of Palestinian Jewry negotiating with Hitler about business instead of demanding justice for the persecuted Jews of Germany is unthinkable."[9] Thus spoke Abba Hillel Silver, noted Cleveland

Reform rabbi and ardent Zionist, who had recently been attracted to the boycott movement by Untermyer. Continuing his conversation with his JTA (Jewish Telegraphic Agency) interviewer, Silver said:

> Palestinian Jewry should be showing the way to unified action and not be willing to victimize the Jews of the rest of the world for a million crates of oranges.
> This is a test case. Always Palestine has asked the Jews of the world to sacrifice for Palestine, now the time has come to ask, will Palestine make a commercial sacrifice for the interests of the fifteen million Jews of the World?[10]

It was in this tone and along this line of questioning that bitter attacks against the *Haavarah* pact were soon to be unleashed by delegates of another important world Jewish body.

The World Jewish Conference

The First Zionist Congress, in 1897, had a twofold purpose: to launch a movement for the establishment of a Jewish state, and to deal with the problems of the Jewish Diaspora. Subsequently, two factions emerged. One strongly urged that Zionism direct all its efforts toward the fostering of a Jewish National Home in Palestine; the other advocated a Zionism co-extensive with a striving for the well-being of Diaspora Jewry.

The first several years of the post–World War I era, which witnessed the staggering problems of securing minority rights for Europe's Jews and afforded a unique opportunity for the upbuilding of the Jewish National Home in Palestine, brought the WZO to the conclusion that it was becoming too arduous a task to also pursue World Jewry's Diaspora problems. The creation of a World Jewish Congress as the proper agency for such problems, a suggestion analogous to a proposal made by the noted Jewish historian Simon Dubnow after the Kishinev pogrom of 1903, began receiving, therefore, a more active response from Zionists. However, it was not until 1932, when the Nazi menace loomed up more than ever before, that it was agreed that the need for the creation of a World Jewish Congress brooked no further delays. So in May of that year, Dr. Nahum Goldmann, leading German Zionist and a spearhead of the World Jewish Congress idea, accepted an invitation by the American Jewish Congress to arrange a preliminary conference for this purpose. As a result of his efforts, the First World Jewish Conference convened in Geneva, Switzerland, from August 14 to August 17 (1933). At the

Conference, Goldmann described the purpose of the World Jewish Congress:

> It is to establish the permanent address of the Jewish people; amidst the fragmentation and atomization of Jewish life and of the Jewish community, it is to establish a real, legitimate, collective representation of Jewry which will be entitled to speak in the name of the 16 million Jews to the nations and governments of the world, as well as to the Jews themselves.[11]

In 1933, when the German-Jewish problem surpassed by far Jewish travails in other lands, the anti-Nazi boycott became a main topic of discussion at the Second World Jewish Conference. Many WZO delegates, Dr. Wise included, felt that it was really the obligation of the World Jewish Conference to adopt a boycott resolution; a view that had influenced a substantial number of Zionist delegates to vote it down at their Congress. Untermyer, who might not have known or appreciated this consideration, singled out Dr. Wise for attack, denouncing his stand as contradictory. However, Dr. Wise "was firmly convinced that a World Jewish boycott could only be declared by a world assembly of Jews."[12]

The Second World Jewish Conference also met in Geneva, this time from September 5 to September 8. At the opening session, Dr. Wise affirmed the appropriateness of having a global boycott declared by the World Jewish Conference rather than the Zionist Congress:

> The World Jewish Congress invites Jews to gather in order to consider and to take action upon all Jewish questions. What the Zionist Congress and the Jewish Agency for Palestine are designed to be and to do in relation to Zionism and the re-establishment of the Jewish Home in Palestine, the World Jewish Congress plans to be and to do in relation to the common Jewish problems of the Diaspora.[13]

Upon the conclusion of his introductory statement, Dr. Wise spoke of the boycott, noting the following:

> We have said tonight that Jews the world over are agreed that the overshadowing problem throughout Jewish life today is bound up with the situation of the German Jews, as it has come into being since the beginning of the Hitler regime. It is no less true, ladies and gentlemen, that the German Jewish problem is itself overshadowed and dominated by one question which must be answered by the World Jewish Congress Executive in conference assembled. That question is: *Shall there be a world Jewish boycott of all goods and wares and products manufactured in Germany?* Put even more simply, shall Jews have any

relation whatever, industrial or economic, with a nation which has declared war against the Jewish people everywhere, by declaring that we Jews are an inferior parasitic empoisoning race of humanity.

With respect to boycott, ladies and gentlemen, certain facts must be borne in mind: first, the Jewish boycott movement from the beginning has been absolutely spontaneous, uninspired and uninstigated. That boycott was not imposed above. It grew out of the anguish of the Jewish masses, who inevitably reacted to the declaration of war against them by taking in hand the only weapon that is accessible to the Jewish masses.

Whatever claims may be made by improvised and improvising Jewish leaders, the boycott movement, I repeat, was the inevitable deadly type of warfare against their very life. Secondly, the boycott movement is, after all, nothing more than a buyers' strike, a strike by possible purchasers, and a solely defensive weapon; not offensive but defensive, even though the high priest of Hitler, Captain Goebbels, maintain as he did at Nuremberg two days ago that the anti-Jewish boycott in Germany was perfected long before the new Germany came into being.

We do not overlook the fact that an anti-German boycott on the part of Jews is bound to affect and injure the Jews as well as non-Jews in Germany. I cannot imagine that any Jew in Germany will be so base as to demand that because Jews will be additionally hurt there shall be no anti-German boycot on the part of Jews in other lands.[14]

In the concluding section of his inspiring message, Dr. Wise discussed the gist of a worldwide anti-Nazi boycott which, he maintained, was now more appropriate and necessary.

To them that cry that German Jews may suffer the penalties of our decision, the answer must in all conscience be given. We are not the authors of the misfortune and the sorrows of the German Jews. We suffer with them. We suffer for them. And God knows that every Jew would like to take his place at the side of the German Jews in their defence.

But the final decision in the matter of a world-wide boycott rests not with German Jews, who are not free, but with World Jewry outside of Germany which *is* free, and which I believe, without anticipating or prejudging the decision of the World Jewish Congress Executive will declare that since the Hitler Reich has taken into its hands every weapon in order to destroy the Jewish people everywhere, we can defend ourselves only in two ways: first, by refusing to have any economic dealings with Germany. Next, by appealing to the conscience of mankind which we believe has been outraged by all that has been done against our fellow Jews in Germany during these terrible months.

We of the American Jewish Congress could not, would not, did not seek to organize and proclaim a world Jewish boycott. We could not until after conference with the representatives of the Jewries of the world. Throughout six months I have maintained because I believed that such a boycott could be declared only by a body such as meets tonight in Geneva and speaks on behalf of millions of Jews. Whatever decision will be reached by the World Jewish Congress, indeed, by all the American Jewry, the largest Jewry on earth, consisting of more than one quarter of the world's Jewish population . . . .[15]

During the last session, Dr. Wise, who had formulated the boycott resolution, introduced it to the conferees:

The World Jewish Conference notes with deepest satisfaction that from the beginning of the Hitler regime and its anti-Jewish laws and acts the Jewish people instinctively and spontaneously resorted to the one immediately accessible weapon of self-defense: a moral and economic boycott. In the spirit of individual and collective self-respect, the Jewish people through the boycott affirms that Jews cannot hold any economic or other relation with the Nazi Government of the Third Reich *and believes that its boycott must continue to be shared by millions of non-Jews in all lands,* who understand and sympathize with the Jewish people's abhorrence of the Nazi and anti-Jewish precept and practice.

When the Jewish boycott of German goods and wares is to be ended depends not upon the Jewish people but the Nazi Government. This instrumentality of moral and economic pressure Jews have been compelled reluctantly to adopt and utilize. But they will not lay this down until such time as the great wrong inflicted upon German Jews is undone and the German Jews once again be placed in the status and position which were rightly their own before the accession of the Hitler Government. The Conference solemnly calls upon the Jewish people loyally to continue in their legitimate, honorable and peaceable resistance against the war waged by Hitlerism upon the German Jews and upon the whole Jewish people.[16]

The resolution was adopted unanimously, after which Dr. Wise had this to say to the Conference:

Ladies and Gentleman: we have just adopted a most important resolution. It is true that in the resolution we have said nothing new to the Jewish people, but we dare believe that we have fulfilled its wish and as representative leaders of Jewries in different lands, we have given our approval to that which the masses of the people have instinctively done from the beginning and demanded of us, namely, moved forward to the boycott as a weapon of self-defence against Hitlerism. Our counter-boycott resolution which we have just adopted does not mean a declaration of war against Germany. No people is farther removed than our own from the idea of warring upon other nations. Nazi Germany declared war against us in April, not only against 600,000 Jews in Germany, but against the whole Jewish people, the honor of which it has violated and the position of which it would destroy throughout the world. We have postponed action as representative leaders for half a year in the hope that a change might come over the situation. Alas, the situation grows graver from day to day, and it is now nothing more but instinctive self-preservation which moves us to resort to the use of the weapon of self-defence, the only weapon which is accessible to us, namely, the moral and material boycott.[17]

The honorary president of the American Jewish Congress also utilized the occasion of his outspoken pro-boycott stand to denounce the Transfer Agreement, terming it a "new golden calf—the golden orange." Heartily applauded, Wise continued: "I think I speak the mind of Jews everywhere when I say we hold in abhorrence any Jew, whether in or out of Palestine, who undertakes to make commercial arrangements with the Nazi government for any reason whatsoever."[18] Thus, the man who had taken so long to agree to the adoption of a boycott against Hitler Germany was now evidently ready to support it "to the limit."

Two other resolutions were unanimously adopted by the World Jewish Conference. One requested the League of Nations to intervene on German Jewry's behalf in a political and humanitarian fashion. It stressed in particular the need of aiding emigration to Palestine. The other resolution averred that the crisis in Germany made the creation of a World Jewish Congress more urgent than ever, and, for this purpose, scheduled its next conference for March, 1934.

In principle, then, agreement was reached by a world Jewish body to conduct a global boycott against Hitler Germany. It remained to be seen, however, just what kind of effect this sort of universal pressure would have against the new and, as yet, undeveloped, but very militant and reprehensible Nazi state.

13

The Last Months of ALDJR

The National Boycott Conference

i.

With the completion of the preparatory work in Europe, Untermyer, Coralnik, and their co-workers called a conference for the coordination of anti-Nazi boycott activities in the United States. Sharing the hope of building a united movement in their country, the JWV and a number of A.J.C. representatives decided in favor of attendance. The conference convened on September 10, with Untermyer presiding.

One of the main points of discussion centered around the question of U.S. representation in the World Jewish Economic Federation. It was raised by George Fredman (p. 30), who claimed that it was his understanding at the World Jewish Economic Conference (p. 75), that an attempt would be made to coordinate the activities of all U.S. boycott organizations under the "banner" of the WJEF (World Jewish Economic Federation). Fredman thought this the only workable plan, for he was convinced that "no one Jewish organization is influential enough to head or direct them."[1] He was further convinced that "only on a world-wide scale would all American Jewish organizations unite." His remarks were followed by the question of whether "these factions" would be coordinated under ALDJR or the WJEF.

Untermyer replied that the work of all interested boycott organizations would be "coordinated" by the WJEF, but that the "autonomy of each country has to be preserved." Fredman pressed on, however, asking Untermyer whether he could get the American Jewish Congress, the Jewish War Veterans, and B'nai B'rith to coordinate under the banner of the ALDJR. Thereupon, Fredman also added that he did not believe this could be done "unless the ALDJR is named a branch of the World Federation."

Untermyer responded that the ALDJR "is one coordinate branch of the World Federation" and "it will preserve its autonomy and be part of the World Federation." He finally got to the heart of Fredman's question by explaining that it "doesn't make any difference under whom we coordinate because we are all coordinated under the World Federation." Untermyer then added:

> But if the American Jewish Congress wants to come in under the World Federation, well and good. We don't care where they come in as long as they promote the boycott and the same is true of all other organizations. All we want is their support, and all we want is that they should come in under the general aegis of the World Federation.[2]

However, Untermyer's concluding remark contained a baseless inference:

> But if Mr. Fredman thinks that we are going to disband the League for the Defense of Jewish Rights after they have done this herculean job, why, he is mistaken, and I am surprised that as one of the vice-presidents of the World Federation, that he should suggest such a course, because it can only lead to discord.[3]

Proceeding to the next order of business, which dealt with the appointment of a Resolutions and Finance Committee, Mr. Untermyer called on Dr. Coralnik, who said the following regarding the anti-Nazi boycott:

> It is not the purpose of the League to somehow monopolize the work of the boycott. It is a nation-wide work....
> We shall today counsel how to construct this boycott in a way that Germany shall feel it. Not only shall we show the public in America and the world that we are fighting not merely [for?] the Jewish cause, which is perhaps not so urgent in the minds of so many of our fellow citizens, but we are the vanguard of the world fight against Hitlerism and against the death of democracy and freedom in the world.[4]

Coralnik also condemned the Transfer Agreement. He called it the "Zionist disgrace," describing it as "ruinous and scandalous." In referring to the Zionists, Coralnik said that he had "pleaded with them in vain."

But to counteract the Zionist-German accord, concluded the League leader, Palestinian Jews should be helped "to widen the market and to procure new facilities, and to help German Jews not to beg the German Government to give them back their money, but we can try to give them this means and to reject all the offers of the Hitler Government and to reject all compromises."⁵

ii.

Untermyer's main point, made before the conferees in his introductory remarks, was undoubtedly well-intentioned, but it was so exaggerated as to amount to an exercise in wishful thinking. "I have said before, and I repeat, that if you gentlemen and our other associates do their duty, Germany will crack this winter from starvation."⁶

Abba Hillel Silver, who was appointed chairman of the Resolutions Committee, justifiably took issue with this prediction, saying that Jews "have to prepare for a long battle." He then gave a view of a boycott which more resembled Dr. Wise's conception: "In a way, this is war; this is a substitute for war; this is a moral substitute for war. That is what boycott is. The League of Nations recognizes it as the moral substitute for physical pressure, in terms of military punitive expeditions."⁷

Rabbi Silver also remarked that just as one cannot conduct an effective war if there is division in the ranks, so American Jewry must avoid division in the conduct of a boycott. He went on to say:

> It is therefore my thought that this body here call upon all other Jewish bodies in this country who have endorsed the boycott, are sympathetic with it, to regard this body as the central authority, the central authoritative and exclusive body in the field of the boycott activity. The subject of representation, et cetera, that is a detail which can be worked out satisfactorily because nobody is particularly interested in control or prestige, or in glory, but what is absolutely important is that for once we establish here one body, one central authority which will speak for the whole of American Israel on this one subject, namely, the successful prosecution of the boycott. If that can't be done, then I believe our task is hopeless.⁸

In addition, Silver reported that his travels had convinced him of the almost unanimous sentiment for boycott. He claimed there was a division of opinion concerning the wisdom of conducting a "public boycott" or a "silent boycott," but the principle of bringing economic pressure on the Nazi regime was almost universally agreed to by American Jews. The Cleveland Reform rabbi concluded by emphasizing the need to direct anti-Nazi sentiment intelligently and constructively. Failure to properly focus so powerful an emotion on a national scale, he warned, would not be the fault of American Jews, but of their leaders.

Rabbi Silver was the last speaker to discuss the unity question. Sometime thereafter, though, five resolutions were read and adopted by the Conference.[9] Yet, neither Silver nor any of the other speakers had really offered a plan for the establishment of "a united front," as called for in Resolution No. III (see p. 405).

Col. Morris Mendelson (p. 45), one of several JWV delegates, interpreted this resolution to mean that, for the price of being accepted into the ALDJR, the applying organization would have to surrender its identity:

> There is no one who regards the ability and capability of Mr. Untermyer more than the JWV. We feel that if there is anyone in this country qualified to lead the Jews at this time, it is he. However, we feel also that it is asking a good deal to ask an organization such as the American Jewish Congress, or other organizations of long standing to give up their identity and come under the banner of the American League for the Defense of Jewish Rights. I say that the resolution that has been passed here inviting these other organizations to come under this banner is just an idle gesture. It will get us nowhere.
>
> Speaking as the Chairman of the Anti-Nazi Boycott Committee of the Jewish War Veterans,[10] I can say quite openly that it would be impossible for us to give up our identity and come under this banner, as much as we would like to do it.[11]

To surmount this hurdle, Mendelson suggested the formation of a Federation of Boycott Committees, which would incorporate "every organization interested in boycott." Untermyer's answer was that "the resolution requires no such thing," but added, though, that the "American Jewish War Veterans will be strongly represented on this or any other committee." As a case in point, Untermyer said that ALDJR was planning to create an Administrative Committee which "will be made up not of the League, but of members who represent other organizations, a good many of them probably in the American Jewish Congress." He then said in conclusion:

> The resolution speaks about coordinating the activities and these have got to be coordinated under some sort of head. You can't coordinate them and have each separate again, or they wouldn't be coordinated. Can you coordinate them under the World Federation? That would be the desirable thing, if it could be done, but the World Federation was not organized for any such purpose and not a country in the World Federation would be willing to subscribe to going under the jurisdiction of the Federation and disposing of and obliterating its

independent action in its own country, so if you take the logical point of view of this thing, in this country we have got to have somebody, or some organization with which these other people can coordinate, and on which they will be represented.

Now, the American League for the Defense of Jewish Rights is not intended to dominate this Administrative Committee or this Executive Committee, let that be clearly understood. I would fight it as hard as anybody would, but you have got to have some sort of a heading of some kind.[12]

In his earlier statement to Fredman (p. 30), Untermyer indicated that the various boycott organizations had the choice of affiliating with the ALDJR or joining the WJEF directly. He now implied, however, that if such organizations did join the World Federation, their activities could not be "coordinated" without the ALDJR. Accordingly, it was not much of a choice; nor did Untermyer clarify just how "a heading of some kind" would "coordinate" rather than "dominate" non-League members.

The next order of business dealt with the problem of funds. Called upon to report, the Finance Committee recommended raising $500,000 "as the initial amount necessary to prosecute the boycott." It believed this amount could be raised "if there is unification of action" on the part of all boycott groups.

Hearing this, Mr. Margolis,[13] a delegate of the American Jewish Congress, asked "whether the campaign will start at once." He wanted to know this because the Congress was conducting its own campaign, and there was the prospect of duplicate money-raising efforts.

Untermyer responded that he did "not think there ought to be two campaigns." He claimed that he had broached the subject to the Congress, and reported that "their proposition to me was that it practically meant that they were to control the funds." Untermyer also disclosed that he had invited Mr. Deutsch and some other Congress members to the Conference; but they had declined the invitation, he said, offering as a reason that "we've got a campaign under way." Irritated by this explanation, Untermyer told the conferees that he had exclaimed: "But your campaign is for other things. You were against the boycott when you started that campaign, now you want to turn it into a boycott campaign so as to interfere with our campaign."[14]

Untermyer then said that he had resigned himself to this situation, adding that the campaign would be conducted without Congress participation. Thereupon, the Finance Committee recommended the appointment of a National Campaign Committee "to provide the necessary machinery for the raising of these funds."

Several delegates, angered by Untermyer's news concerning the Congress, now took turns in strongly censuring this organization. One of them, identified as a "gentleman from Cleveland," chose Mr. Margolis, as the target of his criticism:

> The American Jewish Congress, Mr. Margolis, this is to you, has proved itself to be incapable to lead the fight against Germany, absolutely incapable. You have fought Germany with words, and you can't do that, if you know the Germans, with words. You have to fight the Germans with deeds and the only way you can fight them is by hitting their pockets.[15]

But criticism of this kind was not germane to the discussion; for by now, the Congress had gone on record as supporting the boycott. The main issue at present was boycott unity, and verbal barrages of this kind were not helping to achieve it. On the contrary, it seemed to inspire new outbursts, the next one coming from Judge Hartman,[16] a dissident Congress delegate. Hartman informed the conferees that he had been a member of the Congress' Administrative Committee, and revealed that

> many of us in that Committee fought for a boycott pronouncement, for protests did not prove as effective as we had hoped, and that something more definite must be done by us, and we fought very hard within the Councils of the Administrative Committee for the public declaration of a boycott.
> In the meantime Untermyer came not only to lead the boycott but to typify it and the position of pre-eminence that he won entitled him to be the leader of the entire movement, and we of the American Jewish Congress can say to the Chairman and to this body that we will not brook any interference with the activities of this organization.[17]

Judge Hartman received a hearty applause for his last statement. It was a useless statement, however; or to paraphrase a line of argument mentioned in AJC policy statements, it served as an ineffectual channel for the release of emotion. For Hartman was not threatening in the name of men like Deutsch and Wise, the real powers behind the American Jewish Congress; nor did he serve the cause of unity by concluding with these words:

> The Congress had its chance, and we call the attention of the Congress to that fact. Now that another organization is in the pre-eminent position of leadership under so great a figure in Israel, so great an American as Samuel Untermyer, it is our duty, not only the American Jewish Congress, but all bodies, to cooperate and to enter into the Councils and activities of this wonderful conference of ours.[18]

Before adjourning, the National Conference (p. 97) also resolved "to secure a greater amount of cooperation in preventing sales of German-made goods in the United States." To help accomplish this, the League's Administrative Committee was committed to "formulate a plan to secure the greatest amount of cooperation among organized Jewish women." Mrs. Mark Harris, head of the League's Women's Division, was advised forthwith by Untermyer to enlarge her department.[19]

The knowledge that the American Jewish Congress would not help the League raise the $500,000 it felt was necessary to prosecute the boycott on a nationwide scale made certain Conference delegates uncertain about the possibility of realizing this project. Reacting to this, Judge Hartman said he thought it dangerous to inform the public that there was "doubt of the ability to raise the fund." He suggested that the Conference have faith in the "inherent sense of justice" of both "the American Jewish population and the general population." Hartman admitted, however, that he found "grave danger" in informing the public of the "lack of confidence surrounding the hope for unification."[20]

Fearing that the projected monetary campaign would "fall apart" if the Conference "disbanded with no pledges," Untermyer urged that "each representative pledge his city to a certain amount to raise the $500,000." Some protested that they were not authorized to do this. It did not avail them, however, as attested by Resolution No. II.

The Conference also elected officers. Thus, upon Rabbi Silver's motion, Dr. Coralnik was voted chairman of the League's National Executive Committee. Silver became chairman of the National Administrative Committee, and Untermyer was elected president of the League and ex-officio chairman of all committees.

The National Boycott Conference represented the first concerted effort to centralize the budding boycott movement in the United States. It was an ambitious undertaking, nurtured by the movement's freshness and a great enthusiasm for its success. America, and, indeed, the world, waited to see the fruit it would bear.

Blueprint for Boycott

For the year 1933, the National Boycott Conference of September 10, marked the last in a series of dramatic and headline-making gatherings involving the ALDJR. Also, both the ALDJR and the A.J.C. were soon to be deprived of much of the publicity and political capital that they stood to gain by bringing the German Jewish question before the League of Nations; for in October, Hitler Germany quit this international body. In addition, a London Boycott Conference, which was scheduled for that month and then postponed to November 5, took place without Untermyer's personal participation.[21] He was by that time too busy with his organization's affairs, primarily with the mechanics of boycott.

A report that Ezekiel Rabinowitz (p. 52) submitted to the National Boycott Conference gives an idea of what such "mechanics" involved. It contains a section entitled "Proposals of Major Activities," wherein he said that his "main concern" was the "organization of the consuming public." Proceeding to discuss the consumer, Rabinowitz stated:

> He is important not only because of his direct bearing upon the sale of manufactured articles, of which Germany is one of the largest exporters and which constitutes an important part of Germany's balance of trade, but primarily because the consumer is, in the final analysis, the one who determines the purchasing value of the distributors and importers in all domains of the import trade. The organization of the consumer therefore constitutes the front line of attack upon Germany.[22]

In addition, Rabinowitz urged the organization of various professions and trades, such as textiles, needle-trades, chemical industries, furriers, dentists, physicians, and pharmacists. He considered this the "second large objective of our movement." The League's executive secretary further urged pondering the "thousands of articles which in their finished form are not recognized as German products." The League should use its influence, he added, to hinder the use of German steamers "used in transmitting millions of dollars worth of freight to Europe," "to prevent American freight from being handled by German steam ship companies," and "of course, to influence passengers not to use German lines."[23]

In another section of his report, Rabinowitz listed the "most essential requirements for putting the boycott movement into action":

Executive Department—Propagating the boycott movement,
        a. Circulars,
        b. Placards
        c. Pamphlets
        d. Radio
        e. Talking films
        f. Newspaper publicity
        g. Speaking tours, of leaders of the movement
        h. Headquarters and personnel

Applying the boycott movement throughout the country,
a. Organization of vigilance committees
b. Organization of charge-accounts and deposit accounts
c. Organization of women consumers
d. Organization of trades and industries
e. Legal prosecutions
f. Local organizers
g. Traveling organizers
h. Subsidizing local boycott committees

Information bureau re: replacement of merchandise,
a. Research work
b. Contacts with American manufacturers through Chambers of Commerce
c. Contact with foreign consulates and foreign Chambers of Commerce
d. Weekly trade bulletin
e. Contact with offices of the World Economic Federation

Fund Raising Department—Mail campaign
Local campaign
Local personal solicitation
Speaking tours of leaders of the movement.[24]

Rabinowitz also made a specific suggestion regarding the planned $500,000 campaign. He advised organizing "local campaigns throughout the country," appealing to the Jewish masses in a "mail campaign," and conducting a "silent campaign" among the affluent classes. This approach, he believed, "will bring the best results."

To put the general boycott program into operation, Rabinowitz recommended dividing America into "at least" twelve boycott districts. He said the metropolitan area of New York, "with its enormous market," should be "subdivided" into six such districts. He did not indicate, however, which non–New York states or combinations of states should comprise the six remaining districts; nor did he give an indication as to which regional sections of New York should embrace his proposed six districts.

Dr. Coralnik was more specific on this score, but in a May 15 announcement, a day following ALDJR's official debut. He said then that the city of New York would be divided into fourteen boycott districts: Manhattan into four districts, Brooklyn into six, the Bronx into two, and Queens and Staten Island into one district each. Each district was to be governed by a council whose mission was to persuade consumers not to purchase German commodities or patronize German shops.

The record does not disclose which districting plan, Coralnik's or Rabinowitz's, was adopted for New York. We are told, however, that each such area was assigned a district captain, who, through private investigations, tips, and questionnaires, collected economic data pertaining to the boycott. Since it was impossible for one man to cover an entire district all by himself, he was assigned a vigilance committee, usually selected from student bodies and youth groups. The tactics employed by such committees included entry into stores to check labels and spying on deliveries. Often, under the threat of blacklist, store-owners would permit the inspection of their books by the vigilance committees. Collected data were submitted in weekly reports to the central office for study and action.

Small, obscure establishments, as well as larger, well-known concerns which violated the boycott, were pressured, too. Usually, this commenced with the boycott organization's sending both types of business outfits letters seeking to dissuade them from the continued purchase of German-made goods. League files abound with such letters. The following is the sort of letter generally sent the average boycott-violating entrepeneur(s):

Sand & Siman
38 West 32nd St.
New York, N.Y.

Gentlemen,

We are in receipt of reliable information that you have been, and still are, importing gloves from Germany.

In spite of the unimpeachable source of our information, we find it extremely difficult to credit these reports. It seems to us to be perfectly obvious that no fair-minded and liberty-loving American, least of all a Jew, would knowingly and willfully lend his support to a regime founded on the persecution and suppression of innocent and defenseless citizens on the sole ground of race and religion. Furthermore, the Hitler government is so diametrically opposed to the glorious principles upon which our great country was founded, that it behooves every American to refuse to have any dealings whatsoever with such a regime.

May we cordially invite you to shed some light on the accuracy of these reports.

Very truly yours,

Ezekiel Rabinowitz
Secretary[25]

Boycott breaches by major firms were exposed by the boycott organization, through the newspapers. A description of one such outstanding instance now follows.

First Major Engagement

On August 7 (1933), shortly after Untermyer's return from the Amsterdam Conference, Rabinowitz sent him a copy of a letter that Macy's had addressed to a lady regarding her complaint that the huge department store was selling German-made goods. The woman had mailed this copy to the League's office, where it came to the attention of Abba Hillel Silver. He, in turn, forwarded it to Rabinowitz, adding the following:

> I am enclosing herewith a copy of a letter which was sent out by Macy's of New York to a customer who complained that their department store was buying German goods. It is clear that Macy's is trading with the enemy, and plans to continue. It attempts to justify its action by the well known dodge of "their responsibility to their stock holders." The letter abounds with quietistic phrases about not wanting to hurt the cause of the Jews in Germany etc.
> I would suggest that Mr. Untermyer, upon his return to the United States, be asked to take the matter up with Mr. Straus of Macy's.[26] If he fails to persuade that organization, the Jews of New York ought to bear upon this organization, which by continuing to advertise and sell German-made goods in America, is helping to maintain the present bloody regime in Germany.[27]

It appears that the following July 19 letter, signed by Macy's president, Percy S. Straus, and addressed to a Mrs. Joseph Berlinger, is the "copy" received by the League:[28]

> We are in receipt of your letter taking exception to the sale of German goods by us.
> I, too, am a Jew and it is hardly necessary for me to say to you that I bitterly resent the treatment of the Jews in Germany as much as you, and as much as should any American, be he Jew or Gentile.

As an individual I should not hesitate to express myself with the greatest frankness, but as the President of this corporation, I have a responsibility to a large number of stockholders of all faiths and political creeds, and it is this reponsibility which prevents me from acting simply according to my feelings.

In the first place, were we to order our purchasing office in Berlin, which purchases, as well, in Czech-Slovakia and all other Eastern European countries, to desist from buying in Germany, that fact would immediately become known generally, and would receive considerable publicity. Such action might very definitely put an obstacle in the way of whatever solution this and other Governments might find in mitigating the treatment of Jews by the German Government.

In addition, we find there are still manufacturers in Germany of Jewish faith whom we can help by purchasing from them.

Were we without responsibility in the matter, our first reaction would be to stop buying German goods, but facing our responsibility, we have so far deferred taking any action.

Your letter was discussed at a meeting of the chief executives of this corporation, and it was the unanimous expresssion that individually all of us, both Jew and Gentile, were sympathetic to showing our disgust of the Hitlerite attitude toward the Jews, but as trustees for the stockholders and employees of Macy's, we could not permit our emotions to control our actions.

All our German goods are clearly marked with the country of origin. Therefore, you yourself can exercise your own censorship in this store, a censorship we cannot yet feel justified in exercising.[29]

The record does not show that this letter had evoked a reply from Untermyer; nor does it appear that he undertook any kind of publicized action. But Macy's, pressured by the rise in boycott sentiment, decided on a rather unusual and dramatic step to clarify and justify to the public its German-import policy. On October 2, it published in part of the general and Yiddish press, a full-page notice entitled:

THREE PERSONAL LETTERS

I.

Gentlemen,

From the very first day of my residence in New York which is 1914, I have been a loyal customer of your store. Your record in every department will prove that.

I am writing you to inform you that I have withdrawn my patronage from your store and will continue to do so until you have entirely eliminated all goods made in Germany from your store.

There is nothing of the nature in which Germany is holding a monopoly that is being sold in your store.

Every article which you offer emanating from Germany could easily be replaced either in our own country or in other European countries. It is inconceivable for me to understand why an American concern should support a country ruled by a bloody gang of maniacs who are a menace to civilization and who are seriously threatening our own American constitution by their pernicious and poisonous propaganda which they carry on in our own country.[30]

New York, September 13, 1933   S.T. (—)

II.

Dear Mr. ——,

I have your letter of September 13 and am glad you have written me so frankly.

In view of your desire not to purchase German goods I feel I should explain to you as explicitly as I can exactly what our policy is, and am confident that when you understand it fully you will realize that our sentiments are no different from your own.

I have no desire to conceal the fact that up to the present we have continued to handle a small quantity of goods of German manufacture. However, our purchases in Germany have rapidly diminished and are now being confined to that type of merchandise which we cannot obtain elsewhere, particularly such things as china and glassware, in which we have open stock patterns, which we are obliged to maintain for hundreds of customers who need replacements. Ninety-five percent of all our sales are of American made goods. Our total importations from all foreign countries approximate only about 5 percent of our business. All German goods which we sell are already marked with the name of the country of origin, and no one need buy German goods. We do not press them for sale or advertise them.

This had been our policy up to the moment. I may tell you that it has been the policy, according to my information, of all the other important New York stores (See IV. below). We know of no important store which has entirely discarded the sale of German goods. The subject of our handling German goods is continuing to receive careful attention, and our ultimate policy will be determined by considerations which will in our judgment contribute practically toward accomplishing results which we desire to see realized as much as you do.

As a loyal Jew, it is hardly necessary for me to tell you that personally I bitterly resent the treatment of the Jews in Germany, just as you do and just as should any American, be he Jew or Gentile.

We are, however, deeply concerned with helping the position of the Jews in Germany, with whom we have the greatest sympathy. In so far as we are now making any purchases in Germany, we have instructed our buyers to purchase goods when available, only from Jewish manufacturers, many of whom we are advised are still permitted to function in Germany. If we boycott such firms their plight will be harder than it is now.

The question of general policy in this matter is a very large and serious one, involving many considerations and obligations. My emotions as a Jew are exactly the same as your own, but we do not feel at liberty in view of all our responsibilities to allow our emotions to govern actions which may have far-reaching results, possibly against Jews themselves, without the most careful investigation and deliberate reflection.

We trust that you will realize, therefore, that at heart we have the same purposes which you have, namely, in the interests of humanity to do what we can to help the plight of the Jews in Germany. In our efforts to contribute effectively toward accomplishing that result we cannot allow ourselves to be led into impetuous actions simply because our emotions are stirred with a sense of outrage. We realize that hundreds of thousands of Jews still remain in Germany. My own influence will be exerted toward making the present unbearable lot of these Jews more presently tolerable, and to support influence which will restore to unoffending Jews in Germany the exercise of all the rights as human beings they are entitled.[31]

Sincerely yours,

New York, September 15, 1933   Percy S. Straus, President (—)

III.

Dear M.S.,

I beg to acknowledge your kind letter of September 15, and to thank you heartily for the trouble you have gone to, in explaining to me at length your personal position and that of your company with regard to the sale of German goods.

I am happy to say that the views expressed by you are beyond reproach, that your attitude in the matter is convincing and inspiring.

May I at this occasion reveal to you that I belong to a group of men who are devoting the major part of their time to the promotion of a general boycott of the Nazi Regime in every direction, politically, economically, and culturally. Only when the German people will find out that they are isolated by the civilized world and that a sort of cordon sanitaire has been thrown around that pestilence of

Hitlerism, then they may awake and reconsider their evil doings. As one of the movers of the boycott movement against Germany, I find that one should not press you nor any other New York department store to declare openly a boycott against Germany. I fully realize the complications and I believe that the policy pursued by you if generally adopted by every merchant and executive in the retail and wholesale trade, that Germany will soon feel this visible and indisputable disapproval by civilized men and women the world over the cruel and savage treatment of a helpless minority of their own people.

May I, however, respectfully point out to you that considerations for individual German Jews who are still permitted to continue in business should not in any way modify our general resolution to boycott Germany. German Jews have created the industries in Saxony, in Chemnitz, Annaberg, Plaman, etc. Yet they were the first ones to be arrested at the beginning of the so-called Hitler Revolution, thrown into jail, and their businesses practically confiscated. It is just from that source where most of the textile, glove, articles and embroideries emanate which are offered in American department stores. China and glassware to which you refer in your letter certainly are not articles in which Germany holds a monopoly. To my knowledge some very nice glassware is being manufactured in our own country and very beautiful specimens in Czechoslovakia and France.

Thanking you again for your kind letter and assuring you that I feel very much relieved and happy to be able to continue my purchases in your store, and with all good wishes to you, I am

Sincerely yours,

New York, September 20, 1933. S.L. (—) (The customer)[32]

The notice also carried a reprinted fourth item entitled:

IV.

THE ATTITUDE OF ALL LARGE NEW YORK STORES
(from *The New York Times*, Sept. 19, 1933)

Twenty leading stores here announced yesterday through H. Nelson Street, secretary of the Retail Dry Goods Association of New York that the consumer boycott on German-made merchandise has become so "extensive and effective" that their purchase of such goods "are now confined to a very few essential items which are not obtainable in any other country."

The announcement follows: "at the request of Samuel Untermyer

Esq. the leading New-York retail stores have exchanged experiences on the effect of the consumer boycott on German-made goods.

"They reported that it had become so extensive and effective that sales of German merchandise have decreased to such an extent that purchases by the stores are now confined to a very few essential items which are not obtainable in any other country; that German stocks on hand now are much less than 1%.

"Although they abhor the political and religious persecution in Germany today they feel that a boycott by the stores would create a dangerous precedent."

The statement was issued on behalf of Abraham & Straus Inc., B. Altman & Co., Arnold Constable & Co., Best & Co. Inc., Lord & Taylor, R. H. Macy & Co., Inc., James McGreery & Co., The Nam Store Oppenheim, Collins & Co., (New York & Brooklyn), Ovington's, Saks–Fifth Avenue, & Saks–34th Street., Franklyn Simon & Co., Stern Bros. & John Wanamaker.[33]

In an attempt to counterbalance the effect of this long notice, Untermyer prepared:

AN OPEN LETTER

In reply to the Advertisement of
R. H. Macy & Co. entitled "THREE PERSONAL LETTERS"
Concerning the continued sale by them of German goods

Percy S. Straus Esq.
President, R. H. Macy & Co.

If you had been as frank with your anonymous customer as might have been expected, his answer would doubtless have been very different.

If, for instance, you had, as you should have, told him—

1) That you had no right to speak for the "Department Stores in the United States" and that all of them (including non-Jewish stores), unlike your company, do not, as you imply, continue to buy goods made in Germany. Some of them, including non-Jewish owned stores, have discontinued the practice or are about to do so;
2) That unlike your company, they no longer continue to maintain agencies in Germany for the purchase of goods there;
3) That, unlike your company, they have not recently bought "blocked Marks"[34] in Germany at a heavy discount, which your company has used at par in making large purchases in Germany;

4) That the decision of the New York Department stores to which you refer, against refusing further to handle goods made in Germany, was brought about largely by your influence and leadership as the most important store in the group abetted by another Jewish managed store in New York City; that so long as you persisted in continuing to buy German goods you would have maintained an unfair advantage over them if they had failed to follow your lead; that they dared not object themselves to such unequal competition from your company;

5) That you are managing to hold rather firmly in check your convictions and sympathies as to Judaism, to which you so foolishly refer, since you must know that among the signatures of the Department Stores to your published announcement are those of non-Jewish stores that have ceased to buy goods made in Germany;

6) That Jewish manufacturers are no longer permitted to function in Germany, except very recently and in rare instances, and only under the most stringent Hitler control and conservators who have supplanted and superseded the Jewish owners, and that these few concerns have been forced to discharge all Jewish employees.

7) That there has long existed the most rigid boycott by the German people of the identical concerns from which you say you continue to make your purchases, solely because of their Jewish ownership;

8) That Germany has no monopoly in the manufacture or sale of gloves, textiles, chinaware or any of the articles you continue to buy there. Apparently it is only a question of price, and as the other Department Stores in New York would gladly follow your lead if you took your purchasing agents out of Germany and dealt elsewhere, you would be under no disadvantage in doing so;

9) That the "dangerous precedent" of the boycott, to which you so foolishly refer, is in no respect dangerous nor is it a precedent in that it is *a counter-boycott* against a vastly more impressive and all-embracing boycott, that is being enforced in Germany. It follows the precedent that was set by Germany when it brutally inaugurated and actively continues to prosecute the boycott of Jewish manufacturers and shopkeepers and professionals by the entire German nation for the avowed purpose of destroying their means of living and of ruining and exterminating the German Jews;

10) THAT YOUR STATEMENT THAT—
"All German-made goods we sell are clearly marked with the name of the country of origin" can be, and I supposed it had been, overwhelmingly disproved to your satisfaction. I do not by this mean to imply that you have knowingly been a party to

the continuous violations and evasions of law that have been and are being practiced upon the American public in that respect, some of which have been, as you are well aware, called to the attention of the Federal authorities.

Although this incredible "Crime of the Centuries" is aimed at every loyal unoffending Jewish citizen solely because he or one of his grandparents, happened to be a Jew, this is not, as you seem to assume, a Jewish question. It far transcends in principle and importance all limitations of race and creed. It is the struggle of civilization and humanity against a reversion to bigotry, fanaticism and barbarism of medieval times.

Germany's crime against all womanhood regardless of creeds, in ousting women from all business occupations and condemning them to the fate of breeders of children and household drudges is enlisting, as it is bound to enlist, the outraged protest of men and women the world over as is its suppression of voluntary organized labor and its rigid exclusion of all Jews from labor unions.

With a gagged press and with freedom of speech made a crime punishable by death, this is the only way by which the knowledge of world opinion can reach into Germany. When the world refuses to deal with Germany, when its factories are closed and its workmen unemployed, its people may awaken to the enormity of the crime its Government is perpetrating against civilization. That is the only effective weapon against it and the only language it can be made to understand.

No self-respecting man or woman of any race or creed will, in my judgment, buy German-made goods or patronize a store where they are sold.

It may seem to you ungrateful that your fellow citizens do not appreciate your self-denial in lending the patronage of your company to the defeat of the boycott, by buying goods in Germany and thus prolonging the misery of German Jews and adding to the prosperity of that benighted country whose persecutions of your fellow-Jews you denounce in such eloquent terms, whilst at the same time you continue to maintain your agencies in Germany and to buy German goods. In that connection they are curious to know the amounts of such purchases within the past 90 days and what proportion, if any, was really bought from Jewish manufacturers, of whom they are told that few, if any, are still in existence and that those have been forced to virtually abdicate their control.

This movement has as yet barely begun in this country. It is much further advanced in foreign countries throughout the world. A campaign for funds, strictly confined to the prosecution of the boycott, will be launched throughout the country by the undersigned organizations. It has no connection whatever with appeals for funds of any other organizations. The proceeds will be used strictly for boycott activities.

> World Jewish Economic Federation
> and its American Branch
> American League for the Defense of
> Jewish Rights
> by Samuel Untermyer, President[35]

Untermyer sought to have this reply published in the press a day following the publication of Macy's notice. However, the press rejected his offer, whereupon he wrote Percy Straus the following vigorous and forceful letter on October 4:

> Your Company published at great length and expense on October 2nd in the English and Yiddish text New York and Brooklyn papers, and perhaps in others of which I have no knowledge, advertisements in which, after eloquently denouncing the persecution of the Jews in Germany, you endeavored to justify or excuse your continued sale of German-made goods, denied that the "country of origin" required by law to be stamped upon these goods was illegibly stamped or camouflaged by such terms as "Made in Saxony," "Made in Bavaria" and the like, instead of being, as the law requires, *"conspicuously"* stamped, both on the article and its container, with the *country* of origin, and in which you also sought to excuse the continued maintenance by your Company of a purchasing agency in Germany, apparently for the purpose of picking up bargains there that other stores will not buy.
>
> The World Jewish Economic Federation and the American League for the Defense of Jewish Rights (which is its branch in this country) made desperate attempts to answer your advertisement by another in the same newspapers, the following morning. This proposed answer, I understand, was submitted to your inspection. You not only refused your consent to its publication but declined to point out any specific grounds for your objections, or to withdraw them.
>
> My desire in submitting the reply to your inspection was to get from you an expression on anything that you did not regard as conforming to the facts and in order to be entirely fair to your Company.
>
> Your Company being, as I am informed, by far the most important advertiser in the City, and perhaps in the World, and as the other large department stores of this City (all of whom I understand are members of the Retail Dry Goods Association) are acting as a unit on this and many other subjects, it was impossible to secure the insertion of this advertisement in any English-text newspaper published in the City. These newspapers are so largely dependent upon the patronage

of your associates, and particularly of your Company, that they were unwilling to risk the loss of your goodwill by permitting our organizations to place their version of the issues involved alongside of yours for public judgment.

If I were in the awkward position of these newspapers I would probably have surrendered to the same sort of implied coercion. But if I had occupied your point of vantage, I would have done nothing of the kind. I would, on the contrary, have felt that common justice and the rights of my customers demanded that both sides should be presented.

Having invited this controversy by widely publishing the view that the prosecution of the boycott against handling German goods would be "a dangerous precedent," I would have felt that in all fairness I should not exclude those who are promoting the boycott, and who look at the subject from an entirely different point of view, from the opportunity of setting forth their point of view, which they are now more than ever determined to do, in one form or another, no matter how expensive you see fit to make it.

Owing partly to your attitude and partly to other considerations, these organizations are now about to launch a country-wide campaign for funds, which is to be strictly confined to the legitimate expenses of promoting a lawful boycott of German goods, ships and shipping in this country as it is being made in other lands. Unless you are prepared to withdraw your objections and in all fairness assent to the publication of the reply to your advertisement, these organizations will be put to the enormous expense of circularizing the entire country with their reply, and with such other data as they believe will bring to the American public conviction of the wisdom and necessity of their attitude.

The distribution of 5,000,000 copies of these documents will probably cost $300,000, but I have no doubt that the people of this country, animated by a sense of fair play, will readily support such a movement. A ready way out of the circulation of this reply in the manner indicated would be for your company to permit the publication of the reply that has been suggested, without fear of reprisals against the newspapers for accepting such advertisement.

I do not believe that the American people are so lacking in public spirit and so steeped in callousness that they will sanction the use that you and your associates have made of your power over the press of this country for your own purposes. I note that none of the other members of the Retail Dry Goods Association have found it necessary to publish such an unwarranted assault upon the motives or results of the activities of the organizations of which I am president.

P.S., By the way, it may interest you to learn that the recently appointed Ambassador to France from the United States (who is now visiting in this country) is reported to have answered, when asked why in his opinion the American Government has taken no official action respecting the persecution of the Jews in Germany, that "That is a purely internal affair." "Internal" indeed![36]

Percy Straus responded on October 6:

> I would not want to be discourteous, and yet I cannot feel that the answer I could make to your letter of October 4th would add anything to the actual information which you already have, and which I am sure must make clear to you the unfairness of the implications contained in your communication.
>
> In order, however, that the record may be made perfectly clear, let me set forth three facts:
>
> 1. The action taken by the New York stores followed this sequence of events: A meeting was called to consider the matter, which meeting you addressed; following your departure from that meeting, I stated that Macy's would follow any action taken by the majority of the stores; a committee was appointed to investigate and recommend; no representative of Macy's being on that committee; the unanimous action of the stores followed the recommendation of that committee.
>
> 2. The advertisement published by us was an attack upon no one, but was a frank attempt to make our position plain to the reasonable people of this community. We should not have published such an advertisement as that except for the fact that an apparently inspired whispering campaign was in progress, designed to place the position of Macy's as different from that of the other stores.
>
> 3. The advertisement which you prepared in reply to ours was declined by the New York newspapers wholly upon their own initiative, and without asking our opinion; in fact we had no knowledge of your having prepared this advertisement until we were informed by the newspapers that they had declined to publish it.
>
> You cannot expect me to assent to the publication of a statement of this character when on its face the press considered it unfit for publication.
>
> Much as I would like to allow this letter to stop here, I cannot allow the reference to my brother contained in your postscript to pass without saying that I refuse to dignify it by any comment whatsoever.[37]

More letters of the sort published on October 2 appeared in the press during the next couple of months. However, Untermyer does not appear to have reacted to them in kind, either privately or publicly, as he was waiting to see whether Macy's would, upon reflection, decide to forbear the purchase of German goods. Still, it was not passive "waiting"; for on October 8, at a conference of ALDJR's Women's Division, it was resolved that unless Macy's and similar department stores ceased handling German goods, they would forfeit business relations with the women's organizations affiliated with the League. In addressing the more than 400 female conferees, the chairwoman, Mrs. Mark Harris, stressed the fact that women constituted the overwhelming majority of the consumer public and that it was now essential to take advantage of this by tightening the boycott noose around stores selling German goods and closing all charge accounts kept in them.

Untermyer's endurance held out until November 14, when he addressed the following vigorous letter to the president of R. H. Macy:

> Day by day the evidence seems more and more irresistible that there is no will on the part of your Company to cease selling German goods and there is further evidence that you are continuously in receipt of such goods. From what we are informed, this is especially true as to toys.
>
> The League is waiting impatiently for some evidence on the part of your Company that it is ceasing to handle German goods, but we have finally been forced to give up the attempt.
>
> As one of the hundreds of instances of what seems to be happening daily in your store, we have received a "copy" of a letter written by Mr. Max S. Banner of Banner Bros., Inc., to your company, from which I quote as follows:
>
>> "As a patronizer of Macy's for many years, I was very much astonished yesterday, while in your store, I wanted to buy a few kiddie bags, and, looking over five different styles, I noticed that they were all of German make. I asked the girl to show me domestic products and she answered that almost all of your kiddie bags are German imports. I had no other alternative but to leave the store and go to some other department store where I found quite a large assortment of fine domestic kiddie bags.
>>
>> I very well recall the open letter you had in the New York Times regarding German imports, in which you stated that your store handles only such German wares that cannot be obtained elsewhere. Our line of business is not kiddie bags, yet I know of a good many manufacturers right in this country who can produce these bags as well as Germany."
>
> Apparently you are determined to force the issue and make this a fight to the finish.
> So be it.[38]

With this, the exchange of letters between Samuel Untermyer and Percy Straus came to an end; but the League was not to bear for long the brunt of its "fight to the finish" against Macy's. Added pressure was forthcoming from groups with similar aims.

The Dissolution of the American League for the Defense of Jewish Rights

Almost from the day he joined it, Untermyer, by his indomitable will, fighting spirit, dedication, and fame, had taken over control of the ALDJR; first as honorary president, then as president of the organization. There against Dr. Coralnik, the League's father was shelved into the background. And as the year 1933 neared passage into history, so did the name of the American League for the Defense of Jewish Rights. The prime cause for this was Samuel Untermyer, who began viewing this name as a misnomer. Simultaneously, he was being conquered by a passion to reorganize the ALDJR on a nonsectarian basis. The reconstituted organization, he felt, should be called the Non-Sectarian Anti-Nazi League to Champion Human Rights (NSANL).

This is learned from a November 24 letter that Dr. Coralnik sent Mr. Untermyer after the latter had communicated his intention to him. In his reply, Dr. Coralnik stated he was not opposed to the creation of a nonsectarian league, but that he did oppose the dissolution of his own organization because of it. Instead, he proposed the coexistence of both; the ALDJR as a Jewish organization, and the NSANL, as a liberal pro-Jewish group.

Untermyer responded on the twenty-seventh, saying that he never would have joined ALDJR as a "Jewish organization"; that many of the "original members" were non-Jews and would resent the thought that they were party to a "Jewish organization." He explained that he had maintained "from the very outset" that the boycott was "not a Jewish issue," a view which precluded his acquiescence to maintain ALDJR as a Jewish organization; nor would he consent to the creation of the "new NSANL" as a "pro-Jewish organization," thereby nullifying Coralnik's twin League scheme.

The fact of the matter remains, however, that despite Untermyer's stated reason for joining ALDJR, men much less informed than he could hardly have mistaken it for anything but a "Jewish organization." This, of course, also holds true for the "original members" not of the Jewish faith. Furthermore, there is an ample supply of representative statements to show that Untermyer, in declaring that the boycott was "not a Jewish issue," made no real reference to its being a nonsectarian entity. At best, such statements express his belief that the boycott movement, not the ALDJR, was nonsectarian. Thus, in a June 5 communication to

Rabinowitz, Untermyer wrote: "I have gone into this movement because I have felt that it is the only recourse by which the Jews and non-Jews of America can make plain their disapproval of the cruelties that are being practiced in Germany against the Jews."[39] Nearly two months later, he said: "The spontaneous outpourings by non-Jews as well as Jews confirms the view that it may be regarded as a world-wide uprising of civilization and humanity, regardless of race and creed, against the most incredible crime of many centuries, born of bigotry, fanaticism and savagery, that has reduced a once cultured nation back to the dark ages."[40]

On the other hand, Dr. Wise never attached a nonsectarian label to the boycott movement. Yet, the following statement made by him to a reporter upon his return to New York from the World Jewish Conference differed little from the aforesaid:

> If you ask me, is this to be solely a Jewish boycott, I answer that one of the most grievous disappointments of my life would be the failure of non-Jews, especially of Christian men and women in all lands, to stand by our side and join with us in wielding this weapon of defense against the Third Reich on behalf of the Jewish people. *The truth is that tens of thousands of Christians feel exactly as we do about the crimes planned and perpetrated against Jews by the Nazi Government.*[41]

Yet, granting that Untermyer had completely misunderstood or misinterpreted the character of ALDJR, one might ask why he was instrumental in the creation of a World *Jewish* Economic Federation (WJEF).[42] After all, he claimed that he had held "from the very outset" that the boycott was "not a Jewish issue." The only possible answer, therefore, is that, in his November correspondence with Dr. Coralnik, the renowned lawyer was simply beating around the bush!

Also, the *Morgen Journal* of May 18 claims that Untermyer was in receipt of letters from prominent Christians proposing that he set up a Christian branch of the ALDJR. If so—and this appears to be the only source on the subject—one could hardly take at face value Untermyer's claim that non-Jews would resent being party to a "Jewish organization." On the contrary, the proposal was in harmony with Coralnik's compromise plan of a twin League arrangement.

In any event, on December 16, in an address delivered at the Maccabean Hanukkah celebration at Madison Square Garden, Untermyer again raised the question of Jewish persecution in Germany. This time, however, he did not describe the boycott as being an equally Jewish and non-Jewish "recourse" or "uprising." With his organization now bearing the stamp of a nonsectarian movement and obviously seeking to win over a large number of converts, Untermyer said:

Although the German Jews are the immediate victims of this unspeakable campaign of sadist horrors of a loyal patriotic, inoffensive people, solely because of their race, the fight this time is more than a Jewish fight—it is a struggle in which the Hitler regime is arrayed on one side and all-world civilization on the other. The outcome of that struggle means vastly more to non-Jewish Americans and to American institutions, to the Christian religion, and to all womanhood regardless of race or creed, than it means to the Jewish people, or even to the Jews of the world.[43]

ALDJR's reorganization became official on the twenty-third of that month (December). To no one's surprise, Untermyer was elected president of the infant NSANL. Abba Hillel Silver became first vice-president. Dr. Coralnik swallowed his pride and agreed to serve as second vice-president, an office which he held with a number of other members, Jewish and non-Jewish.[44] However, both he and Silver, respectively, were the presidents of the League's Administrative and Finance Committees. Ezekiel Rabinowitz retained his office of executive secretary.

The organizational change did not mean, however, a change in basic policy. For the next five years, the Non-Sectarian Anti-Nazi League was to stress the boycott as the only effective weapon for the defense of fundamental human rights.

Part III
1934–1937: CONSOLIDATION AND EXPANSION

14

The Boycott Committee of the American Jewish Congress

Preliminary Stage

i.

After having taken so long to decide on the adoption of an anti-Nazi boycott, as well as the great deal of publicity and drama with which it was attended, the American Jewish Congress would have initiated implemental steps soon after Wise's return from the World Jewish Conference. The fact is, however, that it took the Congress about six months to even set its boycott work in motion; whereas at the end of the same interval, ALDJR had evinced marked operational strength.

A memorandum that Lily Shultz, director of publicity for the American Jewish Congress, prepared at the request of Abraham I. Spiro, that organization's treasurer, confirms the impression that the Congress had been idling away its time vis-à-vis the boycott. The memorandum, which was drafted on November 6, 1933, set down Miss Shultz's views regarding her organization's "past performance" and necessary "future action." As such, it covered her reaction to the Congress' April 19 decision to submit petitions to the League of Nations and the President of the United States, asking for aid in behalf of Germany's Jews; a May 21 decision to initiate a $1,000,000 Emergency Fund Drive and the August 20 resolve of the "public sponsorship of the boycott." Reporting on "what has happened," Miss Shultz stated:

The Congress did nothing about either petition. B'nai B'rith undertook the circulation of the petition to the League of Nations; The Free Synagogue[1] undertook the circulation of the petition to the President; the million dollar drive has not been launched openly; To date not a single act has been undertaken to indicate that we are playing any part in the prosecution of the boycott.[2]

Press coverage, or general lack thereof, definitely affirms Miss Shultz's last point. Devoting almost the remainder of her memorandum to "The Boycott," Miss Shultz said:

> There is immediate need for the kind of a boycott program that will release the desire of the masses to take some part in counter-action against Germany.
> If you consult the files of the Congress, you will find constant demands for a program from our out-of-town branches. You will also discover that in almost every city our own constituents are joining with the American League for the Defense of Jewish Rights in the boycott.
> I suggest we get up: A pledge to be sent far and wide—through our affiliated organizations—with the name of the Congress on it, (and to be returned to the local Congress branch) wherein the signatory undertakes not to buy German goods; A list of finished products which constitutes Germany's exports to the United States; A list of raw materials imported from Germany. Both to be listed under some heading like: "Look for the label: MADE IN GERMANY; DO NOT BUY: MADE IN GERMANY"; A bulletin showing American investments made in Germany, Germany's trade balance and her defaulting on payments.
> I think this pledge and circular would aid us considerably in strengthening our organization, inasmuch as it would give us an index of names of interested persons.[3]

The Congress's boycott inertness can partly be explained by the prolonged negotiations it conducted with Untermyer about coordinating activities. At a September 23, 1933, mass meeting of the American Jewish Congress, Dr. Tenenbaum spoke about such negotiations, saying that a committee that included him, Dr. Wise, and Mr. Deutsch had visited with Mr. Untermyer for this very purpose. We have no details concerning the contents of this or similar talks; but it appears that while they were in progress, the Congress thought it best to await their final outcome before investing time, money, and effort on a program which would be duplicated if an accord were reached.

It also appears that the following letter that Dr. Wise addressed to Mr. Untermyer is the one that led to the visit referred to by Dr. Tenenbaum:

> The American Jewish Congress is, as you know, unequivocally committed to the promotion of the boycott against German-made

goods. It regards the boycott as the most effective counter-action and defense against the anti-Semitic policy of the Hitler Government. It has made its position clear in the press and in communications addressed to its branches throughout the country, to which it has appealed for support of the boycott movement through the organization of any number of local boycott committees.

The bold and forceful presentation of the Jewish case, which has been made by you in the press and in addresses delivered by you in various parts of the country, has had a pronounced effect upon American public opinion, and the progress of the boycott movement during the past few months may be attributed to your able and courageous advocacy of the cause. You have established a committee of which you are the distinguished head, and which has assumed the responsibility for organizing the boycott on a national scale. In this effort you are entitled to the fullest support of all those interested in the defense of the Jewish position.

Although the American Jewish Congress has many other activities on its program—the exposure and defeat of anti-Semitism in America, the general defense of Jewish rights in countries other than Germany, the organization of American Jewry for the protection of Jewish rights, the organization of a World Jewish Congress—it is, nevertheless, determined to devote a greater part of its resources and influence to the furtherance of the boycott movement, and assures you that it will give the utmost of its support to the development of the organized resistance to the influx of German-made goods into the United States. Its speakers are being instructed to urge the extension of the boycott when they address Jewish meetings; the literature issued by the Congress will include appeals for the support of the boycott; whatever influence the Congress may have will be utilized both among Jews and non-Jews to stimulate and develop the use of this weapon of self-defense.

I need not assure you that the American Jewish Congress will do its level best to carry on its work in this direction in such a manner as to maintain a united Jewish front. It is hoped thus to augment the power behind the boycott movement and, with coordinated forces, bring about the defeat of our enemies.

In order that we may be assured that our activities shall not overlap, the American Jewish Congress is also prepared to appoint a subcommittee to confer with your committee at any time with reference to coordinating measures to be adopted that will obviate any collision in activities and any discord in the expression of our united desire to further the success of the boycott movement.[4]

Such overtures and the lack of boycott leadership characterized the Congress until shortly after the start of 1934. By then, however, enough time had passed to make some Congress leaders feel that their organization had better assert itself in the boycott, lest the public begin thinking that it was lacking in self-reliance and self-sufficiency.

There might very well have been grounds for such an impression, since the Congress' Boycott Department was not being led during this interval by an aggressive and outspoken fighter. To be sure, Dr. Max Winkler (see p. 80) was an able economist, but it does not appear that he was ready to assume the responsibility of conducting a full-fledged anti-Nazi boycott program. His main interest was preparing statistical compilations on the boycott, and every so often he would announce how effective a medium it was proving to be. However, the conduct of a boycott involved, in the main, executive skill and managerial responsibility. In this respect, Winkler was more the economic consultant than the boycott leader.

This state of affairs displeased Dr. Tenenbaum. For months he had been pressing the Congress leadership to have its boycott conducted on the broadest possible basis, expressing keen personal interest in directing it. As a result, Dr. Wise appointed him chairman of the Boycott Committee of the American Jewish Congress.[5]

ii.

One successful effort of the Congress was in helping to draw the American Federation of Labor into the boycott movement. This, too, was announced by Dr. Tenenbaum at the Congress mass meeting referred to above (pp. 77–82). As a liberal organization, the AFL frequently manifested its opposition to Nazism. We recall, for example (p. 34), that William Green, its president, was a featured speaker at the Madison Square Garden protest rally of March 27, 1933. However, by September of that year, word was out that the AFL was considering joining the boycott movement against the Reich—a step which had already been taken by European trade unionists. Describing conditions under Hitler as "revolting" and "sickening," Green said:

> German trade union executives have disappeared and no one knows where they are. Their great movement, built up by generations of devotion and work, has been virtually destroyed and the rights of collective bargaining and other rights enjoyed by trade unions in every civilized nation have been trampled under foot by men who act like barbarians.
>
> American labor is becoming convinced that something more than protest is needed in dealing with the Nazis. We are being forced to the conclusion that a boycott is the only thing that will bring home to the German tyrants the abhorrence in which their rule is held by the rest of the world. There will need be no surprise in Germany or elsewhere if American Labor turns to the boycott as a weapon in the age-old cause of liberty.
>
> The boycott, if it comes, will not be against the German people. I am

convinced that many millions of them hate the Nazi dictatorship as much as do freedom-loving people in other countries. In the words of the British labor movement in calling for a boycott, it will be a "human protest against the betrayal and denial" by the German government of the "principle of civilized behavior."

When the German masses realize the true state of world opinion, they will act, I am confident, to tear the grip of Nazi labor.[6]

Green's statement was of prime importance to the boycott movement, as it was made in anticipation of his organization's forthcoming convention. During that session, which was held on October 13, 1933, the AFL approved the following boycott recommendation of its Executive Council:

> Owing to the fact that those who are administering the Government of Germany and who are shaping its destinies are pursuing a ruthless campaign of persecution against the Jews of Germany, and because the Hitler Government refused to heed or respect the protests of the people in all nations throughout the world, the Executive Council recommends that the American Federation of Labor join with other public-spirited organizations in our country in officially adopting a boycott against German-made goods and German services, this boycott to continue until the German government recognizes the right of other working people in Germany to organize into bona fide, independent trade unions of their own choosing, and until Germany ceases its repressive policy of persecution of Jewish people.[7]

On December 28, Green not only reaffirmed this resolution, but requested that it be made effective by cooperation with other boycotting groups. Emphasizing again the repression of German unions and the oppression of German Jews, the AFL president declared:

> I ask the officers and members of organizations chartered by the American Federation of Labor, to take such steps as may seem necessary in order to make the boycott on German goods and services as ordered by the Convention effective.
> I suggest that committees be appointed to deal with the problem in accordance with the economic, social and business requirements of each community. Let these communities unite with other communities created for the same purpose representing other groups of people whose opinions are in harmony with the action of the Convention of the American Federation of Labor.
> If the boycott ordered by the Convention can be made effective, the interests of the German workers, the protection of German trade unions and the enjoyment of the rights and privileges to which the Jewish people are entitled in Germany may be safeguarded.[8]

Shortly before the aforesaid was announced, Stephen Wise and Nathan D. Perlman, former U.S. congressman and new vice-president of the American Jewish Congress, had conferred with William Green in Washington and revealed the Congress' readiness to cooperate with the AFL in a joint boycott program. It proved the culmination of an effort begun right after the AFL's adoption of its boycott resolution. Bernard Deutsch confirmed its successful conclusion by announcing on December 29 that the A.J.C. and the AFL had reached an agreement on the conduct of boycott activities.

On February 14, 1934, in an address delivered at a testimonial dinner in his honor, Mr. Green elaborated somewhat on his organization's decision to join the boycott movement. He said that in the wake of its opposition to a policy of persecution directed against Germany's trade unions and Jews, the AFL could not remain silent and yet be true to its own traditions, principles, and policies. Green also said that the action of the central figure who was shaping and directing the destiny of the German people made it clear that any appeal to his heart, conscience, and judgment would have no effect whatever; hence the indispensability of conducting a boycott against him.

About the time that Green was uttering these austere words, Dr. Tenenbaum was preparing to release the earliest available document identifying him as chairman of the Congress' Boycott Committee. This, too, dates to February 14, 1934. It was a memorandum addressed to all organizations affiliated with the American Jewish Congress. Its concluding section informs us that the Congress has organized the boycott "on a nation-wide scale," adding this announcement: "A special Boycott Bureau, in charge of Mr. William Z. Spiegelman, who will direct its activities, has been set up for the purpose of devising plans and disseminating the necessary data and information and cooperating with our constituents and affiliated organizations" (Records of the Joint Boycott Council, Program on the Boycott folder: 1933–1934).

In another February 14 document, contained in the Dr. Max Winkler folder of the Record of the Joint Boycott Council, Spiegelman notified Winkler that he had accepted "several days ago" Dr. Tenenbaum's invitation "to take charge of the activities of the American Jewish Congress Boycott Bureau." Dr. Winkler, upon Tenenbaum's assumption of the chairmanship of the Boycott Committee, undertook to run its Research Bureau, a task that involved the kind of work he was doing as Boycott Department director. Some years later, the NSANL hired him to work in its Research Bureau.

Two other references may be cited in relation to Tenenbaum's appointment as chairman of the Congress' Boycott Committee; one is a March 13, 1934, memorandum drawn up by Spiegelman (contained in the foregoing source) announcing that "this department was organized three and a half weeks ago, the adherence of the American Jewish Congress expressing itself only in a verbal concurrence"; the other is an April 16, 1934, report by Tenenbaum, in which he states: "This Bureau of the Boycott Committee of the American Jewish Congress started functioning on February 21, 1934" (Records of the Joint Boycott Council, May 15, 1933 Minutes folder). And some weeks prior to this, the Congress had called together some 1,300 New York businessmen—buyers, importers, and exporters—and organized them into a Merchandising Council. In the order of importance, this achievement followed the organization of the consumer boycott. For the Congress, however, it proved to be the second major contribution to the boycott movement.

Macy's Surrender

i.

For a little over two months following the Untermyer-Straus quarrel, Macy's president, who had not yielded on the issue in question, had relative peace and quiet. However, January 27, 1934, found Macy's again an object of public altercation; only this time it was a long picket line, not the pen or printed page, that exerted the pressure. Organized and led by Norman Thomas, American Socialist Party leader, hundreds of demonstrators surrounded the Macy store shouting their placards' legends, some of which read: MACY'S BUYS GERMAN GOODS, WE WANT NO FASCISM HERE.

The U.S. Socialist Party had declared a boycott against Nazi Germany on November 7, 1933, on the eve of the fifteenth anniversary of the founding of the Weimar Republic. The boycott declaration, which was made at Madison Square Garden, read: "... We call on Socialists and other liberty-loving Americans to ostracize Hitlerism and to establish and maintain a boycott against all goods made in Hitler Germany" (Records of the Joint Boycott Council, Boycott Resolutions and Statements folder). Its picketing of Macy's was the party's first highly publicized boycott manifestation. For the Congress' Boycott Committee, about to get started under Tenenbaum's leadership, this proved a very timely affair, as Macy's afforded a solid, challenging problem with which to swing into action.

From the files of the Joint Boycott Council, containing the records of the Boycott Committee, it appears that Dr. Tenenbaum initiated negotiations with Macy's during the first week of March. And in contrast to Mr. Untermyer's publicized and belligerent approach, these negotiations were pretty amicable and unostentatious. Discussions were held between Mr. Edwin I. Marks, a Macy's vice-president representing the merchandising colossus and Dr. Jacob Chaitkin, legal subcommittee chairman of the Congress' Boycott Committee.

Basically, Marks's arguments were a rehash of Macy's earlier position; namely, that his company's adoption of a boycott would only produce more antisemitic violence, although he privately expressed his sympathy for the movement. As to the German-made goods contained in his company's store, the Macy's vice-president explained that all such merchandise had been ordered prior to Hitler's taking office and, therefore, could not be canceled. Marks also added that, compared with the orders of previous years, present purchases from Nazi Germany were being pursued on a very limited scale.

In reply, Dr. Chaitkin reminded Mr. Marks that R. H. Macy remained the only large department store that had failed to liquidate its purchasing agency in Germany; one of a long list of grievances with which, as we recall (pp. 112–14), Untermyer had confronted Percy Straus. The somewhat hard-pressed Marks retorted with the unconvincing claim that his company was maintaining this agency to make purchases in Czechoslovakia, not in Hitler Germany. It was more difficult, he explained, to maintain such an agency in Czechoslovakia because, unlike German, the Czech language tended to act as a business barrier.

Needless to say, Dr. Chaitkin, who viewed as unacceptable anything short of absolute business severance with Nazi Germany, rejected the flimsy explanation by the Macy executive. Chaitkin's report to the Boycott Committee included, therefore, a list of stringent conditions which Macy's would have to meet in order to be "white-listed" by the American Jewish Congress. These conditions were that:

> R. H. Macy and Co. agrees to discontinue its purchasing agency in Germany. This is to take effect immediately or within a reasonable period of time, to be agreed upon between R. H. Macy and the Boycott Committee.
>
> Macy's agrees not to place any further orders for German goods in any amount and of any description whatsoever. The term "German goods" shall include not only goods imported from Germany but also goods made in Germany and purchased in this country. The term "German goods" shall further include not only goods wholly made in Germany but goods containing parts or ingredients made in Germany.
>
> R. H. Macy agrees not to use German shipping for any purposes whatsoever.
>
> R. H. Macy agrees not to route through Germany any of its importations from other countries.
>
> The sale of Macy's present large stock of German goods can obvi-

ously not be stopped. However, the sale of any German article inevitably creates a consumer's demand for similar articles. It will therefore be agreed that R. H. Macy shall whenever practicable refrain from displaying German merchandise on its counters and produce such merchandise, only upon specific requests from its customers. Upon receipt of this agreement the Boycott Committee shall be pleased to place R. H. Macy on the "white list."[9]

To a number of his colleagues on the committee, Chaitkin's conditions sounded like a dictate. Dr. Tenenbaum, who attended some, if not all, of the meetings held with Mr. Marks, was of the opinion that the Macy's vice-president was sincere about his claim that his company was decreasing importations from Germany. Marks had also indicated his firm's willingness to discontinue buying German goods, but added that it wished to avoid publicity which could prove detrimental to its business.

Dr. Tenenbaum so informed the Boycott Committee and recommended that a simple statement from R. H. Macy to the effect that it would no longer import any goods from Germany should suffice in the meantime. The giant store was given about three months in which to prove its sincerity. The gentlemen's agreement that followed did not stress Dr. Chaitkin's austere conditions. The Boycott Committee kept them in the "background," but in itself this, of course, proved meaningless.

ii.

On March 17, 1934, the press carried a statement that Macy's had agreed to shut its German office and to cease dealing with German merchandise:

> R. H. Macy & Co., Inc. announced today that instructions had been cabled to the executive vice-president supervising its European offices to close its office in Berlin, which hitherto has functioned in handling merchandise from Germany, Scandinavia and Eastern European countries. A new Macy office shall be established at Prague to cover the same territory excepting Germany.
>
> Consumer resistance to goods of German origin is responsible for the closing of the Berlin office. Macy orders placed in Germany have declined 98 percent for the six months ended February 28, 1934. During this period orders placed in Germany totaled only $2,800 as against $127,000 for the corresponding six months of 1932–33.
>
> The successful search for merchandise which would not meet with consumer resistance has made it possible to replace German products in almost every instance. Cooperation with manufacturers in this country and abroad had been going on for the past eight months and

the progress of these efforts made the closing of the Berlin office advisable.[10]

That day, in response to this release, Bernard Deutsch and Stephen Wise issued the following statement:

> We learn with deepest satisfaction that R. H. Macy & Company, Inc., announce in this morning's press that they have discontinued their Berlin office. This announcement does not surprise us, for we have had reason to know for some time that customer resistance, which is a polite paraphrase for public opinion, has been leading the Macy establishment in this direction. If customer resistance makes it possible for R. H. Macy & Co. to discontinue their Berlin office and to discontinue, as we have reason to know they have discontinued, the use of German shipping, it is clearly revealed that customer resistance in N.Y. grows out irrespective of faith or race to have nothing to do with Nazi goods or services. R. H. Macy & Co. have come to see at last what we have known for some months, that there is a profound unwillingness to deal or traffic with the Hitler Reich in any way. This does not mean a war upon Germany but the rightful and inevitable use of the non-violent instrument of boycott against a nation which has permitted itself to be misled into warring upon civilization and indeed waging an especially violent and bitter war upon liberals, the labor forces, Catholics, Jews, and even their own church. We venture to believe that the action of R. H. Macy & Co. will be followed, as it has in part been preceded, by a discontinuance of the purchase of Nazi goods which cannot be sold and therefore will not be bought. The American people understands that a boycott against Hitler's ways is the least war-like of embargoes against a government which civilization has indicted of betrayal of the basic principles of liberty and justice. This decision seems to us to have been inevitable, even though we understand that normally institutions such as Macy's must be prepared to supply customers with whatever they desire. This norm, however, we have felt, must yield in the presence of the catastrophic shattering of the ideals and standards of civilization by what has happened in Germany.[11]

Among Chaitkin's demands of Macy's, the second condition was not met in the firm's press release. This and related points are discussed in a March 20 memorandum prepared, apparently, by the Boycott Commitee:

> Mr. Jacob Chaitkin has advised Dr. Wise that two of the demands of the American Jewish Congress Boycott Committee of Macy's and other establishments have been met; 1) the termination of a purchasing agency in Hitler Germany; 2) the use of German shipping

facilities, (freight or passenger) for any goods, whether German or other make, for example, the Port wine was carried in German bottoms—came from Portugal and not from Germany and shipments have been coming from Hamburg of goods trans-shipped throughout Europe from all countries, but consigned in German bottoms to America.

We make two demands upon the Macy business:

1) The query is asked what shall we do with the stock in hand made in Germany, how shall we dispose of it? The answer obviously is that the disposition of Nazi-made stock is not a Congress problem. In any event, the goods are not to be displayed. They are to be kept off the counters which display them. Display of goods creates consumer demand.

2) We urge that the reduction of goods to the extent of $60,000 plus in the four months 1933, which was reduced for a corresponding period to less than $2,000 in 1934, shall be eliminated. The important thing is not to create consumer demand by display of goods.

In return the Congress would be prepared to issue a statement, expressing its approval of the policies of Macy, though, of course, it would have to couch that approval in its own terms and interpret the absence of consumer demand as an expression of public opinion in America and of the public conscience which will not permit any great establishment such as Macy's to show German wares or service.[12]

The Boycott Committee did not follow Chaitkin's advice, as it was not interested in driving too hard a bargain with Macy's. Certainly, it would not have been in keeping with Mr. Marks's wish if the Congress had actually issued a statement "expressing its approval of the policies of Macy's." For this was the very kind of publicity Macy's wished to avoid; namely, public notification that it had succumbed, supposedly, to the pressures of a special-interest group. Percy Straus chose to acknowledge this surrender as follows: "It is true that a small stream of German goods, as compared with a veritable flood in previous years, continues to run into our storerooms; but in time, if consumer resistance continues, this will dry up altogether."[13]

The release of Macy's March 17 statement was also followed by statements on the part of America's two principal boycott organizations, each claiming credit for the capitulation of the giant department store. Thus, the Congress' Boycott Committee alleged that it had suggested that Macy's publish its statement. The League complimented Untermyer on Macy's submission. He, however, passed on the credit to the Women's Division.

In any event, the Macy's statement was accompanied by the news that Gimbel's had also ceased dealing in German merchandise "because there was virtually no demand for German goods."[14] However, up until this time, Macy's and Gimbel's had remained virtually alone among New York's biggest department stores still engaged in the sale of these goods. Saks, a giant next-door department store, as well as Hearns' large store, had joined the boycott at the end of February.

Three days after the Macy-Gimbel announcements, Woolworth declared a ban on all German goods for its 1,941 stores. The Woolworth decision was made public by Ezekiel Rabinowitz, who used to good advantage the Macy-Gimbel declarations. For in their wake, Rabinowitz had addressed a telegram to the Woolworth Company inquiring whether the chain stores was still dealing in German goods. The answer dispatched to him by the company president read as follows: "Replying to your wire of today[15] and query as to the policy of this company regarding the importation of goods from Germany, I beg to advise that we have discontinued importation owing to extreme sales resistance."[16] Rabinowitz's telegram was only one of many communications sent to this and many smaller stores requesting them to sever their business ties with Hitler Germany. Most did, according to ANL reports.

At the end of March, John Wanamaker's, one of the few large non-Jewish department stores, also went on record in support of the boycott. It so informed Rabinowitz in a telegram, stating that it had ceased the purchase of German goods in 1933. The telegram further stated that Wanamaker's had no branch office in Germany.

It now remained to keep all these huge stores under check, and the vigilance committees of the boycotting organizations maintained for this purpose a continuous watch to detect any violation of boycott pledges. It was Dr. Tenenbaum's policy to have New York's large department stores inspected quite regularly, if only to convey the impression that they were under constant surveillance. As the minutes of a number of the Boycott Committee's meetings reveal, the department stores often aroused its suspicions. Investigation and alertness were, therefore, always uppermost in the Committee's mind.

The Good-Will Fair

i.

The next major aspect of Boycott Committee action involved a phase of development through which the Anti-Nazi League had passed the previous year at Amsterdam; namely, the exploration of alternative sources of supply for German goods and services. The Merchandising Council (p. 131) was to stand the Boycott Committee in good stead now, since it formed that group through whose hands such substitutes were passed to the public.

The idea was suggested by William Spiegelman, executive secretary of the Boycott Committee, at a February 15 meeting of its newly appointed Administrative Committee. It is reproduced here from a March 13 memorandum outlining some of the Boycott Committee's past achievements and remaining needs:

> The compilation of authentic and reliable data concerning substitutes and equivalent articles produced by American and foreign manufacturers, concerning which, constant inquiries have been received from many quarters.
>
> A radio drive to spread the movement on a large scale.
>
> Steps to secure the effective cooperation of the American Federation of Labor in pursuance to the resolution adopted by them. Contact was made through the good offices of Mr. Nathan Perlman [p. 130], and a joint meeting of the Boycott Committee of the AF of L and our own will take place shortly. The background to this is contained in a subsection of a June 12, 1934 "Confidential Report of the Boycott Committee of the American Jewish Congress for the Period of Three Months." This Confidential Report is contained in the Private Papers of Stephen S. Wise. The subsection under consideration reads:

COOPERATION WITH THE AMERICAN FEDERATION OF LABOR

> On the initiative of this Committee and thanks to the cooperation of Mr. Nathan Perlman, contact was established with the Central Trades and Labor Council of Greater New York, the local affiliate of the A.F. of L. Up to the date of our approach, March 20th, 1934, the local forces of the A.F. of L. had done very little in pursuance of the boycott resolution which had been adopted by the American Federation of Labor Convention.
>
> A plan for the enlistment of all national organizations to secure their support and the support of their membership.
>
> To enlist the cooperation of the Ladies' Auxiliaries, Mens' Councils in Jewish Community Centers, Synagogues and "Chevras" (religious societies), and the like, within the metropolitan district.
>
> Creating pressure on the department stores.
>
> The formulation and preliminary investigation of our plan to arrange for an International Merchandising Good Will Fair based on the idea of enlisting the active aid of those who have an economic rather than an emotional interest in the success of the boycott movement, namely, the American and foreign manufacturers of equivalent and substitute articles.[17]

Spiegelman wanted the Fair to have a "positive" rather than a "negative" character; and by using words like "Good-Will" to describe it, he hoped to elicit the interest and cooperation of American and foreign importing concerns.

Ambitious and praiseworthy project that it was, its organization required secure financial backing. But it was thought that, more than likely, the necessary sums would be underwritten in advance by an accommodating businessmen's committee. This did, in fact, happen in the end; however, it proved to be more troublesome a task than at first anticipated. Dr. Wise, as honorary chairman of the Merchandising Council, and subsequently chairman of the Fair's Sponsorship Committee, had to spend many hours with prospective financial sponsors to help raise the necessary monies.

Part of Wise's difficulty was due to the fact that, in the early phase of this undertaking, he could not pinpoint for prospective contributors the exact amount of required cash; nor had the Boycott Committee then come to terms with a business firm which would help it set up this operation. By April, however, the latter problem had been resolved. Opening arrangements were concluded with Samuel E. Kimball, president of the Commercial Exposition Company, a local New York corporation. The Fair was to be held in this city at the Grand Central Palace for a fee of $4,000.

All likely exhibitors, both American and foreign, could now be approached by the sales force of Kimball's staff. The Boycott Committee, on the other hand, acted more as a liaison with this group by trying to promote and publicize the Fair. Thus, contact was not only made with individual concerns, but also with foreign consuls and foreign chambers of commerce. And while such government agencies could not go on record in support of the Fair, they did, in many instances, promise their unofficial cooperation.[18]

For the community at large, the Fair was to serve as a medium for rallying public sentiment behind the boycott movement. Its Sponsorship Committee was to function on a nationwide basis in keeping with the aim of emphasizing the idea of boycott on the broadest level possible. To this end, many out-of-town concerns were contacted. However, Dr. Tenenbaum's main interest in the Fair was the enlistment of all organizations supporting the boycott. He so wrote Louis Segal, Dr. Chaim Zhitlowsky, and Baruch Charney Vladeck (p. 178), all prominent leaders in the ranks of Jewish labor: "The American Jewish Congress does not desire to be the sole promoter and sponsor of the exhibit and wishes to secure all organizations, Jewish and non-Jewish, which have adopted the boycott policy to participate as sponsors without any financial liability or obligation on their part."[19]

A parallel note was struck by Spiegelman in a letter drawn up for the Sponsorship Committee. It was sent to Dr. Wise for approval, reading as follows:

> The purpose of the Fair is to meet the demands of an aroused buying public for information concerning the products and services of nations whose policies are in accord with the principles of modern civilization. Such an exposition has become imperative as a result of continuous increase of customers' resistance, irrespective of race or creed, to the purchase of goods made in Nazi Germany.
> It is our conviction that the Fair will serve a two-fold purpose. It will help to stimulate trade recovery throughout the world and at the same time, isolate Hitler Germany, which is retarding trade recovery as it is threatening international peace through its oppressive policy.
> The American Jewish Congress has been constrained to take this step as a logical outcome of the resolution adopted at Madison Square Garden, on March 7, where the "Case of civilization against Hitlerism" was presented and where 19,000 persons with one voice echoed the demand of Judge Seabury "for a boycott as wide as civilization and as powerful and as strong as humanity."[20]

Spiegelman was referring here to Judge Samuel Seabury, who participated in a mock trial of Hitler held at Madison Square Garden on the occasion marking the first anniversary of the Nazi victory at the polls. Judge Seabury, whose investigation of New York City's courts and politics resulted in the resignation of Mayor James J. Walker in 1932, turned the eyes of civilization to the full significance of Hilterism in his summation as counsel for public opinion at large. His angry charges reviewed the indictments handed down by some twenty "witnesses" who preceded him. Rev. John Haynes Holmes, minister of the Community Church of New York and personal friend of Stephen Wise, presented the resolution and passed sentence.

Spiegelman's quotation was taken from the concluding section of Seabury's speech, which read as follows:

> The emergency is great; the need for immediate action vital. It must be crystallized at once and it must find expression in a boycott against Hitlerism—a boycott as wide as civilization and as powerful and as strong as humanity.
> Public opinion as the force and boycott as the weapon will break the power of Hitlerism. It will clear it from the pathway of the developing and advancing civilization which it now obstructs and thus accord to the world the only opportunity it has for the preservation of world peace. (*NYT,* March 8, 1934)

ii.

The contract signed with Kimball called for scheduling the opening of the Fair in the month of June under Congress auspices. On May 11, when it was becoming evident that Kimball's corporation was actually running behind schedule, Dr. Tenenbaum sent Dr. Wise a communication expressing the following note of concern:

> And I am very much afraid that he may be inclined to charge to our account his own failure to go ahead as speedily as possible with the physical arrangements of the Fair. It is now five weeks since we have signed the contract and rumors have begun to come back to us that we have abandoned the Fair altogether, which shows that further delay in giving the matter the necessary publicity and attention may jeopardize the whole undertaking and give time to our Jewish enemies to gather all their forces to discourage the Fair.[21]

Tenenbaum added that unless Dr. Wise took this matter "energetically" into his hands, the Fair might become "a thing of the past." He therefore suggested that the Congress' honorary president use his influence to have either Seabury or LaGuardia placed on the Sponsorship Committee.[22] Believing that the New York mayor was "the best bet," Tenenbaum wrote that only Wise's "intervention could get President Deutsch to use his influence with LaGuardia."

Just what Dr. Wise did regarding this is not known; but it is clear from Kimball's counter-charges that he would not allow himself to be pressured even if his corporation was behind schedule. The summer vacation was approaching, and it was decided, therefore, that it would be best to reschedule the Fair in the fall. In the last week of October, the Good-Will Fair was held without much further ado.[23]

In the interim, however, the Boycott Committee, which had already taken steps to enlist the participation of the AFL, Jewish labor unions, and many national Jewish organizations, also made overtures to the NSANL. It proposed the establishment of a mode of cooperation between them, suggesting that the Trade Fair serve as a means of forming a Joint Boycott Committee. This was then discussed at length with Untermyer. The ANL chief proved sympathetic toward the idea of the Fair, but found it necessary to reject the participation of his organization in it along lines that were becoming very familiar to the Boycott Committee. His reply, dated July 24, read:

> Whilst we have decided, after considerable hesitation, not to join you in your undertaking, we shall be glad to give you any help or cooperation which in your judgment may be of use to you. As to your

other suggestion regarding the appointment of a Joint Boycott Committee, which would in many respects be desirable, there is a fundamental objection which I am sure you have already considered—that we are constantly insisting that our movement is non-sectarian in character and that this is of the utmost importance for the successful prosecution of our boycott work and is, I think, also useful to you. That advantage would be destroyed or gravely imperilled if we were to enter a joint committee. The existence of several boycott committees cannot harm that cause, and may be of great aid to it.[24]

Committee minutes also reveal that there was no universal agreement among staff members regarding the wisdom of having a Fair—at least during the early stages of the discussions of this subject. A recent Committee addition, Israel Posnansky, a Zionist Revisionist, who had formerly served with ALDJR as Rabinowitz's assistant, and was viewed, therefore, as a man of experience, held that the Fair was a good idea in theory only. For past field investigations had led him to distrust many Jewish manufacturers, whom he charged with pretending that their latest German shipments were old. He explained that such shipments were being delivered to these manufacturers surreptitiously in the early morning hours and that they imported these wares under assumed names.

Posnansky's charges were directed particularly against the large manufacturers. The boycott movement sought to make more easily accessible goods of American or foreign manufacture for the German ones. However, the large manufacturers, thought Posnansky, had an insincere attitude toward this policy and were apt to find "ethical" reasons for declining to cooperate publicly with the Boycott Committee.

Posnansky also believed it would be difficult to obtain the cooperation of the importers. He, therefore, suggested that the consumer be tackled instead—through radio talks, picketing, and the publication of a boycott bulletin.

Part of the business world was also represented at these deliberations. Thus, at a June 15 luncheon discussion with Spiegelman, several Macy's spokesmen[25] argued against the Fair. They contended that, firstly, the boycott was "one-hundred percent successful," and there was no need, therefore, to intensify it by a Fair; secondly, the Fair might fail to display a sufficiently large, impressive number of equivalents for German goods; thirdly, they expressed fear that such an enterprise could irritate the AFL, since the Fair would encourage, ipso facto, the importation of articles of foreign manufacture from countries of a lower living standard and labor wage. To illustrate this, reference was made to the complications that might arise as a result of Japanese participation.

Fear was also expressed that the Fair might prove too great a success, and thus furnish antisemites with a conspicuous example of so-called Jewish economic power; so that rather than benefit American Jews, the Fair would boomerang against them. The Macy's officials declared, though, that should the Boycott Committee carry out its plan of holding the projected Fair, their company would be represented, but reluctantly so.

Macy's attitude was not surprising in view of its half-hearted adherence to the boycott.[26] Its "fears" seemed to reflect this attitude, as well as its business interests and stereotype. The next few months were to prove, however, that there was really nothing to "fear"; for in the end, Macy's subscribed to the boycott at long last.

15

At the World Jewish Conference

Boycott Reaffirmation

In spite of hopes that 1934 would finally mark the founding of the World Jewish Congress, that year saw the holding of yet a third, albeit the last, of the Preliminary Conferences to this aspiring event. But unlike 1933, it offered the only opportunity to discuss the boycott in an international Jewish forum, as a Zionist Congress had not been scheduled for 1934.

As in the past two years, the World Jewish Conference of 1934 was held in Geneva, Switzerland. And again, like the year before, the boycott was one of the leading subjects of a four-day meeting session, from August 20 to August 23. Dr. Nahum Goldmann, who, during the course of the year, had established his residence in Paris, was among the non-American delegates who denounced Nazi brutality and warned that the boycott would continue until Jewish rights in Germany were fully restored. Goldmann spoke on the twentieth, saying:

> There are some differences among Jewish groups as to whether the boycott should have been proclaimed officially or unofficially. These are questions of tactic, which are of small measure in relation to the magnitude of the problem. But all Jews, including the leaders of those organizations, who, up to now could not come to a decision about the official boycott, do not become tired from declaring that every self-respecting Jew must boycott Germany. Next to our spiritual and

political struggle against the principles and methods of the Third Reich, the boycott stands as the only weapon at our disposal. No one will expect us to lay it aside, so long as there remains a battle to wage and the minimum of our demands: the restoration of Jewish equality, which is not completely fulfilled.[1]

Dr. Margoshes also attended the Conference, rendering at the second session a statistical account of the general American participation in the boycott movement and its damaging effect on German exports. As presiding chairman of the third session, he introduced Dr. Wise, who gave the most definitive and inspiring boycott pronouncement of all:

Ours it is to consider what attitude shall World Jewry take with regard to the Hitler Reich, which name may yet be officially adopted. Two years ago when the earlier preliminary World Jewish Conference was held, we were assured, especially by German Jews, that Hitler would never come to power: one year ago there was the general and lamentable admission that Hitlerism had attained to power and could not be dislodged for many years. To-day, eighteen months after the accession of Hitlerism to dominance, it may truly be said that Hitlerism is still sovereign over the Germany of yesterday's pseudo-election to the presidency,[2] It may for a number of reasons be on the eve of dislodgment.

To-day, in the presence of such Nazi aggression and bullying as, to quote the "London Times" of July 29, "are provoking anti-German repercussions, even in places where Germanism is nationally strong," it might be urged that Jews could and should be silent, in any event, for a time. But if we long remain silent, will not the cries of protest against Nazi wrong after a time die down? One remembers that such Jewish leadership as was opposed to the World Jewish Congress urged silence on the part of the forces of civilization. We did not beg, least of all could we coerce these, to speak. We would not and we could not. But we in America, perhaps more than in any other land, made clear, not in the cries of anguished pain but in the accents of prophetic insight, what this evil thing meant. . . .

It must be made clear with respect to the anti-German boycott or counter-boycott, that the aroused Jewish consciousness began the boycott, in my country for example, but the American conscience, and indeed the human conscience, now carry on the boycott in all lands. The American conscience has expressed itself in the Resolutions of the American Federation of Labour, adopted one year ago, and in the action of those Christian groups, Catholic and Protestant alike, which will not have any dealings whatsoever with a land subversive of all we know and cherish under the name of civilization. How little Jews are disposed to stand and to battle together comes to light in the circumstance that to this day the boycott stands unapproved, if not formally disapproved, in certain Jewish quarters: though members of these groups personally admit that they share in the boycott from day to day, but cannot give it their explicit and public approval.

The boycott against German wares and services will not be given up. It will not be given up until the Hitler regime shall either have been ended, or shall have cancelled every law and practice in violation of human freedom, political equality, and the ideals of civilization. How often must certain things be repeated? The boycott is the one weapon of non-violence, the moral effect of the use of which outweighs its material effect. Supremely and incomparably it is the non-violent instrument which can be used by all those upon whom non-cooperation has been forced.

The Jewish boycott could not have been averted by us any more than it could to-day be halted by super-cautious bodies in Paris, London and New York. If proof were needed (as we need it not) of the rightful instinct of the Jewish masses, such proof is to be found in the way in which, without leadership or suggestion, these turned to the boycott and adopted it as the answer to the crimes of Hitlerism. To their credit be it said, Untermyer, and Melchett for a lesser period, intensified the Jewish boycott consciousness. Following the Geneva Conference of one year ago, our Second World Jewish Conference, the American Jewish Congress took over the leadership of the boycott and has, in co-operation with the American Federation of Labour and other bodies, devoted time, strength, funds and infinite devotion to this essential task.[3]

Therewithal, Dr. Wise rendered the following judgment and scheme:

Three or four attitudes are possible on the part of the World Jewish Conference and Congress with respect to Hitlerism. It must be borne in mind that the World Jewish Congress movement was pre-Hitler. The World Jewish Congress is not a Hitler evoked palliative, any more than the Zionist movement was Herzl's response to Czarist persecution of Russo-Jewry.

I. Jews may do nothing, save extend relief, meagre or adequate, because of Hitler and Hitlerism, A purely nihilistic position which is not far removed from that which many Jews accept as the most prudent and innocuous course. This was frankly and undisguisedly suicidal—the acceptance of the counsel of the post-Hitler Marranos.

II. The second proposal is that nothing be done contrary to the actual or imagined will of Hitlerism, which were cowardice and self-degradation at their basest.

III. The third course for World Jewry is to continue to do what has heretofore been prescribed for us by those who, for any reason of their own devising, are powerful in the conduct of Jewish affairs.

IV. The fourth possibility is to summon Jews of all lands together by their chosen representatives, and to lead them after full, frank and responsible discussion to decide for themselves what should be done in this our time of most desperate need.

Undeniable is the fundamental thesis that every Jew, whether he know it or not, has a stake in the outcome of whatever decision may be reached by Jewry, not only has a stake, but that his all is at stake therein. We hold that every Jew who has a stake, and there are none who have not, must directly or indirectly be helped to have a part in reaching these decisions. All Jews cannot have part unless there be representative, democratically organized elections where those are legally permissible. So that this becomes the next step, and we in America are resolved that it shall be the next step in our collective procedure.[4]

Rabbi Wise also took occasion to denounce the Transfer Agreement, saying:

> One year ago, under the joint influence of German Zionists, who were not free agents and should not have been in evidence at the Prague Zionist Congress, and of certain representatives of the *Yishub*,[5] we made the woeful blunder of withholding our condemnation from certain German Palestinian undertakings which involved a breach of the boycott. That breach, I grieve to state, is being continued and even widened. Every manner of reason and excuse is being offered—as centering on the emigration of Jews from Germany, who hoped in this way to have their flight to Palestine furthered or made possible. One leading Palestinian put it over and over again at Prague: "Palestina hat Primat," that is, Palestine has primacy. This Conference must clearly state that, while Palestine has primacy over all other factors in the Jewish equation, its primacy ceases when it comes into conflict with the moral law. If we had been prepared to gain Palestine on lower terms, it might have been encompassed sooner and more easily.
>
> The moral law has primacy even over Palestine and its needs, and the needs of them who would pilgrim thither. Palestine primacy halts at the threshold of moral sovereignty. The moral law made Palestine as truly as Palestine is the author of the moral law. Why *cavil* at minor social and moral infractions of the law in Palestine and stoop to the gravest breaches in the moral world? This trafficking of Jewish Palestine with Nazi Germany must cease at once. There is something worse than entering Zion with bowed heads, to paraphrase Theodore Herzl, and that is with unclean hands. One does not thus "ascend the Hill of the Lord, nor stand at His holy place" . . .
>
> The boycott is declared by not a few Jews to be a species of war, and that like every "violence of war" it is not "nice and peaceable." "If there must be a boycott, let non-Jews lead it." This I declare to be the worse type of parasitism. Timidity to copy and seek to excel in the pursuit of

quasi-Christian teaching not even daring moral and spiritual resistance of non-contact and non-cooperation with the land, which has become the scourge of mankind.[6]

During the course of this oration, the following telegram, addressed to Stephen Wise by Samuel Untermyer, arrived:

> As president American nonsectarian boycott league and World boycott Federation organized Amsterdam last August, I earnestly urge Conference against creating damaging misleading World impression that boycott is distinctly Jewish. It is civilization's protest and only weapon regardless of creed its support comes.
> Largely from Catholics, Protestants, churches and labor unions, Jews alone could not have accomplished present results. Whilst Jewish masses are unanimously enthusiastically behind boycott, few influential Jews are supporting us. No Jewish banker is on any boycott Committee or has openly dared support or contribute from fear of German reprisals or because of German connection.
> When our organization inaugurated movement single-handed eighteen months ago, every powerful American Jewish organization opposed us. All are still doing so under these malign influences with honorable exception of Jewish Congress which courageously changed its policy six months later and is now helpfully cooperating. Of course, our race will survive but boycott cannot succeed without continued non-Jewish World support for which we are deeply grateful and which Conference will I hope recognize by appropriate resolutions. Please read this message to Conference. Regards.[7]

Untermyer received a reply to his message from Dr. Goldmann:

> Wise read your message and praised your work which Conference unanimously and enthusiastically approved. Conference agrees with you, boycott no[t] chiefly Jewish but moral and material self-defense of civilization against Nazi forces of darkness and enslavement. Pledge ourselves together with all freedom enjoying and justice loving people and faiths to stand thru the boycott and other lawful and peaceful means against Hitlerism. Conference earnestly hopes that American Boycott League and American Federation of Labor and American Jewish Congress continue all cooperation.[8]

On August 23, the last day of the Conference, the following resolutions were adopted:

> The Third World Jewish Conference solemnly confirms the boycott, proclaimed last year by the Second World Jewish Conference against National-Socialist Germany. The causes which led to that proclama-

tion still subsist in all their intensity. The Conference states that, thanks particularly to participation in the boycott movement by such large non-Jewish organizations as the International Trade Union movement, the British Labour Party, the American Federation of Labor and other sections of the population in other countries, the boycott against National-Socialist Germany has made considerable progress. The Conference earnestly appeals to the entire Jewish people in all the countries of the world, as also to all those who are enlisted in the fight for liberty and justice for all races, religions and peoples, to organize and carry through the boycott with all their energy.

The Third World Jewish Conference regrets to draw the attention of the leading organizations of Zionist organization and Palestinian Jewry to the sad fact that the import of German goods into Palestine, in spite of the boycott of World Jewry against National-Socialist Germany and the Boycott Resolution of the "Assefath Hanivcharim" (organ representing Palestinian Jewry), has increased since last year.

The Conference empowers the Executive which it will elect to get in touch with the relevant Zionist Palestinian organizations, in order to put an end to this regrettable situation and find a solution to the problem of Jewish emigration from Germany to Palestine which will be in conformity with the general boycott movement of World Jewry.[9]

Conference Reverberations

As propounded in a resolution of the World Jewish Conference of 1932, the establishment of a World Jewish Congress was to be "based on the conception of the Jewish people as a unified national organism."[10] According to this resolution, the proposed Congress was to be "a legitimate representation, authorized and in duty bound to deal with all questions of Jewish life, and to represent the Jewish people to the outside world, in a struggle for its civil and national rights."[11] This resolve was confirmed at both the 1933 and 1934 sessions.

However, the American Jewish Committee, which had been invited to participate in the Preliminary Conference of the projected World Jewish Congress organization, declined acceptance on the grounds

> that such a Conference would not be truly representative of the Jews of the world; that in most countries, including those in which Jewish problems are acute, the Jews have established national and local committees headed by capable and distinguished men, many of whom hold important posts in the legislative and administrative services of their respective countries, and that these organizations are better able to cope with internal problems than an outside conference; that no helpful action would possibly result from the conference of persons

from many parts of the world to discuss the peculiar economic and political and social conditions affecting the Jews in various countries, as such a conference would be nothing but a forum for speeches, and a welter of talk is far from the kind of cooperation and assistance that the Jews of Germany and Eastern Europe require; that the assembling of such an international body at this time will be seized upon by the enemies of Jews in various parts of Central and Eastern Europe as convincing proof of the charge that they have made repeatedly that the Jews are an international body without local or civic patriotism.[12]

Regarding the last of the aforesaid charges, the Committee cited a United Press report from Geneva declaring that "a super-government of Judaism, representative of Jews in every country, was in process of formation."[13] To this was added the statement that "Plans were formulated by the World Jewish Congress for the government, actually a Jewish Parliament, with delegates from every country and with permanent headquarters in Geneva."[14] In some of America's newspapers, this appeared in the form of streamer headlines, reading: "JEWS TO FIGHT OPPRESSION WITH 'SUPER-GOVERNMENT'."[15]

When news of this piece of slander reached the Jewish Conference in Geneva, Dr. Wise had this to say about it to his interviewer:

> This report is so absurd that you may be astonished that I refer to it at all. There are doubtless Jews in New York, London and Paris who are not so enthusiastic as we about the projected World Jewish Conference. But there is not a man or woman in this room who would be guilty of saying such a foolish thing as that we favor a World Super-government. We do not favor any Jewish government. We do favor Jewish self-respect and the idea that Jews shall cease to be victims of hatred. As far as a super-government is concerned, we merely ask that every government on earth be just, not merely to Jewish, but to all peoples and all religions. More than that we do not ask.[16]

But the American Jewish Committee took a much dimmer view of a headline imputing to Jews the myth of planning the creation of a super-government. Indignant and anxious about the possible harmful effects of such a vilifying allegation, the Committee hurriedly informed the press through its secretary, Morris D. Waldman, that it was in no manner, shape, or form affiliated with the Geneva World Jewish Conference. Its statement read:

> In view of the erroneous headlines and statements contained in some press reports of a conference of Jews now being held in Geneva, attention is drawn to the fact that the American Jewish Committee, which is made up of representatives in every important city in the

United States, has not indorsed and is not participating in the World Conference, and that important organizations abroad, among them the Board of Deputies of England and the Alliance Israelite Universaille of France, have declined to send delegates to represent them.

In light of these facts, the conference cannot truthfully be described as representative of the opinion of Jews of the world or as expressing the viewpoint of Jewish citizens of the United States.[17]

This statement was expounded as follows:

> A Jewish parliament would give aid and comfort to those who promote hostility to the Jews, on the ground of alleged international solidarity and super-loyalty. It would sow doubts in the minds of our fellow-citizens in all countries as to the precise status of the Jew as citizen.
>
> These dangerous consequences will follow, although the Congress will in fact be not representative of all the Jews, and will have no power to enforce its decisions even upon those individuals who vote for its representatives, and who, by so doing, are implying the acceptance of an obligation to an extra-national authority. These consequences are inevitable, although in practice the Congress can be nothing more than a platform for the making of speeches, and a convocation for the passage of resolutions . . . .
>
> The Committee believes that, animated by their love of country and their devotion to the highest conception of patriotism, American Jews will recognize the menace to their status inherent in the proposed World Congress and will declare their opposition to it.[18]

The Committee's Report expounded this stand as follows:

> The American Jewish Committee holds it to be self-evident that U.S. Jews have here established a permanent home for themselves and their children, have acquired the rights and assumed the duties of American citizenship, and recognize their unqualified allegiance to this country and of whose citizens they regard themselves as a loyal and integral part. The Committee believes that as American citizens, Jews have the right, individually or associated in groups, to approach the U.S. government and solicit its good offices in behalf of the betterment of the lot of oppressed Jews in other lands. The Committee does not believe, however, that it is consistent with these principles for them to associate themselves with the citizens of other countries in creating an international body which will assume or attempt to speak for the Jews of this country.
>
> The Committee believes that, animated by their love of country and their devotion to the highest conception of patriotism, American Jews

will recognize the menace to their status inherent in the proposed World Congress and will declare their opposition to it.[19]

Judge Proskauer, who, in December 1933, had been elected a member of the Committee's Board of Directors, made a similar statement, accentuating the antisemitic dangers with which the creation of a World Jewish Congress was fraught.

> To foment what is called a World-Congress, with delegates to be elected, is just to play into the hands of our adversaries. As Jews, we have a right to meet through our various communal organizations to confer with our fellow Jews of other countries for the aid of our unfortunate brethren and the furtherance of our spiritual and cultural ideals. But this is a very different thing from acting through the process of the election of delegates to what is inaccurately called a Congress–a process which carries with it the implication that there should be a democratic representation, as though we were really a political unit. Nothing is further from the truth. There is no international political Jewry, and the best protection for our people in every land is that there is no such political organization.[20]

Publicity around the World Jewish Conference also occasioned a public response from Samuel Untermyer, who was likewise opposed to the creation of a World Jewish Congress. He accounted for his position in a statement which set forth his analysis of antisemitism.

> I do not favor a World Jewish Conference, or any sort of action by the Jews of the world to combat anti-Semitism. The problem is different in each country and should be separately treated. Such a World Conference would serve only to concentrate attention upon the subject and to magnify it.
> The question of what measures should be taken as an effective means of combatting the spread of anti-Semitism throughout the world and especially in America, opens up an unlimited field. The Jews of each country have their own problem, which must be treated according to the conditions prevailing in that country, and differently from the problems in other countries. So far as concerns America, the rise of this feeling has been due mainly to the lying and vicious propaganda circulated here by the Hitler Government through its paid propagandists and agents in America. If American Jewry could or would, on any proposition, act as a unit it could readily be overcome.
> The minority rights of Jews in the countries in which they are threatened can be protected only with the assistance of our Government, and then only to a limited extent. Our State Department might demand that every treaty shall contain safeguards for minorities.[21]

Considering his efforts to coordinate the boycott activities of every country under the aegis of the World Jewish Economic Federation, it can hardly be said that Untermyer was showing consistency by not favoring the creation of a World Jewish Congress because "the Jews of each country have their own problem." However, Untermyer was showing consistency in the area of nonsectarianism, which had become a near-obsession with him; for as shall presently be seen, he was soon to alter the "Jewish" character of the World Jewish Economic Federation as he had that of the American League for the Defense of Jewish Rights.

16

Legal Activities

ANL Phase

In addition to using moral suasion and economic pressure to stave off the ever-growing Nazi menace, the NSANL took recourse to the law in order to make more effective the conduct of its anti-Nazi boycott. To this end, it sought to use to good advantage its inherent American right to wield this medium in a way that suited the best interests of its cause.

Essentially, this defensive battle was waged in two ways: by fighting for the enforcement of existing legislation which could be applied to the detriment of Germany's financial interests, and by pressing, on either ethical or patriotic grounds, for new legislation to serve similar ends. As a matter of logic and opportunity, the easier of the two, namely, pressing for the enforcement of previously enacted laws, was pursued first.

Several June 7, 1933, pieces of correspondence, written by Jacob Chaitkin[1] (p. 132) in reply to two letters from Ezekiel Rabinowitz, constitute the earliest available documents on this subject. We do not possess Rabinowitz's letters. However, the Chaitkin correspondence does tell us that one of them was written on June 6. From them it is learned, in any event, that Rabinowitz had contacted Chaitkin for legal advice regarding Hitler Germany's practice of mislabeling its exported goods. Germany had been compelled to adopt this devious method as a result of the growing strength of the boycott movement; and Rabinowitz, almost simultaneously with the founding of ALDJR, acted swiftly in an attempt to seal up this breach in the not too impregnable boycott wall.

Chaitkin's reply to Rabinowitz's "general questions" is of particular interest because it reveals how an attorney-at-law viewed the legality of a movement of which he was himself a leading member, and, perhaps, explains why boycott leaders were not afraid to espouse it.

In order to understand the legal aspect of these questions, one must have a clear idea of the legal definitions of a boycott. These definitions vary with different jurisdictions and different types of judicial mind. New York is one of the most liberal jurisdictions in this respect.

The law of New York provides the same test for boycotts, strikes and lockouts. Their legality depends on the approval of the courts of (1) the object in view and, (2) the means of attainment of said object (Gill Engraving Co. vs. Doerr, 214 Fed. III, S.D.N.Y.). Under the New York law the word boycott in and of itself does not imply illegality: "It cannot be said that to boycott is to offend the law" (Mills vs. U.S. Printing Co., 99 A.D. 611, aff'd 199 N.Y. 76).

Applying the above test to the boycott sponsored by the ALDJR we are confronted at the outset by the utter lack of precedents as to the position of the courts towards the object of the boycott. However, for the purpose of this opinion, I must assume that the object will be provided in any fair juridical contest. This will not be a question of law, it will be a question of principle and policy with the courts. It cannot be said without a court test that the anti-German boycott is illegal because the legality of its object has not yet been approved by the courts. We must assume that we shall sustain the legality of the boycott on this aspect of the question.

Passing on to the question of the legality "of the means of attainment," our path is somewhat better chartered by precedents and legislation.

As a general rule, the courts have disapproved and condemned what is known as the "secondary boycott," which has been defined as an attempt to procure or coerce parties outside the combination to cease dealings with the antagonist.

Even New York, one of the most liberal states in permitting organized labor to use the boycott weapon, frowns upon the "secondary boycott." In the United States generally, the secondary boycott is clearly illegal (cf. dissenting opinion of Mr. Justice Brandeis in Traux vs. Corrigan, 257 U.S. 312, at p. 364, where he collates all the cases; Duplex Printing Press vs. Deering, 254 U.S. 443). In the last cited case, the secondary boycott was defined as "a combination not merely to refrain from dealings with the person aimed at, or to advise, or by peaceful means to persuade his customers to refrain (primary boycott) but to exercise coercive pressure upon such customers, actual or prospective, in order to cause them to withhold or withdraw patronage through fear of loss or damage to themselves." The case cited held that secondary boycott would be illegal even if the object of the primary boycott was legal.

In condemning the secondary boycott, the courts frequently take the position that the object of the boycott itself becomes improper when third persons are coerced into joining the original combination. As was said in one of the leading New York cases: "An action for a direct and primary purpose in the interest of individuals or a combination of individuals taken in good faith to advance the interest of the individuals or combination may be lawful, while a remote and secondary action which carries with it a degree of malice is illegal" (Bossert vs. Dhuy, 221 N.Y. 342).

It has been held that a boycott must not be for oppression's sake only but must further a lawful purpose. Neither punishment nor revenge is a proper purpose (Auburn vs. Wadell, 178 A.D. 270). The secondary boycott, as a means to promote the objects of the primary boycott, is illegal because it involves the unlawful objects of oppression, punishment and revenge.

The foregoing does not mean that it is absolutely prohibited to give full publicity to the objects of the boycott. Judge Cardozo has said (in Nann vs. Raimist, 255 N.Y. 307) that the "pressure of notoriety and persuasion" is a legitimate means of bringing about a lawful object. It is in the final analysis a question of degree rather than of kind as to whether the means employed are legal or illegal.[2]

We also learn from Chaitkin's correspondence that on May 22, Rabinowitz—as might have been expected—had addressed himself to Untermyer as well on the mislabeling question. But there is no record of a reply to this from Untermyer, either in his capacity as ANL president or as attorney-at-law.

The first we hear of Untermyer taking up this matter is at the National Boycott Conference of September 10, 1933 (p. 97). The most common of the mislabeling practices, he said there, was the German manufacturer's deceptive method of stamping his goods as "Made in Saxony," "Made in Bavaria," or "Made in Duesseldorf." The uninformed might fail to associate such German provinces and cities with the mother country; hence Untermyer's reaction:

> This is contrary to law specification; so I have notified the Treasury Department that if they don't stop that, that I shall begin a suit in the Federal Court to compel them to stop it; stop cheating the American people by being a party to this fraud upon American industry. And they will either stop or the subject will be dragged through the courts.[3]

A couple of months later, Untermyer was already concentrating his efforts on this matter. He wrote as follows to Rabinowitz on November 8:

> If there is going to be such a thing as a Law Committee, I am

enclosing a letter for its action. I think this committee should bring a test case against the Treasury Department in the form of a suit to mandamus or enjoin that Department from continuing to pass through this port and admit goods marked "Made in Baden" or "Made in Saxony," etc. We might as well have a ruling on this subject in the courts.

If the Law Committee will submit to me a proposed complaint on those lines, together with a brief on the subject and I find that my impression is confirmed by an examination of the law, I will participate in the argument of the case in court.

Besides being a wholesome thing, it would involve considerable publicity so that the American people would understand that goods marked "Made in Baden" are German goods, which they do not now realize.[4]

Though no copies have been preserved in the ANL archives, we know that Untermyer wrote the Treasury Department letters of complaint relating to Nazi Germany's deceptive export practices. Such correspondence is mentioned in one of the Department's replies to Mr. Untermyer, written on November 20:

Reference is made to your communication of the 16th instant, which related further to the importation of German-made merchandise into the United States. You quote from a letter received by you to the effect that merchandise labeled "Made in Baden" is being passed by Customs officers as properly labeled with the country of origin.

In previous communications I have pointed out that Section 304 of the Tariff Act of 1930 requires that "imported merchandise shall be marked so as to indicate the country of origin." [See Document No. XIV.] From time to time the Treasury Department at Washington has ruled that the names of certain well-known capital cities and provinces when appearing upon imported merchandise may be taken as a sufficient indication of the country of origin. Many of these cities and provinces are listed in Article 509 of the Customs Regulations of 1931. [See Document No. XV.] To these names was added the name of the province of Baden in Germany by Treasury Decision 46515. An examination of the law will indicate to you that the use of such well-known cities and provinces is fully authorized.

It would seem that a remedy for the condition now existing can be obtained only through an amendment to Section 304 of the Tariff Act so as to provide that imported articles may be marked with the name of the country of origin only.[5]

This was good advice, as part (b) under Article 509 of the Customs Regulations of 1931 did list such provinces as Bavaria and Saxony "to be a sufficient indication of the country of origin." But because this issue apparently caught him during the transitional stage between the planned liquidation of the ALDJR and substitution of the NSANL, Untermyer left it again in a state of abeyance.

However, on the night of January 3, 1934, the reconstituted League revived the mislabeling question as its first order of business at a meeting at the New York Astor Hotel. The participants, mostly lawyers, were shown sample articles on which markings of "Made in Germany" were inconspicuously placed and the name of a German city, state, or province was used prominently to mislead would-be boycotters. It was resolved to seek the elimination of these fraudulent methods by an insistence on the strict enforcement of the labeling law. Untermyer, decrying the decision of the Treasury Department to accept certain territorial regions as sufficent denotations of the country of origin, repeated his readiness to battle this ruling in the courts.

This did not prove necessary, however; for as a result of Untermyer's loud protestations, his convincing case, and probably the Treasury Department's desire to avoid undesirable publicity, the requested change was entered that month. As amended by the Treasury Department, the text of Article 509b read:

> To collectors of Customs and Others Concerned—
> Article 509b of the Customs Regulations of 1931 is amended to read as follows:
> (b) The marking required by Sec. 304 shall include the name of the country of origin. The name of a subdivision such as a kingdom, principality, state, or province, or of a city within the country of origin is not alone sufficient. The term "country" as used in Sec. 304 is held to mean the political unity known as nation. However, colonies, possessions or protectorates outside of the boundaries of a mother country shall be considered separate countries.
> All Bureau and Departmental rulings inconsistent with Art. 509b as hereby amended are revoked.
> The decision shall take effect ninety days after its publication in the weekly Treasury Decisions.
>
> J. H. Moyle, Commissioner of Customs

Approved January 31 1934
H. Morgenthau, Jr.
Secretary Treasurer.[6]

Untermyer sponsored a similar, but even more strongly worded measure for passage in the New York State Legislature. It was introduced by State Senator Albert Wald, and referred to thereafter as the "Wald Act" or "Wald Bill." The bill, under Sec. 435, of the Penal Code,[7] made it a misdemeanor to remove from any article of merchandise marks indicating the country of origin. It also made the owner of a business personally responsible for the defacement of labels on articles bearing the country of origin. If found culpable, the guilty party could be fined, imprisoned, or both. The boycott movement was thus provided with two deterrents designed to halt tampering with labels by merchants and importers.

17

The Non-Sectarian World Conference

i.

In early November, it was announced that a Non-Sectarian World Conference would be held in London, beginning on the twenty-fifth of that month. Untermyer, heading a five-man delegation selected to sail for England, was invited to preside over the international meeting. It was expected that delegates from at least a dozen countries would take part in the scheduled four-day conference.

The issuance in mid-November of a new anti-Nazi booklet by the NSANL was especially timed to increase the publicity being given this latest of World Conferences. The purposes of this publication were set forth in the preface:

> To demonstrate to the world that an effective substitute for war has been found, through the boycott, to prevent a nation from violating its treaty rights or its world obligations; to render impossible through the success of the boycott (in crushing Hitlerism),[1] the continuation of Germany's vast foreign propaganda which is spreading among our people (to) the poisonous germs of race and religious hatred; . . .
> Another equally important purpose of this publication is to disprove, demonstrate and set at rest for all time the utter falsity and absurdity of the widespread, constantly repeated German propaganda that the ever-increasing worldwide boycott of German goods is a Jewish movement. This is not and was at no time a Jewish question, although the Jews were the first victims and have been in proportion to their numbers the greatest sufferers from the reign of terror and lawlessness that now holds the German people in its grip.[2]

Boycotting labor organizations, boasting a membership figure surpassing that of World Jewry itself, were set forth as an example to bring this claim home. There was also put forward the idea that should the boycott succeed in forcing Germany to renounce her policies of oppression and discrimination, it would have been proven that economic sanctions were a potent combative method upon the nation against which they were directed.

As announced from ANL headquarters, the Conference was scheduled to hear and discuss the following outline program:

> Presentation of reports giving up-to-date resumes of boycott progress; Information exchange relating to the substitution of German products; Ways and means of offsetting the effect of Nazi racial hatred propaganda; The establishment of a permanent world boycott organization; The organization of an information bureau.[3]

The purpose of the Conference, said Untermyer, was "to devise and put into effect means of coordinating and intensifying the activities of the existing world boycott against Germany which is steadily growing in scope and effectiveness."[4] The Conference was also expected to demonstrate, he added, that "boycott is an effective substitute for war."[5]

The call for yet another World Boycott Conference, whatever the motivation, drew criticism from some quarters[6] that this movement was deteriorating into a severe retributive measure for the persecution of German Jews. It was added, moreover, that the boycott had not convinced Germans of their error and that Christian communities did not recognize revenge as a principle in social action.

Ever sensitive to such censure, and deeming it necessary to underscore again the raison d'etre of an anti-Nazi boycott, Abba Hillel Silver responded:

> The boycott is an economic offensive against the most dangerous enemy of twentieth century civilization—Hitlerism. It is aimed through economic pressure, to contribute to the undermining of a regime which has destroyed human freedom, robbed men of their elementary human rights, revived the darkest prejudices and intolerances of the Middle Ages and consigned hundred of thousands of innocent men, women and children to spiritual degradation and economic annihilation. The boycott is a bloodless war of self-defense in behalf of the rights of labor, the rights of a free church, the inalienable rights of man to life, liberty and the pursuit of happiness.[7]

Along the same lines, Silver said to a Cleveland audience: "When we fight Nazism, we are fighting for basic human ideals. The boycott is a matter of demanding our elementary human rights, not a matter of revenge."[8] Of course, there was nothing new in all this; but, then, again, it was important to stimulate the boycott movement by maintaining the freshness of its objectives and justification. This was especially the case now that one of the two main boycott groups was undergoing reorganization and expansion.

ii.

Tedious as was Untermyer's insistence that the boycott movement be nonsectarian in character, it must be admitted that the delegates presently gathering in London supported such a view, despite a considerable Jewish representation. This is not to say, however, that Protestantism, Catholicism, and Labor were not very well represented too. But most surprising, perhaps, of all, although their cultural and religious backgrounds proved quite diverse, the attending delegates reached political unity through their common liberal and democratic bonds.

The AFL was not directly represented at the World Conference. However, William Green did address a letter to the Conference expressing his labor force's "deep interest in its deliberations and entire sympathy and accord with its aims and purposes."[9] He then added:

> The rights of minorities in all countries must be respected and preserved if international good-will and peace are to be promoted and maintained. Labor in the United States has regarded the persecution of the Jewish people in Germany merely because they were Jews with feelings of resentment and horror.
>
> The recital of these facts and these principles for which organized labor in the United States and Canada firmly stands will convey to your Conference the real basis for the declarations successively made by conventions of the American Federation of Labor in opposition to the restriction of trade unions and the persecution of their members and of minorities in Germany.[10]

Most of the discussion at the Conference centered around subjects which, however important, were by now routine to the movement. One of the highlights was a report by the American delegation that over 500 articles formerly imported from Germany into the United States were already being manufactured in the home country.

One of the Conference's more ambitious resolutions[11] provided for the organization, in all countries other than Germany, of school and college youth in support of boycott activities. One also notes that all resolutions reflected the nonsectarianism which formed the basis for calling the Conference together.

At the close of this grandiose meeting, a new organization emerged in place of the World Jewish Economic Federation. It was named the World Non-Sectarian Anti-Nazi Council to Champion Human Rights and voted Samuel Untermyer as its president.[12]

18

The Phase of Decline

i.

The success of the American Anti-Nazi boycott in 1933 and in much of 1934 was partly due to the clamorous and sensational manner in which this movement was covered in the press. However, front-page coverage, such as the boycott had received in the Yiddish and Anglo-Jewish press, and more reserved reporting in the general press, ceased in the latter half of 1934. And since the boycott had not succeeded in toppling or crippling the Hitler regime by 1935, nor even in wringing from it fundamental concessions for German Jewry, it ran the gamut of much of its newsworthiness.

According to the editorial of an erstwhile Chicago newspaper, the loss of newsworthiness was not the principal inadequacy:

> We had thought that after the World Boycott Conference in London had created the International Boycott Commission, the boycott work would become vigorous on all fronts, in all countries; and the boycott activities would be intensified. It appears, however, that the London meeting exhausted the energies of the movement; all over the world and in America, too, it is functioning very weakly.
>
> Even the doughty Untermyer in New York seems lately to have become indifferent. Is it because the movement is now under the supervision of the World Boycott Committee and that it is a hindrance to the American work? Or has the brave battler become fatigued and his enthusiasm cooled off?[1]

The editorial concluded with the complaint that it heard "little of the boycott movement in New York—and just at a time when the undertaking should have gotten additional power."

Four days later, George E. Harriman, who was the ANL's executive scretary in the middle-thirties, wrote Untermyer a confidential letter which confirms and partly explains to us the reason for the assessment of the foregoing editorial:

> Regarding your question as to my attitude towards the Women's Division:
>
> Mrs. Harris is a delightful person; She is tremendously enthusiastic and possesses a most wonderful personality. But, so far as I can learn, she does not cooperate with many of the women who are eager to work for the boycott.
>
> Today the Women's Division is producing absolutely no revenue. Whereas every organization depends largely upon its women's groups for fund-raising. This may not be Mrs. Harris' fault, but in many of our interviews, she has found one reason or another for objecting to money-raising plans for the Women's Division. Mrs. Harris seems to feel that so long as women talk boycott and do a little store checking, they are fulfilling their duties towards the League.
>
> Of all the Women's Divisions, I am sorry to say, that the Bronx is the only one that shows any real activity. The Chairman of the Manhattan Division is a very charming lady but does not impress me as an organizer or as having any particular force. The Brooklyn situation is even worse. Certain sections of Brooklyn are just ripe for us but nothing has been done. Naturally, I am loath to criticize Mrs. Harris, but in the final analysis, mine is the responsibility and I think it only fair to you and to myself to put this on record. Basically, I believe the whole problem is one of getting Mrs. Harris to cooperate with the women who want to be helpful.[2]

Also in conformity with the opinion of the aforesaid editorial, a February 4, 1935, communication by Untermyer reflects the weak state of boycott outside the immediate environs of New York City—a circumstance which was to plague this movement throughout its existence. The communication was sent to Harriman from Palm Springs, California:

> I am not at all satisfied with Boycott conditions out here. The movement seems to have died down, owing to the absolute inefficiency of the local committees, both at Los Angeles and San Francisco. I shall see what can be done toward reviving and strengthening them. That is our trouble throughout the country. We never had proper local organization. Until you can get to work on that and establish such movements that extend its effectiveness. Our most fertile soil should be the labor unions in the several localities, but I have seen no indication on our part of any effective activity in that direction. That is

where I expect you to enlarge your field of usefulness. The disposition to treat this as a local situation and to give almost exclusive attention to New York City and its suburbs, seems to be irresistible. Not even other cities of the state, such as Buffalo, Albany, Syracuse etc., have been organized, although that would be a simple matter. We need someone who will devote himself especially to that purpose, and who is accustomed to that sort of work.[3]

Dr. Tenenbaum was also dissatisfied with "Boycott conditions," and in an August 9, 1934, memorandum dealing with "the progress of the Anti-Nazi Boycott in the United States," he informed his associates that the boycott was in need of a new stimulus because it was "no longer a novelty." The Boycott Committee chairman felt that the needed incentive could "be gotten through the coordination of activities and through the accession of new forces." He recommended a "courageous worldwide public appeal, emanating from a conference of an international character, backed by signatures of people of world-wide repute." This, believed Tenenbaum, "will at this time be greatly effective."

For the League, however, its conduct of a World Boycott Conference less than a year before was to be the last "conference of an international character." And for many months thereafter, the extent of Untermyer's boycott action hardly amounted to more than the prosaic advocacy of its intensification. This may have led Ira Hirschman (see p. 80) to charge that "Untermyer talks more than he does."[4] The accusation was cited by a Yiddish journalist who also found fault with Untermyer, stating that he "does not have too good a staff."[5]

One is tempted to agree with at least the second of the aforesaid charges; for if anything, Untermyer helped to alienate, rather than to retain, his co-workers. A number of documents will now be introduced in support of this contention.

On January 27, 1934, Untermyer addressed a communication to Ezekiel Rabinowitz expressing regret for not having joined with the American Jewish Congress in raising the $500,000 resolved upon at the National Boycott Conference:

> I note the comparatively meager response to my appeal you have thus far received in the way of campaign contributions, but do not share your elation at the results in view of the information that the American Jewish Congress, which only recently came into the boycott field, had the vision to put out a plan by which $25,000 or more was without great difficulty subscribed to its fund, whilst we have been kicking around for almost a year, spending all kinds of money and lacking the ingenuity to do anything substantial in that direction. I am so thoroughly disappointed at the complete flop we have made in our

efforts to raise money that I feel we have made a mistake in not joining with the Congress. . . . I feel you are getting nowhere.[6]

The Jewish Congress concentrated its efforts on Jews, of course, in order to raise money. However, in voicing his disappointment at not having teamed up with the Congress in behalf of the League's money-raising effort, Untermyer either ignored or simply failed to see this as a glaring contradiction to what he stated in the second half of the aforesaid communication:

If you could only be stirred up to the realizing sense of the possibilities of this movement for attracting campaign funds, as well as country-wide support, I think we should make more progress; but unfortunately you persist in hanging on to the view that we want only to reach the Jews. We want nothing of the kind. They have long since been reached to the extent to which we shall ever be able to interest them. What we want to do is to reach the American public. That can only be done by wide publicity on the lines that will appeal to them and I appear to be unable to hammer that into your head.[7]

The insulting remark made by Untermyer in this communication is nothing compared to the manner in which he belittled Rabinowitz's successor:

December 10 1934

B. G. Richards, Esq.,
729 Seventh Ave.,
N.Y.C.

Dear Mr. Richards,

So far as concerns your office, the boycott might be said to have completely broken down, through the inaction there . . .

Complaints are coming here from every direction. I understand that the Schwartz store is now openly selling German-made toys, which they did not do last year. But nobody takes a step, and nothing is done. Your place up there might just as well be dead as the way things are going on. You do not lift a finger.

I am told German knives are being sold by Macy's, and am communicating with them on the subject. I am afraid we shall have to make a radical change. It is the only alternative to going out of business. I can get no action out of you.

Mr. Marks of Macy's tells me that an importer here, named Rosenthal (I believe it is the Rosenthal China Co.) claims to have had orders for German china from Wanamaker and a half dozen other New York stores.

Why all this information comes to me, and why you never find out anything is a mystery to me. Don't you realize that the place might as well be closed as to go on as it is now being conducted? You are just in a state of complete coma.

Very truly yours,
Samuel Untermyer[8]

Nor did Richards's successor, George Harriman (p. 164), escape Untermyer's crass criticism. Thus, on May 29 1935, the ANL chief wrote:

> I sent the office a copy of my letter to Mr. Sanford Bates of May 23rd, protesting against the meeting of the International Prison Reform Association that is scheduled to be held in Berlin in August. It is impossible for me personally to follow up these things. That is the business of your organization, but you are doing so little of it that the burden falls on me, and I am not willing or able to bear it. This is a prolific subject of publicity, but it is apparently hopeless to expect anything from your office or that it will properly appraise the news value of such things.[9]

On a number of occasions, Dr. Wise received letters of complaint from Dr. Tenenbaum and Lily Shultz, each accusing the other of inefficiency, interference, bungling, and the like; but never did a Congress officer connected with the boycott sink to the uncivil level of the aforegoing "Untermyerada."

ii.

The downward trend of boycott interest was by no means limited to the continental United States. By 1935, Europe, as well, was witnessing a sharp decline in boycott activities.

Indications of this could already be noted at the World Non-Sectarian Boycott Conference, since the English press completely ignored this affair. It is true that national excitement over a royal wedding which coincided with the holding of the Conference distracted newspaper interest from the latter. But Untermyer's explanation that London's Nazi agents bribed the English press to ignore the Conference, is, of course, completely untenable; as if an entire nation's press could be bought off.

Imaginary as Untermyer's interpretation may be, it does not disclose how the Conference fared. To judge from one of the on-the-scene-reports,[10] the gathering did not fare so well. For example, most Jewish organizations which had up to now been active in the boycott, failed to be represented; nor, with the exception of Britain's Walter Citrine, was labor truly represented. Furthermore, those organizations which did participate acted perfunctorily, not enthusiastically.

Moreover, at about the time this unimpressive Conference was taking place, Germany began making an economic comeback. Partly this was due to its rearmament program, but partly also to the economic peace which it had succeeded in making with leading European countries.

Germany achieved this peace by means of barter agreements. According to these agreements, Germany no longer had to sell its merchandise to individual merchants in the various countries. To the boycotting Jew this posed a twofold problem: on the one hand, boycott often meant sacrificing one's personal interests; and on the other hand, as a citizen of a country that had concluded barter agreements with the Nazis, the conduct of an anti-Nazi boycott would thenceforward be viewed by such a country as an unpatriotic act.

Poland affords an illustrative example of a country where Jewry was so affected. There, the Central Boycott Committee had been organized in 1933 with the tacit approval of the government, inasmuch as, at the time, Poland feared German ambitions of gaining mastery over Danzig and Upper Silesia. But in January, 1934, Poland signed a ten-year Non-Aggression Pact with Hitler, and so Polish fears appeared allayed. The pact, which called for the renewal of German-Polish trade, stipulated the cessation of boycott interference as a precondition. This was agreed to by the Poles, and gradually, Poland's Boycott Committee fell into government disfavor. However, Joseph Pilsudski, Poland's benevolent marshal and statesman, who had proclaimed an independent Polish republic in 1918, with himself as Chief of State, kept the Committee alive until his death in May of 1935. But a month later, it was no more.[11]

19

Renewed Boycott Unity Quest

On March 17, 1935, significant administrative changes took place within the American Jewish Congress, the most notable being the reelection, after a lapse of six years, of Stephen Wise to the presidency. Dr. Wise, who was reelected at a Congress convention that met in Philadelphia, was cheered by some 600 delegates when he declared in his acceptance speech that:

> American Jews as represented in the American Jewish Congress will not compromise with Hitlerism, but will go forward and fight it until Hitlerism is banished from the face of the earth.
> If a few German bankers send us word that maybe they can get a few more Jewish lawyers and a few more Jewish doctors admitted into the professions in Germany provided we end the boycott, I say no-no-no.
> I will not assent to this betrayal of civilization by the Jews of America. We do not fight for the Jews alone. Thank God that in this time of unprecedented crisis we Jews will battle always for freedom, justice and civilization.[1]

Representing the Boycott Committee, Dr. Tenenbaum read a report which said in part:

> The bitter truth is that there is not enough of the Jewish boycott, and were the 16,000,000 Jews scattered throughout the world, where lie the nerve centers of commerce, really boycotting, there could have been an end to Hitlerism after the first anniversary and we would have no need to speak of boycott after the second anniversary.[2]

After hearing Dr. Tenenbaum's report, the convention voted to continue to enlarge the boycott and adopted a resolution pledging its cooperation with all agencies conducting it.

Almost a month later, the NSANL, under the joint auspices of the AFL, conducted what probably was its grandest and most imposing rally of the year. It took place on the night of April 10 at the New York Hippodrome, where "a capacity mass meeting" was presented a resolution drawn up by Samuel Untermyer, calling upon the League of Nations to apply economic sanctions against Germany. Such a measure, the resolution pointed out, was stipulated in the covenant of the world organization and should be applied to prevent the outbreak of war. It was the second time in two years that Untermyer made what turned out to be a vain, albeit dramatic, attempt to impel the League of Nations to act on Nazi Germany's persecution of Jews and other minorities. Also, in line with some of his previous extravagant prognostications, Untermyer could not resist the temptation to predict that a boycott invoked by the League of Nations would end "within three months" the German war threat.

Actually, Untermyer did not attend the mass meeting, having been ordered by his physicians to remain home because of illness. In his place, the meeting was chaired by George Gordon Battle, New York lawyer, liberal, and one of the gentile members of the League's Board of Directors. He proclaimed the text of the Untermyer resolution, which read as follows:

> Whereas the attitude of the present German Government and its consistent violation of its solemn contract obligations contained in the Covenant of the League of Nations and its adoption of measures that steadily increase the probabilities of and incite to a catastrophic war in the near future;
>
> And whereas the Covenant of the League of Nations authorizes it to employ "Economic Sanctions," which is another phrase for a boycott to curb the war-like tendencies of governments;
>
> Now therefore be it resolved that this meeting of liberty-loving, peace-loving Americans, assembled under the joint auspices of the American Federation of Labor and the Non-Sectarian Anti-Nazi League to Champion Human Rights, irrespective of race or creed, supported by Labor and other organizations of other countries that are now actively engaged in the boycott of all German merchandise, calls upon the League of Nations and the members thereof, as the most effective weapon against war, to now enforce such "economic sanctions," in the form of the recommendations of a world boycott against the purchase by their respective citizens and residents, of German merchandise and the use of the German services, such boycott to be continued until the Government of Germany shall have

given binding guarantees to preserve the peace of the world and to restore to its racial, religious, industrial and religious minorities those rights of which it has deprived them.³

On May 16, a testimonial dinner was tendered at New York's Hotel Commodore to Bernard Deutsch upon his retirement from the presidency of the American Jewish Congress. Stephen Wise, Louis Lipsky, as well as the outgoing A.J.C. president, took the occasion to make an impassioned plea to the American people to join in an organized, nationwide anti-Nazi boycott. They also urgently requested the League of Nations to apply economic sanctions against Hitler Germany, so as to isolate it, and thus prevent a second world conflagration. The top Congress leaders emphasized that theirs was not a partisan appeal on behalf of Germany's Jews, as these were doomed whether there was peace or war, so long as Nazism remained entrenched in the "Vaterland."

In addition, Lipsky expressed his disappointment at the nations of the world which, after denouncing Hitler's violations of the Versailles Treaty, had failed "to speak also for an outraged civilization protesting against the lawlessness of the leaders of the German government."⁴ The Congress vice-president also made the following pronouncement:

> The American Jewish Congress continues its efforts to secure justice for Jews in all lands in which their rights are being denied. . . . It will align itself with all liberal forces in their battle with the destructive influences of the Nazi government. It looks forward to the time when the League of Nations will invoke the use of economic weapons against all nations that seek to achieve their own ends through planning the destruction of those who do not sympathize with their ambitions.⁵

The slackening pace of the boycott, particularly the heavy blow administered by its dissolution in Poland, stimulated, in July and August, a renewed attempt at boycott unity between the League and the Congress. However, this time the Congress' leading officers did not take charge of the deliberations. These were left entirely up to Dr. Tenenbaum, who initiated them of his own accord.

The Boycott Committee assented to taking this step at the end of June, at a meeting in which it was agreed that the boycott in America was not being intensified in proportion to the worsening conditions in Germany. It was also agreed that the two major boycotting organizations were falling short of their goal because of a lack of coordinated action.

As the first move toward the direction of coordination, the Boycott Committee decided that a letter be sent to Mr. Untermyer, communicating its desire to reach a mode of cooperation with the League.

The letter, dispatched by Dr. Tenenbaum on July 2, called Untermyer's attention to the dissolution of Poland's Boycott Committee and warned that, as a result, the burden of boycotting now more than ever fell on the shoulders of American sympathizers:

> The American market is at present flooded with German goods, more than ever since the inception of the boycott. Dr. Schacht is fighting the boycott with tremendous financial resources at his command. It is to be feared that other European countries may follow the example set by Poland and if those carrying on the boycott in America will not double their efforts, the whole boycott movement may fall to pieces.
>
> It is greatly to be deplored that after two years of intensive boycott work, the country at large, outside of New York, is totally disorganized. I personally have felt from the outset that we cannot afford to split our forces, especially in view of the extensive resources of the German government and the lukewarm response of the non-Jewish population of the United States.[6]

Dr. Tenenbaum concluded with the opinion that a budget of $100,000 a year was necessary in order to prosecute the boycott successfully, and that such a sum could be raised through a united effort. Untermyer received the letter from Harriman with a critical analysis attached. It stated that Tenenbaum's evaluation of the boycott was "unduly pessimistic" and concluded with the following suspicious observation:

> On the whole I believe that this letter is largely prompted by the fact that the Congress boycott has petered out and that they are desperately in need of funds and that they would like to hang on to another organization in order to carry it on. I may be mistaken in these premises, but this is the situation as I see it.[7]

A news release concerning Tenenbaum's letter to Untermyer was sent out by the Congress' publicity department and appeared in the July 4 edition of the New York Yiddish daily, the *Morning Journal*. Harriman, distrustful as ever, apprized his chief of this development, commenting as follows:

> The whole purpose appears to be an attempt to drive us into an untenable position by announcing the Congress' desire to cooperate, leaving the onus, in the event that this plan falls through, upon us. We have tried to get in touch with Dr. Tenenbaum to put our position before him and are continuing to do so.[8]

Lastly, on July 17, Harriman sent Untermyer an outline of a proposed plan for coordinating the League's boycott work with that of the Congress. It stipulated the following conditions:

That the Congress turn over to the Non-Sectarian Anti-Nazi League their boycott work; That while the Congress will preach boycott, they will not solicit funds for this purpose, leaving this to our organization; That they announce that they are turning over the boycott work to us because our organization is concerned solely with that effort, and they believe that our structure is such as to make our appeals to all sects of the community stronger than those of merely one definitely sectarian group. That the Congress be represented on our Board by one or more of their members to prove their enlistment under our banner; That other organizations be approached with the proposal that they turn over their boycott activities to our organization.[9]

Harriman's terms were tantamount to asking the Boycott Committee to cooperate in its own disintegration. Untermyer, in a scornful July 20 reply, pointed this out to his somewhat naive secretary:

Referring to your letter of the 17th inst.,—I don't know why you are always deprecating and criticizing what other people do. If you make no move, this is no reason they should not . . .

It would be gratifying to find you doing something yourself, instead of criticizing everything that is being done.

Your proposed letter to Dr. Tenenbaum is not satisfactory. There was no idea of the Congress turning over the entire Boycott work, nor could we expect any such complete surrender as you are suggesting.

I am enclosing the form of arrangement that I would approve. You may take this as a basis and reach some agreement with Dr. Tenenbaum, if possible, before I sail on Tuesday.[10]

Untermyer's file does not contain this "form of arrangement." In any event, on July 26, Harriman prepared a report for his chief, part of which read:

I contacted Dr. Tenenbaum and suggested that he appoint a committee to meet a committee of ours. Our committee gentlemen feel, however, that it would be better that before such a meeting takes place, that Dr. Tenenbaum set forth in writing his proposals regarding the coordination of our work in a definite form.[11]

That day, Harriman sent Dr. Tenenbaum a letter to this effect. The Boycott Committee chairman replied on the thirty-first:

I am glad to have the opportunity given to me by your letter of July 26th to reaffirm the great interests which the Boycott Committee of the American Jewish Congress has in effecting a united boycott front against the products and services of Nazi Germany.

In this connection, I am taking the liberty of reiterating the proposals of the American Jewish Congress as to the way in which this united front may best be effected. These suggestions, as you are aware, have already been made verbally to Mr. Untermyer and to other members of your organization.

In order to widen the boycott front and to draw in those elements which have recently been moved to favor boycott of Nazi Germany as the result of the most recent developments in that country affecting Jews, Catholics and other minority opinion, we propose:

1. The organization of a coordinated boycott league to be known as the American League for Boycott. Such league to be comprised of the American Jewish Congress, the Non-Sectarian Anti-Nazi League, the Jewish Labor Committee, and other national organizations now engaged in boycott activity, or interested in promoting such activity.
2. It is understood that the boycott activities shall be directed through this organization with the understanding that each member group of this League shall extend to the League the cooperation of this organization.
3. The machinery for the conducting of the boycott and the raising of funds to finance this work shall be entrusted to a committee representative of all the member groups in the American League for Boycott.
4. As soon as the American League for Boycott shall have been established there shall be called a large conference or convention whose principal purpose shall be to enlist the cooperation of the widest possible public in pursuing the boycott.

May I request the appointment of a committee by your organization to meet with a committee of the American Jewish Congress for discussion of these proposals and a clarification of them, and the proposals made by Mr. Untermyer in his letter of July 22, 1935.[12]

We have no record of the discussions that followed.[13] However, their highlights are preserved in a report which Harriman submitted to Untermyer on August 13:

You will recall that our Executive Committee suggested that Dr. Tenenbaum of the American Jewish Congress, put before us his proposals regarding the coordination of the work of our organization and that of the American Jewish Congress.

We approached Dr. Tenenbaum in this connection and received from him a letter, copy of which is enclosed.

On receipt of this letter and after a discussion with Messrs. Louis Meyers, Dr. B. Dubovsky and J. George Fredman, we arranged to meet the committee of the American Jewish Congress for the purpose of discussing their and our proposals.

This meeting was held yesterday afternoon at the office of the American Jewish Congress. Dr. Tenenbaum is away and Dr. Jacob Chaitkin represented the American Jewish Congress as its principal spokesman, assisted by Messrs. Tygel, Carmel, Posnansky and Miss Schultz, Acting-Secretary of the Congress. Messrs. Meyers, Dubovsky, Fredman and I represented our organization.

The interview did not take us much further. The main proposal of the Congress seems to be a supervisory group under a new name, such as, for example, "The American Boycott League." Such group to obtain the affiliation of all groups interested in boycott work, including our organization. The individual groups would, for the moment, be left as they are, but the controlling body would have the right to allocate the work to each individual group or discontinue the work of any group, as they saw fit.

The practical results would be that we would lose our identity as we are the only group mentioned which is devoted entirely or even mainly to boycott activities. The other groups, such as the American Jewish Congress, the Jewish Labor Committee, the I.O.B.A.[14] etc., all have other special activities to which they devote time and propaganda. Also, we would be at the mercy of all groups, for each organization would be represented on this plenary committee by a maximum of 5–6 members and it is easy to foresee that on any question of policy, we could be overridden by a majority vote.

Further, as at present projected, the controlling body would be definitely of a Jewish character, our group being the only one with a non-sectarian color. Therefore such a coordination would mean a negation of all that you have fought for so long and valiantly, a swing of the boycott back into Jewish hands and a stressing of the Jewish angle of the boycott, giving only lip-service to the plight of all other oppressed German religious, political and industrial minorities, although it was suggested, that other than Jews be approached with the idea of their affiliation.

The whole project is very vague and it hardly seemed, from the character of the delegates present, that they were really authorized to present any definite proposition.

The question of leadership was barely touched on and it seemed as if the gentlemen representing the Congress were anxious to leave this important question, definitely up in the air.

I will, naturally, report any further developments but, I believe, that I am expressing the opinion of our Committee when I say that it seems extremely doubtful that anything may come out of the negotiations as at present outlined by the American Jewish Congress.[15]

Harriman was right, as once again negotiations between the Congress and the League proved to be an exercise in futility.

20

The Birth of the Joint Boycott Council

The Jewish Labor Committee

i.

The last two decades of the nineteenth century and the first two decades of the twentieth, years which witnessed the zenith of Jewish mass immigration into the United States from Eastern Europe, also gave rise to an impressive number of Jewish labor unions that grew out of the ranks of a swelling Jewish labor force. Generally, the Jewish workers and their Jewish leaders, though trying to preserve their ethnic origin and socialist outlook, did not set themselves apart from the burgeoning American labor movement. Thus, they affiliated themselves with such central American labor bodies as the Knights of Labor and the American Federation of Labor. By the eve of the outbreak of World War I, the ever-expanding Jewish labor movement included such organizations as the United Hebrew Trades, the Workmen's Circle, the International Ladies' Garment Workers' Union, the Amalgamated Clothing Workers of America, the Jewish Socialist Farband, the Jewish National Workers' Alliance (Poale Zion), and the Forverts Association. All told, these organizations represented several hundred thousand Jewish workers.

In the eyes of organized labor, the rise of Hitlerism, with its destruction of German trade unionism, was viewed as a grave threat to the labor movement as a whole. Jewish labor, however, by virtue of the Fuehrer's total war against the Jewish people, saw in Hitlerism a double threat. To help combat it, a thousand delegates, representing the Jewish labor groups listed above, met at a special conference in New York City on February 25, 1934, and established a new Jewish-American defense organization named the Jewish Labor Committee (JLC).

From its inception, the JLC had the strong backing of the AFL, with whose help it initiated its anti-Nazi program. A notable case in point is the Labor Chest Fund, an endowment established by and directed under AFL auspices in support of the union victims of the Hitler-Mussolini dictatorships. After its founding in 1935, the CIO,[1] just as staunch a defender of human and labor rights, likewise supported the anti-Nazi activities of JLC.

The raison d'etre of the Labor Committee is clearly expressed in Part II of its constitution: "To give aid to Jewish and non-Jewish labor institutions overseas; provide succor to victims of oppression and persecution and to combat anti-Semitism and racial and religious intolerance abroad and in the United States."[2] In keeping with this clause, the JLC sought to convey to both Jewish and Gentile Americans the obvious point that Nazism was the archenemy of mankind, particularly of the Jew, socialist, and liberal. To this end, in addition to supporting the Labor Chest, the JLC was also instrumental in persuading the AFL, in 1936, to organize a Committee for the Victims of Nazism and Fascism.

As its first major activity, the Jewish Labor Committee embarked on an all-out drive for the boycott of Nazi goods. It conducted this mainly in union shops, hurting the Germans most in the area of machinery. Otherwise, its conduct of the boycott followed the course of the other boycotting organizations. We herewith cite a letter typical of many other communications sent by the JLC leadership to owners of concerns dealing, or suspected of dealing, in Nazi-made goods:

August 31st 1934

May Glove Company
204 Fourth Avenue
New York, N.Y.

Gentlemen:

Our office sent you a letter on August 16th, asking you to furnish us with (a) definite information whether your concerns manufactures kid gloves of German origin.

Our Committee, which represents bonafide Labor, affiliated with the American Federation of Labor is vitally interested in an effective boycott of German goods.

We have not received as yet any reply from you. Several other manufacturers of gloves responded to our inquiry and cooperated with us fully in the boycott movement.

We wonder what can be the reason for your silence. We expect a definite reply from you to our inquiry within a week, not later. If your concern will still abstain from replying to us, we shall be compelled to take all the necessary steps within our reach, in the matter of the boycott of German goods.

We are of the opinion that your concern, as well as others, has to be interested in boycotting goods of the Hitler Germany, which persecutes everyone and everything, which strives to real democracy.

Expecting your reply, we remain,

          Very truly yours

          Jewish Labor Committee
          B. C. Vladeck, Chairman
          B. Gebiner, Executive Secretary[3]

To the Yiddish-speaking labor masses, Baruch Charney Vladeck was one of America's most famous figures. He was born in Russia into a Hassidic family named Charney; but like many a Jewish lad of the East European ghetto, Vladeck left the traditional-religious path to join the Socialist Bund, a Yiddishist-secularist workers' party which was on the Tsar's long list of subversive organizations. He assumed the name "Vladeck" to elude his sovereign's secret police, whose displeasure he had aroused by his "revolutionary" activities. In 1908, upon deciding that Russia was too dangerous a land in which to foster his ideals, Vladeck left for America.

America enabled the "young Lassalle," as Vladeck had come to be called in socialist circles, to develop and fully express his great talents. He was an accomplished orator, and in time, evinced a brilliant faculty for belles-lettres, journalism, and organization. Eventually, he became managing editor of the *Jewish Daily Forward,* a Yiddish paper. His versatility also included prominence in the civic affairs of New York City, especially in the area of housing.

It was under Vladeck's inspiring leadership that the idea of forming a Jewish Labor Committee materialized. Its official inception in the winter of 1934 came after Vladeck had formed a provisional Jewish Labor Committee the previous fall to represent the Jewish worker in the fight against Nazism. An affiliated organization of the AFL representing nearly 400,000 members, JLC proved a mighty addition to America's family of Jewish defense organizations. It was to Vladeck, therefore, that Dr. Tenenbaum was now to turn in a new attempt at effecting a united anti-Nazi boycott front.

ii.

As a distinct body within the American Jewish Congress, the Boycott Committee was given considerable freedom in determining and conducting its business. Officially, however, decision-making rested finally with the parent organization. For as we have already observed, the Congress, often in the person of Dr. Wise, was consulted by the Boycott Committee regarding major issues. Of course, the action Dr. Tenenbaum was now contemplating constituted a major undertaking, ultimately requiring, therefore, Congress approval. However, the sure chance of obtaining this was complicated by the fact that conflicting, and, at times, antagonistic, views had strained A.J.C.-JLC relations. But as we shall presently see, on July 31, the day Dr. Tenenbaum addressed himself to Vladeck, he had good grounds for expecting Congress support in case his Boycott Committee reached an agreement with the Labor Committee.

iii.

In theory, the American Jewish Congress was supposed to be fully representative of all U.S. Jews. But only during World War I, when the movement for the creation of an American Jewish Congress was in its formative stage, had this really been the case, more or less.

The American Jewish Congress movement got under way at the Zionist Conference of August, 1914, where it was proposed to convene a "Congress" which would embrace the non-Zionist as well as the Zionist American Jew. The proposal, which divided Conference opinion, was not resolved until the following year, when the contra-Congress elements yielded to its proponents. But the task remained, as yet, only half-finished because the projected American Jewish Congress still did not embody the non-Zionist organizations, principally the American Jewish Committee and the various labor groups.

The Committee viewed with alarm the prospect of being a co-member in an organization with a Zionist majority. It rightly feared that in such a situation the Zionists would be in a position to push through resolutions and decisions diametrically opposed to its thinking. The Committee also opposed a Jewish Congress, afraid lest the name "Congress" imply that Jews constituted a separate nation with distinct national interests. Mention has already been made (pp. 92–96) that the Committee opposed the World Jewish Congress movement on these grounds.

In lieu of the word "Congress," the Committee urged the use of the word "Conference," as the latter usually connotes an ad hoc setup; that is to say, the Committee wanted the proposed gathering to deal solely with the postwar problems of Jewish rights, and to be dissolved after these had been resolved, increasing thereby its chances of perpetuity.

The second major non-Zionist organization which entered this controversy was the National Workmen's Committee on Jewish Rights in the Countries at War and in Rumania. It was formed at a September, 1914, convention representing the various labor groups[4] which met to voice their concern over the danger to East European Jewry—particularly in Rumania—as a result of the outbreak of the World War. At the time, as in the case of the American Jewish Committee, a majority opposed the Congress plan out of fear of being overwhelmed by a Zionist plurality. However, mounting Jewish suffering in Europe and a Zionist propaganda barrage at home, caused the Workmen's Committee to reexamine and thereupon alter its position. For it had become convinced that only through a united Jewish American stand would the chance of obtaining Jewish minority rights in Europe be enhanced. This made it easier for the Zionist faction of the Workmen's Committee to drive through a pro-Congress vote at the organization's next conference in September, 1915.

General agreement was finally reached along the following lines: The name "Congress" would be approved, but the organization would have to be dissolved as soon as its mission had been fulfilled. Three-quarters of its members were to be chosen directly through general elections and the remaining quarter was to be designated by organizational appointment.

Elections were held in 1917, with 335,000 Jews casting their votes. The balloting resulted in the election of 300 representatives. These were joined by 100 delegates appointed by thirty national Jewish organizations.

The opening session took place in December, 1918. At its close, nine delegates were selected to express the Congress' demands at the Paris Peace Conference which would take place the following month. In 1920, the Congress convened again to hear the report of its Paris delegation. Soon thereafter, though, because most delegates refused to view it as other than an ad hoc organization, the Congress was summarily dissolved.

However, the Congress' Zionist delegates refused to accept the demise of this organization. So while the non-Zionist delegates prepared to leave the gathering, the Zionists began drawing up plans to set up a permanent Congress. Their purpose was not realized, however, until 1922, when a new American Jewish Congress conference was convened in Philadelphia.

Much had changed by now, however. The Workmen's Committee, the one group which really did turn out to be an ad hoc assemblage, was already defunct. Also, the unequivocally pro-Zionist outlook of the new Congress was not at all in agreement with the non-Zionist view of B'nai B'rith and American Jewish Committee representatives. And since these no longer felt it necessary to discard the ideologies of their organizations in behalf of the European and Palestinian Jewish communities, they refused to be a part of the reorganized Congress. Without the B'nai B'rith, the American Jewish Committee, and most of the Jewish labor organizations, it could not be said that the reconstituted Congress was a truly representative body of all American Jews.

A.J.C.-JLC Relations

The argument over the issue of genuine organizational representation was one of the cardinal reasons why the JLC had rejected Congress offers to become one of its affiliates. A document regarding this issue has been preserved. It renders the Labor Committee's position with regard to this issue, having been drawn up by Mr. Vladeck on December 12, 1934, who addressed himself to Mr. Deutsch as follows:

> At the last meeting of the Executive Committee of the Jewish Labor Committee, your letter of November 30th was submitted for consideration and action. After a lengthy discussion, it was decided not to accept your invitation and not to negotiate with the American Jewish Congress about participation in the projected elections. In informing you of this decision, I take the liberty to recapitulate briefly the reasons cited for this action during the discussion.
>
> 1) The Jewish Labor Committee feels that the American Jewish Congress has not established the necessity for its existence. It has not offered any program in regard to the Jewish problem that has not already been offered by one or the other of existing Jewish organizations.
>
> 2) In regard to the situation in Germany, the American Jewish Congress has stressed the fight against Hitlerism as a purely Jewish issue. The Jewish Labor Committee considers the Jewish plight in Germany as only one angle of Fascism and is of the opinion that only by conducting our campaign as a part of a general labor campaign against Fascism, can we succeed.
>
> 3) The slogan of democratic elections does not impress us much. First of all there is no possibility of a real democratic election under circumstances under which it is impossible to register and control the voters. Any small group bent on victory can get a large vote by means

which are impossible in a regular political election. Besides the American Jewish Congress has for several years now assumed to be speaking for the whole Jewish community without practically having been elected by anybody. This makes it possible for some of us to think that the slogan of democratic elections is nothing but a political move on the part of some leaders of the Congress who feel that the Congress has been compromised and needs new sanction. That some aspects of the activities of the Congress are purely political and are motivated not by a desire to serve the Jewish people but by a desire to clinch leadership in Jewish life, is obvious to many impartial observers. The Jewish Labor Committee is composed of organizations managed along strictly democratic lines.

Please do not interpret the foregoing as an indication that the Jewish Labor Committee is unwilling to cooperate with other Jewish bodies. Just the contrary. We are more than even convinced that in matters of real importance there should be cooperation between all Jewish agencies and for the ten months of our existence we have proven our willingness to cooperate and our desire to limit ourselves to the sphere of activity which we have originally undertaken, claiming to represent nobody else but our constituents.[5]

But several weeks later, A.J.C.-JLC relations reached the nadir of mutual distrust and discord, after Vladeck wrote an article in the *Forward,* bitterly denouncing the Congress. His scathing attack so infuriated Wise that he sought to damage Vladeck's reputation with LaGuardia. In a "Personal and Confidential" communication to the New York mayor, dated January 4, 1935, Dr. Wise wrote:

I feel you ought to know that a day or two ago, Vladeck in the "Forwards" not only wrote a ten column article against the American Jewish Congress of which I am Honorary President and Deutsch the President, but that his article is filthy and a foul attack upon all of us personally. He used terms which I think render him criminally liable, terms such as "racketeering." I mention this to you because you know I was ready to meet with him and you to talk things over. Now I cannot. It will be a very great hurt to the work of the Congress which means everything to me, that he who has written about us as no man has, should be singled out for honor at your hands, whether on the Charter Board or anything else. Let us talk it over.[6]

Vladeck's opposition to the creation of a World Jewish Congress and his being a non-Zionist set him apart from Wise on the role of Jewish nationalism. However, the present recourse to innuendo by the Labor Committee president only served to exasperate relations already strained by ideological disharmony. But as we shall presently see, events in Hitler Germany had a way of occasioning the unification of incongruous groups.

The Berlin Riots

In the summer of 1935, some two months prior to the legal despoilment of German Jewry's citizenship rights by the Nuremberg Laws, bloody anti-Jewish disorders broke out in Berlin's fashionable Kurfuerstendamm. These riots were, in all likelihood, organized in reprisal for the protests voiced by some Berlin Jews against a showing of an antisemitic film. The violence took place on July 15 and 19, and was executed by SS brutes, who, as on previous occasions, were permitted to vent their savage passions against the Jewish populace. They did not shame their past record, considering the brutal results: sadistic beatings, torn limbs, and broken heads and necks.

Decent humanity was shocked. In America, an outraged Emmanuel Celler, the noted Jewish congressman from New York, threw the House into a tumultuous debate after angrily stating:

> I am sure that Americans everywhere deplore and denounce the terrifying scenes that have occurred in Berlin in the last few days.
> The bullying, the bloody deeds and atrocities which the Hitler hoodlums and the Storm Troopers are guilty of cannot go unnoticed in this House.
> I speak not only for my own race, but for Catholics who are the latest to fall under Hitler's disfavor.
> I hereby call upon all Americans, Catholics, Protestants and Jews, to join in an economic boycott against Germany to show how this nation feels about these atrocious deeds.[7]

The congressman's forceful words touched off the question of American intervention in the affairs of other nations. It was raised several days later in the Senate when Senator William H. King of Utah introduced a resolution proposing that the Senate Foreign Relations Committee study the advisability of severing U.S.-German relations. Assailing Hitler, Senator King incisively remarked: "I regard the conduct of Hitler as brutal, cruel and barbarous. I don't want it to go on record that not a single person in this nation protested."[8]

Thereupon, Celler was asked why he had not introduced his boycott proposal in the form of a resolution. He responded that he did not consider it proper to initiate so overt an act against a "friendly" power, also adding:

> I am very much in sympathy with the spirit of Senator King's proposal. Until something else can be done, however, I feel that an economic boycott will be the most effective means of ending the deplorable conditions in Germany. Should that fail, I think it the duty of the President to protest against Nazi persecution through the customary diplomatic channels.[9]

A week later, in a similar statement, Celler called upon Cordell Hull to voice "at least a protest" to the Nazi Reich against the persecution of its Jews and Catholics. The New York congressman pointed out that the Secretary of State had ample precedent in this regard since, in the past, eminent heads of the Department of State had interceded in behalf of persecuted minorities in other lands. Celler also used this opportunity to make a more vigorous statement on the subject of the anti-Nazi boycott:

> I ask Catholics, I ask Jews, I ask Protestants everywhere to mete out some punishment to Germany. It is within our right to do so. I believe that Germany should be thoroughly boycotted. Germany is an industrial nation. She would feel, indeed, the scourge of a boycott. Not until she is deeply stirred will she come back to the sense of responsibility and cease these brutal attacks upon defenseless people of the Catholic faith and the Jewish faith.[10]

To all appearances, Germany ignored Celler's statements. However, in response to King's proposal, one of its spokesmen for the Ministry of Propaganda commented arrogantly: "Is there a heat wave in America? I'll bet some of Senator King's colleagues will be chuckling about his proposition the same as I. Tell them in America Germany doesn't feel the least bit alarmed at Senator King's threat—if it is a threat."[11]

American Jewry, however, was very much alarmed. It viewed the renewed terror in Germany with great anxiety and anger. Propelled by the A.J.C.-JLC, close to 2,000 Jewish organizations, representative of all sections and factions in Jewish communal life in America, convened on July 21 in a Joint Emergency Conference to arouse public opinion against the latest outbreak in Germany.

The Joint Conference adopted a program of action designed to bring about "the organized resistance of all American citizens, regardless of faith or race, to the destruction of the foundations of democratic civilization by the present regime in Germany."[12] The addresses of the speakers and the resolutions[13] called for the cooperation of all nations, particularly the United States, in making known to the Hitler government the abhorrence of civilized mankind for the brutal policy of persecution of Jews and other religious groups, workmen, and all minority opinion in Germany.

Further, the Conference urged the League of Nations to invoke economic sanctions against Nazi Germany, and called on the U.S. government to revoke its commercial treaties with the Hitler government. It also urged the U.S. government to refuse to renew these treaties as long as the Nazi regime continued its policy of persecution. In addition, the American public at large was urged to support a policy of isolating Germany through the boycott as "a most effective weapon in combatting the Hitler menace . . . as an expression of the condemnation of the American people of the revolting practices of the Hitler Government and as a means of liberating the German people from oppression."[14] Finally, all organizations directing the boycott were called upon to present "a consolidated front" and take "immediate steps" to achieve it.

This resolution was in keeping with one of the chief purposes of the Conference, which was to show the world a united front. The American Jewish Congress and the Jewish Labor Committee had such unity in mind and hoped that their quick joint action would produce a similar response from other Jewish groups. Unfortunately, though, a tiny, undisciplined, and irresponsible element, instigated and led by Communists and Revisionists, disrupted the proceedings by yelling and jeering at some of their political opponents who happened to be among the scheduled speakers.[15] Fistfights broke out as a result, depriving the Conference of its dignity. The emergency session was thus turned into a pageant of disunity rather than a demonstration characterized by a solidly united Jewish front.

Vladeck, one of the chief organizers of the extraordinary session, and Tenenbaum, as a leading Congress official, also attended it. Of course, both pressed vigorously for the adoption of the boycott. However, Vladeck was particularly outspoken, urging unremitting battle against Fascism and Hitlerism, the formation of a united Jewish front, and condemning those who broke it "whether these be Federation of Labor officials sailing on German boats, or Palestine representatives seeking to make business arrangements with the Hitler Government."[16]

BC-JLC Negotiations

i.

It was as a result of this new spirit of A.J.C.-JLC unity, rather than the mere fruitlessness of his negotiations with the Untermyer organization, that Tenenbaum addressed himself to Vladeck on July 31. His letter pressed for the union that the JLC president had advocated so passionately at the Joint Emergency Conference (p. 184), which he helped bring about:

> Referring to our conversation, we feel that the time has come to unite forces for the intensification of the boycott movement in America.
> My two years' experience with boycott work has impressed me with the fact that the masses are enthusiastically for the boycott and ready to make every sacrifice towards its success. There is no difficulty in marshalling great forces and material support for the boycott. The great difficulty which has made the boycott look like a rather feeble attempt in comparison with the great aim before us, lies in the lack of determined leadership to see the boycott through at all costs and the fact that there are several agencies, each one pulling in a different direction with no provision for cooperation with each other.
> It is my strong conviction, based on experience, that we could have, with a little more effort, a boycott organization second to none, which could serve as a model and an inspiration for other countries.
> It is with this in view that I am appealing to you to make a start in the right direction. Specifically, I propose that the Boycott Committee of the American Jewish Congress and a Committee of your organization should come together to work out a plan for cooperation and joint action.
> I am convinced that having such a nucleus of a united boycott front other organizations will join forces so that in time there may be formed one agency for boycott throughout the United States.[17]

Vladeck's reply came on August 7:

> At last night's meeting of the Executive Committee of the Jewish Labor Committee, we took up for action your letter of July 31st, suggesting a Joint Committee on the Boycott. The Committee was in agreement with this suggestion and the Action Committee has been instructed to communicate with you for the purpose of carrying it out.[18]

But Vladeck and his organization proved slow in acting upon Tenenbaum's proposal, whereupon, on November 7, the Boycott Committee chairman dispatched still another letter to his Jewish Labor Committee counterpart:

> It is nearly four months since we have started negotiations on the possibility of a united boycott front.
> I am sure that your decision taken a few months ago still stands and that your organization as well as mine are most anxious to consummate such a union of forces.

Unfortunately, there has been a delay of months which has caused neglect in capitalizing on the sentiment of the masses and it is only natural that the initial enthusiasm may be cooling off to the detriment of the boycott possibilities which a united front would hope to achieve. As you know, I approach this whole project in an utterly unselfish and patriotic spirit, but there may be people who will see in this a political motive, an impression which I am most anxious to avoid.

I personally know how busy you have been in the last few weeks and realize only too well that extended activities have made it impossible for you to act with your usual speed. However, it seems to me it is only a matter of a meeting for an hour or so, and everything could be settled to the satisfaction of everybody. Perhaps, I should be more explicit and tell you quite frankly that some of our people are beginning to lose patience with this constant delay.

I appeal to you, therefore, personally to call the meeting at your earliest convenience so that the matter may be settled once and for all.[19]

Tenenbaum and his "people" were "beginning to lose patience," indeed, as about two months had passed since the Jewish Congress and Labor Committee had stated that a united front of the two bodies had been effectuated. But aside from a "Declaration of the Jewish Labor Committee and American Jewish Congress Concerning a United Boycott Action," there was little else to indicate that this was so in fact:

From day to day, it is becoming more and more clear that the boycott is one of the strongest weapons which the Jewish and progressive world can employ against Hitler and his regime. Very often the Nazi leaders themselves are forced to admit that the boycott hinders them in the execution of their program. It is, therefore, necessary, now more than ever before, that organizations which carry on in a constructive way the boycott against Germany, should coordinate their work and strengthen and spread it. In connection with this, we have made an agreement to conduct unitedly the work of the boycott and we shall call upon all our affiliated organizations to join this united action.[20]

It now remained to be seen if the nerve-racking struggle would actually bear fruit.

ii.

In the weeks thereafter, though, talks between the two boycotting organizations began in earnest. The Governing Council of the American Jewish Congress appointed a committee of three, the Honorable Carl

Sherman, Dr. Samuel Margoshes, and Dr. Joseph Tenenbaum, to represent it in the deliberations. The record does not state who, besides B. C. Vladeck, represented the Jewish Labor Committee.

Furthermore, it is not known if the JLC set forth any conditions for entering into a boycott union with the American Jewish Congress. As far as can be ascertained from archival sources, the Labor Committee simply wanted the Congress to let it know what conditions—if any—it had for the consummation of the contemplated union. In reply, the Congress trio informed the Labor Committee that its organizations did have some conditions, outlining them as follows:

1) A joint call should be issued to the organizations and to the public at large for the widest possible participation in picketing of stores which continue to sell German merchandise.

2) A circular letter should be sent out to the constituencies of the Congress and the Labor unions as well as women committee branches out of town, with a program of cooperative or joint efforts to strengthen the boycott in their respective localities, including picketing, organization of vigilance committees, joint conferences, etc.

3) The calling of the women's organizations which you suggested is undoubtedly the right step and we welcome this suggestion. We should, however, meet as soon as possible to decide on the means of implementation of this resolution.

4) I still believe that a national conference of our joint organizations with the participation of representatives of the American Federation of Labor to consider the program of boycott work on a national scope would be most helpful and should not be unduly delayed.

5) A call issued to the unions to cease work in shops and concerns where German raw material, half finished goods or machinery are being employed would be of inestimable value.

6) There are many other items which I think could be tackled by a Joint Committee, or deemed best by your committee, in cooperation with the Central Labor Trades Council. One of them is an appeal to the longshoremen to cease unloading German goods. I know this thing is not easy, still it seems to me worthwhile considering.

7) I further propose that a call should be issued to other national organizations to join forces with us—our two organizations serving as the nucleus of attraction. The Independent Order Brith Abraham and the Women's Division of the American Jewish Congress have recently summoned all its constituencies to designate a contingent of volunteers for picketing.

8) Inasmuch as we are mutually interested in having all labor groups share in the boycott work—with exception of these groups whose affiliation, as we have agreed, are undesirable on account of their known tactics and partisan motives—it is essential that we invite the Jewish Labor Bloc[21] to join as a unit in the united boycott front.

9) I have enumerated those activities which could be accomplished without a joint office and without great cost. The expenses accruing even from those activities will be shared by all organizations jointly at a proportion to be agreed upon.[22]

These conditions were set forth by the Congress on January 24, 1936, at a special meeting with the Labor Committee. However, they were not altogether acceptable to the JLC, disagreement centering chiefly around items 7–8.

As articulated by Vladeck, the JLC contended that it would be unfair to include the IOBA (Independent Order Brith Abraham)[23] and the Jewish Labor Bloc as equal partners in any agreement regarding the proposed joint boycott agency. As he understood it, only such organizations as were "engaged in the boycott work per se could be parties to the agreement."[24] To comply, therefore, with the Congress request that it, its Labor Bloc, and the IOBA be granted separate representation in the proposed boycott agency, was tantamount to entering into agreement with the whole plus some of its parts.

Subsequently, the Labor Bloc withdrew its demand for co-partnership, with the understanding that it was to be granted representational rights by the American Jewish Congress in the new boycott body. The IOBA followed suit with a similar request.

Item 6, though not objectionable in principle, was objected to, nevertheless, as a practical measure "on the ground that it would be impossible for the unions, in view of their present difficulties, to call upon the longshoremen to cease unloading German goods."[25]

Just what the Congress delegates had to say with regard to this is not known. They probably took it at face value, expecting the matter to be resolved in due course. In view of their good faith in the organization with which they were meeting to achieve union, the issue from a practical standpoint was too trifling to impair such union. The much-sought-after union was achieved at the termination of the meeting. The new resultant organization was named the Joint Boycott Council.[26]

Finally, so serious a step as union between the American Jewish Congress and another organization had also to meet with the approval of Dr. Wise, especially where a Vladeck was concerned. For the Congress president had not forgotten the blistering attack of a year before against him, his close co-workers, and his organization by Mr. Vladeck. And as far as we can tell, Dr. Wise avoided coming into personal contact with Vladeck. However, during the latter's negotiations with Dr. Tenenbaum, Rabbi Wise examined at least part of the BC-JLC correspondence. Upon one such an occasion, Rabbi Wise reacted to Tenenbaum as follows:

"They will use us, but believe me, no good will come from any project which is under the leadership of one as bitterly opposed to the Congress and as hostile to nationalism as is Vladeck."[27]

Tenenbaum, at any rate, was not dismayed, for he was not necessarily seeking Wise's blessings. His interest in the boycott was so intense that it transcended the basic divisive points between the A.J.C.-JLC and their presidents. And as long as Wise did not block his efforts at union between his Boycott Committee and that of the JLC, Tenenbaum was free to try to consummate it. Thanks to his assiduity, his labors bore fruit.

21

Last Major Boycott Unity Quest

Judging from a February 23, 1936, statement released by the NSANL on the occasion of the A.J.C.-JLC merger, the Untermyer organization—as might very well have been expected—was not delighted to learn of the birth of the Joint Boycott Council. In the eyes of the League, JBC was but a "Jewish" child of parent organizations that were "Jewish in aim and name"; and as such, it felt that its creation would have a deleterious, rather than a salutary, effect upon the American boycott movement. To the League's way of thinking, the amalgamation of two separate "Jewish" boycott groups would at best confuse the masses, and, therefore, weaken, not strengthen, the boycott movement. So, for example, argued the *American Israelite* of Cincinnati, Ohio, perhaps, one of several Anglo-Jewish periodicals representative of such thinking. Part of its inquiry, addressed to the JBC on December 3, 1936, read: "Is there any reason why the Congress cannot or should not regard the League as the organization to head-up the boycott in the thought that the boycott against Germany is more than a matter for a Jewish organization, whether it be the Congress or any other body?"[1] Hence, if Tenenbaum and Vladeck, inspired by the successful merger of their respective organizations, had entertained any immediate hopes of adding Untermyer's organization to their Boycott Council, the League's statement certainly wrecked their aspirations. For with the exception of two lesser attempts, more than a year would pass before the JBC engaged again in intense negotiations with the NSANL on the question of all-out boycott unity.

The first such attempt occurred on March 25, 1936, when Tenenbaum and Vladeck responded to a seemingly innocent inquiry by League Secretary Harriman concerning the underlying motive for the establishment of the Joint Boycott Council. Their reply, while not really revealing anything new, did express a strong desire to see the boycott movement strengthened through an effectuation of absolute boycott unity, irrespective of party affiliations. To this end, the two Boycott Council chairmen extended the League an invitation to join their newly formed body by assigning to it delegates "to help formulate plans and undertake common action."[2] Harriman was assured, moreover, that it was not the Council's aim to interfere with the activities of any other organization, "but solely to unite all the available forces for the greater effectiveness of the boycott movement in this country."[3]

With this, however, correspondence on the subject draws to a close until December of that year, when, for obscure reasons, the ice broke, finding the League and the Council once again engaged in unity talks. But, for equally obscure reasons, the archival records of both organizations are silent on the progress of these talks during their preliminary stage. Some information regarding this phase is contained, though, in the February 11, 1937, issue of the New York Yiddish daily, *Der Tog*. It appears in the form of an "Open Letter" by Dr. Benjamin Dubovsky, chairman of the League's Executive Committee. Dubovsky was granted the opportunity of replying to the following accusation made four days earlier in *Der Tog* by the English-writing columnist Dr. Samuel Margoshes (p. 29):

> While Samuel Untermyer has, no doubt, been a pillar of strength to the boycott of German-made goods and services, he has constantly and consistently retarded all efforts in the direction of a unification of all agencies engaged in the boycott movement in this country.[4]

In response to this charge, Dr. Dubovsky wrote:

> Yes, there were unsuccessful attempts to unite the boycott activities of both organizations. Conferences were held at the home of Mr. Untermyer and elsewhere; many conferences, the last one held only recently, during December, 1936, between our League and the Joint Boycott Council, of which the American Jewish Congress is a 5% partner,[5] attended all of them.
>
> At those early conferences, it was clear that our League could not become a part of the American Jewish Congress, but the boycott activities and the Boycott Committee of the American Jewish Congress could become part of our League, thus forming a united organization to conduct all boycott activities. But the representatives of the Con-

gress asked as a "compensation" for giving up their separate boycott activities—25% of all the funds collected by the united boycott appeal to be used by the Congress for its other activities.

To this "compensation" Mr. Untermyer and our committee objected, stating that all money raised for boycott activities must be spent for only such activities, and for no other.

The same problem wrecked our last conference with the Joint Boycott Council. We suggested the fusion of all groups into one; a complete united front under one leadership for the boycott. While both partners to the JBC insisted on reserving the right for their organizations to solicit funds separately on the claim that they are doing boycott work, and then allocate part of such funds to the Coordinated Boycott Committee. How these facts can be interpreted into meaning that "Mr. Untermyer has constantly" and "consistently retarded all efforts in the direction of a unification of all agencies engaged in the boycott movement in this country," needs a new Einstein to explain.[6]

The conferences described in the aforesaid continued during the next several months. The record is incomplete on this score, too, but it does indicate, however, that it was Vladeck who took the initiative this time; perhaps because both he and Tenenbaum felt that a "new man" might have better luck with this heretofore impossible task.[7]

A March 16, 1937, cabled address from Untermyer to Vladeck seems to bear this out. However, the arguments that it lists are all too familiar from the abortive experiences with the Boycott Committee:

> I have, as you know, felt from the inception of the Hitler regime, and the inauguration of the boycott by our League, that there should be but one boycott organization in existence, and we have made frequent efforts to bring about that result, but it seems that the Congress is not yet ready to separate the boycott activities from its other work. The result is that the boycott has not been extended throughout the country as it should have been and that we are scattering oranges [sic].
>
> There are two controlling reasons why I think that the League should be retained as the sole instrumentality for the boycott:
>
> 1) It was the first in the field, and for eight months thereafter we were unable to enlist the cooperation of the Congress in the boycott movement.
>
> 2) The Congress is engaged in so many activities apart from the boycott, that it is not fair that those who want to support the boycott should have to subscribe to these other activities, or to those that are purely Jewish.

3) I believe that we can get wider support for a non-sectarian movement than for one that is purely Jewish, especially at this time when we should be able to secure substantial financial support from the Labor movement, and from the Catholics and Protestants against whom the Hitler campaign is still being waged, and will, I believe, continue to be waged.

4) I believe, and of course I may be mistaken, that the League is, whether rightly or wrongly, recognized throughout the country as *the* boycott organization, probably by reason of the fact that it was first in the field, and that it has strictly confined its activities to the boycott.[8]

In conclusion, Untermyer advised: "I think we should again take up with Dr. Wise, Dr. Tenenbaum and yourself the question of unifying our boycott activities under the leadership of the League, and try again to bring all elements into that union.[9] Untermyer's concluding stipulation meant at least League supremacy in any future agreement. Despite this, the Boycott Council, at a meeting held on March 30, agreed to meet with his organization. But by making the following decision, it obviated the League's probable intention of demanding the Council's dissolution as a prerequisite for complete boycott unity: "It was moved and unanimously carried that a Committee be appointed to negotiate with the Non-Sectarian Anti-Nazi League on the basis of cooperation, with the understanding that the Joint Boycott Council will not give up its identity."[10]

We have no details regarding the negotiations that followed. What we do know is that the League refused to be part of any new boycott organization which was not non-sectarian at least in name. This is borne out by a statement made by the special JLC committee which conducted the negotiations with the League. It was forwarded to Tenenbaum by Vladeck on May 26:

> The Jewish Labor Committee sees no reason why a merger of these organizations, so essential to the efficiency and effectiveness of the boycott work, should not come to be realized because of a difference of opinion on the name of the new organization. It was the impression of the committee participating in the negotiations that the name was the greatest stumbling block to unity.[11]

Upon Vladeck's request, this opinion was presented to the Congress authorities with a proposal to meet with the League again in order to reach a complete understanding.

On June 2, Tenenbaum dispatched the first of two replies to Vladeck, saying that he, as well as the Congress leaders, were "heart and soul for unity"; the question being: "Unity at what price?" Then adding his own feeling with regard to this matter, Tenenbaum wrote: "I, personally knowing the policies and the leadership of the Anti-Nazi League, have deep misgivings on this point. Frankly, it is not only the name—but the platform; the methods of approach and the policies and the tactics of the 'Non-Sectarians' that make us hesitate."[12] In association with Untermyer, Tenenbaum was also sure to include the personality problem which played a decisive role in forestalling unity. Untermyer "conducted himself with irresponsible bossism," he felt. "Unfortunately, the League is Mr. Untermyer and Mr. Untermyer is the League," concluded the Boycott Council chairman.

It was becoming apparent anew, as it had time and time again, that the same issues that had impeded a union between the Boycott Committee and the Anti-Nazi League were acting once more as insurmountable obstacles to the latter's union with the Joint Boycott Council. Now, though, Vladeck and his Labor Committee colleagues had also gotten the taste of fruitless bargaining with the Untermyer League. More importantly, however, by now the American Jewish Congress, and seemingly, even Dr. Tenenbaum, had enough of these futile merger negotiations. The matter received official consideration at a June 8 meeting of the Congress' Governing Council. It did not get too far, however, and as a result, Lily Shultz was instructed to convey the following message to Dr. Tenenbaum, which he, in turn, promptly passed on to Mr. Vladeck: "It was decided that while the American Jewish Congress is in favor of cooperation with agencies working on behalf of the boycott, it refused to enter into any further mergers."[13]

A mode of cooperation was worked out, though, in the area of boycott cases. But even this agreement, into which the JWV was also incorporated, was reached only after the passing of many valuable months. The effort can be traced to a November 2, 1936, JBC communication to the NSANL, advising it that the Council favored the establishment of a joint-committee "for the purpose of deciding the status of important cases as regards the Anti-Nazi Boycott." On June 28 of the following year, JBC Executive Secretary Posnansky (see p. 141) apprized Isaiah Minkoff, his counterpart in the JLC, of this communication; Posnansky further adding that "the Non-Sectarian League refused the establishment of such a Committee." He therewith stated that somewhat over a month earlier, the chairman of the Boycott Council's Film Division had addressed a "lengthy" letter to the League, "asking its Film Division for close cooperation in matters pertaining to the Film Industry." But "up to the present," concluded Posnansky, "no reply was recieved from the League."[14]

However, not too long thereafter, an "Actions Committee on Boycott Cases of the JWV, JBC and the NSANL" was formed (see Document No.

XX) after all. This is learned from a December 1937 document mentioning for the first time, apparently, the existence of a "Joint Action Committee." But just as the record does not disclose exactly what kept the three boycott organizations from creating their Action Committee sooner, so it is equally silent as to what led them to finally agree to its formation. Whatever the reason or reasons, in the wake of the hopeless discord and dissension that characterized America's three major boycott organizations, the establishment of a representative combative body seemed the best alternative course to actual unity.

22

Legal Activities

JBC Phase

i.

The damning, angry words which Congressman Celler voiced in the aftermath of the Berlin Riots in July of 1935, were followed up by legislative action half a year later. We recall (p. 183) that Mr. Celler did not consider it proper to introduce an anti-Nazi boycott bill into the House; but this did not mean that he relinquished the use of other media to harm German interests. The Brooklyn representative sought to achieve this by proposing bills which were damaging to German trade, on the one hand, and advantageous to American business, on the other hand.

Celler's action commenced with the introduction on February 26, 1936, of HR 11475, a bill designed primarily to aid American labor and industry by guarding them against the unfair competition of foreign countries. However, it was also designed to hurt Germany, which, on account of the boycott, had embarked on a policy of increased subsidization of industry.

In a formal statement appended to this bill, Celler explained that he proposed it to amend Sec. #303 of the Customs Tariff Law. According to Celler, this Tariff Law, commonly referred to as the "Dumping Act," was being violated with impunity through various subterfuges. His new bill, the New York congressman asserted, would only serve to amplify the provisions of the Customs Tariff Law.

Celler's statement also pointed out the known fact that most of Germany's larger industries were receiving government subsidies on all export goods in order to procure foreign exchange which, in turn, was used to purchase needed raw materials. One of the examples cited by him dealt with an American steel venture in which German manufacturers underbid their American competitors by 40 percent; this, despite the fact that only the Germans were confronted with such expenses as rail charges, ocean freight, and additional delivery charges within the United States. These, Celler concluded, could not possibly have been sustained without a direct, generous subsidy.

To right many of these wrongs, Celler's bill made it mandatory upon the foreign exporter to state on the consular invoice whether he had received a government subsidy. It also required American consulate officials in foreign countries to ascertain if subsidies had been given. The bill further provided that any foreign manufacturer who refused to give such information was to have his goods barred from the United States, and that no consular invoice should be certified for him. Also, Celler considered it only fair that the amount of the subsidy should be added to the duties in cases of this sort because it was impossible for an American manufacturer to compete with government-subsidized firms. In citing Germany's notorious policy of subsidization, Celler charged that the Nazi regime did not hesitate to confiscate the property of its opponents to obtain funds. And, although, his bill was directed primarily against the Third Reich, it, of course, did not mention Germany by name. Thus, on the face of it, HR 11475 sought only to protect the rights of American workers and manufacturers.

ii.

This piece of legislation, and some others which Celler subsequently introduced, was authored by none other than Dr. Joseph Tenenbaum. For the legislation folder of the JBC archives contains a letter which Tenenbaum wrote Celler on February 3, 1936, wherein he informs the Brooklyn congressman that he is forwarding him a "rough draft" of the bill that he—Tenenbaum—had just drawn up, "and which had been approved in principle by the Economic Committee."[1] This "rough draft" was nearly word for word the bill Celler introduced into the House later that month. Tenenbaum also included a "background" statement which, with the exception of but a few slight modifications, read word for word like the introductory statement that Celler had appended to his bill.

In accordance with House procedure, HR 11475 was referred to the Committee on Ways and Means. In the interval preceding its discussion on the House floor, Tenenbaum worked hard to obtain support from many patriotic organizations for the bill's passage. To cite but one example of the publicity and propaganda given this bill, we quote the following statement that the American Jewish Congress made over the radio (Station WMCA) on March 10:

> This bill will make it possible for the United States to bar foreign merchandise competing with our own goods, when the price of such foreign merchandise has been cheapened because of government export subsidies. The bill is plainly aimed at German goods which are being "dumped" all over the world with the aid of German government funds. The American Jewish Congress urges all those interested in the boycott of Nazi goods to write their Congressmen to support this bill.[2]

Celler helped his own cause by informing Tenenbaum just which congressmen to concentrate most of his efforts on, and precisely which of them were sympathetic to his bill. He explained that "if sufficient pressure is put behind it, we should not have difficulty in getting a hearing on this measure."[3]

HR 11475 did not receive a hearing at the Seventy-fourth Congress session. And inasmuch as biennial elections took place in 1936, it had to be reintroduced the following year, thereby being assigned the new number of HR 6743. Like HR 11475, HR 6743, which contained some additional sections, was drawn up by Dr. Tenenbaum in collaboration with the Legislative Committee of the Joint Boycott Council. It is herewith reproduced in its entirety:

75th CONGRESS, *1st Session* H.R. 6743
IN THE HOUSE OF REPRESENTATIVES
April 28, 1937

Mr. Celler introduced the following bill; which was referred to the Committee on Ways and Means and ordered to be printed

A BILL

To regulate foreign commerce, and for other purposes.

Sec. 1. Be it enacted by the Senate and House of Representatives of the United States of America in Congress assembled, that whenever any subsidy shall be granted by any foreign government, corporation, or other private agency, to a producer of manufacturer of any article, item, or product, dutiable or nondutiable, it shall be required that the amount of such subsidy shall be stated on the consular invoice; and that such subsidy or bonus be considered as part of the value of the article or item and therefore dutiable. It shall be the duty of the American Consul or any other duly appointed officers of the Secretary of the Treasury to make proper investigation of any such alleged subsidy or bonus and duly report to the Secretary of the Treasury.

Sec. 2. In cases where such subsidy has been granted, the customs duty shall be increased by an amount equal to the subsidy.

(a) In cases where the article, object, or material is nondutiable, there shall be assessed an amount equivalent to the amount of the subsidy.

Sec. 3. Any manufacturer, producer, or shipper of merchandise in a foreign country shall be required to give any agent of the United States the required information as to subsidies; and if such producer, manufacturer, or shipper refuses to give such information or withholds such information, the Secretary of the Treasury shall refuse entry of such goods into the United States, or assess an amount equal to 100 per centum of the value of the shipment ad valorem.

Sec. 4. A subsidy within the meaning of this Act shall be considered as being any of the following:

(a) A grant by any foreign government, corporation, or individual which shall enable the grantees to sell below the open market value of such merchandise in their country or other countries where similar conditions prevail.

(b) A special remission or exemption of taxes.

(c) The purchase of goods by any foreign government or corporation at a price higher than the prevailing market rate from a manufacturer or producer selling the same product below the open market value of merchandise in other countries.

(d) The issuance of special currency for the express purpose of facilitating exports.

Sec. 5. The foregoing shall apply to all transactions, including barter, or such trading transactions where currency is used in the purchase of goods in whole or part, or where foreign goods are bought and paid for with goods shipped from this country.

Sec. 6. Any article containing more than 75 per centum foreign materials in terms of value (not including the container) shall be so marked. The name of the foreign country which has contributed the greatest amount of foreign material must also be prominently stated on the container.

(a) This section shall not apply to medicine compounded by a pharmacist for a particular individual.

Sec. 7. Any manufactured product which contains 75 per centum or more of imported parts in terms of value shall be so marked in a prominent place. The name of the country which has contributed the greatest amount of the parts must be prominently stated on said article.

Sec. 8. Values in sections 6 and 7 shall be taken as the values of such materials or parts in the United States.

Sec. 9. Whenever bulk material is imported and afterward placed in containers, such containers shall be plainly marked with the country of origin.[4]

Subsequently, however, HR 6743 died in the Committee on Ways and Means.

iii.

Besides Celler, there were also other congressmen who, during the Seventy-fourth and Seventy-fifth Congresses, presented bills which went against German economic interests. Unlike Celler, however, it seems they were not motivated primarily by strong anti-German considerations. Nor, in drawing up their bills, did the congressmen, as far as we know, collaborate with representatives of the boycott movement. But the fact that their action stemmed more, perhaps, out of domestic concerns than empathic or ethnic identification in no way lessened the value of their legislation for the boycott cause.

One of these bills, HR 11477, like HR 11475, was also dated February 26, 1936, and was introduced by Congressman Dow W. Harter of Ohio. The opening paragraph described it as: "*A BILL* to foster industry and fair competition, to promote and encourage employment, and to prevent the dumping of foreign merchandise on the markets of the United States."

The next item and the Section (2) that follows explains why this bill was named the "Anti-Dumping Act of 1936":

> Be it enacted by the Senate and House of Representatives of the United States of America in Congress assembled, that the Antidumping Act, 1921, (19 U.S.C., Annotated, secs. 160 to 173, inclusive), is hereby repealed.

NOTICE OF DUMPING

> Sec. 2. Whenever, in the case of any merchandise, whether dutiable or free, which is being or is likely to be imported into the United States from any foreign country, of a class or kind like, similar to, or competitive with any merchandise manufactured or produced in the United States, the Secretary of the Treasury, or other official of the Treasury Department acting under the Secretary's direction or designation for the purposes of this Act, may have reason to believe or suspect from the invoice covering the shipment, or from other documents, or from any information furnished by an appraising officer, or upon any complaint presented to him, that the export or actual selling price, or price at which such merchandise is agreed to be sold, to an

importer in the United States is less than the fair value, as defined herein, of the same or similar or competitive merchandise, the Secretary shall publish or cause to be published in the same manner as other Treasury Decisions a notice of suspected dumping covering the class or kind of merchandise involved, to such extent as he may deem necessary for the guidance of customs officers; and shall direct all appraising officers to withhold appraisement reports on such merchandise to collectors of customs until all investigations regarding foreign values, sales prices, production costs, and all other matters which the Secretary may deem necessary for all purposes herein shall be completed, under such regulations as the Secretary may prescribe.[5]

In cases like the aforesaid, the Harter bill (Sec. 6) provided that:

If the export or actual selling price or price at which such merchandise is agreed to be sold to an importer in the United States is less than the fair value therof, as defined herein, there shall be levied, collected and paid, in addition to the regular duties imposed thereon by law, a special dumping duty in an amount equal to such difference. In such case, the special dumping duty so accruing shall be levied, collected and paid even though the merchandise is not otherwise dutiable.[6]

Though it was intended, basically, to help counteract Nazi propaganda activities in the United States, mention should also be made of HR 4960. This was a legislative bill which Congressman Joseph W. Martin of Massachusetts introduced at the Seventy-fifth Congress on February 19, 1937. It was "A bill to Regulate Advertising of Imported Articles," and was referred to the Committee on Interstate and Foreign Commerce.

The substantive text of HR 4960 read as follows:

Be it enacted by the Senate and House of Representatives of the U.S.A. in Congress assembled that, no person shall advertise in any form or manner any articles imported into the U.S. for sale unless such advertising shall contain, in legible English words, in a conspicuous place that shall not be covered or obscured in any statement to be nearly indelible and permanent as the nature of the article will permit.[7]

Sections 2 and 3 of the bill explained that

This Act shall apply to advertising of imported merchandise in Daily, Weekly, Monthly, Bi-Weekly, Bi-Monthly and Sunday newspapers, magazines, both of national and local publication, pamphlets, books, booklets, brochures, circulars, envelope stuffers, outdoor painted display signs, billboards, posters, window displays, lope stuffers, outdoor counter displays and advertising media or any description such as calendars, buttons and so forth.

In radio broadcasting where commercial broadcasting is used in the promotion of and to advertise for sale in the U.S. any imported article or material, a broadcasting announcer shall at the beginning and end of each broadcast period, clearly state the name of the country of origin of the article or material advertised.[8]

The introduction of this bill and others like it reflected the growing awareness of the Nazi danger on the part of an increasing number of American public servants. More and more of them were beginning to come to grips with a problem which until now had evoked response and action from such special-interest groups as the Non-Sectarian Anti-Nazi League and the Joint Boycott Council.

23

The JBC and the U.S. Post Office

The maritime vigil which the boycott movement observed in order to thwart the entry of German-made goods into the United States also encompassed the mails and various cargoes heading for Hitler Germany. Such vigilance was applied to non-German as well as German ships leaving or entering American ports and destined ultimately for the Fatherland.

This activity, like the travel on German ships, was an important source of revenue to the German government. But beyond its reliance on the power of moral suasion, there was little the boycott movement could do to hinder such traffic. Mail shipment by land, sea, and air, was governed by Post Office rules and regulations, both national and international. Moreover, the Post Office Department, unlike the House or Senate, was a branch of the federal government, and as such, consisted of appointed and not elected officials. Further, with the exception of the Postmaster General, postal officials were barely known and were dissociated from political embroilments; hence their immunity, from the ordinary postal clerk to the head of the postal system, to the socioeconomic pressures that plagued congressmen and senators. But for reasons which we shall presently see, this circumstance did not prove to be the rule in the case of the anti-Nazi boycott.

On February 7, 1936, as one of his first steps in his capacity as JBC chairman, Dr. Tenenbaum addressed an inquiry to the then U.S. Postmaster General, James A. Farley, regarding information pertaining "to accepted postal regulations which would help those in sympathy with the boycott to avoid the sending of mail on German boats."[1] The Post Office Department reply to this was that "it was Post Office policy to expedite the dispatch of mail as far as is practicable."[2] To realize this aim of his, Tenenbaum was further informed that it would be necessary to have the mails deposited at such a time as to connect with ships flying colors other than the German flag. Otherwise, concluded the Post Office Department letter, there was substantially nothing in the domestic postal laws to authorize endorsements such as "Not to be forwarded by German steamship."[3]

With this, the matter came to a rapid close. However, friction commenced the following year with the introduction of a new Post Office Department ruling which provided that fast steamers, regardless of registry, would be given preference over slower ones. This at once produced the double effect of American-flag ships losing a large share of the mails, with German ships filling in the vacuum.

Under the previous arrangements, mail addressed to Europe was kept at port up to seven days in wait for an American ship to pick it up. However, the new ruling reduced this to only a two-day wait, whereafter mail would be sent with any ship available.

Naturally, American steamship lines bitterly resented this ruling. Some of them warned that feeling of hostility on their part toward the Post Office Department would be created as a result, proving costly to the U.S. government. Others acknowledged that a reasonable delay in mail delivery could slightly annoy and inconvenience some Americans; but they felt that such hardship was more than compensated by the ultimate gain of the general public welfare.

Whatever the merits of these arguments, the fact remained that Germany, because she had the fastest steamers and the most frequent sailings, stood the chance of benefiting most under the new ruling. The resentful steamship companies were very well aware of this, and some, supposing correctly that they would find in him a sympathetic ally, apprized Tenenbaum of their grievances.

They did not have to wait long for a reaction. Immediately, Tenenbaum dispatched letters to the various steamship lines informing them of the opposition of the JBC to the new Post Office Department ruling and its readiness for common action to have it rescinded. Many senators and congressmen also became recipients of JBC mail on this matter. The Post Office Department, with which the JBC chairman initiated a correspondence exchange that ranged over almost the entire summer of 1937, was, of course, his principal target.

Tenenbaum's main contention was the the recent ruling by the Post Office Department was a disservice to America because "no other country permits any of its mails to be shipped on other than its own vessels."[4] In his opinion, moreover, such a ruling was tantamount to an indirect subsidy of foreign lines. In time, he pointed out most emphatically, "the Government would be forced to re-imburse the American Lines to the extent of the loss resulting from a shrinkage in their mail carrying."[5] Such were the more patriotic-sounding arguments which, in contrast to his letter of inquiry the year before, Tenenbaum presently summoned in order to declare the Post Office Department's new ruling unfair to America's merchant marine. Now the parochial argument of the boycott, which appealed almost exclusively on moral grounds to "avoid the sending of mail on German boats," could be blended with a charge which appealed to all Americans by its allusion to the national interest; that is to say, that the new ruling, aside from discriminating against one of America's own commercial industries, was also "at the same time a source of financial assistance to a system of Government completely intolerant of the democratic system of Government."[6]

Under separate cover, on July 20, the Post Office Department dispatched to Tenenbaum two replies in answer to his protests. One succinctly presented the Department's view by stating that:

> No one, of course, could object to the operators of American flag vessels making every possible effort to obtain pay cargo and certainly, the Post Office desires to employ American flag vessels in transporting its foreign mails wherever such vessels can provide a reasonably expeditious service. It is the obligation of the department, however, to expedite the mails and it does seem that the time preferentials allowed—twenty-four hours in one case and forty-eight hours in the other—is as much delay as the Department would be justified in permitting, even to favor American flag vessels.[7]

In the concluding section of this reply, Tenenbaum was informed that the Department regretted to inform him "that there are no vessels in the U.S.-European service flying the American flag comparable to the fastest steamships flying the flags of other countries."[8]

The other reply was more elaborate and stated essentially that:

> The schedule of preferentials prior to July first was provided principally for the reason that most of the American flag ships were operating under Post Office Department subsidy contracts, and under the terms of their respective contracts the contractors were required to carry all mails tendered them and payment had to be made regardless of the volume of mail carried. The problem which faced the Department under the old subsidy contract system was whether the department should pay extra poundage rated to foreign vessels and non-contract American vessels when it was paying a high subsidy rate to American vessels operating under these contracts, while the American

vessels under their contracts were obliged to carry all of the mail tendered them for their contract pay.

The Post Office Department subsidy contracts referred to above were all terminated, effective June 30 1937. The Merchant Marine Act of 1928, under which Act the subsidy contracts were let, was superseded by the Merchant Marine Act of 1936. Under the first mentioned Act subsidies to American steamship companies were paid by the Post Office Department under their ocean mail contracts, but all subsidies are now being paid direct to the Maritime Commission operating under the said Merchant Marine Act of 1936. Therefore, the Post Office Department is no longer obligated to pay in any form subsidies to United States steamship companies.[9]

But the charge which motivated Tenenbaum to write the Post Office Department in the first place, namely, that its new ruling was "a source of financial assistance" to a tyrannical regime; this charge was dismissed most dispassionately of all. It had been made in a July 14 communication and controverted by the following comment:

> With respect to your statement in the last paragraph of your letter, regarding dispatching mails on German vessels, I have to state that there is nothing in the Universal Postal Union convention under which our postal service operates, authorizing discrimination against vessels of any country for the reasons cited by you.[10]

Tenenbaum himself, however, was not to be dismissed as lightly as some of his charges. During this period of his controversy with the Post Office Department, the JBC chairman gathered evidence to prove that its new ruling had resulted in a decrease in the pieces of mail carried by U.S.-flag ships. To that end, printed circulars were disseminated by JBC, claiming that during the month of July, as compared to May, there was more than a 50 percent decrease in the mails carried on the vessels of the United States Lines; while during the same period the North German Lloyd enjoyed an increase of more than 30 percent in mails carried from New York.

This trend continued into August, and on the eighteenth of that month, Tenenbaum thought it was time to act once more. Again he dispatched a letter to the Post Office Department, informing it that, because of its new ruling, American-flag lines were still undergoing "hardships." This new ruling, he tirelessly continued to contend, was illegal. Herein really lay the crux of this entire controversy, with the legality or illegality of the new ruling depending on which of two sections of the Merchant Marine Act of 1936 (HR 8555) one chose to base oneself upon. Thus, Sec. 212(b), (1) and (d), read:

The Commission is authorized and directed—(b) To study and to cooperate with vessel owners in devising means by which—
(1) the importers and the exporters of the United States can be induced to give preference to vessels under United States registry.
(d) To establish and maintain liaison with other boards commissions, independent establishments, and department of the United States Government, and with such representative trade organizations through the United States as may be concerned, directly or indirectly, with any movement of commodities in the water-borne export and import foreign commerce of the United States, for the purpose of securing preference to vessels of United States registry in the shipment of such commodities . . .[11]

Dr. Tenenbaum, ever interested to deny German vessels the right to carry U.S. mail, based himself on the aforesaid. But the Post Office Department felt justified in adopting its new ruling because of Sec. 405(a) of HR 8555, which read as follows:

All mails of the United States carried on vessels between ports between which it is lawful under the navigation laws for a vessel not documented under the laws of the United States to carry merchandise shall, *insofar as practicable,* be carried on vessels of United States registry.[12]

In its reply of the twenty-fifth, the Department finally began showing conciliatory signs. Though it did not admit the "illegality" of the new ruling, it did freely disclose that ever since its enactment, it had received many letters of complaint on this subject. Furthermore, it seems that the Post Office Department tried to assuage Tenenbaum's resentment by emphasizing that its new ruling affected parcel post mail only. The Department informed him, moreover, that it was conducting a survey "to better determine just how far it can favor American vessels without neglecting its duty to provide a reasonable dispatch for the mails entrusted to it."[13] Hence it commented that: "It would seem, therefore, that there is but one question to be considered and that is: whether a delay of several days in dispatch of parcel post mail would seriously affect the interests of the senders and recipients of such mail."[14]

This candid reply, which seemed to express a sincere desire to cooperate and find a workable solution, appears to have calmed Tenenbaum down; at least to the extent of abandonment of the belligerent tone which, up to the present time, had characterized his correspondence with the Post Office Department. However, in the closing week of September, this issue was definitely settled to Tenenbaum's satisfaction. This was due to the fact that he had received a letter from Joseph

Kennedy,[15] then chairman of the U.S. Maritime Commission, who informed him that he had been apprized by the Post Office Department that a decision had been reached "to allow a preference, as related to parcel post, of seven days at destination to United States flag seapost and United States non-seapost steamships over foreign registry seapost and non-seapost steamships, which should materially increase the quantity of parcel post mails dispatched on lines operating steamships under United States registry."[16] With this promise by the Post Office Department to return to its original commitment to delay for seven days at port all European-bound mails, JBC's increasing perturbation over this matter was assuaged.

24

The Opening of the World Jewish Congress

With Jabotinsky's secession from the World Zionist Organization in the spring of 1935, the Nineteenth Zionist Congress, convening in the summer of that year, was spared the hotly contested boycott and transfer battles that had characterized its 1933 meetings. Even the World Jewish Congress, opening at last in the summer of 1936, spared relatively little of its time for a discussion of the boycott and disregarded the transfer issue.

Dr. Wise, who, during the Congress' previous two sessions had spoken so passionately on the subjects of boycott and transfer, typified this change of emphasis.[1] This may be exemplified by one of his main speeches which, while explaining and defending the idea and purpose of a World Jewish Congress, only mentioned the subject of boycott in passing:

> We do not believe in the use of physical force, but there are too many Jews who carry the reluctance to wage even defensive war into the spiritual realm. Such are those Jews, who have refused to have any part in an anti-Nazi boycott, although the boycott is a perfect expression of non-violent, that is to say, economic and moral resistance to evil . . .
> The World Jewish Congress is a purely voluntary and cooperative association of representatives of those Jewries throughout the world which have chosen to have part therein. It can have no more power than is entrusted to it by the Jewries it represents, no more authority than will derive from the wisdom of its deliberations and the loftiness of its purposes.

The World Jewish Conference represents great masses of Jewish people in a number of lands in which the Jewish masses live, such as the United States, Poland and Palestine. That in these lands there are groups or bodies which refuse to participate in a World Jewish Congress in order to make impossible any and every public Jewish assembly, does not alter the fact of mass support in these same lands by large and diversified groups.

What do we expect of a World Jewish Congress? We answer: NO MIRACLES. The World Jewish Congress will not solve all, or most nor even many of the unsolved problems of the Jewish people. But a World Jewish Congress may perform these functions:

1. Bring Jews together of many different lands and many different views who do not meet together in any other way;

2. Bring Jews together on a new plane, not that of giving and receiving, but for an interchange of views touching every manner of Jewish problems with a view to their solution;

3. Jews of one land will face the problems of Jews of other lands, invite their counsel and invoke their experience.

All these will derive from our faith that Jews may and should have relations with their fellow-Jews in other lands on all questions of affecting their life as Jews, including the problem of special status accorded to or inflicted upon them as Jews. We understand that, as Jews, we cannot postpone our concern with the lot of other Jews until this has become catastrophic in quality and measure. When calamity befalls Jews in other lands, we are not to bear ourselves as neutral or friendly observers, but to labor earnestly and effectively in every possible way to redress wrong as well as to mitigate distress.[2]

In view of the continued Hitler threat and the two Preliminary Conferences that preceded its founding, it was only fitting that the World Jewish Congress also go on record as having adopted the anti-Nazi boycott. Stephen Wise, who had portrayed the achievements of this movement before the conferees, was called upon to read the boycott resolution:

> German National-Socialism has declared war on the whole Jewish people, and in the three and a half years of its regime has carried on this war with unexampled severity. The Jewish Minority in Germany has been deprived of its most elementary civil rights, systematically eliminated from the economic life of the country, reduced to the status of pariahs by the senseless race theory, and driven back to a new ghetto.
>
> National-Socialism has, furthermore, developed an unprecedented propaganda of hatred and incitement against the Jews of the whole world, not shrinking from defamatory literature and agitation in their efforts to infect all the nations of the world with the poison of race hatred and anti-Semitism.

> The first World Jewish Congress declares that the Jewish people will take up the challenge which has been forced upon it, and proclaims its solidarity with the anti-Nazi Boycott movement as a spontaneous weapon in its defense. It earnestly calls upon Jewish communities throughout the world to prosecute with energy the boycott of goods and services of Nazi Germany within the framework of the legal conditions and regulations of the individual countries, as a measure in defence of Jewish honour.
>
> The World Jewish Congress expresses its sympathy and its solidarity with all the other classes and communities who are suffering persecution in Germany for political, religious or economic reasons, and appeal to all friends of humanity and justice who are interested in the maintenance of the highest values of civilization to associate themselves in the fight against the principles and anti-Semitic policy of National-Soclialist Germany.[3]

Presupposing, however, the accuracy of Tenenbaum's foregoing report, one is tempted to ask: was the boycott as effective and potent a force as it had been earlier? Apparently not, if we are to be guided by the diary of William E. Dodd, U.S. ambassador to Germany at this time. According to Dodd, from 1933 to 1935, regarded as the most intensive and extensive period of the boycott, some of Germany's leading officials believed that this movement was capable of toppling the Nazi regime. The ominous foreboding which is contained in the following May 13, 1934, "Last Warning" speech by Goebbels, clearly reflects this fear:

> All Germany is aware of the fact that if part of the outside world continues the anonymous boycott against German goods, this is due to our own Jewish fellow-citizens.
>
> If the boycott were carried to lengths actually endangering our economic situation, it would not mean that we should let the Jews go free! No! The hatred of the German people would first of all vent itself on those who can be grabbed in the homeland.[4]

In 1936, however, Hitler actually began to make his power felt outside Germany, winning political successes that assured the continuance of his Nazi regime. Economic recovery went hand in hand with these victories, prompting Rudolf Hoess, the subsequent commandant of Auschwitz, to brag on October 11 of that year, that the boycott had been defeated. As to the World Jewish Congress, twelve years would pass before it would meet again and be presided over for the last time by Stephen Wise, the man who contributed so much to its creation and continued progress.

25

Boycott Enforcement

Picketing

The mechanics of the boycott, in their day-to-day operation, were last examined for the year 1933. The tactics then employed by the two principal boycott organizations were, of course, still in the formative and experimental stages. But on the whole, their choice of tactics was the same, with no one weapon markedly differentiating one boycott organization from the other.

By 1934, however, this was no longer the case. Picketing had become a distinguishing mark of the Boycott Committee, dramatizing the difference between its fighting style and that of the ANL. It was used primarily as a retaliatory measure against incorrigible boycott violators. It was also intended to act as a deterrent against potential offenders.

The actual attitude of the League toward picketing can be traced to 1933 itself. On November 3 of that year, Untermyer, in writing to Rabinowitz on Woolworth's standing with the boycott, affirmed that company's good intentions. However, under no circumstances, warned the hoary ANL leader, should there be a recourse to picketing: "Unlike other American businesses, they (i.e. Woolworth) are in a precarious situation in that they have a number of stores and an investment of $5,000,000 in Germany, but not withstanding all this they are really anxious to help. Whether that is so or not this proposed picketing is illegal and contrary to the best traditions of American institutions." [1]

Years later, in complete concurrence, Tenenbaum expressed himself as follows:

> An essential ingredient of the boycott action is publicity. Next to publicity, picketing of the boycott violators has a powerful deterrent

effect. Picketing, which is today a legally recognized medium of retaliation in labour disputes, was resorted to extensively in the American pre-revolutionary boycott, before it was ever employed as labour ammunition. However, the nature of the boycott, its aim, its method and sweep, differ sharply from the tactics and strict limitation of target in the case of employer-labour conflicts. So is boycott picketing, despite its primacy over its labour parallel, a weapon of a different kind. For, unlike labour picketing, boycott has no legal status. The boycott as well as picketing is in conflict not only with the law but with authority.[2]

Dr. Tenenbaum certainly concealed his real thinking on this subject in the boycott report he submitted to the first World Jewish Congress:

> Concerns which continue to be sales drummers of the Hitler trade are being picketed systematically or periodically by men and women of all walks of life. We have had such pickets before the doors and show windows of some of the biggest concerns in the country, including the billion dollar chain stores. It usually proved successful where persuasion had failed.[3]

However, for the first eight months or so after its establishment in February 1934, picketing did not constitute a part of the Boycott Committee's program. The earliest available document advocating the initiation of picketing is a Boycott Committee communication, dated October 10, 1934. Its message is directed to the Congress' Women's Division, informing it that it "can extend the following co-operation to the Boycott Department—picketing."[4] The rest of the document sets forth the background to the adoption of this decision, stating specifically that "The boycott has reached a stage where letters and committees sent to importers and department stores are ineffectual. Firms are used to them and ignore them."[5]

It was a statement that postdated Tenenbaum's opinion on the state of the boycott, as cited above (p. 165) in an August 9, 1934, memorandum. It may therefore be safely assumed that up to early October of that year, Dr. Tenenbaum and his associates were still in search of a new boycott stimulus. Then word reached them that a young Poale Zion group had had success in a picket demonstration against a Bronx branch of the Kresge department store chain. The October 10 communication which reports this states that the picketing proved "an effective means to get attention." To the Boycott Committee, the event was especially noteworthy and newsworthy because "this place never discontinued importing German merchandise nor did they reply to any of the letters sent them." As a result, Dr. Tenenbaum, who had been hard-pressed to find an effective modus operandi in dealing with such defiant concerns, decided to incorporate picketing into the boycott program.

The demonstration that led to this judgment was portrayed as follows: "But when two Jewish girls were placed in front of their store wearing picket signs reading 'For Humanity's sake, do not buy Nazi-made merchandise—this store continues to sell German goods,' we could see how many people who were ready to enter the store refused to do so upon seeing the signs which the pickets wore."[6]

From a JBC document, dated July 22, 1937, it is learned that, eventually, picket captains were appointed to take charge of demonstrations like the aforesaid. However, because women had more free time to spare for such purposes, picketing became a main activity of the Women's Division of the American Jewish Congress. After its initiation, scores at a time would be seen parading in front of boycott-violating establishments to protest the importation and sale of German-made goods.

Pressure and Persuasion

i.

Picketing was used by the Boycott Committee as a last resort. The phase that generally preceded the recourse to this measure is contained in the following descriptive statement:

> Every shipment coming from Germany is scrutinized by the Boycott Committee. The importers and buyers are interviewed and appealed to stop importing German goods. The stores, wholesale and retail, are being supervised by special vigilance committees, and where the appeal to the conscience fails, the sales resistance of the buying public can be relied upon to hit through the more sensitive medium of the cash register. Lists are distributed to the press and to the local newspapers, containing the roster of concerns dealing with German goods and services.[7]

Clearly, though, before the boycott offender could be appealed to by persuasive methods, one had to ferret him out. The Boycott Committee did this by sending the various jobbers and importers specially prepared questionnaires, which they were requested to fill out and return to its office. A sample of one such questionnaire follows:

Name, Address, Nature of Business;
Of what business association are you a member?
Are you handling any German made goods? If so, why?
Are you willing to submit a list of merchandise already purchased, and identify such, by special label as having been bought before given date?
Would you pledge not to display German made merchandise you have in stock?

Which articles have you difficulty in replacing?
In boycotting articles imported from Germany which countries do you buy from instead?
Do you know of any cases where German merchandise
  (a) is falsely stamped
  (b) where stamp "Made in Germany" is omitted
  (c) where stamp is tampered with and merchandise is restamped?
Are you willing to display a card indicating your adherence to the Anti-Nazi Boycott?
Signature, Date.
Name of Vigilant, Address, Captain of Team, District,
Remarks.[8]

Those answering in the affirmative the question that inquired about their willingness to "pledge not to display German made merchandise," more than likely, became recipients of the following pledge card form:

> We the undersigned, hereby declare that we will not import, purchase, handle, or distribute any merchandise manufactured in Nazi Germany or make use of any service furnished within or subject to the control of the German Reich, as long as the oppressive laws and acts against Jews and other sections of the population in Germany have not been revoked and nullified.[9]

The following communication, written by William Speigelman (p. 130) on July 19, 1934, shows the Boycott Committee acting with reference to merchandise "where stamp 'Made in Germany' is omitted":

> Our Boycott Committee is taking action against a firm which has established a practice of erasing the words "Made in Germany" on sewing machine parts, and selling them to customers who would not make purchase of such articles were they to know that the articles are of German origin. We need an expert mechanic who would be able to identify such article(s) and to render testimony.[10]

On April 21, 1936, at the request of the president of the Baltimore branch of the American Jewish Congress, Dr. Tenenbaum prepared for him an outline of the procedure for conducting a boycott campaign. This sketch is of interest, since it offers in some detail a methodical sequence of the coercive steps that the JBC employed against boycott offenders:

> Through the public at large asking it to refrain from buying Nazi-made merchandise, or using Nazi services. This can be accomplished through articles in the press, mass meetings, conference and radio talks.
> By bringing moral pressure to bear on importers and storekeepers, not to sell German-made merchandise. For this purpose letters must be sent to those importers, department stores, jobbers and retailers

who handle Nazi-made merchandise, and appeals made to them to discontinue doing so.

In many cases those handling German merchandise, insist on having a conference with the representatives of the Boycott Committee. In these cases your Committee will have to designate one or two members to meet with them.

In the event that merchants refuse to cooperate with the boycott movement, the following procedure is usually carried out:

1) A whispering campaign against the particular party is inaugurated.[11]
2) His name is publicized through circulars, e.g. why such and such firm is still handling Nazi-made merchandise? or in case they use vessels controlled by the Nazi Government—why does the particular firm still use Nazi vessels?
3) Placing pickets in front of the firm which violates the boycott—this is the most effective course. The pickets are provided with signs on which the following inscriptions are written: FOR HUMANITY'S SAKE STOP BUYING NAZI-MADE MERCHANDISE, OR, THIS FIRM TRADES WITH THE ENEMY OF CIVILIZATION—NAZI GERMANY, or signs of a similar nature.[12]

In conclusion, Dr. Tenenbaum discussed the legality of picketing, an activity which, as was noted above (pp. 213–15), was regarded as illegal by the respective chiefs of the two major boycott organizations. However, by citing the Minute Men of the JWV, "an organization cooperating with the Boycott Committee" that "specializes in picketing boycott violators," Tenenbaum explained his success with this medium:

> They have had no trouble whatsoever with the police. If taken in for picketing, they are released immediately after with impunity. It is important for you to know that Mr. Fiorello H. LaGuardia, Mayor of New York City, is one of the vice-presidents of the Anti-Nazi Boycott Committee. His connection may be responsible for the leniency of police treatment. Since the inception of the boycott, no picketing case has been tested in court.[13]

ii.

JBC archives contain several "case histories" describing the manner in which the Boycott Council brought into line recalcitrant offenders. In one of the more dramatic cases that follows, the boycott violator did not prove vulnerable to picketing, which, as has been noted, was regarded as "the most effective course." We shall presently see, however, how the Council's policy of acquiring as complete an account as possible on its subject's background helped it play upon his other weaknesses and susceptibilities.

A. D. Jacoby, the owner of two needlework concerns in New York

City, was discovered by the Council to be dealing in German-made products. On March 3, 1936, on the heels of Council pressure, Mr. Jacoby signed a statement saying that he "solemnly" swore "not to handle any German merchandise."[14] But in the summer of the following year, a JBC surveillance committee which was keeping Jacoby in check, reported, much to Posnansky's chagrin, that "he had since purchased thousands of dollars worth of German needles and thumb tacks."[15] Jacoby had either been bluffing all along or had recently succumbed to an attractive business offer.

Posnansky now took personal charge of the case, embarking on a campaign of singling out Jacoby for a sundry number of vitiating and harassing experiences. For two consecutive weeks, with the aid of the Council's Youth and Women's Divisions, he led daily mass picketing in front of Jacoby's establishments. And on two occasions during this period, in a further effort to humiliate Jacoby, the JBC executive secretary placed pickets around the offender's home to apprize his neighbors of their social *yichus* (i.e., Hebrew and Yiddish for one's lineage).

But this was not all. Learning that Jacoby worshipped at and was a member of the Brooklyn Jewish Center, Posnansky addressed a passionate letter to its president, which began with a discourse on the meaning and purpose of the boycott, especially as concerned Jews. This part of the letter, which was written on August 6, 1937, read as follows:

> The Boycott is not only the only non-violent method that we can accept in our fight against the Nazis. It is also the only course of action that can be accepted by self-respecting Jews. For there is also a moral question involved. No loyal Jew who has not completely forgotten his Jewish heritage, his Jewish parents, his Jewish education, will permit himself to handle or barter in goods which are soaked in the tears, sufferings and the humiliations of his co-religionists.[16]

Posnansky then came directly to the point and informed the president of the Center that one of its members, A. D. Jacoby, "continues to handle large quantities of this blood-soaked merchandise because of its comparative cheapness of price due to the sales resistance resulting from the Boycott."[17] He also informed the president of the "precedent" set by other congregations in such cases; namely, "expelling members who dealt with German goods." Posnansky's letter concluded with a request to be apprized of the decision that the Center's Board of Directors would arrive at.

How did Jacoby react to all this? To be sure, he let it be known that he would not be "intimidated" and refused to be taught "how to run my business." But, in due time, Posnansky "broke" him.[18]

Posnansky's resoluteness in the handling of this and other cases was in keeping with a view which Dr. Tenenbaum had expressed in a March 3,

1937, letter, informing the addressee that he was being placed on the Boycott Violators list: "To our mind, Jews who break the Boycott Front are enemies within our midst, and as such, constitute the greatest menace to our people everywhere."[19]

iii.

For the period under consideration, ANL archives, unlike the files of the Joint Boycott Council, contain no record of such devices as pledge-card forms, questionnaires, or detailed periodic reports concerning boycott vigilance. Nor are case histories available for concerns other than some of the giant department stores. A couple of manuscripts that could be summoned, in this connection, embody program outlines, rather than documentations of events. The outlines, which are found among 1935–36 material, carry no specific dates, however. One, entitled, "Boycott Work in Its Daily Operation," reads as follows:

I. *Mobilizing the Consumer*
   A. Consumers en masse
      1. Oral propaganda, pamphlets, circulars, posters, Newspapers, pins, automobile plate, movies, information on boycott, information how to carry on boycott, data regarding the progress of boycott.
   B. Consumers Collectively
      1. Appeals through circulars, correspondence, speakers, to various social, civic, fraternal and religious organizations to join the League for boycott purposes.
   C. Organization of Women
      1. Central Board of various women's organizations throughout the country.

II. *Mobilizing the Business-men*
   A. Organization of Retailers
               Wholesalers
               Manufacturers
               Importers
               Brokers
               Shippers
               Various Trades & Professions
               Importers of raw material
               Freight and Passenger Service
               Tourist Service
               Insurance Service
               Bond Holders

III. *Enforcement of Boycott*
     Vigilance Committees
     Investigators
     Black and White Lists
     Law Department
     Charge and D.A. Accounts

>   Secondary Boycott
> IV. *Replacement of Boycotted German Articles*
>   Information Bureau
>   Economic Bulletin
>   Research Work
>   Contact with Boycott-committee of Foreign countries
>   Contact with Chambers of Commerce and Manufacturers in the U.S.
>   Contact with Commission Houses in Europe
>   Contact with Chambers of Commerce and Manufacturers in Foreign Countries
>   Contact with Buyers in America[20]

The other outline is entitled, "Instructions and Suggestions to Regional and Local Units of the Non-Sectarian Anti-Nazi League to Champion Human Rights, Inc." This is a most important document, since it suggests what NSANL organizational features should devolve on local, affiliated units. A salient introductory selection reads as follows:

> *Organization:* If your locality does not yet have an organization for anti-Nazi activity, take the initiative in creating one. Communicate with the National Office in New York for special instructions. Call together the leading figures in all local organizations or local units of national bodies that are in sympathy with our work, regardless of creed and race. These groups include—Catholic, Protestant, Jewish and other religious bodies. Trade Unions, Fraternal Organizations, Social Groups, Commercial Bodies, Women's Clubs, Youth Organizations. Contact Parent-Teacher organizations and Ministers in your district.
>
> The participation in the activities of the Non-Sectarian Anti-Nazi League must be as broad as possible. Wherever existing agencies are already at work, there must be no encroachment or needless duplication. An effort should be made instead to consolidate the activities of single groups under the leadership of a general front under a strictly non-sectarian, interdenominational and un-political point of view.
>
> In many instances, local units will be found ready to cooperate in activities endorsed by their national bodies. A plethora of nationwide organizations are affiliated with the League. Local unions can be relied on to support the anti-Nazi boycott as suggested in the American Federation of Labor resolution endorsing the aims of the League.[21]

In its formulation, the aforesaid represents one of the League's most definitive statements on boycott programming.

Radio

The radio, as we recall (p. 104), was one of a long list of "Major Activities" that Rabinowitz had recommended "for putting the boycott movement into action." And rightly so, as the influence of the spoken word, by its eloquence and emotional impact, added a dimension lacking in the printed page. A radio had another quality not inherent in the general press. For whereas the latter could not be expected to feature, say, a weekly or bi-weekly boycott column, the former could be utilized for comparable broadcast purposes. More importantly, therefore, the radio served as a supplement to and an ally of the public prints. Thus, the advantages of the one were complemented by the drawbacks of the other.

Broadcasting on a regular basis became an integral part of the Congress boycott program which Tenenbaum and Spiegelman had reorganized in early 1934. It was launched in the form of a campaign designed to alert the Jewish public to the realization that Nazism was becoming a worldwide danger to Jews everywhere. The broadcasting got under way in April that year.

By contacting large business concerns and requesting them to cooperate with the Boycott Committee by securing "one or more fifteen minute broadcasts over metropolitan stations,"[22] Tenenbaum and Spiegelman obtained the necessary funds to cover the expenses incurred for radio time. The campaign was given wide publicity, and if they so desired, the backers' names were listed in the press. The undertaking proved a success, and on May 23, the Boycott Committee announced its intention of making its broadcasts a weekly feature "for the purpose of keeping the objects of the boycott movement before the public and of repulsing the attacks of the Nazi propaganda here and abroad."[23]

Some further light on this subject is shed in the second of Dr. Tenenbaum's "Confidential" reports covering the months of June 12–August 2, 1934. In a section called "Boycott Radio Drive," the boycott action initiated by the Boycott Committee is described as follows:

> For the purpose of maintaining the customers' resistance towards German goods and for the purpose of keeping the boycott work of the American Jewish Congress before the public eye, this Bureau has been able to arrange during the period under review, sixty-eight broadcasts over eight stations, consuming at least twenty hours of radio time without cost to the Congress, facilitates having been contributed: either by the stations themselves or by Jewish radio advertisers. In addition, four special broadcasts of considerable length for the above purpose and for a direct appeal for boycott funds, were arranged. Forty speakers, Jews, as well as non-Jews, spoke.[24]

Such broadcasts originated from Manhattan and Brooklyn in both English and Yiddish. However, before long, the Federal Communications Commission, established by the Federal Communications Act of

1934, informed Dr. Tenenbaum of its intention to shut down the Brooklyn stations that he had at his disposal. The reason given was that they were not serving the best interests of the listening public. On October 1, 1935, ignoring Boycott Committee protests, the FCC liquidated the aforesaid stations.

From some of the 1934–35 correspondence of the JBC, it is learned that the Boycott Committee's Manhattan programs were broadcasted on Saturday nights between 10:00 and 12:00 P.M. on stations WEVD and WMCA. Although each program featured a guest as the main attraction, a lighter side, in the form of musical entertainment, was provided as well. In time, broadcast hours and days were changed, while other radio stations were utilized as well. Furthermore, WEVD and WMCA remained in the employ of the Boycott Committee throughout its existence.

Aside from the fact that the NSANL also conducted periodic radio programs, too little information is available to enable us to recount or analyze some of its activities via this medium.

Department Store Vigil

i.

The effectiveness of picketing and its advantage to the Boycott Council was regulated, in most cases, either by the size of the picketed concern or its distance from the New York metropolitan area; for the larger the concern and the further its distance from the New York metropolitan area, the less effective the picketing. In such cases, the JBC and ANL often found themselves employing the identical weapons of moral persuasion and blacklisting.

Of the various business establishments accused during this period of breaking the boycott, Sears Roebuck & Co. and the Woolworth chain stores were the largest and the most conspicuous. As late as the middle thirties, Sears had still not officially acceded to the anti-Nazi boycott, while Woolworth was accused by both the League and the Council of failing to remain faithful to its boycott pledge of March 1934.

Sears presented a twofold problem: on the one hand, its main offices were located in Chicago, hence out of the immediate reach of New York's ANL and JBC central headquarters. On the other hand, and of a more central consequence, Lessing J. Rosenwald, Sears' chairman of the board, took the position that he had no right to decide single-handedly to embrace the anti-Nazi boycott in his corporation's name. This attitude came as a disappointment to boycott leaders; for many of them were former associates or admirers of Lessing Rosenwald's father, Julius Rosenwald, a Sears builder, famed Negro benefactor, and charitable espouser of Jewish causes.

The seemingly earliest available document stating Lessing Rosenwald's position on the boycott is an October 2, 1933, communication, written in reply to an inquiry about Sears' policy regarding the importation of German-made goods. Rosenwald's explanation was that up to that year, his company had been purchasing annually about $1 million worth of German merchandise. Ever since, he continued, Sears was acquiring very few German items. Rosenwald added that it was a German Jew who was handling this phase of his company's business. Whereupon, Rosenwald concluded with the rather flimsy excuse that he feared that this Jew would become a victim of foul play if the company stopped buying from Germany completely; an excuse that brings to mind the second of Percy Strauss' Three Personal Letters (pp. 108–12).

Some further elucidation of Sears' stand may be brought forth from an August 8, 1934, communication by Rabbi Joseph Shubow, secretary of the New England Congress Committee, an A.J.C. branch with headquarters in Boston, Massachusetts. In this missive, which is preserved in JBC's Boycott Correspondence file of 1934, Rabbi Shubow after reporting of the adherence to the boycott by "a number of large Boston stores and suburbs," claimed that Sears had explained to him that, due to the nationwide character of its mail orders, it could not exclude products from "certain countries." However, in order to accommodate customers refusing to buy German products, Sears agreed to insert in its catalogues, as well as on its merchandise, the name of the country of manufacture.

Rosenwald's boycott policy underwent no noticeable change in the next several years. This is quite evident from some of his replies to letters by various boycott leaders. One such exchange was with Salmon O. Levinson, chairman of the Chicago Committee for the Defense of Human Rights against Nazism,[25] an organization which was independent of, though in outlook sympathetic to, the Non-Sectarian Anti-Nazi League. The Levinson letter, written on October 7, 1935, is absent from the record. However, Rosenwald's answer, which was written on November 14, read as follows:

> I want to apologize sincerely for not having previously replied to your letter of October 7th, but during the past few weeks I have been able to spend very little time in the office.
> The principle involved has been given a great deal of consideration by the officers of this company.
> The amount of goods imported from all countries is exceedingly small, and from Germany alone our imports are insignificant. Being a national institution, and serving people from coast to coast, we have

come to the conclusion that it would be inadvisable for our company to attempt to eliminate any certain class of goods simply because a certain portion of our customers desired us to do so.

As an individual, I believe I am as ardently Jewish as any one with my background could possibly be. Personally I do not knowingly purchase goods from Germany. I consider this my personal affair and can exercise my own judgment as an individual in purchasing what I desire.

Insofar as the company is concerned, I am, as an officer of the company, forced to have different views from those which I hold as an individual. We have a large number of stockholders and have the entire population of the United States purchasing from us. As a consequence, I do not feel it incumbent upon me to use my position as an officer of the company to force my opinion on our stockholders and customers, possibly to the detriment of the company.

In the above, I have tried to give you as clearly as I possibly could my personal and the company's position with regard to this rather difficult problem, I trust this will be of some assistance to you in answering the correspondence which you have received on this subject, the copies of which are being returned to you herewith.

Please accept my thanks for bringing this matter to my attention.[26]

Levinson replied to this letter on December 30. His effort to negate Rosenwald's arguments may be illustrated by the two following excerpted paragraphs:

The only way in which Hitler and his tribe can be stopped within a reasonable time is by economic pressure. That is an effective and legitimate weapon. It merely constitutes a refusal to deal with a man, or a corporation, or a nation, that is criminal, cruel, or fraudulent. I can not imagine you, Lessing, buying anything yourself for your own personal use made in Germany. Our protest can be heard in no other way inside Germany, for public opinion is blindfolded and freedom of the press is extinct.

The fact that your imports "from Germany alone are insignificant" would seem to relieve you altogether of any business reason. But in these times when the world is all agog, when the very fabric of civilization is being torn to tatters, when the theory of totalitarian government is even making headway in its economic aspects in this country, we must look to the high-minded businessmen of the country to put on such economic pressure as may be necessary to destroy the last vestige of this imminent peril. If it succeeds in Germany, it is bound to succeed in other countries. According to a recent great British authority, there is only one third of civilization that is free, only one third of the people of this earth who really enjoy liberty. We are trustees for them. We are trustees for one another and we must subordinate every motive of materialism to this call to the spirit, if we would protect and preserve our beloved America.[27]

The Jewish War Veterans also tried to induce Mr. Rosenwald to rid his company of German-made merchandise; and there is a record of Rosenwald's reaction to this attempt as well. He stated it in a July 28, 1937, letter to Edgar H. Berman, then the acting chairman of JWV's Boycott Committee. Written nearly two years after Levinson's abortive overtures, the letter shows that the Sears executive had still not been prevailed upon to cease the importation of German goods;

> Concerning the matter of the purchase of German merchandise by our company, I should like to be quite frank in answering you and giving you my carefully considered opinion on this subject. As an individual, I am decidedly opposed to the purchase of German merchandise, and since the Hitler regime, I have never knowingly bought German-made goods. I feel that this is a matter which is entirely within my own judgment and discretion and for which no one can criticize me.
>
> In so far as our company is concerned, I feel very strongly that, as an officer of the company and acting in the capacity of a trustee for our stockholders, I do not have the right to impose my personal opinion upon the company, our stockholders and our customers. We have thousands of stockholders and several millions of customers throughout the nation. Some of these stockholders and some of these customers are unquestionably [as] much in favor of purchasing goods from Germany as I am opposed to it. I feel, therefore, that I would be usurping my authority if I were to demand that the company follow a policy which is contrary to the will of its owners and customers, even though I myself do not encourage the purchase of German-made goods as an individual. Furthermore, I am of the opinion that any goods imported from any country should be properly labeled, and that when a customer buys an article, he should know that such an article is obtained from a foreign country. He is then at liberty to use his own judgment as to whether or not he desires to purchase it. Both in our catalog and in our retail stores, in all cases where the merchandise is not manufactured in the United States, the country of origin is shown.[28]

Yet, about three months later, the ANL decided to drop Sears from its Boycott Violators list. A League statement accompanying this decision said that Sears "had given decisive proof of their wish to cooperate."[29] Some background to this "decisive proof" is provided in the October 29, 1937, minutes of the League's Executive Committee meetings. Dr. L Ertinger, the central figure of the following minuted passage, was then the League's executive secretary:

Dr. Ertinger read to the meeting a letter of October 6 from Sears Roebuck & Co. In this letter, Sears Roebuck & Co. said that they have closed their German buying office. They have reduced purchases from German sources during 1936 to 1/6 of 1%. The Company has furthermore decided that from 1937, no more German gloves should be purchased. They have put it on record that Sears Roebuck are sympathetic to our work and that we shall receive every possible cooperation in the future. Dr. Ertinger in supplementing this letter reported in detail the lengthy conversation he had with Sears, and it was unanimously decided to remove their name for the time being from the boycott list of the League.[30]

This League action incurred the wrath of both the JBC and JWV. The latter vented its anger against the League in the October–November 1937 issue of its organ, the *Jewish Veteran*, in a critical article appearing in the regularly featured column, "On the Boycott Front." The most telling point was that a "decisive wish" on the part of a firm "to cooperate" with the boycott movement was far from sufficient to warrant its removal from a Boycott Violators list. And while conceding that a small number of Sears stores had, in fact, liquidated their German-imported stocks, the article charged that the great majority of the firm's branches continued importing annually an estimated $500,000 worth of German goods.[31]

In reply to this charge, which was probably addressed to the League under separate cover, Dr. Ertinger wrote Chairman Berman as follows on October 25:

> We note that Sears and Roebuck is still importing a few lines from Germany. We know that their total imports from Germany do not exceed 1/6 of 1% of their remaining business. We further know that prior to our pleading with them, they were importing many millions of dollars worth of German merchandise. They have expressed and demonstrated willingness to cooperate.[32]

The NSANL file in the JBC archives reveals that the Council vented its anger against Untermyer personally, saddling him with the responsibility for Sears' removal from the League's Boycott Violators list. Untermyer, the Council charged, had not rendered good judgment on a decision which, it felt, had been reached prematurely.

ii.

Certainly toward the end of the middle thirties, F. W. Woolworth, over which ANL and JBC expended a good deal of their time and energy, became a disappointing and irritating problem. Just how long and to what extent Woolworth lived up to its boycott pledge is a moot question.[33] The League's *Economic Bulletin* of May 1936 reported that Woolworth had discontinued selling German merchandise in most of its New York stores, but was selling all kinds of such wares in its out-of-town branches. But JBC's investigation of Woolworth, cited in a document one month earlier, made no such distinction. It simply stated that, of the various chain stores, Woolworth's was one of the greatest importers of German-made goods.

A detailed account of what transpired soon thereafter is wanting. What little information is available stems from the aforesaid JBC source, stating that negotiations were "in progress." During this period, it was Council policy "not to picket them, though not to deal with them either." However, a later source, dated January 20, 1937, does describe anti-Woolworth picketing by the Boycott Council. Negotiations had obviously collapsed in the interim.

One might ponder, in this connection, the advantage and relevance of Jewishness as a contributing factor to the outcome of pressure tactics. Imponderable as this might seem, we have at least seen that the Jewishness of a boycott offender did prove consequential enough to bring about a confrontation with the boycott leadership. One then noted—witness Percy Straus and Lessing Rosenwald—that the argument of German Jewish persecution tended to put the offender on the defensive; and it mattered little, really, whether such an argument originated from a prominent boycott leader or from an ordinary boycott adherent.

Not so with Woolworth. The Woolworth chain was under Christian ownership, hence, inadvertently, weakening the appeal of the Joint Boycott Council on the powerful, emotional grounds of Jewish ethnicism. For in contraposition to the Jewish owner of a given enterprise, who could be shamed and made an overt target of disapprobation before Jew and Gentile alike, the non-Jewish owner of such an enterprise was far less vulnerable to this sort of strain and vexation. To, therefore, bring him into line, one had to count more heavily than usual on the force of moral persuasion. And if urgent enough, it could be expected that JBC would call for the aid of Stephen S. Wise, the one man who, by virtue of his prestige and the deep respect that he commanded, was in a singular position to effect the conclusion of a pro-boycott settlement in such cases.

But as of the middle of 1937, Dr. Wise had still not persuaded the Woolworth management to cease violating the boycott. This is learned from a July 8 statement sent by Dr. Tenenbaum to Rabbi Wise's wife, Louise Waterman Wise, whom he informed that if Woolworth were to just import a minimum of German goods, the boycott against it would be terminated.[34] To bring this about, he explained, all that would be required was that Woolworth produce "satisfactory evidence" that it was steadily reducing its purchases of German commodities, and that in time, it would cease handling them altogether. But "up to the present," Dr. Tenenbaum added, "no such evidence has been given by them." His note concluded with the comment that, on a number of occasions, communications, including a letter by Dr. Wise himself, "were not accorded the courtesy of a reply."[35]

The Furriery Scandal

i.

Although the JBC was not worldwide in scope and organization as was the NSANL, still, through the cooperation of aides operating in many European capitals, the Council, in order to detect boycott violations, kept a tight vigilance over trade relations with Hitler Germany. However, if evidence to this effect were discovered, the by-now-familiar countermeasures of blacklisting and picketing would be applied against the "guilty" firm(s), usually, until agreement was reached to resolve the issue through arbitration.

The most shocking and most publicized case of this kind was uncovered in May of 1937 by Tenenbaum's European co-workers, who were long puzzled by the handsome profits made by some American importers of Rumanian furs. Much to the chagrin of the former, further investigation revealed that Hitler Germany was also receiving a substantial share of these profits. The question was how.

The scheme was discovered in an action which implicated the Eitingon Schild Fur Corporation, the Alexander Bernstein Company, and the Balkan Importing Corporation, a New York branch of Pellimpex, the large Rumanian fur firm. All three were accused of being involved in a deal in which Eitingon and Bernstein received an estimated $800,000 worth of Rumanian-imported Persian lamb skins that were shipped to the United States via Germany. Balkan's role in this was to assist its sister companies in the sale of these skins.

The collusive procedure that the threesome worked out was the following: Eitingon and Bernstein forwarded the American dollars used as payment for the Rumanian furs to a number of London banks, wherewith Pellimpex, apparently, had special accounts. These dollars were then sent to the Reich, which would, in the meanwhile, buy these furs with Rumanian lei currency credited to it in Rumania through barter agreements. But because Rumanian lei had very little value in the foreign-exchange marts, it was Hitler Germany which profited considerably by the exchange of this currency for American currency. As for Eitingon and Bernstein, they were free from any suspicion, since the records of their canceled checks showed them dealing not with Germany, but with Rumania. It was a shrewd scheme, which the Boycott Council described as "one of the most carefully planned and seemingly fool-proof devices yet evolved by the Nazis in an effort to improve their foreign exchange position."[36]

The beguiling plot turned out to be a very scandalous affair, not so much because the accused offenders were Jews who had signed boycott pledges, but because they were engaged in a multi-million-dollar business whose publicity greatly magnified the enormity of their offense. This applied particularly to Eitingon, whose earnings of $9,789,000 the year before qualified it as the world's largest fur dealer.

The allegedly guilty firms denied having any knowledge of the violation with which they were being charged and resisted for six months any attempt to settle the dispute by arbitration. However, the continued refusal of the Furriers' Union to handle any of their merchandise during this interval finally compelled them to submit to arbitration. Their case was adjudicated on November 7 and 8 (1937) by an arbitration board composed of a special Furriers Committee and JBC representatives. All the defendants were found guilty of the "obnoxious practice" of importing German goods and punished with a fine of $75,000.

ii.

Ordinarily, Untermyer did not make public statements as regards boycott violators. However, he could not ignore the foregoing scandalous case. For aside from having rocked Jewish circles and having been publicized in the general press,[37] the affair proved embarrassing to him personally because the penalized importers were League patrons. Of them, Untermyer said: "They are men of high character and unblemished reputation who are and have long been heavy contributors to our charities and who would not, in my judgment, knowingly have stooped to such methods."[38]

Untermyer also claimed to have made this *cause célèbre* an object of investigation which, upon completion, satisfied him "that the guilty parties were innocent of any knowledge of the means which were employed and by which Germany profited."[39] The most he would concede, however, was that "they were apparently negligent in not having been informed about the deception."[40] He further asserted that "they would doubtless have refused to receive the goods, had they known."[41] At any rate, Untermyer refused to recognize the decision of the Board of Arbitration, "which acted on charges presented by an organization not in any way affiliated with the League."[42]

Untermyer was not content, however, with just making a deprecatory statement about the fining of the furriers. In his singular manner, he availed himself of the opportunity to blast this procedure, saying:

> I am not familiar with all the details of the transaction resulting in the imposition upon these New York fur merchants of this fine for alleged violation of the boycott against Germany. It is not the first case in which boycott violators have been able to buy themselves out for sinning against their fellow men.
>
> Our League does not approve of fining violators. It reminds us of the practice in Luther's time, when throwing coins into a church box was supposed to clean them of all sins. It converts dealing with Germany into a question of dollars and cents, instead of dealing with it on principle.[43]

Untermyer's caustic assessment implied that fining hardly acted as a deterrent against boycott violations. To him, the furriers' fine was an example par excellence that merely confirmed his analogy; for if caught that the perpetrator had only to fear a fine of 10 percent forfeiture of his profits, after which he was free again to violate the boycott.

In the final analysis, the ANL chief placed the blame for the furriers' scandal on the Customs Department, noting with asperity that "This situation furnishes just another illustration of the laxity and incompetency of the Customs Department of the U.S. Treasury Department in permitting these constantly recurring frauds upon our Customs laws on the part of Germany, against which we have been protesting without avail."[44]

Untermyer singled out for particular condemnation German-American barter arrangements which facilitated the entry into the United States of all kinds of Nazi ware on a noncash, noncredit basis. This, the ANL chief maintained, abetted the contrivance of fraudulent schemes, "of which the fur transaction is a striking illustration." Further, the Treasury Department, Untermyer rightly asserted, was responsible for the detection of fraudulent schemes. If so, he reasoned, it should have uncovered the furriers' plot. And since it failed, Untermyer continued, the Treasury Department is to blame "for our being victims of Germany's devious methods." This seemingly plausible charge lacked but one thing: documentary proof that the Rumanian fur had actually come into the United States by means of barter or a method other than the one which Dr. Tenenbaum's European aides had uncovered.

The 1936 Olympics Episode

In 1896, in keeping with the tradition of the ancient Greeks, the Olympic Games were revived, and as a symbolic gesture, held in Athens, Greece. Thenceforward, they were scheduled every fourth year and usually held at some chosen capital city. Such meets were decided by a World Olympic Committee, which, in 1932, chose Berlin as the site of the international sports event for 1936.

With the launching of the boycott movement, it was only natural that an attempt be considered to get this decision overruled. There was but one way to achieve this, and that was the nigh-impossible task of getting the sports leaders from the fifty nations that had approved the decision to rescind it. The next best course was therefore pondered; namely, inducing the Amateur Athletic Union (AAU), which organization was the official representative body of America's major sports clubs, to announce its withdrawal from the forthcoming Olympics.

In this field of endeavor, the most potent weapon at the disposal of America's two major boycott groups was the so-called Kirby Resolution, which the AAU had passed in 1933 as a precondition to its participation in the 1936 Olympics.[45] This resolution stated that American athletes would not be "certified for the Olympics unless the position of the German Olympic Committee of the Organizing Committee of Berlin and the German Government is so changed in fact as well as in theory as to both permit and encourage German athletes of Jewish faith or heritage to train, prepare for and participate in the Olympic Games of 1936."[46]

But whether or not America would act in accordance with this resolution was largely up to Avery Brundage, president of the American Olympic Association, who showed complete disregard for the Kirby Resolution[47] by committing the United States, as early as 1934, to participation in the next Olympics. This is not surprising, as all available records show Brundage unalterably opposed to all entreaties or demands to keep American athletes out of the Olympics. He did, however, have the following to say about it:

> The time and place for the Olympic Games of 1936 were fixed by the International Olympic Committee, composed of impartial representatives of 50 different countries, long before the present German government came into power. Olympic regulations provide that this decision must be reached at least three years in advance since it takes at least that long to prepare for this great enterprise.[48]

Brundage summed up his stand on this matter in an American

Olympic Committee pamphlet entitled *Fair Play for American Athletes*. His opening statement, "The Issue," read:

> The future of amateur sport in the United States is now being threatened as a result of the efforts of certain individuals and groups to involve sport in foreign political affairs, and to keep American athletes out of the Olympic Games. It becomes the duty of those charged with the administration of amateur sport to fight off this invasion. "Shall the American athlete be made a martyr to a cause not his own?"
> The Olympic Games were revived in order to encourage the development and extension of international amity and good will in a world filled with intolerance, persecution, hatred and war. The great success of the Games is due to the precautions taken to guard them against entanglement in political, religious or class controversies. To involve them in the present Jew-Nazi altercation would completely invert the object of the Games.[49]

The AOC president concluded with a couplet that smacked of anti-semitic innuendo: "Upon the altars of these peaceful Games let no usury be committed."[50]

"The Facts," Brundage's next statement, is also spiced with an unrestrained bias and bellicosity:

> The Games of the Eleventh Olympiad are an international and not a German enterprise. They are entirely and exclusively controlled by international committees who make all the rules and handle all the competitions. The Games will be held in Germany whether the United States is represented or not, and from present indications will be a brilliant success since more countries and more athletes than ever before are entered.
> The International Olympic Committee and twenty-three international federations composed of the impartial, unbiased sport leaders of fifty nations have sanctioned these Games and approved their location. These men, noted for fairness and sportsmanship, are quite competent to weigh the facts and issues involved.
> As always the American team will be selected from the best athletes of this country including Jews, with character and amateur standing the only restriction.
> Full courtesy and hospitality in Germany are assured to all Olympic athletes and visitors, no matter what race, color or creed.
> Berlin was chosen as the site of the Olympic Games long before Hitler became established in power. When the Nazis took over the German Government the International Olympic Committee in no uncertain terms served notice that there must be no political interference. Jews the world over greeted this warning with great enthusiasm.

Certain Jews must now understand that they cannot use these Games as a weapon in their boycott against the Nazis.[51]

In another statement which is not, however, acknowledged by name, the anonymous writer professed a knowledge of "Jewish Opinion," proceeding to diagnose it as follows:

> It would be an injustice to an intelligent race to assume that Jews as a whole approve of the propaganda against United States participation in the Olympic Games. The misinformation circulated, the false logic, the attempts to intimidate, the hysteria and specious appeals to emotion, and the political and economic coercion employed in the campaign must be deplored by all fair-minded and level-headed Jews.... Jewry suffers from the radicalism and the self-seeking of a few in its ranks who put personal advantages before the welfare of the race. It also is the victim of unscrupulous politicians of other faiths. The Olympic boycott will be repudiated by all intelligent Jews when they learn the facts and issues involved.[52]

To be sure, Brundage had some opposition from influential AAU leaders, Jew and Gentile alike. The most prominent of these was Judge Jeremiah T. Mahoney, an Irish Catholic, who was elected AAU president in January 1935. Mahoney, through the press, radio, and the organization he now headed, conducted a vigorous campaign to alter the location of the 1936 Olympics. But his efforts, which were directed against Nazi Germany in the name of religious and racial tolerance, came to naught. In December of 1935, the AAU, succumbing to too strong a penchant for U.S. participation in the approaching Olympics, voted in favor of it.

With the 1936 Olympics drawing nearer and nearer, German Jewish athletes, under one pretext or another, were ruthlessly eliminated by the Nazi policy of exclusion. But this hardly impressed Brundage, who coldly wrote:

> In accepting the invitation to compete in the 1936 Olympic Games the American Olympic Committee, like the Olympic committees of 48 other nations which have accepted, does not endorse the policies of any government. The Committee considered nothing but sport and its requirements. Germany's political policy within or without its borders has no bearing on the subject. The Committee only followed the universal and unbroken Olympic precedent of forty years and ignored irrelevant political, racial and religious affairs. Attempts to twist and distort the unanimous decision of the committee into an endorsement of Nazi policies are nothing but bare-faced effrontery.[53]

Brundage's last point was an obvious slap in the face to boycott leaders, who were vainly complaining that Germany's Olympic authorities were not honoring their country's pledge not to interfere with the free entry and participation of Jews. A March 5, 1935, communication by Harriman states, in this connection, that "we have industriously been garnering proofs that Germany is not living up to these pledges and that the United States should stay out of the games on this account alone."[54] The League secretary then went on to explain:

> Another point that impels us to continue our anti-Olympic work is that the patronage and attendance at the games will violate the boycott and provide the Nazis with important quantities of foreign exchange, a thing which we are dedicated to prevent. . . . It strikes us that when we are practicing a general boycott against anything German, we would be omitting an essential element on our program were we to neglect so well publicized and so profitable a feature as the forthcoming Olympiad.[55]

A Fair Play in Sports Committee that was organized within AAU ranks because of Brundage's intransigence proved too small and feeble a body to overcome the pro-Olympics group. An undated League report entitled "Memorandum on Olympic Games" gives us an idea what the contra group was up against. The telling argument is found in a subsection called "Methods of Protest":

> It must be understood that Amateur Athletics in this country are controlled by the Amateur Athletic Union, an organization which rules with an iron hand. For an athlete or a club to defy the AAU means to be barred from all athletic competition. The AAU and the Olympic Committee are practically the same bodies under different titles. Neither the AAU nor the athletes are ever likely to support any movement which may disrupt the regular holding of the Olympic games, no matter what ideals may be at stake. The athletes are youngsters and the athletic officials are old men who find in their Olympic activities a sense of power and importance. Their primary objects would naturally be defeated if the games were not held and therefore they are naturally opposed to any cause that is likely to prvent them from being held.
> The psychology of the athlete too must be understood. It is the ambition of every youngster with athletic abilities to make the Olympic team. It is the goal of a lifetime, and they are not likely to support any movement which will thwart that ambition. In fact there is a danger in constant protest of arousing antagonism towards Jews in this country rather than towards the Nazis.
> Under the circumstances it is impossible to obtain the support of such athletes who have a chance of making the American Olympic

team in an organized protest. The same is true of the major clubs, all of which are and must be affiliated with the AAU. They would be unwilling to endanger their positions.

On the 1932 Olympic team there were only two Jewish athletes, a runner and a boxer. It would therefore of course sound ridiculous to conduct a boycott by Jewish athletes. The Jewish athletes in the Olympics are not important enough to carry any weight. I spoke with one of the two Jews of the last Olympic team and he was unwilling to jeopardize his position.

The only form of protest that could be organized is that of older men, once famous athletes, like Benny Leonard, Benny Friedman etc. With them we could create a noise in the press. But in effect such a protest would be useless. We could also organize some of the smaller distinctly Jewish athletic clubs in a protest movement, but they too would carry no weight, because they have no athletes in their ranks that can make the Olympic team.

If we are to continue any anti-Olympic activity at all, the following idea must be stressed; that all the basic principles of fellowship, fair play, international amity and friendship for which the Olympics stand are being violated by the nation in which the next Olympiad will be held. We can safely use the Olympic games to make anti-Nazi propaganda but we can not afford to make anti-Olympic propaganda without doing more harm than good.[56]

Congressman Celler sought to be of help by introducing, on August 15, 1935, a House resolution barring the use of public funds to defray the expenses of American Olympic athletes. The measure did not pass, however.

It soon became painfully clear to the two major boycott organizations that they could do nothing to reverse the AAU decision to participate in the 1936 Olympics. However, to demonstrate their disappointment and protest, they supported a drive to hold a Jewish Olympiad under JLC auspices. The games took place at New York's Randall's Island, and were presided over by Charles L. Ornstein, one of Mahoney's right-hand men and long-time AOC member.

Boxing

i.

To Americans, Germany's Max Schmeling became well known from his fights with Jack Sharkey, to whom, in 1932, Schmeling lost the heavyweight title that he had won two years earlier. In 1936, however, at the relatively old boxing age of thirty-one, Schmeling made a sensational comeback by regaining the heavyweight crown, thereby becoming the first fighter to defeat the then twenty-two-year-old black American, Joe Louis. In a Hitler Germany, the event was marked with more than the usual ostentation accorded such an occasion. After all, had not a "true" Aryan averted the unpleasantness—which he did not two years later—of losing a championship fight to an "inferior" Negro?

There was some debate in boycott circles as to whether Schmeling was or was not pro-Nazi; but this remained, by and large, an academic question. For what interested the boycott leadership most was to prevent the Nazi regime from receiving a handsome slice of Schmeling's U.S. earnings.

A comparison between the ANL and JBC records, which indicates, incidentally, that it was Untermyer, who took the initiative in the Olympics question, discloses that he also did the spadework in the Schmeling case, waging an organized campaign to have all his contests boycotted. In a November 29, 1937, communication to the promoter and boxing manager Mike Jacobs, Untermyer said that he held nothing per se against Schmeling, and would be satisfied if the German pugilist agreed to leave in the United States such monies that accrued from his bouts with American prizefighters. However, Schmeling made it clear that he had no intention of meeting such a condition. He brooked no interference in his financial affairs, insisting that it was his own private business. Schmeling also commented that he viewed the boycott as a political matter, hence irrelevant to the world of sports which he was representing. In any event, judging from attendance figures at his matches, the Schmeling boycott, which managed to stir up some publicity, turned out to be a failure.

ii.

In the meanwhile, Adolf Hitler had apprized an intimate political circle that he was ready to go to war in order to secure for Germany the territory to which she was "entitled" for her "rightful" political and economic expansion. The American anti-Nazi boycott movement would be entering a more critical and even unpredictable stage under this menacing circumstance.

Of much greater significance, of course, was the question of the very continuation of Western civilization itself; for so fateful and destructive a menace as an international war could obviously disengage a boycott from active or meaningful continuity. And so, before long, this question became a real pressing issue for America's boycott leaders. It was until the next decisive and final stage of the American anti-Nazi boycott movement that this critical possibility haunted the professional arbiters of continued, active anti-Nazi resistance.

Part IV
1938–1939: PRELUDE TO WAR

A.
THE DRIVE FOR LEBENSRAUM

26

Incipients of Nazi Expansion: From Vienna to Munich to Prague

i.

Never in history did a leader announce to the entire world in as much detail, through both the written and spoken word, his dictatorial aims and expansionist goals, as did Adolf Hitler. And never did the world's leading statesmen, knowing the plans for aggression, so underestimate them or make light of them. Rearmament, conscription, the reoccupation of the Rhineland: all carried out with impunity in defiance of the Versailles Treaty; so that by January 30, 1937, when Hitler informed the Reichstag that Germany was withdrawing from this Treaty, his nation was again a world power. By now, however, such notification no longer rang as a daring threat, but was just a formal gesture. For to the Germany which had befriended Benito Mussolini, the Italian dictator, tested its air power in Spain, and in great measure isolated Poland from France, the Versailles *Diktat* was a dead letter anyway.

On November 5, 1937, as we now know from captured German documents, Hitler informed his General Staff that he was prepared to go to war to give Germany the *Lebensraum* he felt she deserved. This was not to be in far-off Asia or Africa, but right in the heart of Europe, in countries contiguous to the Reich. Austria was to be the first guinea pig in this expansionist experiment.

The moment was most propitious, with Hitler having a choice of annexing the former Hapsburg state either through internal political subversion or actual military invasion. But warlike though he was, Hitler possessed enough sense to attempt a bloodless conquest where this was practicable. And practicable it was in the Fuehrer's native land, where throughout 1937, Austrian Nazis had subjected their Chancellor, Dr. Kurt von Schuschnigg, to riotous demonstrations and incessant acts of sabotage. This campaign of terror weakened considerably the internal political structure of Austria, which could not now expect great-power intervention, as in 1934, to insure its survival.[1] The attempt in 1934 to seize power in Austria had occurred on July 25, when, after subversive action, Engelbert Dollfuss, Austria's diminutive Chancellor, was mortally wounded by his country's Nazi followers. But Schuschnigg, then Minister of Justice, foiled the putsch by quickly dispatching government forces which regained control of the situation. However, he became Chancellor about six hours after the Dollfuss assassination. Hitler, because Germany was still militarily weak, and because Britain, France, and even Italy had declared their support of continued Austrian independence, was compelled to postpone his plan for Anschluss. Anschluss was forbidden by the Versailles Treaty.

On the other hand, the Italo-German accord of 1936 precluded Mussolini's intervention. France was beset with internal strife. As for Britain, she was rendered quite impotent by the appeasement policy adopted by Neville Chamberlain, who, in 1937, replaced Stanley Baldwin as Prime Minister.

Austria escaped an attemped takeover in 1937, only inciting Hitler to apply more drastic measures in 1938. Wasting little time, the Nazi chieftain announced to the Reichstag on February 20 that Germany intended to take under her wing the over ten million "Germans" living in "two of the States adjoining our frontiers." It was a clear reference to the seven million Austrians and the three million Sudeten Germans of Czechoslovakia. They were to be taken over one at a time within a twelve-month period.

With Austria first in line, its Nazis were called to stage an open revolt in the spring of 1938. If Schuschnigg attempted to quell it, German troops would enter Austria to prevent "German blood from being spilled by Germans."

Hitler, however, would make a final attempt to annex Austria by "peaceful" means. Schuschnigg was, therefore, invited, or rather summoned, to the mountain retreat in Berchtesgaden to discuss the Austrian question face to face with the Fuehrer on February 12, 1938. The Fuehrer's demands, however, were tantamount to ordering the dissolution of the Austrian state. Schuschnigg explained he could not personally assume the entire responsibility for acceptance; that Wilhelm Miklas, Austria's President, would also have to approve them. But Hitler laid down an ultimatum requiring Schuschnigg to sign immediately and secure Miklas's signature within three days, or see the German army march into Austria.

Upon hearing Hitler's terms, Miklas refused to capitulate to them in toto. Thus, Hitler demanded that pro-Nazis be appointed to the Ministries of War, Finance, and the Interior. But the two Austrian leaders agreed to only one such appointment, that of Dr. Seyss-Inquart to the latter office. For the appointment of pro-Nazis to the remaining posts obviously would have meant the Reich's absorption of Austria's tiny economic and defense system; hence, its certain demise.

In a last, desperate attempt to save his country from either an internal or external takeover by the Nazis, Schuschnigg decided to gamble its future on a plebiscite which he set for March 13, 1938. The unexpected move threw Hitler into one of his celebrated fits. Immediately, the Nazi dictator demanded cancellation of the plebiscite and ordered his troops concentrated on the Austrian border. In the face of an actual threat of invasion, Schuschnigg, who had, perhaps, misjudged Hitler's firm resolve on an Anschluss, at long last announced his forced resignation. Completely abandoned, Miklas signed Inquart's appointment as Federal Chancellor of Austria, thereby dooming the little country. In any event, on the very day that Schuschnigg's plebiscite was to be held, the former Hapsburg state became by proclamation "a province of the German Reich." For a moment, Austria left the stage of history.[2]

ii.

By late summer, a repeat performance was prepared for Czechoslovakia. There, ever since Hitler's rise to power, the Sudeten Germans had posed a serious threat to this rather artificial state. Up to the Anschluss, however, the Sudetens pursued a policy of restraint. But soon thereafter they began conspiring with the Fuehrer, whose ravenous territorial appetite was far from satiated by the Austrian serving he had just gobbled up.

The campaign got under way on March 28, 1938, with a secret visit to Berlin by Konrad Henlein, leader of the Sudeten Germans Party. Hitherto it had been the party's policy to avoid acts that would cast suspicion on the fealty of the Sudeten Germans to Czechoslovakia. Now, open defiance of the Czech regime was determined upon. Life was also to be made intolerable for this regime by making impossible demands upon it. The strategy was to wait for internal deterioriation to set in, at which time the Greater Reich would intervene to defend the rights of an oppressed and persecuted minority.

The new tactics of the Sudeten Party had the desired effect. On May 20, apprehension over rumors of an imminent German invasion prompted the Prague government to order immediate partial mobilization. Czechoslovakia's action, supported by Britain and France, threw

Hitler into a raging, ugly fit. He felt humiliated because the Czechs had dared to issue a call to arms at a time when he was not, as yet, prepared to smash them. Their readiness to fight seemed to the world a sign of strength and was a blow to his own and Germany's prestige. Hitler, thereupon, made detailed plans for the dissolution of Czechoslovakia. His "irrevocable" decision, issued in a special directive to the Wehrmacht on May 30, 1938, called for the breakup of the Czechoslovakian state beginning October 1.

Military intervention by either England, France, or Russia seemed unlikely.[3] In fact, England had made it quite plain to the Prague government that she approved the granting of concessions to the Sudeten Germans. Under separate treaties, both France and Russia were committed to the protection of Czechoslovakia's territorial integrity. However, the thought of having to depend on Russian help placed France in a predicament; for even if Russia could be trusted, it could not possibly render effective help unless Poland permitted Soviet troops to cross its territory. Poland was not prepared to do this, as it feared the Soviet Union no less than it did Nazi Germany. Poland even had an interest in Czechoslovakia's collapse, which could conceivably bring it territorial gains. Hence, relations between the two countries were far from amicable. In fact, subsequent developments made such a possibility remote, as England, whom Hitler feared most, was unusually pacifistic, convincing him that it was unwilling to risk a war over Czechoslovakia. For Chamberlain, who, in a despondent bid to settle the Czechoslovak crisis, had backed Hitler's demand for an autonomous Sudetenland at a September 15 meeting with the German dictator, then advised the Prague government to cede the Sudeten areas to Germany. French concurrence left the Czechs no choice but to yield.

Hitler was satisfied for about a week, after which a now stunned and angry Chamberlain was informed that the Nazi tyrant insisted on the immediate occupancy of the Sudeten territory by his troops. In a last desperate effort to save the peace, the British head of state, with Mussolini's help, arranged for a fresh conference held at Munich on September 29–30. It concluded with an agreement that Germany would approve a gradual transference of the Sudetenland, in return for which Germany obligated itself to guarantee Czechoslovakia's new frontiers.

How much such a guarantee was worth became known in mid-March 1939, when German troops occupied Prague. Like Austria, almost to the day of the month of the year before, Czechoslovakia ceased to exist.

27

The Worsening Jewish Plight

i.

Although by the time of the Czech collapse flight had reduced the Jews of Germany proper to about three-fifths their former number—to some 325,000 souls—the incorporation of the various territories into the Greater German Reich had nearly trebled this figure. Thus, the annexation of Austria brought in 180,000 Jews, the Sudetenland, 350,000, and the disintegration of Czechoslovakia, around 250,000. All told, in the spring of 1939, the fate of nearly 800,000 Jews lay in the hands of, perhaps, the most inhuman tyrant in history. For the more Jews came within Hitler's expanding reach, the more ruthlessly did he treat them. Their swift state of decline went hand in hand with the rapidly deteriorating political situation in Europe.

It started in Austria, where an anti-Jewish wave of terror, unlike anything Reich Jewry had heretofore experienced, was organized soon after the appearance of German troops. It was as if the various developmental stages in the science of Jewish degradation through which the German heartland had gone during the past five years were all applied simultaneously in their full horror and intensity. An eye witness described it as follows:

> The Austrian National Socialists broke loose and avenged themselves with truly bestial cruelty upon their opponents. Large numbers of the leading men of old Austria were literally mown down. But those who suffered most were the Austrian Jews. For weeks the Jewish inhabitants of Vienna—apart from those who had been immediately killed and arrested—were beaten and robbed; their homes were

plundered and their businesses confiscated. They were caught in the streets and compelled to wash the Austrian Storm Troopers' motorcars, to clean out the lavatories in the barracks, to scrape the political slogans of the former regime from the roads and pavements. Neither children nor old women were spared. Many died in the concentration camps at Dachau and Buchenwald; many took their own lives.[1]

These bestial acts were accompanied by the introduction of the Nuremberg Laws; so that within a matter of weeks, Austrian Jewry was reduced to a state of utter destitution. Needless to say, a similar fate befell Czech Jewry when Hitler devoured their land.

If the world would not dare to stop him from seizing Austria, it certainly would not dare or care to stop him from increasing the ferocity of his anti-Jewish policy, thought Hitler. Here, too, Austria acted as the guinea pig, and again the experiment proved a success. The Fuehrer visited barbarities upon Austria's Jews with impunity, hence his conviction that the same could certainly be applied to the Jews of the old Fatherland. A series of new decrees now followed, tightening even more securely the noose that was strangling the German Jewish community.

It began with a law requiring the registration of Jewish-owned property. By a decree announced by Goering on April 26, 1938, all Jews (including three-quarter Jews, half-Jews, as well as non-Jewish consorts of Jews) holding property worth over 5,000 RM were ordered to declare their possessions to the Reich. The next day there was a mass deportation of Jews to Dachau, which was followed by the sequestration of their property. It was the prelude to the virtual sequestration of the remainder of Jewish wealth in Germany.

In June, the month of the deadline for property registration, another decree was issued, suspending the modest property allowance hitherto granted Jewish emigrants. This was followed by a July 22 decree ordering the issue of special identity cards (*Kennkarten*) for all Jews. On August 18, another measure was introduced enjoining every Jew and Jewess to use respectively the middle names of Israel and Sarah. This was supplemented by an October 7 measure requiring all passports and identity papers possessed by Jews to bear for racial identification the letter "J" (*Jude*), thus isolating German Jews as an identifiable mass, and facilitating their slaughter when it should please the Fuehrer to order it.

ii.

On the same day, October 7, 1938, the Polish government, which had begun making veiled overtures to Hitler Germany, adopted a law prohibiting passport renewal for nationals who had been living abroad for more than five years. Furthermore, those nationals who, by virtue of this new ruling, proved ineligible for passport renewal, forfeited their citizenship.

The new ruling, scheduled to go into effect on the twenty-eighth of the month, threatened with statelessness nearly 20,000 Polish Jews who had been living in Germany for decades. Many of them had been residing in Germany since World War I. To retain their citizenship, they had but to renew their passports at the nearest Polish consulate. Now this was no longer possible, for Polish consulates were under strict orders to enforce the new ruling. As for the Nazis, they welcomed a decree which served to rid them of Jews; for they loathed the fact that *Polnische Ost Juden* (Polish Eastern Jews) were privileged to reside in their land. On the effective date of the decree, the stateless Jews fell under the jurisdiction of Germany's dreaded SD (*Sicherheitsdienst*, or Security Service).

And so on the night of October 28, with ruthless German *Puenktlichkeit* (precision), some 15,000 "foreign" Jews were loaded into buses and freight trains, and driven to the Polish frontier. Much to the displeasure of Reinhardt Heydrich, Germany's cold-blooded Chief of Security Police, this was found to be closed. However, some days later, he tried once more. Now around 10,000 Jews were herded together, driven again toward the Polish frontier, but dumped this time in the cold, open fields near a town called Zbonszyn. Many of the hapless victims, who included old and young, the infirm and the chronically ill, were clubbed across the frontier. Only the quick action of the American Joint Distribution Committee, which furnished the bare necessities of life, saved them from certain death.[2] Ultimately, most of these refugees were resettled in Poland. A portion were granted entry certificates for Palestine. Some were even permitted to reenter Germany. But there was little consolation in this, as in the interim, their means of livelihood had been destroyed.

Still, this was hardly the close of the tragedy, proving only a brief overture to another display of bestiality that surpassed what had passed over Austrian Jewry in the spring. The violence was touched off when, on November 7, seventeen-year-old Herschel Grynszpan, whose parents were among the many thousands of Jews summarily expelled beyond the German border into Poland, fatally wounded Ernst vom Rath, an attaché of the German embassy in Paris. Himself a German Jewish refugee who had made his residence with a Parisian uncle, Grynszpan "could bear it no longer," and in a fit of unconquerable despair, shot an innocent German official to draw the attention of the world to the Nazi horror.

Vom Rath died on November 9, giving the Nazis an ideal pretext for their craving savagery. That very evening, Goebbels issued instructions for the organization of "spontaneous" reprisals. The popular outburst was stage-managed by Heydrich, whose men acted as liaison for contacting the rioters and obviating local police intervention. Captured German archives contain his instructions, teletyped at 1:20 A.M. on November 10:

> Only such measures should be taken which do not involve danger to German life or property. For instance synagogues are to be burned down only when there is no danger of fire to the surroundings.
> Business and private apartments of Jews may be destroyed but not looted.
> The demonstrations which are going to take place should not be hindered by police.
> As many Jews, especially rich ones, are to be arrested as can be accommodated in the existing prisons. Upon their arrest, the appropriate concentration camps should be contacted immediately in order to confine them in these camps as soon as possible.[3]

When the night of horror was over, Heydrich sent Goering the following dispatch:

> The extent of the destruction of Jewish shops and houses cannot yet be verified by figures . . . 815 shops destroyed, 171 dwelling houses set on fire or destroyed only indicate a fraction of the actual damage so far as arson is concerned . . . 119 synagogues were set on fire, and another 76 completely destroyed . . . 20,000 Jews were arrested. 36 deaths were reported and those seriously injured were also numbered at 36. Those killed and injured are Jews . . .[4]

Actually, the tragic import of this abhorrent episode lay not so much in being the worst anti-Jewish pogrom yet perpetrated by the Nazi regime, but in marking the transition from a policy of legal restriction to sheer physical violence, and thereby heralding the advent of genocidal slaughter. But there was also an ironic side to this tragedy. Most of the damage affected insured Aryan-owned establishments. However, in the haggling that followed between Goering, as Germany's economic plenipotentiary, and a representative of the insurance companies, Nazi policy proved again that it could be counted upon to victimize the Jews.

The total bill for the orgy of violence and spoliation was about 25 million RM. The insurance companies were enabled to provide compensation without loss, obtaining their funds from a billion-RM fine that Goering imposed on the Jewish community, which he charged, had revealed a "hostile attitude towards the German nation and the Reich." Goering's announcement of the billion-RM fine was accompanied by the following remark:

> That will work. The pigs will not commit another murder. Inciden-

tally, I would like to say that I would not like to be a Jew in Germany now. The second point is this. If in the near future the German Reich should come into conflict with foreign Powers, it goes without saying that we in Germany would first of all let it come to a reckoning with the Jews (Gerald Reitlinger, *The Final Solution,* p. 17).

To add even more insult to injury, Jewish store-owners were also warned to repair, at their own expense, their damaged establishments. Together with the community fine, this was more than enough to despoil German Jews of their entire property.

A Decree for the Elimination of the Jews from German Economic Life, issued conjointly with the Jewish community fine, was a clear warning that German Jews had reached the end of the road under the Nazis. "Elimination from economic life" was but a euphemism for a campaign which meant the total extinction of German Jewish life. For the new decree stipulated the liquidation of all Jewish businesses after January 1, 1939, a fitting sequel to the decree of April 26, 1938 (p. 246). It also gave rise to active discussions about extending a forced-labor law to Jews, banning their children from the public schools, creating ghettoes; and last but not least, forced emigration. But those Jews who had experienced the recent interval of terror needed little prodding to induce them to emigrate. Panic produced a new wave of refugees fleeing for their lives.

To a world which had grown accustomed to Nazi outrages, the events of November 9–10 and their aftermath, called invariably Black Thursday or the *Kristallnacht*,[5] were evidence that Germany had reached new depths of barbarity. Even Germans recoiled in disgust. President Roosevelt, who had not issued an official anti-Nazi denunciation during his whole tenure of office, expressed the revulsion and indignation of the American people in these words: "The news of the last few days from Germany had deeply shocked public opinion in the United States. I, myself, could scarcely believe that such things could occur in a twentieth century civilization."[6] In a singular act of determination among the statesmen of the world, Roosevelt proceeded from words to deeds by recalling the American ambassador in Berlin.

Germany likewise recalled its ambassador in Washington. Goering, on being informed of the indignation of American public opinion, angrily referred to the United States as a gangster state and a country of scoundrels. Hitler also flew into a rage, and in his inimitable manner, reassured himself that the reaction simply corroborated his charges regarding "the Jewish conspiracy." His response was only to intensify the actions which were pushing the Jews and the world ever closer to the final disaster.[7]

28

The Swelling Refugee Problem: From Departure to Flight

If emigration means a voluntary movement of people to countries of their choice, then the years 1933 to 1937 can still be said to fall under this rubric with regard to German Jewry. In late 1938, however, when Hitler first began toying with the Madagascar Plan,[1] the word "evacuation" was added to the current usage of "emigration." For by the end of that year, forced Jewish emigration became the order of the day in Nazi policy.

Figures bear this out quite clearly. From 1933 to 1937, the emigration of German Jews totaled some 135,000. However, in 1938 alone, nearly 100,000 Jews fled the Nazi state. While the latter figure is based on the enlarged Jewish population of a Greater German Reich, it reflects not only the established Nazi policy of restriction, but also the intensification of terror. For not political and economic disabilities, but the fear for personal safety, preoccupied the heart and mind of the "Greater German Jew," and what ensued was a panicky flight rather than the erstwhile, relatively orderly exodus from the pre-1938 Germany. Yet, for all his augmenting troubles, the Jew, in the great majority of cases, had neither a place nor the means to go. And by 1938, all the world was the setting of his tragedy.

To be sure, attempts on a worldwide scale had been made to come to the rescue of German Jewry. But stringent immigration laws and the disinclination of governments to receive a sudden influx of large waves of aliens blocked the admission of Jews into most countries. While many Jewish organizations—boycott included—refused, out of self-respect and sheer distrust, to consider a plan to ransom their coreligionists, enough funds could have been raised to effect their release if they had been granted permission to disembark in sufficient numbers on the shores of receptive host countries. But, alas, this was not possible to obtain.

A substantial part of the discussions that led to this sorry state of indirection transpired in the assembly halls of the League of Nations. Here, nations unwilling to absorb the Jews—the one alternative to their annihilation—could express humanitarian sympathy for their terrible lot in the very act of rejecting any appeal for direct mass entry.[2]

Such were the circumstances under which James G. MacDonald, the League's first High Commissioner for Refugees,[3] was forced to carry out the functions of his office. An American, MacDonald was appointed on October 11, 1933, to head an agency which, by general consensus, was needed to help solve, through international collaboration, the socioeconomic and financial problems of the refugees. MacDonald was authorized to negotiate with the several governments on technical matters like passports, identification papers, and work permits. In addition, he was empowered to deal with questions concerning the admission of refugees into countries with a favorable absorptive capacity and the alleviation in the acquisition of decent living quarters. An Advisory Council, consisting of representatives of private organizations, both Jewish and non-Jewish, was also organized to assist him in the performance of his duties. It helped legalize the status of many refugees, but ultimately proved powerless to change their fate. In 1935, when it became very evident to him that he was unable to carry out the obligations of his office, MacDonald resigned. He was replaced by a Britisher, who gloried in the fact that he helped rescue 5,000 refugees. It was little to brag about for a three-year term of office.

The Evian Conference

i.

Two things became very evident in 1938; first, that the problem of Jewish emigration from a Greater Germany could not be solved by charity and routine relief work alone; and second, that the Jews' need for a place of refuge had become a distinct international issue, and would have to be dealt with accordingly. The Anschluss, attended by a brutality and terror that put tens of thousands of Austrian Jews to flight, was the first alarming sign which made this painfully clear.

In the past, the simplest way to have called the attention of the world to such an emergency would have been to present it before the League of Nations. However, this emergency required prompt action, whereas the League was wont to act at a snail's pace. By now, moreover, the League had suffered an irreparable loss in authority and prestige. Furthermore, American Jews, who had at long last prevailed upon their government to act, were confronted with the embarrassment that America was not a League member. They overcame this, though, by beseeching President Roosevelt to undertake the role normally assumed by the League. He viewed the request sympathetically, calling for an international conference which met in Evian, France, in July of 1938. There seemed to be hope at last that some countries would open up their gates to Jewish entry.

World Jewry watched tensely as representatives from thirty-two countries assembled in an attempt to find a solution to the woeful refugee problem. In theory, all refugees, irrespective of nationality or religion, were on the agenda. In practice, however, all realized that it was the pitiable dilemma of the German Jewish refugee that was really responsible for this pressing session.

Twenty-one Jewish organizations, among them the World Jewish Congress (WJC), were represented. And, yet, even this desperate situation failed to obtain from them a joint policy statement. The official historian of the World Jewish Congress described this glaring display of disunity as follows:

> The Congress sought to have a single, common delegation of all the major Jewish organizations at the Evian Conference; it also advocated that a single, joint memorandum be submitted in the name of all the associations concerned. In both of these endeavors it was defeated by Jewish disunity, rarely more in evidence than on this occasion. It was a sorry spectacle to see each of the Jewish organizations insist on appearing separately before the special subcommittee of the Evian Conference and stating its own views on how to solve the refugee problem, in the space of the three minutes allotted to each delegation.[4]

Constrained to act alone, WJC delegates, headed by Dr. Nahum Goldmann, sought to convince the Evian representatives of the dire need to make the Jewish refugee problem the main topic at the Conference. However, they took care to draw the attention of the representatives to persecuted Jews in countries other than Germany, like Poland, Rumania, and Hungary. Antisemitic to begin with, and encouraged by the Nazi example, these countries had helped to create additional masses of refugees. Congress officials, therefore, sought to obtain the recognition of these classes of refugees as well, pleading that such homeless Jews be included in any measures that the Conference would adopt in favor of political refugees. They urgently asked that these be included within the purview of the organizations which it would create.

Thus, officially, WJC spokesmen had deemed it proper to demand the reaffirmation of the principle of the "equality of rights" of Jews in all countries. But since such a doctrine had become in Hitler Germany both a misnomer and an anachronism, the Congress delegation decided that it was best to beseech Conference representatives to do everything possible to get the Nazi government to modify its emigration policy by permitting Jews to depart with at least a modicum of their property. By now Jews left with scarcely the shirts on their backs. However, emigration was only part of the staggering problem. The other part included the need to support penniless pariahs until the end of their adjustment period in the various countries of immigration. Considering that a mass emigration of around 250,000 Austro-German Jews was being contemplated, the problem was staggering, indeed. Hitler, in any event, in his January 30, 1939, address, told World Jewry how he felt about its predicament. Directing his words at the "democracies," he cited them as saying: "First, 'We',—that is, the democracies—'are not in a position to take in the Jews.' . . . Second, they assure us: 'We allow them a certain amount of capital to bring with them as immigrants.' For hundreds of years," Hitler went on, "Germany was good enough to receive these elements, although they possessed nothing except infectious political and physical diseases. What they possess today, they have by far the largest extent gained at the cost of the less astute German nation by the most reprehensible manipulations. Today we are merely paying this people what they deserve."

The Congress delegation also counseled that the most productive form of immigration was land settlement in hitherto uncultivated areas. Palestine was underscored, in this connection, as occupying a central place in the heart and mind of the Jew.

ii.

When the Evian Conference ended, it left posterity a legacy of lofty sentiments, deep sympathy, and profound regrets. Just about every representative had a plausible reason why all other countries, save his own, should come to the rescue of Hitler's victims. With the exception of the appointment of a Permanent Committee—the so-called Intergovernmental Committee for Refugees (IGC)—little in the way of practical results was achieved.

The IGC was chaired by a Britisher named Lord Winterton. The office of vice-chairman was filled by an American, Myron C. Taylor. At its first meeting, on August 3, 1938, George Rublee, an American lawyer and presidential advisor, was chosen as director. He was assigned the task of conducting "negotiations to improve the circumstances of exodus and to replace them by conditions of orderly emigration" from Nazi Germany, as well as "to approach the governments of the countries of refuge and settlement with a veiw to developing opportunities for permanent settlement."[5] To help him carry out this mission, Lord William Robert Peel, of Palestine Royal Commission fame, was chosen as assistant director.

The appeal the World Jewish Congress made on behalf of the refugees was also discussed at the meeting. After due deliberation, the IGC affirmed the "importance of inducing the countries of origin of the refugees to assist in their settlement by permitting them to take with them the property that they owned and which was their only means of livelihood."[6] A very cheerful note was struck when this was followed by an announcement by the representative of the Dominican Republic that his country was ready to admit 100,000 refugees, the majority of whom would be absorbed on a land-settlement basis. What else remained, but that Rublee set out immediately for Berlin and negotiate a deal?

In Berlin, however, the mission of the Intergovernmental troubleshooter was viewed with misgivings. For following an October 18 request by the American and British ambassadors in Berlin that Mr. Rublee be invited to the Reich capital. Germany's State Secretary, Baron Ernst von Weizaecker, sent the following memorandum to Foreign Minister Joachim von Ribbentrop:

> The Committee had intended, in order to prove its worth, to enter into discussions with the German Government. It would then be established in Germany that we—for obvious reasons—were not willing to provide the Jews with foreign currency and thus the committee would reach its ultimate object, namely, to prove that it was again German obstinacy which was responsible for the misery of the Jews. I was not able to recommend Mr. Rublee's journey simply for the sake of making Germany the scapegoat.[7]

This report, coupled with the strained atmosphere that followed in the wake of the Kristallnacht nightmare, delayed Rublee's visit. During this period, the American troubleshooter remained stranded in London.

Two Ransom Plans: Rublee vs. Schacht

i.

Rublee was not only well-trained in the law, but was also well-equipped to discuss economic issues with the foxy Dr. Hjalmar Schacht, outstanding financier and erstwhile president of the Reichsbank, whom he was soon to confront. And during his long period of waiting, Rublee had ample time to work out a plan to finance Jewish emigration from Hitler Germany. On October 27, after nearly three months, it was made public.[8]

The central idea of Rublee's plan, which remained constant throughout subsequent changes and modifications, revolved around German exports. Under this plan, both Germany and the involuntary emigrant shared in the proceeds resulting from the increases in Reich exports. This meant that Germany would confiscate surplus supplies remaining from the emigrant's export sales after deducting the funds needed to cover his emigration expenses and a sufficient amount of capital to secure him passage into countries which, otherwise, would block his entry.

Nothing further was done about this scheme until November 12, when Goering suddenly became concerned with the economic consequences of Heydrich's holding as hostages the 20,000 Jews (p. 248) arrested during the Kristallnacht. Heydrich's strategy was to pressure rich Jews to collect payments on their foreign-exchange holdings in order to expedite the emigration of the poor of their race. Goering, however, was apprehensive lest Heydrich's extortionate plan further offend world opinion. In such an event, Goering thought, Heydrich's plan would boomerang and cause the Reich to lose more foreign exchange than it would otherwise acquire. The ensuring damage to the country's economy would, in turn, do irreparable harm to its military buildup, something Goering wanted to avoid at all costs. Goering's apprehension was communicated to Hitler, who promptly approved the suggestion of sending Dr. Schacht to London to introduce a German plan of emigration before the Intergovernmental Committee.

ii.

Unlike the recognized gangster variety, to the world, Dr. Hjalmar Schacht symbolized the "respectable" Nazi. With him as its representative, thought Hitler and his closest party cronies, Germany would regain the prestige of which she was so badly in need.

The cunning supersalesman arrived in London on December 15 and presented a plan that consisted, basically, in a demand for payment of 1,500 million RM to ransom Germany's 600,000 Jews. The following rough outline summarizes the various estimates and conditions upon which Schacht proferred his proposal for consideration.

Out of the total German Jewish population, which included so-called *Mischlinge*—persons of mixed racial blood—there were 250,000 women and children, 200,000 aged and infirm, and 150,000 wage-earners. Arrangements were to be made for at least 30,000 of the latter category to leave annually over a three- to five-year period. After a reasonable interval, their families would be permitted to join them. The expatriated inhabitants could then rest assured that the aged and infirm of their "race" would be vouchsafed the right to end their lives in Germany with no abuse of their persons.

All this would be financed by a special trust fund which the Nazi regime could create by freezing German Jewish assets. At first, this proposed fund was to consist of one-fourth of German Jewry's collective wealth. Later, though, the Germans insisted that the aggregate of Jewish wealth go into the fund. However, either way, the Germans had no intention whatever of advancing the cash value of such a fund. Instead, it was proposed that Jewish assets become the security for an international loan, to be paid up in twenty to twenty-five years. Only by raising the loan, it was emphasized, could World Jewry hope to expedite the emigration of their German brethren. Jewish financiers, Schacht remarked artfully and stingingly, should be willing to accept the onus of providing the sum necessary for their departure.

The Schacht Plan was given serious study and immediate consideration. Only a day after Schacht's arrival, Rublee and Winterton appointed a technical-financial committee and a committee of private individuals to help launch it. The governments of the United Kingdom, the Netherlands, and France tried to help by appointing financial experts who extended their cooperation in the effort to solve the refugee problem. But within a week after the disclosure of Schacht's ransom scheme, it was becoming increasingly clear that its conditions were unacceptable both on financial and ideological grounds.

Nonetheless, when Schacht reported to Hitler on January 2, 1939, on his dealings with the IGC, the Fuehrer appeared keenly interested in the progress of his financial expert. Next, the stage was promptly set for a visit by Rublee, who, over Ribbentrop's opposition, was extended an invitation to come to Berlin. However, a little over a fortnight later, Hitler ousted Schacht from his post as Reichsbank president for protesting against the inflationary consequences he anticipated from Goering's recent acceleration of the rearmament program. This resulted in a temporary suspension of the negotiations in which Helmuth Wohltat, head of the Foreign Credits Control Office and a Goering confidant, succeeded Schacht as Germany's chief representative. The resumption of negotiations proved quite futile, however, since Hitler, in a vindictive and irrational response to his feud with Schacht, now became unalterably opposed to surrendering the assets of the German Jewish community. By February, Rublee had had enough. Perceiving the hopelessness of the situation, he resigned himself to failure and tendered his resignation.[9]

In April, Wohltat went to London to negotiate a limited Jewish settlement in Rhodesia and British Guiana. However, this new confrontation yielded no better results than the old one. In fact, it made any solution to the refugee problem well-nigh impossible, for by itself, the IGC was, at best, making modest progress. Yet, it must be said that there was very little the committee could do in a situation involving Nazi gangsterism and extortion on the one hand, and a lack of determination and conscience in the democracies, on the other.[10] In any event, in July, at the initiative of the Joint Distribution Committee, the Intergovernmental Committee created a Coordinating Foundation designed to make less troublesome the emigration of the refugees. The Foundation proved to be the IGC's last major prewar act. It was headed by Paul Van Zeeland, ex-Premier of Belgium, and enjoyed the support of both Jewish and Christian organizations. But the Foundation had only a reserve of a million dollars for a task requiring, perhaps, hundreds of millions. It had barely begun functioning when its work was cut off by the outbreak of World War II.

Time was now rapidly running out for Reich Jewry, and, indeed, for European Jewry as well. The failure of diplomatic negotiations to resolve the emigration problem of the German Jews only caused them to be secured more tightly in the clutches of the Gestapo, which had been wielding almost absolute authority over them since 1936. Gestapo power became a crucial factor to Jews after Austria's annexation, when it was made sole agency that could issue them exit permits. On January 24, 1939, this arrangement was sanctioned by decree; for Goering, assuming the duplicitous role of statesman and hangman, invested Heydrich with the power to "solve the Jewish question by emigration and evacuation." The prototypes of Zbonszyn and Black Thursday were vivid indications of what awaited those Jews whose problems would be "solved" by evacuation. But unknown to the world—including the Jews—the matter had deteriorated to the most unfathomable development. As Hitler himself clearly enunciated six days later, on January 30, to the Reichstag: "Today I will once more be a prophet. If the international Jewish financiers in and outside Europe should suceed in plunging the nations once more into a world war, then the result will not be the bolshevization of the earth, and thus the victory of Jewry, but the annihilation of the Jewish race in Europe!"[11]

At the time of its enunciation, the catastrophic import of Hitler's "prophecy" was generally missed by Jew and Gentile alike. And when Hitler attacked Poland, thereby "plunging the nations once more into a world war," he convinced himself, as he was later to say in his *Political*

Testament, that "it was desired and instigated by those international statesmen who were either of Jewish descent or worked for Jewish interests." It made little difference to him that it was he, and not "International Jewry and its helpers," who was "finally responsible for everything."

B.
THE RESPONSE IN AMERICA

29

The Growing Resentment of American Public Opinion

The Increase in Boycott Sentiment

In June of 1936, the NSANL sent a questionnaire to approximately 4,000 notables in every state of the Union in an effort "to determine the informed opinion in America" by posing the general question: "What to do about the Ugliest Menace to our Civilization?"[1]

This question was, in turn, subdivided as follows: Should the people of America join in an organized effort to protest Hitlerism? Should the organized protest take the form of a general boycott of German goods? If you do not approve the boycott, what alternative do you suggest?

The eminent people to whom these questions were addressed included all state governors, senators and congressmen, thirty university presidents, clergymen, writers, artists, newspapermen, publishers, professors, actors, theatrical producers, prominent businessmen, and other professionals. Most of these favored making a protest against Germany. By contrast, only a few called for a hands-off policy, and but one issued a statement that might have been construed as approving Hitlerism. Over 71 percent of the responses agreed that the anti-Nazi boycott should be prosecuted, with many offering interesting suggestions for the extension of such boycott work. Those who did oppose the implementation of a boycott expressed their unequivocal opposition to Hitlerism by suggesting the use of "moral suasion" instead. To the ANL, for example, this survey proved that at least the overwhelming majority of the American intelligentsia agreed that something had to be done about Hitler and Hitlerism.

In 1939, the results of a similar survey revealed that, as of April 11 of that year, sixty-five out of every hundred persons interviewed agreed to "join a movement to stop buying German-made goods." The survey, directed by Dr. George Gallup's American Institute of Public Opinion, found that anti-Nazi boycott sentiment had started showing an upward trend beginning with the Munich crisis. It culminated with Hitler's seizure of Memel on March 23 (1939), the last of his "bloodless" conquests.

In addition, the survey disclosed that no important difference of opinion existed on the boycott issue by virtue of age, political affiliation, or geographic distribution. Throughout the United States, boycott sentiment was running at least 60 percent. However, some differences of opinion were obtained from diverse economic groups. Thus, lower-income groups were more in favor of using the boycott as a weapon of protest than were upper-income groups.

The main reason for pro-boycott sentiment was noted as well; and this was that Nazi aggression should be crushed. Typical comments were: "Boycott is our most powerful and convenient means of criticizing aggression!" and, "Somebody should teach Hitler a lesson."

The minority that was opposed to participation in an anti-Nazi boycott took this position not because it sided with Germany's policies, but because it feared lest such action involve America still further in Europe's troubles. The comment typical of this view was: "Boycott is an act of warfare. It would be the first step toward war with Germany."

Growing disapproval of German actions was also reflected in a companion survey conducted by the Gallup Institute. This survey concerned itself specifically with the duty increase on German-made goods which the State Department introduced three days after Hitler's army marched into Prague. The added levy had the backing of an overwhelming majority of Americans. According to the survey, nearly eight out of every ten voters endorsed this increment.

The following table sums up the percentile results of the two surveys conducted by the Gallup poll. Each category is preceded by the question asked by the surveyors. The first of these was referred to the voters at regular intervals during a six-month period.

Question: Would you join in a movement in this country to stop buying German-made goods?

	YES	NO
October, 1938	56%	44%
December, 1938	61%	39%
April, 1939	65%	35%

Question: Our government is showing its disapproval of Germany's policies by putting a special tax on German-made goods brought into the U.S. Are you in favor of this special tax?

YES	NO
78%	22%[2]

These figures remained constant throughout America, clearly indicating the growing concern over and opposition to Hitler's continued policy of aggression. They demonstrated, moreover, that the boycott cause had gained a moral victory. It must, therefore, have been with a sense of pride and satisfaction that G. E. Harriman (p. 164) wrote: "The League, since its formation in 1933, has consistently maintained that once aware of the true situation in Germany and the world aspirations of Hitler, the American public would rally behind the boycott movement regardless of race or creed."[3]

The Founding of the Volunteer Christian Committee

i.

President Roosevelt was undoubtedly correct when he declared during the aftermath of Black Thursday that "the news of the last few days from Germany had deeply shocked public opinion in the United States" (see p. 249). On November 15, only a day following this utterance, a group of Americans founded the Volunteer Christian Committee to Boycott Nazi Germany.[4]

The new boycott organization represented several hundred leaders in the educational, religious, scientific, and labor fields. It was fathered by Christopher T. Emmet, Jr., free-lance writer and liberal, who served as its secretary. Its chairman was Dr. William Jay Schieffelin, noted New York civic leader. The organization had very modest beginnings, however, starting out with a membership of some sixty people and using Dr. Schieffelin's home as its headquarters.

In a speech which he delivered in March of 1939, Schieffelin explained that the formation of the Christian Committee was an expression of the change of attitude on the part of numberless Americans from passive disapproval of Nazism to an active boycott of the Hitler government. This change of attitude was depicted in the opening statement of a pamphlet that the VCC issued about two months after its creation:

> Inasmuch as the Nazi persecution of Jews and Christians in Germany violates every principle of our political and religious heritage, and since this pagan religion is spreading to Hitler's totalitarian allies and through his agents over the earth, we feel we must protest not

only by word but by deed. It is not enough to help the victims of persecution; we must strike at the root of the persecution itself.

While the rest of the world trembles, we alone, because of our distance and our economic strength, have a great opportunity to rally the shattered force of world opinion and speak with a voice which even dictators cannot ignore.... A widespread American boycott of Germany and German goods would not only substantially curtail German trade, but injure the Nazi Government's credit.

How many of us realize that half of every American dollar spent in Germany or on German ships or for German goods goes into the hands of the Nazi Government to strengthen its arms, its persecution and its hold over the German people? Of what use is it to protest if at the same time we subsidize the very things we protest against? Does it make sense to pay taxes for a great increase in our armaments to guard against future danger from Germany and her ally Japan with one hand, while with the other we give them money for the very arms we fear? By merely protesting we provoke Hitler but do nothing to weaken him, the very opposite of Theodore Roosevelt's injunction, "Speak softly, but carry a big stick"....[5]

And like the ANL and JBC which preceded it, the VCC also deemed it proper to explain why and against whom its boycott was being directed.

We pledge ourselves to do this not in hatred of the German people but in sympathy, because since their Government holds their minds in a spiritual prison which is hermetically sealed, they cannot know the truth, and are at the mercy of every vicious lie backed by the most powerful propaganda machine the world has ever known. Since we cannot communicate with them by word we can only open their eyes by our deeds. And though at first the German people may suffer with their masters from a boycott, it is the only way to save them and ourselves from the spread of a deadly disease which, if not checked, must lead eventually to war or slavery or perhaps both, over the whole earth. The modern world has grown too small to live for long half slave and half free.

A great start has already been made, for never before has so unanimous and so spontaneous a protest rung out in America. We must act to organize it while the horror and the pity are still intense and the tragedy still so dramatic.[6]

The VCC did not solicit funds as a sign of commitment to its cause. It solicited instead moral commitment to the following pledge:

Inasmuch as the persecution of Jews and Christians violates and threatens every principle which as Americans and Christians we hold most dear, we feel we must protest not only by word but by deed.

We therefore pledge ourselves to do nothing, either directly or indirectly, which can aid the German Government as long as it maintains three principles which lie at the very heart of Nazi doctrine: First, violation of religious freedom; second, racial persecution; third, glorification of war and inculcation of race hatred into the minds of little children.

As long as these doctrines prevail we pledge ourselves not to travel on German ships, knowingly buy German goods or visit the territory of the Third Reich.

We pledge this not in the hatred of the German people, but because we are not allowed to communicate with them by word. We can only open their eyes by letting our actions speak for us.[7]

The following observation was made in this connection:

There is the danger that many people who refuse to buy German goods still are reluctant to sign a boycott pledge. But if the Christian boycott remains secret and unavowed, it plays into the hands of Hitler, his agents and his sympathizers here by enabling them to blame it all on the Jews; whereas if American Christians are willing to stand up and be counted by signing our pledge it will prove that the opposition to Hitler is neither confined to Jews nor led by them.

The Gallup Poll proves that Jews are only a fraction of those who are boycotting Germany, so why should they have to bear the whole burden of the Nazi attack in what is really our fight as much as theirs?[8]

Also noted was the "Progress of the Pledge":

Since the Volunteer Christian Committee to Boycott Nazi Germany was formed two months ago, the pledge has been signed among others by over 300 leading Americans from 117 cities in 39 states, representing the world of science, education, art, literature, labor and the professions. Thousands of pledges have been signed and every day more are coming in.

Among the signers are 122 distinguised scientists, associated with 47 different institutions of learning; also 25 presidents of colleges, and 52 professors. There are also well known authors, Bishops, some of the most prominent leaders of the women's peace movement in America, and many of the country's leading economists.

The endorsement of so many economists, educators, churchmen and pacifists is not only confirmation of the practicality of the boycott, but of its moral justification as a peaceful substitute for war.

Mr. William Green, President of the American Federation of Labor, has personally signed the Christian Boycott Pledge and has offered the cooperation of his organization in furthering the pledge and the boycott throughout the nation. Mr. Green and the American Federation of Labor were the pioneers among non-Jews in this field . . .[9]

Specific details concerning Green's involvement in the new boycott organization are wanting. On March 8, in any case, Shieffelin wrote the AFL executive, asking him to link up his labor group with the VCC, and pointing out that such a joint venture would "strengthen and consolidate" the boycott in America. A week later, Green replied:

> I acknowledge receipt of your letter dated March 8th.
> It is quite evident that you and your organization and the American Federation of Labor are in thorough accord so far as our joint desires to make the boycott against German goods and German service effective are concerned. We are each seeking to make this boycott effective. I will gladly render all service possible in this direction.
> I am planning to again call upon the membership of the American Federation of Labor to renew their determination to make the boycott against German goods and German service effective. I feel, however, that the American Federation of Labor can exercise a greater influence by pursuing its own independent course in this particular matter rather than to join with other organizations. Our membership, in my opinion, and their families, will be more impressed by an appeal directly from the American Federation of Labor rather than by a joint appeal in which the American Federation of Labor, along with other organizations, might participate . . .[10]

In apparent acceptance of Green's preference for a continued independent boycott course, Dr. Schieffelin wrote him on the thirty-first: "The Volunteer Christian Committee to Boycott Nazi Germany has limited financial resources and we hope, by securing the cooperation of such organizations as yours, to avoid the necessity for a great money raising and organizing campaign all over the country."[11]

The subject of contributions, among others, is cited in "How You Can Cooperate," the concluding subtitle of the aforesaid VCC pamphlet:

> Contribute to our expenses if you can for we need funds, but more important still, contribute some of your time. We want above all to make this a volunteer cooperative and Christian effort, with no hate but with no compromise on principle.
> Please bring the pledge to the attention not only of your friends but of any organization you belong to, in order to have it introduced at meetings or distributed by mail. We are especially anxious to have it read in churches or at meetings connected with church activities and distributed afterwards.
> Try to have it posted on the bulletin boards of churches, schools, meeting halls and other public places. Try to have it printed in local newspapers and in the publications of different organizations, if possible, in a box that can be torn out for signature. Finally, friends of

the movement can keep it in their homes for signature and distribute it from hand to hand.

Labor must be made to realize the danger from the competition of Nazi and Fascist wage slavery. Businessmen can be aroused to the menace of unfair and subsidized competition. Christians must be made to know what is happening to their brothers in Germany and also to remember that, if we are truly Christian, what is done against the Jews is done against us. Negroes should learn what the spread of Nazi race doctrines here would mean to them.

It can be shown that even to such organizations as the Rotarians or Masons, opposition to the Nazis and Fascists is also a matter of self-preservation. The ideals which inspire scientists, teachers, writers, artists, and even sportsmen, are all denied today in Nazi Germany.

It is encouraging to remember that long before the word "boycott" was used, our forefathers made great sacrifices in forcing a general popular embargo against trade with Great Britain, and in 1768, the people of Boston were asked to sign a pledge to buy no more goods imported contrary to this agreement. George Washington, Thomas Jefferson and Patrick Henry were its ardent supporters in Virginia. The boycott, therefore, is in the oldest American tradition.

We believe the Christian Boycott pledge will not only help to restrain Hitler, but act as a symbol of our own unity against prejudice and intolerance here.[12]

The Coordinated Boycott Committee

i.

Another non-Jewish boycott organization, named the American Boycott Against Aggressor Nations (ABAAN), also came into being during this period. Its purpose differed from the VCC, JBC, and ANL in that it pursued a policy of boycotting all three Axis powers. It was an understandable, even useful move, considering the fact that, in the second half of the 1930's, more and more, the Axis countries began menacing world peace. Consequently, the Volunteer Christian Committee and the American Boycott group united with the Joint Boycott Council to form the Coordinated Boycott Committee (CBC), chaired by Dr. Schieffelin. The aim of this threefold organization was to make the boycott more powerful through coordination and to eliminate the useless duplication of efforts. On the day of the merger, the CBC issued a statement saying:

> The struggle between the totalitarian powers and the democracies is now entering the decisive stage. We in the United States are not without responsibility for the wars of aggression that are being waged

against all freedom loving peoples. The Fascist powers are still at the mercy of the democracies economically, as they furnish Germany a field of 75% of its exports and with all her foreign exchange which enables her to buy materials for her war machine. That could be stopped if the democracies make the boycott air-tight.

As it is, the American boycott alone made real inroads in Nazi economics. Last year Germany was forced to absorb an unfavorable balance of 43 million dollars, and Germany cannot stand such blows too long. Even isolationists can agree on a principle of stopping to finance an aggression. The boycott is a means for united action by believers in democracy the world over, while waiting for their government to act.[13]

In a luncheon address three days later, Dr. Tenenbaum outlined CBC's tasks. They are cited as follows in an undated report:

> The Volunteer Christian Committee to Boycott Nazi Germany, the American Boycott Against Aggressor Nations and Joint Boycott Council of the American Jewish Congress are hereby entering in an agreement to form a joint agency known as the Coordinated Committee for Boycott.
> The purpose of this Committee is to coordinate all activities of the above-mentioned organizations, to cooperate to the fullest extent in all boycott problems and activities and to pool all available information, resources, research and office facilities for joint and common action to the extent that such unification of action seem desirable.
> Three officers of each organization will be delegated to constitute the permanent representatives on the Coordinated Committees for Boycott.
> The organization will endeavor (a) to promote and expand the boycott among all the sections of the people of the United States. (b) to foster and promote a strong Pan-American Boycott movement. (c) to cooperate with the existing boycott organizations in Europe and overseas countries and establish strict control over the transport movements of Nazi made goods, in order to prevent the Nazi practices of bogus sales and relabeling of merchandise in the countries of transit, or having factories abroad for the finishing of goods transported from Germany, in order to conceal the country of origin.[14]

ii.

Had such a plan or development actually taken place soon after the rise of Hitler to power, the results might, indeed, have been detrimental to the German economy. But at this late stage, the truth of the matter is that Hitler Germany was too powerful militarily and economically to be affected seriously enough even by a keen boycott. Besides—and this is the main point to bear in mind—the military option was soon to play the decisive role in the rapidly deteriorating political arena. For by 1938-39, Hitler Germany was too powerful militarily to be frightened or cowed into submission. Indeed, now it was Hitler Germany which was making and carrying out military threats. In short, by now, the boycott movement had definitely been supplanted by the military option.

League Aloofness

i.

Only the NSANL kept out of the newly expanded boycott organization described above (p. 268). To be sure, there had been no dearth of proposals and discussions regarding an amalgamation with the JBC, but these fell short of fruition for reasons already familiar. And they appear to have collapsed for good upon the advent of the Coordinated Boycott Committee.

We recall (p. 192) that Dr. Benjamin Dubovsky, chairman of the League's Executive Committee, participated in an abortive attempt at union with the Joint Boycott Council in the latter part of 1936 and early 1937. At the end of 1938, which witnessed an increase in crises to the Jewish and non-Jewish world alike, Dr. Dubovsky and his faction called for a renewal of the unity talks. ANL sources contain ample information regarding the response of its leadership to his invitation.[15] JBC sources are very meager on this point, probably because Council representatives anticipated the usual unacceptable proposals. The following draft of March 14, 1939, drawn up, apparently, by the Dubovsky faction, seems to confirm this:

> It is understood that a new organization is to be organized which is to be non-sectarian in its character for the purpose of continuing and intensifying the boycott against Nazi Germany.
> In order to launch and develop the new organization, the two outstanding organizations, namely—the NSANL and the JBC—will cease to exist.
> The name of the new organization is to be *The American Anti-Nazi Boycott League.*
> It is understood that the body which is to govern for the present (until a joint convention will be held) is to consist of equal representation by the NSANL and JBC (consisting of the Boycott Committee of the American Jewish Congress and the Boycott Committee of the Jewish Labor Organization).

It is further understood that the former boycott organizations (the NSANL and the JBC) being dissolved, the policies of the new organization shall not depend or be limited in any way by the decisions or policies of the national bodies which sponsored the activities of the various groups now being merged into the new organization.[16]

This set of proposals was followed by a March 29 communication from Harriman to Dr. Robert Marcus, Posnansky's successor as executive secretary of the Joint Boycott Council. It stated that the "time has arrived for the coordination of boycott activities," and that the "only possible way of effectuating such coordination is by preliminary and frank discussions." Marcus was, therefore, invited to send representatives to an "informal" conference on the thirty-first to consider "whether it is possible to form a united boycott organization, or how can the boycott activities of the organizations represented be coordinated."[17]

At this juncture, the Harriman communication must have sounded platitudinous and stereotyped to the Boycott Council leaders. A penciled remark that, apparently, either Dr. Marcus or Dr. Tenenbaum wrote on it, makes this very plain: "Not Debatable."

ii.

In a number of ways, the year 1938 also marked a turning point for the Non-Sectarian Anti-Nazi League. For one thing, the once stalwart Untermyer, "whose name," to quote Tenenbaum, "became a challenge and a symbol of boycott,"[18] started succumbing to old age; as he was now eighty and in a deteriorative state of health. His last recorded, politically important act was the dispatch on March 16 (1938) of the following cablegram to State Secretary Hull, in reaction to Hitler's occupation of Austria:

> Since Nazi Germany in defiance of international law and by force of arms has annexed the free and independent Austrian nation, we must demand on behalf of our members and supporters the immediate abrogation of our commercial treaty with Austria with its provisions for unconditional most-favored nation treatment at the hands of the United States. Unless the annexation is not recognized by the United States, Austria cannot be treated as free and independent in trade and tariff matters, because Germany could then flood this country with goods by way of Austria to the detriment of manufacturers and to the end that she will acquire American exchange to carry on her ruthless aggression. Furthermore, we must urge that you demand on behalf of the American people full recognition by Nazi Germany of Austria's so-called war debt to us of $26,000,000 together with payments on the

$18,000,000 of bonds issued by the Austrian national, municipal and other subsidiary governments and held by the American people, and that you demand of the representatives of the Austrian people in this country whether and when these obligations will be met.[19]

Abba Hillel Silver, the one NSANL officer with eloquence and prestige comparable to a Stephen Wise, had for the past two years shown signs of coolness toward Untermyer and the boycott activities of the League. The loss of Silver's services is traceable to the following communication that Harriman wrote him on January 27, 1936:

> I had some letters from Mr. Untermyer this morning, the first word we have had from him since he left for the coast. He is evidently in a little better shape. In one of them he expressed his high regard for you and his deep appreciation of the services you have rendered in the cause of the boycott. He complains rather plaintively, however, that you have ceased communicating with him and that he valued your advice and assistance very highly, and feels rather lost without it.[20]

Rabbi Silver tersely replied that he was very busy. If so, then he remained "very busy" for the remainder of that year and into the year after, for on May 25, 1937, Untermyer addressed himself to him in language similar to the aforesaid. But the noted Cleveland rabbi continued to remain distant.

With Untermyer's retirement in 1939, and his death a year later, the League had lost its leading figure, a man of national renown. Of the remaining League leaders, only Rabbi Silver, at least by virtue of his distinction and fame, was qualified to inherit his mantle. But he does not appear to have been interested in the mantle; nor, for that matter, does it appear that the League leadership showed any interest in bestowing it upon him. Rabbi Silver continued his association with the League, but did not do much beyond attending board meetings.[21]

Yet, the crisis of leadership was but one of two factors that signified a turning point for the League. The second was even more far-reaching, since it affected the very character of the League. For during 1938, due to the ever-increasing Nazi danger, the League shifted from a course that had accentuated boycott activities in order to concentrate on baring subversive Nazi activities in America. More and more, its propaganda material, correspondence, and especially its monthly publication, became replete with general anti-Nazi subject matter. The boycott commenced to be treated more as a matter of course and given less stress and publicity. But what is more, unlike former years, the ANL no longer responded with the same degree of outspokenness to the politically explosive events of the day. And as we shall presently see, it became nowhere involved like the JBC and VCC in such momentous issues as the Rublee and Schacht Plans and their implications for the boycott movement. The following selection, reproduced from a 1938 ANL pamphlet, is typical of this detachment and represents one of a decreasing number of documents focusing on the subject of boycott:

BUY THE DEMOCRATIC WAY

Protests should be made against the cruel deeds of the Nazi regime. Hitler has disgraced the German nation.

A one-hundred percent boycott of German goods will block Hitler from the biggest resources of raw materials, the United States. Hitler's economic defeat, the stoppage of his rearmament, his persecution of German, Austrian, Polish and Czechoslovakian citizens, Jews or Gentiles, can be achieved by boycotting German goods.

Use your power as a free citizen. Boycott German goods; for as long as Hitler is in power the world is threatened with brutal terror and war.

Are you an American businessman interested in America's prosperity? Boycott Germany for it is unfair to trade. Germany by forced barter trade with creditors, disregard of payment of debts, and dumping made possible by governmental aid, has introduced unfair competition on the world market and conquers by such methods Mexico and South America.

Are you a true American citizen? Boycott German goods, for Hitler violates the Monroe Doctrine by propagandizing throughout the American continent his doctrines of suppression of democratic rights and by direct interference in internal political affairs in providing political groups, as proven in Mexico and Brazil, with arms and organized leadership.

Are you an American working man? Boycott German goods, for their production violates labor's fundamental rights of freebargaining. German goods are produced under the lowest wage rates and enslavement of your fellow workers in Germany. Are you a Christian? Boycott German goods, for Hitler is persecuting the Protestants and Catholics alike.

Are you a Jew? Boycott German goods, for Hitler is murdering your fellow Jews throughout Europe.

Are you an intellectual and professional? Boycott German goods, for Hitler wipes out the science and culture for which you have striven. Are you a Mason? Boycott German goods, for Hitler has destroyed Masonry.

Are you a traveler? Don't travel on German ships, for Nazi spies are employed on these ships to check up on all your affairs . . .

Does your business involve foreign correspondence? Don't mail it on Nazi ships for your mail will be opened.

Examine all purchases. All imported merchandise must be stamped clearly with the name of country of its origin.

Nazism is a disease, attack the disease. Do not let it spread. Boycott Nazi Germany.[22]

The change of boycott focus was clearly expressed in a communication addressed to the managing secretary of the Amalgamated Ladies' Garment Cutters' Union by Dr. Dubovsky on June 26, 1940:

> For the last seven years, ever since Hitler came to power, the League, which was organized under the late Samuel Untermyer, has conducted the fight against Nazism at first, by an economic boycott of Nazi-made goods and services, and for the last two years, by investigating and exposing Nazi and Nazi inspired activities in the United States.[23]

30

Contra Ransom

A fortnight after Rublee's appointment as IGC director, Dr. Tenenbaum hurriedly wrote to Stephen Wise:

> I am sorry to disturb your well deserved vacation, especially since I know that you are not feeling very well; but I must bring to your attention a matter which does not brook delay.
>
> I am reliably informed that the International Committee for Refugees is negotiating with the Nazi Government to permit the refugees to take out part of their property in merchandise. Moreover, the arrangement that the Nazis are likely to make is a sort of Haavarah agreement [p. 90] extended to the entire world. This means but one thing that as a result of what the refugees will be able to take out of Germany, the entire world will be flooded with Nazi-made merchandise on a scale which will completely vitiate the efficacy of the Boycott. The likely arrangements will be to set up a credit of 10 or 15% of the proceeds for the benefit of the refugees.
>
> I have personally sent a cable to Goldman asking him to watch out during the negotiations, but, frankly, have very little faith in his pro-Boycott sentiment. Perhaps, you will be more impressed by this procedure which will make the Jewish victims agents of the Nazi Government, if I tell you that according to what I have read and information received, Germany is almost on its last legs economically. The financial crashes on the German stock exchange which is as tightly controlled as anything imaginable, only confirm the disastrous condition now prevailing in Germany.
>
> Naturally, Germany will do everything possible to use the refugee

question as a means of dumping all that Germany can produce for export without anyone being able to interfere or limit the German flood. I don't know what we can do about it, but I know that you are the only man who has the courage, even at the chance of courting unpopularity, to say the right word at the right moment. As a member of the Refugee Committee set up by President Roosevelt, you, more than anyone else, is able and, I am sure, willing to do what is in your power, to stop or limit this nefarious scheme of getting out some refugees at the cost of helping to build up Hitler's war machine to an unparalleled strength and removing whatever obstacles Hitler might find in the unwillingness of democratic elements to buy German merchandise and subsidize German armament.

I enclose a letter received from Dr. Knopfmacher[1] which has been sent to me confidentially and which I should appreciate your returning to me after you have read it through. This letter will only confirm what I have said above.[2]

Upon receiving Tenenbaum's communication, Wise inscribed upon it the following message to Justice Brandeis:

Will you be good enough, after reading the two items, to give me confidentially your judgment on this problem, I do not feel I can act, 1) because we have not sufficient information, 2) Rublee may be trusted to make best possible bargain, 3) the Reich will grant no favors without a consideration. I shall be grateful for your judgment.[3]

But as we now know from the sequence of events that followed, ultimately, it was not the Rublee Plan, but the Schacht Plan, upon which an accord would have to be reached in order to partially solve the refugee problem. And the Schacht Plan, as soon as it was released, received a very hostile reception in many quarters, both Jewish and non-Jewish.

We also recall (p. 256) that one of the two committees that Winterton and Rublee appointed consisted of private individuals dedicated to help make Schacht's scheme operational. On December 18, 1938, Rublee apprized the State Department of the Jewish reaction to this act: "We have consulted privately with prominent Jewish leaders here and have heard from Jewish leaders in Paris. They are categorically opposed to the setting up of a private committee which would lend an air of credibility to the area that there is such a thing as World Jewry. They believe that the matter should be considered exclusively by the governments."[4]

Undersecretary of State Sumner Welles responded the next day: "No one who has been consulted believes that it would be possible to raise the sum mentioned, or even an appreciable part of it, under the terms outlined. The plan is generally considered as asking the world to pay a ransom for the release of hostages in Germany and barter human misery for increased exports."[5]

Tenenbaum actively opposed the Schacht Plan by launching a one-man crusade against it, whatever its subsequent modifications. In memoranda, the radio, the press, and gatherings of boycott interest, until war inadvertently put an end to the plan forever, he fought it bitterly and unconditionally.

Possibly anticipating that his position might be condemned as heartless, Tenenbaum observed, a day after the release of the Schacht Plan: "The pity of it all is that the more responsive we become to the heartrendering appeals of our tortured relatives and fellow Jews, the more we endanger the lives and liberty of the very people we intend to help, because the more we pay, the more insatiable become the demands on them."[6]

Dr. Tenenbaum believed "that this is part of a new Nazi extortion plan and will pave the way for new and larger demands, if we yield."[7] In addition, the Schacht Plan was fraught with danger to boycott progress, and any hazard to this movement Dr. Tenenbaum was determined to prevent or eliminate almost at any price. Addressing on December 18 a conference of more than 1,200 representatives of Jewish organizations that gathered at New York's Hotel Astor to deliberate on Schacht's proposals, Tenenbaum said:

> The newest Schacht offensive to barter human misery for increased exports will fail dismally, as have failed all previous efforts to break the boycott. . . . But lest someone be naive enough to take the Schacht negotiations seriously, we here utter a warning: Nothing can induce or terrorize us into giving up the boycott. No Jew will dare give up one penny for the newest Schacht offensive to break up the boycott. . . . Millions for the refugees, and not one cent as tribute![8]

At the close of the conference, the delegates rejected "categorically and finally any proposal which would make of our tortured brethren agents for the promotion of Nazi export dumping and thus provide foreign exchange for a regime which is today stooping to the depths of a huge international kidnapping racket."[9]

Well-intentioned people engaged in rescue work could, due to naivete or human weakness, yield to the temptation of nibbling at Schacht's bait. To prevent this, Dr. Tenenbaum circulated a memorandum among all the German Refugee Aid Societies, warning that the Nazi refugee barter plan was a "monstrous fraud" and that the German government did not have the "slightest intention of permitting the Jews to leave Germany." Its officials he angrily branded as "master gansters" who had developed a "highly efficient, methodical and gigantic blackmail and extortion industry." Their true intentions Dr. Tenenbaum depicted as follows: "The Nazis need the Jews as scapegoats to sate their brutal sadistic impulses of hate and hurt. They intend to use the Jews as an almost inexhaustible source of ransom and blackmail to fill the gap of their failing economic resources."[10]

This memorandum was also released to the press; and in conclusion, the JBC chieftain made certain to remind the readers of their obligations to the movement he was so valiantly, even fanatically, trying to defend:

> Every dollar which we permit to enter Germany, every compromise from which Germany will gain trade benefits, is tantamount to desertion of our sacred cause, the cause of self-defense. Breaking the boycott now, when the entire world seems to have realized the importance of this weapon, would be a deadly blow to our common cause. We have no right to do that even for the sake of the unfortunate refugees.[11]

Contrary to the thinking of the various World Jewish organizations, but motivated, nevertheless, by the best of intentions, the American Joint Distribution Committee took it upon itself to try to strike a bargain with the Nazis. Therewithal, upon the heels of Schacht's announced trip to London, its chairman, Felix M. Warburg, journeyed forthwith to participate in the IGC negotiations with Nazidom's supersalesman. Before long, Warburg announced that the JDC would pay the ransom money Schacht was demanding. This stirred up a storm of protest and indignation in the United States and Britain, and Warburg and the JDC were denounced for misrepresenting Jewish public opinion and assuming the self-assigned role of guardians of the Jewish people.

No one was more in agreement with these charges than Dr. Tenenbaum. On December 20, in a communication to Dr. Wise, in which he also denounced Warburg's role in the Schacht-IGC negotiations, the JBC chairman tried to convince the American Jewish Congress president that Germany merely intended "to make World Jewry its agents for increased exports." He proceeded to prove this charge by way of the following assessment:

> Assuming that Jewish property in Germany amounts to 2 billion RM, which means $800,000,000 at par and deducting from that 25% capital flight tax, the amount that the Jews possess in Germany, is at the most liberal estimate, only about $600,000,000. At the prevailing transfer rates, which have been up till now 14% of par, this would be equivalent to no more than $84,000,000, which sum, of course, will be further reduced every month that the Jews continue to live in Ger-

many. At the current rate of the depredatory transfer of Jewish property into Aryan hands, this sum will probably shrink to one half in less than a year's time.

But accepting the figures as they are now and that we will be able to take out, say, even 200,000 Jews during the next year, which, of course, you know we can't, the amount of Jewish property now available in Germany will not be even enough to care for the aged and other elements that cannot leave Germany under any circumstances. Would it not be so much better if we should tell to Germany right now to choke on Jewish property in Germany and leave the Jews out just as they are? This would not only remove the last shred of justification of the Nazi Germans to keep the Jewish hostages in Germany, but would very much strengthen our hand to start an appeal for money for refugees without any division of opinion or antagonism which would surely arise if we go in any such scheme suggested by Germany.

I am writing you now very urgently because I believe that you ought to cable immediately to Myron Taylor and George Rublee advising them of the feeling in this country and asking them to flatly refuse any such scheme as the one termed the Warburg-Schacht Plan. (What a combination!)[12]

The record does not reveal how Dr. Wise felt about the Schacht Plan at this time.[13] But in the months that followed, while Tenenbaum continued to oppose it in whatever shape or form, it appears that Wise grew inclined to work out an agreement. Tenenbaum, however, tried to dissuade him from adopting such a course. On May 1, 1939, he wrote:

With every Jewish emigrant leaving Germany, 75% of his property will simply melt away before any substantial number of Jews can leave Germany. In view of the fact that the Jewish Community in Germany lives solely on its accumulated capital, this property cannot even last long enough to maintain the Jews of the Nazi Gehenna for a period of 2–3 years, necessary to get 100,000 Jews out of Germany. Thus, by the magic of Nazi accounting, for every single dollar "saved" for the refugees we shall have to feed back 4–5 dollars into the maw of the hungry Nazi wolf, including the private charity dollars and support money by relatives which will flow increasingly each year into Germany, as long as this scheme will continue to operate . . .

Had the Refugee Committee, instead of bargaining for "Jewish property" simply insisted on an orderly process of emigration, with the refugees permitted to take out some of their belongings and the German Government providing land and sea transportation into the places of destination, we could have been able to "save" fully as much or more on some of the property without any obligation on our part to keep Germany supplied with fresh money each time the Jewish property reserve will become empty. We could have raised enough money and a substantial loan for resettlement and equipment of the refugees, who in 2–3 years or less, would become self-supporting and able to amortize gradually loan and interest which they shall have contracted in order to start a new life. In that way, we could have started a real exodus which to a large extent would have been self-supporting. Instead, we have now been saddled with an "agreement" which is a monstrosity from a moral and business viewpoint alike . . .[14]

Next, the zealous Boycott Council chairman sharply attacked the creation of the then contemplated Coordinating Foundation (p. 257).

There is another phase which seems to have been completely overlooked in the shuffle. As you remember, I have asked the question what the aim and purpose of the envisaged corporation is to be. I received an answer which did not satisfy me at all and nobody else, I am sure, could feel relieved by its nebulous status. Foundation or Corporation are but names for seasoning the same unpalatable dish. The purpose of this ambiguous body, whatever title one may choose, is expressly stated in the "agreement."
Forgetting for the moment about the questionable authority or power to secure "fair treatment" of the remaining Jews (a task which the intervention of the most powerful governments failed to accomplish), the corporation will have to transact the business of property transfer in goods and to recompensate Germany in foreign exchange for the cost of raw materials which go into the manufacture of these goods. By this single provision, the Nazi negotiators skillfully smuggled through the two chief objectives of the Schacht ransom plan, i.e. increased German exports, and at the same time it will supply the Nazi Treasury with much needed foreign exchange (the price and amount of the used raw materials in the transfer goods will be fixed by the Nazis or trustees, two of whom will be Nazis).
I do not want to analyze this scheme in detail, but it seems to me that even a cursory recital of its functions suffices to show in what labyrinth this innocent "Foundation" may lead us. The question is: What can we do in order to have the Foundation and not lose our wits about it? Frankly, I do not see how we shall be able to extricate ourselves. The Nazis have the cat in the bag and they mean to hold on to what they have. This explains their insistence that the existence of such a corporation is the sine qua non of the entire "agreement."[15]

Turning to his key subtitle, "Shall We Give up the Boycott," Tenenbaum said:

I think we ought to be clear that we cannot preach the Boycott of Nazi goods and increase Nazi exports at the same time. There is no better salesman than a sale. Every machine, every tool bought from Germany, means opening the door for future replacements, for repairs and the acquisition of a great many other parts and goods suitable for this particular piece of equipment. It means creating new opportunities for Nazi dumping above the limit of this one sale. We have one Haavarah (see p. 90) for Palestine, and we are now reaping the weeds of this hybrid plantation. Not only is the entire Near East flooded with German merchandise, but it has enabled the Nazis to gain an economic foothold in Palestine and to subsidize, finance and equip the Arab revolt which has imperilled our Yishub [The Jewish population in Palestine] and put our hard won position in jeopardy. A Haavarah of world-wide dimensions will not only weaken the defensive forces, Jewish and non-Jewish, now arrayed against Nazi oppression, but will destroy the morale and safety of our people. Believing as I do that economic pressure can defeat Hiterlism, I feel that we have no right to sacrifice the fate of the Jewish people, the cause of liberalism and indeed of the world, no matter how vital may be the cause or how pressing the necessity. One thing, I am sure, we all realize by now, and that is: the stronger Hitler grows, the weaker we are as a people. The people everywhere and in a dilemma of this kind the choice cannot be subject to much hesitation.[16]

As late as July 5, Tenenbaum noted in a communication that Wise had still not sent him a reply to his May 1 letter. By that summer date, it was slightly less than a fortnight before a revised Rublee Plan was to be proposed at an IGC conference in London. Dr. Wise, in league with the Joint, and independently of the Congress, was now apparently ready to support it. In a fit of indignation and bitter disappointment, Dr. Tenenbaum sent Dr. Wise what was perhaps, the strongest personal letter that he had ever written him in his capacity of Boycott Committee chairman. The paucity of pertinent informational background is quite evident, however:

> I really believe that you have taken a great responsibility which I deeply regret to say, you shouldn't have, as head of the Congress, without consultation . . .
> I believe the action taken by a handful of people and by the JDC to be disastrous to our cause, calculated to make the Boycott a mock gesture to injure the cause of the democratic front. Moreover, I believe that whatever the motives, it is sheer nonsense to endorse the Hitler Refugee Transfer Plan at a time when either we'll have a war or a final appeasement. In the first case, it wouldn't perhaps matter so much. But in a case of "a peace conference before war," we shall have prejudiced and grievously injured our entire cause with this kind of precedent. To such a conference we ought to come with "clean hands" insisting not on a settlement of the refugee question but on the Jewish

question in Germany in general, so that there shall be no refugee problem left . . .

I consider this deal the greatest blunder of our blundering age and leadership and I for one who has stood for six years and fought for the Boycott against all odds, I shall not stop the fight now in view of this insidious attempt at annihilation of the very basic principle of the Boycott. Unless and until I am assured that this abominable scheme is being abandoned to the shade and fates of the original Warburg-Samuel-Marx etc. plan, I shall use every legitimate means at my disposal to discredit the contemplated Corporation and those connected with it, even if it would mean my leaving the Congress. I hope you'll understand my feelings in the matter and appreciate my motive.[17]

Tenenbaum was true to his word. At a JBC Executive Committee meeting of the week before, he had already helped lay the policy for future independent action. After due consideration of the "New Refugee Transfer Plan," the group passed unanimously the following resolution:

Since information has reached the Joint Boycott Council that certain members of the Jewish Community of the United States are contemplating the formation of a Corporation to promote a certain kind of transfer of German goods through the medium of German Jewish refugees, it is the consensus of opinion of the JBC that such an undertaking will undermine the promotion of Boycott activities not only in the United States, but the world over. The representatives of the constituent bodies on the Joint Boycott Council are requested to take up this matter with their respective organizations.[18]

But the Congress, which, about half a year earlier, had condemned the Schacht Plan, now thought it best, in view of the endeavors of the Joint, not to take sides. Tenenbaum reacted to this in a memorandum that he prepared in order to circulate the JBC resolution: "The American Jewish Congress has, as yet, not taken any stand in this matter. I, myself, as you know, feel very strongly about the consequences of this deal and it is my contention that the strongest protest is not strong enough, in view of this attempt to break the Boycott front with no real improvement in the refugee situation."[19]

While the Congress failed to take a position on this matter, some of the constituent bodies of the Joint Boycott Council issued statements in support of Tenenbaum's stand. The first of these came from the JLC, which, on July 12, reacted to the Rublee Program's proposal to "facilitate" the emigration of Jews from Germany "in a uniform and orderly manner." The statement was sent to the Joint by Adolph Held, who, on

November 15, 1938, a fortnight after Vladeck's death, had replaced the renowned Bundist and Jewish labor leader as JLC president:

> Careful consideration of the Program fails to point out any benefit to the emigrating Jews which would justify our acceptance of the dangerous precedents it establishes. The Program implies tacit recognition, on the part of World Jewry, of the right of the German Government to confiscate Jewish property. It will encourage *anti-Semitic* governments in other lands to treat their Jewish populations in the same manner that Hitler treats the German Jews. It will affect the rights and interests of millions of Jews in Poland, Roumania, Hungary and other countries, and will expose them to the danger of being held for ransom. The Rublee Program will destroy the boycott against Hitler Germany, and will undermine the struggle of the labor and progressive movement against Hitlerism and anti-Semitism. Rather than help German Jews, the Program will tend to alienate the best friends we have in our fight for existence.[20]

Held also pointed out that the real problem was not to obtain the release of the German Jews, but to find a haven of refuge for them. For no time, he argued, did Hitler prevent Jews from leaving Germany. The point was not in need of corroboration, but proved timely in view of a recent news item which the Labor Committee now made use of. It was a quotation from the *Voelkischer Beobachter* which was cited by the *New York Times* on July 7, 1939: "We desire once more to make ourselves perfectly clear. The aim of National Socialism remains the eviction from the Reich of these Jews to the last man. We are giving them our attention once more only to speed up their emigration. We think this is worth the effort."[21]

Reflecting on the financial arrangements of such an exodus, Held explained that it would be more economical for the relief agencies to give the refugees cash aid after they left Germany than to reimburse the Hitler regime for the goods taken out by them. "This," he declared, "will at least not necessitate our providing Hitler with foreign exchange, of which he is so greatly in need."[22] Held then added: "Before giving our consent to the Rublee Plan which is but a modified version of the notorious Schacht Plan, we should at least try to find an answer to the most burning question of the day: Where will the emigrants, supposedly helped by the Rublee Plan, go!"[23]

In directing the next part of his lengthy statement to the Joint, the JLC president took it to task for underwriting "the funds necessary to set up the Corporation," especially after the refusal of British Jewry "to become party to this dangerous unilateral arrangement." He concluded with the following observation:

The Rublee Program presents not merely a relief problem. It confronts us with a political problem which involves the interests of the Jewish people as a whole, and will have wide repercussions the world over. Finally, the cause would have been served much better if a subject of such vital importance would have been submitted to the various central Jewish organizations for discussion and action.[24]

The VCC was next to state its position on the Rublee Plan. On July 18, the opening day of the IGC conference, Christopher Emmet (p. 263) sent an "open letter" to Myron Taylor, pleading that the contemplated plan be rejected or at least changed. After listing opposing views familiar to us from Tenenbaum, Emmet noted: "Even if the alleviation offered under this plan were real and not illusory, it would be folly to weaken the boycott, for if Hitler is not stopped, Jews and democrats all over the world will eventually become refugees, as they are today in Central Europe."[25] The letter concluded with a plea to all refugee agencies to use their influence to demand an end to the persecution of Jews, Czechs, and other Nazi victims as their condition for giving up the boycott and for any eventual economic concessions to Germany.

The next day the Christian Committee released a statement which branded the Rublee Plan a "misnomer" because "many of its provisions were accepted by Rublee with reluctance on the insistence of Herr Wohlthat acting for the Nazi Government." But while the VCC remained opposed to the Rublee Plan, it wished "to pay tribute to the energetic and unselfish efforts of Rublee and Taylor to secure the best terms from the Nazis." It admitted that this plan was "a distinct improvement upon the Schacht Plan," but also charged that it was a modification of that "notorious scheme," nevertheless:

> As a boycott organization, it is the main function of the Volunteer Christian Committee to Boycott Nazi Germany to prevent the supply of foreign exchange to the Hitler Government, hence we feel bound to oppose this plan. We believe that its greatest beneficiaries will be the Nazis rather than their victims.
>
> If there is every indication that Germany today is not in a position to start a major war with any prospect of success, a larger measure of credit for this must go to the boycott. The peaceful economic weapons of boycott and embargo are the hope of the democratic world to prevent war, or to insure victory if war should come.
>
> Contrary to popular belief, the refugees can really be a source of wealth to the country to which they come, but under the Rublee Plan, instead of being absorbed into the economy of the land of their adoption, they would remain adjuncts of the Nazi economic barter system. They would have to remit a large part of their earnings to Germany in the foreign exchange which Hitler needs for his arma-

ments instead of spending their money as consumers. This would be calculated not only to help Hitler, but to increase local prejudice against the refugees.

Christian opponents of Hitlerism admire American Jews in refusing to be blackmailed into giving up boycott, however terrible Nazi pressure. Homes for the emigrants have not as yet been found, so there is no need to rush the adoption of the Rublee Plan now, even if it were desirable.

We believe Germany's economic position to be so insecure that if the democratic world stands firm and refuses to compromise, not only military, but moral disarmament can be achieved without war.[26]

Such were the opinions of at least some boycott leaders on the eve of the Second World War; namely, that Germany was "not in a position to start a major war with any prospect of success"; that Germany was "almost on its last legs economically." We now know—better, perhaps, than even Germany itself knew—that it had an excellent "prospect of success" in winning a "major war." What we do not know for sure is whether Germany really was "almost on its last legs economically" in the months preceding that war; for Hitler would shortly obtain by conquest, plunder, and terror the raw materials and consumer goods that the boycott, purportedly, had been peaceably placing out of his reach. Actually, the boycott might have been taking its toll of Nazi Germany, if Hitler's warning on January 30, 1939, that "we must export or die," can be taken at face value.

But even as Hitler was uttering these words, it was becoming painfully clear that, if the world ever did have an opportunity of crushing Germany economically, such a prospect was already a thing of the past. Presently, the world would have to crush Germany militarily in engagements of cataclysmic proportions.

31

Legal Activity and Department Store Vigil

Bill HR 8099

On August 3, 1937, Representative Robert L. Doughton of North Carolina introduced HR 8099 "to amend certain administrative provisions of the Tariff Act of 1930, and for other purposes." This measure, also described as the Customs Administrative Act of 1937, amending Sec. 304 of the 1930 Tariff Act, included the following substantive provision:

> Marking of Articles: Except as hereinafter provided, every article of foreign origin (or its container), imported into the United States shall be marked in a conspicuous place as legibly, indelibly, and permanently as the nature of the article (or container) will permit in such manner as to indicate to an ultimate purchaser in the United States the English name of the country of origin of the article. Otherwise, delivery is ordered to be withheld until marked.[1]

Doughton's bill was passed by the House on August 19 without amendment. Thence it went to the Senate Finance Committee, which took it up for consideration at the next Congress session in January, 1938.

During that session, Senator David I. Walsh of Massachusetts proposed that certain articles be exempted from Doughton's provisions for marking with the country of origin. This suggestion was viewed by boycott leaders as almost sounding the death knell of their movement. Thus, on April 22, an alarmed American Jewish Congress sent Walsh a telegram claiming that his proposed changes would permit between 60 percent and 75 percent of the goods entering the United States to be unmarked. Similar charges were made in a flood of communications from the AFL, the JLC, a host of local unions, and other objectors all over the country.

Tenenbaum's letter, which was dispatched on April 27, was probably the most explicit and analytical of all. It dissected and refuted, section by section, the logic behind Walsh's amendment, in an attempt to demonstrate that it would do a disservice to the interests of American labor and the American public: "We hold, and we are sure you likewise agree, that the American purchaser has the right to know whether the article he is buying is of foreign or of American manufacture, and that the American manufacturer and producer is entitled to the protection given to him by the present law, which this amendment would vitiate."[2]

As regards specific points, Dr. Tenenbaum took the Senator to task for stating that "crude substances" (Sec. E) need not be marked with the country of origin. Possibly the bulk of American imports, suggested the energetic boycott leader, were crude substances in active competition with similar materials produced in the United States. As a case in point, Tenenbaum cited the then struggling phosphate and nitrate industries, which shipped their materials in bags, for the most part. "Why," he asked, "should not our American industries be entitled to the protection of having German and other goods marked with their country of origin?"[3] For under the 1930 Tariff Act, Tenenbaum argued, save for shipments that came in bulk,[4] the country of origin had to be marked on all foreign merchandise.

Next, Tenenbaum criticized the portion (Sec. F) which stated that an article did not have to be marked with the country of origin if it was for the use of the importer, and not intended for sale. How, he asked, could the government check such claims? For the importer, he said, might in absolute good faith purchase a large quantity of material for his own use; and then, with a slump coming on, and finding that he needed cash, be compelled to sell the material. Unless new or additional government supervision were created after the initial importation had taken place, the importer would be free to sell his goods, Tenenbaum pointed out.

The Boycott Council chairman also found fault with the assertion that "an ultimate purchaser, by reason of the character of such article or by reason of the circumstances of its importation, must necessarily know the country of origin of such article even though it is not marked to indicate its origin" (Sec. H., subdivision 3). In rebuttal, Tenenbaum said he did not understand how anyone could know whether the ultimate purchaser was aware of the origin of the product; some people, obviously, might, others might not. Certainly, claimed the JBC chairman, this would give enormous latitude for marking evasions. He closed his argument with the charge that "this bill is of such a nature as to practically nullify the Marking Act completely."[5]

In addition, Tenenbaum expressed his surprise at the Treasury Department for saying that Walsh's amendment would strengthen the marking provisions rather than weaken them. Tenenbaum reacted to this by saying: "The very fact that exceptions are now being made would of itself be prima facie evidence that the intention of the act is to weaken these provisions, rather than strengthen them."[6]

As of April 19 (1938), HR 8099 was in the Conference Committee, the last legislative station prior to its enactment into law. In desperation, Dr. Wise sent a personal representative to talk things over with Walsh and Conference Committee members. Walsh, Council records show, received him "graciously" on May 2. In the meantime, though, the JBC sent all House and Senate members communications protesting against the objectionable features of Walsh's amendment. The measure was eventually passed, and "the most obnoxious provision, according to which containers would not be required to be marked even where the article itself would not have to show the country of origin, was stricken from the measure."[7] Thus, in the end, pressure and the force of argument had the desired effect. The following year, a similar measure—the Lake Bill—was proposed for New York State. It required "marks of origin" on all imported articles sold therein. But Governor Lehman (p. 34) vetoed the bill on May 29, 1939, saying: "In view of the Federal Statute already existing, this bill appears to be unnecessary and in the opinion of Secretary of State Hull, would be harmful" (*NYT*, May 30, 1939). Lehman felt that in view of the efforts by the federal government to restore American foreign commerce by the removal of excessive and discriminatory barriers to the sale of American products abroad, the impositions of the Lake Bill would be most unfortunate. He also felt that passage of the bill would invite retaliatory measures against American exporters in foreign countries.

Two other bills, introduced in the House earlier that year by Representative Celler, are also worthy of mention. The first of these, HR 219, was presented on January 3. HR 219 was another abortive attempt to enact into law the legislation contained in HR 6743, and HR 11475, which preceded it. The second bill, HR 2638, was introduced on January 16, and came to amend a June 8, 1938, law entitled "An Act to require the registration of certain persons employed by agencies to disseminate propaganda in the United States and for other purposes." The added section (8) read:

For the purpose of protecting, conserving, and advancing the interests of American citizens who are holders of German securities partially or completely in default, German corporations in default on bonds, as to interest or principal, or both, owned by American citizens, shall register all assets located in the United States as may be owned by them directly or indirectly, and irrespective of the nature name or description of such assets, with the Secretary of State or such agent or agencies as the said Secretary of State may designate. The said German corporation shall give an itemized and detailed account of such assets as of the day on which the present measure becomes law and also as of June 1, 1933, together with details as to how the assets, in the intervening period, may have been sold, disposed of, or transferred, and the person or persons to whom such assets may have been thus sold, disposed of, or transferred . . .

The same applied to American banks and financial institutions, as well as agents or agencies, connected or identified with or acting for German corporations guilty of default as to interest or principal.

This amendment came as a response to Germany's intention to compel American citizens to register with the designated Reich authorities every type of property owned by them in Germany in excess of 5,000 RM. It stated, moreover, that such a decree was designed to enable the Nazi government to eventually deprive Americans of property owned by them in Germany. The bill explained that the Hitler regime could do this by invoking either one of its laws already in existence, by creating new legislation to that end, or by penalizing American citizens for wrongs of which they might become guilty at a later date.

The list of grievances included Germany's failure to pay full interest to thousands of American investors holding German bonds aggregating about $600,000,000. Further, a strong protest was registered because no interest whatsoever had been paid American investors since January 1, 1937, and only part of the interest prior to that date, following the Nazis' coming to power. In addition, the bill tried to protect American citizens by stating that Germany's laws were not binding for them, since they were not subject to German "Jurisdiction."

The bill also cited other points unfavorable to the Nazis: hence, inadvertently, helpful to the boycott movement. But unlike HR 11475 or its variant, it does not appear that Celler and the boycott leadership collaborated in the preparation of HR 2638.

Sears and Woolworth

The December 10, 1937, minutes of the Joint Committee on Cases (see Document No. XX) reveal that, as a result of a discussion with a worker for the United Palestine Appeal, Dr. Robert Marcus (p. 270) was prevailed upon to request an appointment with a Sears representative for the purpose of "clarifying" the Council's boycott against it. It was agreed, furthermore, that two members of the Joint Action Committee would attend such a session.

In a matter of days, all JBC auxiliary units in communities having Sears branches were contacted for information regarding the state of the company's German merchandise. To carry this through, communications were to be addressed to the local store manager and the main Sears store in Chicago, with copies to the Joint Action Committee.

We recall (p. 225) that in the fall of 1937, Sears was dropped from the League's Boycott Violators list. This move was strongly resented by both the JBC and JWV, as they were far from satisfied with Sears' record at that time. But as the year 1937 neared its end, JBC indicated a willingness to reconsider. It felt that after the company's entire purchasing record of that year became available, it would be in a better position to render an accurate judgment. Thus, if it was found, said the Council's Action Committee members in January 1938, that Sears' figures of German importations for fiscal 1937 showed "a considerable decline," the chain store would be whitelisted.

Official discussions began in March 1938, when a Sears representative appeared before the Actions Committee and produced German importation figures that showed "a distinct drop in comparison with 1936 importations"; whereupon it was decided to remove Sears from the Boycott list for a six-month period, provided the following assurances were received: "That the figures submitted by the Company as being imports from Nazi Germany constitute the complete amount of German goods handled in the specific period; that the Company will cooperate in bringing about a reduction in the amount of German ships used in the transportation of the merchandise."[8]

It now remained to also try and get Woolworth in line. We recall (pp. 226–28) that, up to our period, repeated efforts by Wise, Tenenbaum, and, presumably, League leaders, failed to persuade F. W. Woolworth to cease its handling of German merchandise. Nor was any headway made in 1938. The concluding section of a June 2 communication of that year, which Dr. Marcus addressed to an inquirer, typifies this lack of progress: "The Woolworth Company offers no alibis. It simply disregards the anti-Nazi Boycott Movement."[9]

The first progress report we hear of is contained in the January 13, 1939, minutes of the Actions Committee, where it is noted that Woolworth was reducing its German importations. On the basis of this new development, it was decided to seek an appointment with the "Woolworth people" to discuss this "matter." It was also decided, though, that "until a statement was received from them embodying the facts reported, they were not to be taken off the list."[10]

The matter was settled in less than a month, however; for on February 3, a Woolworth representative met with the Joint Committee on Cases, with the result that his company was taken off the list of Boycott Violators.[11] In discussing the Woolworth Company, a Council source dealing with the subject of "Department and Chain Stores" offers the following reason for this step:

> The Council's investigation indicated that German purchases decreased progressively from 1933 until the present time and now amount to only fifty-nine hundredths of one percent of the total merchandise purchased. In addition, it was shown that the Company had been influencing American manufactories to produce merchandise formerly purchased abroad; also, that it was not buying German merchandise domestically.[12]

An exemplary letter of good-will, intimating continued cooperation, was also received by the Boycott Council from the management of the John Wanamaker stores. It was written on April 21, 1939, and read as follows:

> Since the Board of Directors of John Wanamaker, N.Y., established the policy of discontinuing the purchase of German merchandise, the store has not made any purchase of German merchandise, directly or indirectly. Moreover, we have carried out the spirit of this policy by refraining from having German merchandise shipped to neighboring countries for final processing before importation.[13]

"We have done little picketing in the last year." So said Dr. Tenenbaum in an October 30, 1938, address entitled "The Boycott of Nazi Germany," which he delivered at a Congress session at the Hotel Biltmore in New York. "It was not necessary," Tenenbaum continued, because "the biggest concerns and the smallest have become boycott-conscious."[14]

This trend was gaining even more strength in 1939, with the various stores showing either a "great decline or complete severance with German importations."[15] It was a distinct achievement, though its more tangible effects must, due partly to the outbreak of World War II, be consigned to the realm of speculation and conjecture.

Part V
1939–1941: IN WAR

32

The Joint Boycott Council

The Crisis of Obsolescence

On September 27, 1939, at a meeting of the A.J.C. and JLC representation on the Actions Committee, it was decided "to liquidate the JBC office effective October 15,"[1] as it was assumed that the British naval blockade would be capable of keeping German goods out of the United States. A few days later, the Joint Boycott Council suspended its activities.

However, on December 4, came the following announcement: "Because of the tremendous infiltration of German goods in the past two months, in spite of the British Blockade, the American Jewish Congress, in conjunction with the Jewish Labor Committee, has again taken the field to prosecute the Boycott of Nazi goods."[2]

The Council estimated that in September alone, $2,000,000 worth of German goods had entered the United States, adding "that there is now in this country $10,000,000 worth of German goods."[3] The JBC also complained that many firms that had signed boycott pledges had ceased fulfilling their commitments as soon as they received word that Council activities would be suspended.

These external problems were now aggravated and complicated by internal troubles; for documents dating from the late thirties reveal that the Council was increasingly plagued by financial difficulties. A May 19, 1939, memorandum, drawn up by Dr. Tenenbaum, states that the Council was operating on an annual budget of $15,000 paid out equally by the A.J.C. and the JLC. "Yet," complains the JBC chairman, "it is impossible to meet the most pressing expenses."[4]

The situation had deteriorated completely by the outbreak of World War II. A December 1, 1939, document described as follows the Council's financial straits:

> Immediately after the war broke out, a committee (of which Dr. Tenenbaum was the chairman) was formed to investigate what effect the war would have upon the conduct of the boycott and what changes in the organization should be made. At that particular time, the funds of the organization were at their lowest point. The rent had not been paid, and neither had employees received salaries for two weeks.
>
> In submitting this report, the committee was very little influenced by the last named fact, because it was understood that if the need for vigorously pursuing the boycott existed, some means for raising funds would be obtained. In submitting its final report for the curtailment of boycott activities, the only determining factor was whether it was necessary to maintain a large office and a staff in view of the fact that German imports would be drastically curtailed by the British Blockade. . . . As a result of this study, the Committee unanimously recommended to the JBC that the staff be reduced and expenses curtailed.[5]

The January 17, 1940, minutes of the Coordinated Boycott Committee contain specific information relating to the curtailment of expenses. They state that "in view of the limited field left to the Boycott, the parent organizations voluntarily reduced to $200 per month the budget from each parent organization."[6] The CBC minutes of September 18 of that year point to a further reduction by stating that "the American Jewish Congress is prepared to give $150 a month for the next three months, until the end of the year, if the Jewish Labor Committee is willing to do likewise."[7] Thus, not only was the Boycott Council being operated on a reduced basis, but on an extension arrangement as well; one that began when the Council again took to the field, and which was renewable every three months.

Such a setup was, of course, not to Tenenbaum's liking; but, after all, these were times that challenged repeatedly the purpose and justification of the boycott. And even Tenenbaum eventually had to question its usefulness. Thus, on June 5, in a report that he made to the Council on the morrow of the evacuation of Dunkirk, Tenenbaum examined afresh the status of the boycott and informed his colleagues that, in view of the new emergency:

> Boycott activities, as such, had become limited in their usefulness and that it would be necessary for our organization to take on other

functions and activities. We face this problem: activities in some other field. The Boycott is now a negative activity. The positive activity could include action against the Fifth Column and the possibility of more positive help to the Allies.[8]

One should now note with interest the similarity of the foregoing statement to the new and similar course of action adopted by the NSANL (see p. 273). Nevertheless in actual practice, a perusal of the documentation clearly shows that whereas the ANL almost ceased, albeit it did not actually end, its boycott effort, JBC definitely continued on a more balanced policy course involving both the boycott and general anti-Nazi activities.

However, considering that a prior decision had already been made to liquidate the JBC office, the last-mentioned declaration should not be regarded as a drastic statement; for the vicissitudes of war were having a radical effect on the boycott movement. Britain, about to be thrown into the convulsions of a life-and-death struggle, could no longer be expected to maintain an effective blockade against Nazi Germany. Besides, the imminent French capitulation, which marked Germany's virtual conquest of Western Europe, enabled Hitler to obtain just about any commodity he wanted.

This is why Tenenbaum suggested "action against the Fifth Column," an alternative course engaged in by the Congress, and adopted, as previously mentioned (pp. 272–73), by the NSANL in 1938. This is not to say, however, that either the Congress or the League had a direct bearing on the direction in which Tenenbaum now sought to lead his organization. Council minutes show that it was inspired by some CBC members who "had become active in organizing the William Allen White Committee to Defend America by Aiding the Allies."[9] The work of this new organization overlapped both that of the JBC and the A.J.C., and of the League, for that matter, in its active support of the Allies in general and Great Britain in particular, through an embargo on war materials and by standing guard against the subversive action of the Fifth Column. However, the blending of these two activities involved extra expenditures, which the Congress adamantly refused to appropriate. This not only made it impossible for Dr. Tenenbaum to expand into Fifth Column activities, but barely enabled him, with the skeleton staff to which he was reduced, to engage in boycott action.

What a harrowing and frustrating experience it was to try to preserve the Joint Boycott Council during this period, Tenenbaum stated in a report that he submitted to the Congress on September 11, 1941:

> In submitting this report, I wish to emphasize that since the beginning of the war the Joint Boycott Council has passed through a period

of uncertainty caused by the very nature of the blockade and also by the erroneous opinion that the British Blockade makes Boycott obsolete.... Unfortunately, the notion was too deeply ingrained that Boycott during the war is to be more of a demonstration than a redoubled effort to contribute our share to Nazi defeat.[10]

With the boycott movement on the wane, coupled with the Council's inability to "enlarge the scope of activities," JBC became with every passing day a dying organization. Yet, for about two years, Tenenbaum, torn as he was between his zeal for the boycott and recurring reservations about the Council's near-anachronistic character, bade the tattering organization to weather through the storms of war. Behind this unyielding position lay the seeming perpetuity of extension renewal, a required waiting period "until the international situation became more clear,"[11] and a fervent desire that "the preservation of the idea of boycott, both as a weapon of Jewish Defense and as a weapon against Nazism during the prewar years, should be kept alive."[12] The chapters that follow, dealing as they do with the few and unfinished activities that remained open to the Boycott Council in the war years, reflect this effort.

33

Boycott and Embargo

Neutrality and Boycott

In addition to the charge that the British blockade had occasioned the obsolescence of the American anti-Nazi boycott movement, the Council had also to contend with and rebut the new argument that the boycott constituted a violation of the Neutrality Act.[1] For now that a war was actually raging on the European continent, boycott opponents became even more vocal in their claim that the anti-Nazi boycott was actually an act of war. To them the claim that boycott and neutrality were mutually exclusive was a forgone conclusion, a position diametrically opposed to the assertion that boycott was an act of self-defense.

Tenenbaum challenged this contention in a memorandum entitled "The Boycott in the Light of War Experiences,"[2] in which he asserted that "the Boycott existed before any neutrality laws were enacted." Paraphrasing President Roosevelt, the veteran boycott chieftain also argued that just as there is no neutrality in "thought," so "there is none obligating the consumer to buy Nazi goods in the United States."

In an ensuing outburst of emotion, Tenenbaum revealed his true feelings about this subject: "No Jew can hide his indignation under the cloak of neutrality, seeing what Hitler is doing to Polish Jewry. The least we can do is to boycott, boycott more than ever, harder than ever and with as much force as we can marshall at the moment."[3]

The Council chairman also stated that, "until shortly," it had not "generally" been realized that the British blockade did not extend to

German exports carried on neutral ships. Consequently, he argued, in addition to German dumping at any price and risk, "there was nothing to prevent the reshipment of German merchandise to America as neutral cargo."[4]

Tenenbaum's concluding criticism pointed to the "desperate need of Germany for foreign exchange which drives the Nazis to ever greater efforts to maintain their foreign trade despite the war and blockade." Asserting that the Nazis would "go to any length" to secure U.S. dollars, Tenenbaum exhorted that it was the duty of the boycott movement "here" to prevent the "conversion into dollars" of Nazi goods for the Nazi "war chest"; hence his insistence that "The Boycott was never more necessary than today when every dollar that Germany can lay its hand on through trade or otherwise is of such vital importance for Herr Hitler's war machine."[5]

The Moral Embargo Campaign

i.

Up to 1938, the call by boycott leaders for a U.S. embargo on German trade was rather sporadic. After Munich and the Kristallnacht, however, one finds these leaders beginning to underscore this demand; and following the outbreak of the European conflict, an effort was made to make use of it in the nature of an organized campaign.

It should be realized, however, that embargo, as such, was not a particularly potent catchword before 1938; and it certainly was not popular with the State Department. Thus, in September of 1934, when AFL Vice-President Matthew Woll proposed to Cordell Hull that the United States place an embargo on all imports competing with American-made goods, the Secretary of State rejected the idea and used the occasion to denounce all racial and political boycotts as "economically unwise"—more costly to the boycotters than to the boycotted. And although he did not mention the anti-Nazi boycott by name, he intimated that this boycott came within the purview of his remarks. Hull also explained that the United States had had enough experience with boycotts not to get entangled in another one. In addition, he claimed that American industry stood to lose five dollars for every dollar of foreign imports it boycotted, and that, since the United States sold more abroad than it bought, retaliatory measures would cost it more than the boycott would cost the foreign nation. Untermyer and Tenenbaum challenged this conclusion, however. Even if it were based on accurate facts and figures, Untermyer contended, Americans could still find substitutes for their U.S. products. Hull, he added, misinterpreted the temper of America.

Tenenbaum reacted by saying:

> The statement of Secretary of State Hull condemning "boycotts as economically unwise" whether they be "from political or racial motives" is a most amazing document of utter disregard for public opinion, and violates both diplomatic prudence and the plain logic of facts. Hull must have known that the anti-Nazi boycott movement is not the result of racial or political scheming of revenge, but a spontaneous and invincible desire of the American people to protect all that is valuable and durable in civilization—the very life blood of democracy—from the onslaught of the most ruthless clique of blood-thirsty autocrats bent on war and destruction. (Records of the Joint Boycott Council, Dr. Joseph Tenenbaum file, Boycott Speeches, 1933–1938, NYPL.)

ii.

The earliest apparent reference and call to an embargo by Dr. Tenenbaum came in a November 24, 1938, address. In it, after accusing the very countries which feared Nazi Germany most of supplying it with the weapons for their own destruction, he exaggerated the power of the boycott and its capability.

> It is a sad commentary on our contemporary statesmanship that the very same countries which dread the German menace most, supply Germany with the means of their own destruction. The democratic countries account for more than three-quarters of the total German export trade. The share of the British Empire, Netherlands, Scandinavia, France, Switzerland, Belgium—to take only some of the immediate neighbors and future victims of Hitler—accounts for 55% of all German exports. Economically, Germany is still at the mercy of the democracies. Instead of a bloodless trade embargo, they prefer to subsidize an enemy who converts every available pound, franc and dollar into bombs to kill and maim the very hands that feed him and his army . . .
>
> An embargo of German goods by the democratic powers would bring Hitler to his knees in less than one year's time, and if governments don't act, a voluntary embargo by the consuming public of the democratic countries would accomplish the same thing without any of the customary diplomatic hazards.[6]

In conclusion, Dr. Tenenbaum revealed the name of the man who had inspired his call for an embargo, claiming that it was already reaching popular proportions:

A well organized World-Boycott Movement means the end of Hitlerism. In the United States, lately, there has been a wide-spread movement for such an embargo, the genuine resentment of the public demands it. William Green, President of the American Federation of Labor has sounded the keynote. We respond enthusiastically to his call and await his leadership.[7]

As for Dr. William Schieffelin (p. 263), his earliest recorded reference to the embargo was apparently made in a March 5, 1939, speech. Therein, the VCC chief contrasted boycott and embargo and explained why, while favoring the latter, he found the former more effective. He disclosed several reasons in which he enumerated the "advantages" of boycott over embargo; among these were that

> it takes place immediately without waiting for the long fight in Congress; a really widespread popular boycott here is bound to extend to Canada and probably to England and South America, which the Government embargo could not do; whereas some people will raise the war bogie against embargo, they cannot effectively attack a private boycott, or deny the constitutional right of Americans to buy where and what they choose.[8]

Of course, the advent of war radically altered this analysis. For now the boycott, basically a movement to halt the sale and purchase of ordinary household goods, began sharing much, if not most, of the spotlight with the call for a governmental and "moral embargo" against strategic war materials.

The term "moral embargo" was actually coined by President Roosevelt in October of 1935. The coinage was born out of both the passage of the Neutrality Act in August of 1935 and Mussolini's invasion of Ethiopia the following October. Angered by Rome's dastardly act, Roosevelt immediately prepared to have Italy cut off from the supply of U.S. arms and munitions. However, the Neutrality Act did not provide for an embargo on raw materials which Italy could easily convert into implements of war. Well aware of this, Roosevelt asked the State Department to investigate the possibility of including copper and steel on the roster of restricted items. Advised, however, that the Neutrality Act was not that flexible, the American President sought recourse in an appeal to his country's business world for a "moral embargo" based on the spirit of the Act.

In 1940, probably at the March 3 meeting initiating the opening of the Council's annual Anti-Nazi Week campaign, which included radio talks and symposia, the distribution of anti-Nazi literature, and mass rally meetings, Dr. Schieffelin suggested waging "a voluntary moral Embargo

Campaign."[9] In any case, one of two adopted resolutions demanded to "immediately organize a national campaign to impose a moral embargo against furnishing American materials and other resources to Nazi Germany."[10] The other was "that the Boycott hitherto applied to imports from Germany to the United States be extended to exporters who allow Germany to obtain such American materials, goods and services as may benefit the Nazi regime and help prolong the war."[11]

An actual reference to the contemplated embargo drive had been released to the press on February 27, 1940, by Abe Bluestein, newly appointed executive secretary of the Boycott Council. "We plan to launch a popular campaign on a national scale," he informed a reporter of the *New York Post,* "to curb the export of our American materials directly or indirectly to Germany." In the context of a statement that the Anti-Nazi Week "this year" was "of particular importance for the movement,"[12] Bluestein added: "We aim to stress the point that our Neutrality Act does not prevent the people from acting in accordance with their conscience and does not demand that the American public remain indifferent to the dangers of a Nazi victory in Europe."[13] It was a point which Tenenbaum, as Boycott Council chairman, was drumming into the reading and listening public so as to obviate war-mongering charges.

iii.

The Moral Embargo Campaign was scheduled to last about three months. Its program included the following:

> A pledge to be signed by exporters not to sell American materials and merchandise to Nazi Germany; An appeal to prominent organizations and individuals throughout the country for support of the Moral Embargo against Nazi Germany; An attempt to obtain at least five million signatures from the general public in support of the Moral Embargo.[14]

To help realize these aims, Tenenbaum drew up an ambitious program in which he recommended contacting all affiliated organizations, especially the AFL unions of every community. He then urged that radio broadcast time be purchased to bring into the home the message of and intent behind the moral embargo. He also suggested enlistment of the support of ethnic groups—Polish, Czech, Danish, Norwegian, Finnish, Swedish—whose ancestral lands had suffered by Nazi hands.

It is nowhere indicated, however, that in the early and middle planning stages of the Moral Embargo Campaign, Tenenbaum intended to get the American government to officially sponsor such action.[15] We first come across such a request in an April 16, 1940, report on the "intensification of activities in the past few months" that Dr. Tenenbaum sent to Dr. Ernst Knopfmacher (see p. 369), one of his closest European collaborators. Among other things, mention is even made of an attempt to secure the cooperation of the American Jewish Committee in the new venture:

> We are engaged at present in an attempt to organize the American Jewish Committee for a Moral Embargo against Nazi Germany, which will be headed by prominent American clergymen, statesmen and men prominent in civic and public life, whose aim will be to urge the U.S. Government to proclaim a Moral Embargo against Nazi Germany.[16]

However, the AJC continued refusing to cooperate in an organized fashion in any project—no matter what one called it—that was either a form of boycott or was sponsored by a boycott organization. This hardly daunted Dr. Tenenbaum, whose present campaign depended on so many organizations other than the Committee, upon whom he could rarely, if ever, depend. Moreover, it was for this campaign that he had suggested about a month before (i.e., February 1940) the creation of a Moral Embargo Committee which a reorganized CBC was instrumental in forming and which Dr. Schieffelin had agreed to chair. Into it now filed "representatives of American citizens and organizations representing Federations and Landsmanschaften of former citizens of nations menaced or invaded by the Nazis."[17] Tenenbaum estimated that this body represented nearly 20 million U.S. citizens; "so that," in his words, "our voice will be authoritative wherever we appeal."[18]

However, in the final analysis, JBC records do not reveal whether the subject of embargo was actually broached to the State Department. The minutes of a March 19 (1940) CBC meeting do report, though, that "the question was raised whether the signatures gathered in support of an embargo should be sent to the State Department in Washington." AFL Vice-President Matthew Woll "felt this would not bring any results but that the campaign itself and the amassing of signatures" could be of help to the boycott organizations by enabling them "to bring pressure upon any exporter or exporters who would not support the Moral Embargo."[19] Whether Mr. Woll's advice was followed is not known. But the fact that Council archives do not expressly state that the American government was approached "to proclaim a Moral Embargo against Nazi Germany" is an indication that no ultimate decision was reached to do so; for it would have been too important an event to omit from the record altogether had such a resolve actually been carried out.

Officially, though, the Moral Embargo Campaign was launched on April 28, 1940, at a mass meeting entitled the Embargo Nazi Germany Conference; this was some two months after Bluestein had announced it to the press. The sponsoring organizations and the reason for the delay are cited in the September 30, 1940, minutes of the Council's Action Committee:

> The Campaign was to be sponsored by the American Federation of Labor, the League for Human Rights, Freedom and Democracy,[20] and the Coordinated Boycott Committees, including the Volunteer Christian Committee to Boycott Nazi Germany, the American Boycott Against Aggressor Nations [p. 267], and the Joint Boycott Council.
>
> Due to negotiations in which members of the Volunteer Christian Committee and American Boycott Against Aggressor Nations were participating, that led to the formation of the William Allen White Committee [pp. 295, 411–14], there was an undue delay in initiating the Campaign for the Moral Embargo.
>
> The Campaign, however, was finally started and was just getting under way on a national scale when Germany's big offensive started and Italy entered the war. The surrender of France and the domination of all of Europe by Germany confused an otherwise fairly clear picture. The British Blockade was applied against the entire continent and there were no more neutrals to buy for Germany's account.
>
> There was fear, however, that the British would be unable to maintain a blockade against the entire continent with its extremely long coast line ranging from the North to Norway through to Spain. The situation is still unclear.[21]

One thing was clear, though. Due to the destructive waves of war, the Council was no longer the master of its charted course. Nevertheless, the foregoing report concludes with a satisfactory note; namely, that "the statistics to date bear evidence that Germany's share in American trade has become negligible."[22]

Supplemental Arm

It was only natural, after the Boycott Council again took to the "field," that it should wish to avoid an overlapping into the sphere of activities of the British blockade. This was in keeping with the Council's self-explanatory policy of avoiding duplication of efforts. Dr. Tenenbaum discussed this problem in a March 23, 1940, evaluation report which he prepared for the *Congress Bulletin*. He began with the subject of American exports to Nazi Germany:

> The six-month old war has not succeeded in eliminating German-American trade. Imports from Germany to the United States are still higher—more than half—than last year's average. This figure is prob-

ably exceeded by bootleg imports via Holland, Belgium, Italy. Thus, while sales to Germany are negligible in official statistics, they are in reality a flourishing business and millions of dollars worth of vital American raw materials reach Germany via neutral shipping centers. The chief profiteer in exporting American materials to Germany has become Joseph Stalin.[23]

In view of the inadequacy of the British blockade, Dr. Tenenbaum made two observations specifying the kind of role that the Council should play:

> The importance of the Boycott is to supplement the effect of the blockade. For the Boycott can reach out where the arm of this blockade is powerless.
> The apparent limitation at this juncture of a Boycott against Nazi Germany alone; for now Russia has become the economic backyard of Germany. The problem would be in extending the moral embargo to Russia and against other aggressor nations. In my eyes it constitutes a logical extension of the pre-war anti-Nazi Boycott. This is one of the problems which the leadership of the American Jewish Congress and Jewish Labor Committee will have to decide soon as a matter of policy and expediency.[24]

One might now justifiably ask whether such action would not have meant overdrawing boycott strength and reducing its effectiveness. While this may very well have been the case—even if it is a difficult thing to gauge—it is not really the point; for one should bear in mind that the boycott, from its very inception, was conceived as the ideological struggle of the few and the weak against the many and the mighty; and as such, the overly zealous Tenenbaum was prepared to scruple at nothing to add his modest contribution toward Hitler's defeat, no matter what the odds.

Even so, Tenenbaum's inclusion of Russia in the boycott must not be construed as an empty symbolic gesture of some kind, nor as an overexertion of his organization's power; nor, for that matter, as an isolated act. On the contrary, he was thereby but joining a boycott and embargo Russia movement which, apparently, came into being on the heels of the Nazi-Soviet Pact of August 1939. Tenenbaum decided on this move in the late winter or early spring of 1940, probably because thereabouts did it become plainly evident to him that Russia had "become the economic backyard of Germany."

The specific charge with which Russia was indicted by the Council was the purchase of large quantities of oil which, ultimately, reached German ports. Also, in connection with its extension of the boycott against firms exporting raw materials and semi-finished goods to Germany,

Council investigations disclosed that cargoes of such articles were being sent to Germany by nonbelligerent countries since the beginning of the war. This included, besides Russia, Italy, Sweden, and the Netherlands. Other countries also showed increased U.S. purchases which, the Boycott Council charged, were made for the benefit of Nazi Germany. Thus, in its Preliminary Draft of the Moral Embargo Campaign (prepared sometime in early 1940), JBC included "a study of American export trends since the outbreak of the war," which indicated that also Belgium, Hungary, Switzerland, Rumania, Yugoslavia, and Denmark had increased "tremendously" their purchases in the United States. Moreover, these increased purchases, this study revealed, "were concentrated mainly in war materials and raw materials for war industries." Therefore, "it was suspected that these excessive acquisitions of war materials were reaching Nazi Germany." The official figures for 1939, which were released by the Department of Commerce, confirmed this suspicion. They showed an increase in exports to these countries in ferro-alloys, cotton, petroleum, and copper; all vital war materials which, in the past, had been imported directly by Nazi Germany.

The role that the boycott would play in these circumstances was stated by Dr. Tenenbaum in a September 9, 1939, memorandum entitled "Boycott and War." He remarked that there was not the "slightest indication that German dumping in this country will be affected as nearly as it was in 1914–1915."[25] He then went on to say:

> Also, with many "neutrals" in the field, she will be able to use foreign tonnage for the shipment and trans-shipment of German goods through foreign ports. Italy's "neutrality" may prove of great advantage to her in this respect, and it is problematical if Britain would dare to be too exacting in the search of contraband on Italian or other neutral boats. It is here where the Boycott can render a service by making it impossible for Germany to sell here or in Latin America and obtain cash or barter for indispensable war materials.[26]

It must be added, however, that the Boycott Council chairman was puzzled by "the question of why Britain permitted such excessive exports of war materials to neutral countries adjacent to Nazi Germany."[27] The deliberation of this question is set forth as follows in his Preliminary Draft to the Moral Embargo Campaign:

> Was it that they feared to antagonize the neutral countries, thereby driving them into the Nazi camp or did they fear to alienate American businessmen by "interfering" with their legitimate business? Whatever the reason, we in this country must share part of the responsibility for the suspicious and excessive shipments of war materials to the neutral countries.[28]

But the Hitler hordes, which, by overrunning Europe, had turned the subsequent campaign for a Moral Embargo into an anachronistic project, likewise rendered almost useless the idea of using JBC as a liaison for the British blockade. The reason, according to the Action Committee minutes of September 30, 1940, was the same; namely, "there were no more neutrals to buy for Germany's account."[29]

34

The Jewelry Industry Vigil

i.

In July of 1938, owing to the absorption of Austria by the Nazis and in anticipation of a similar fate for the Sudetenland, Dr. Marcus began exploring the possibility of forming a Businessmen's Advisory Council to help offset a great increase in the U.S. imports of diamonds and semiprecious stones from these two regions. However, the creation of this Council, or Committee, as it was also called, proceeded at a snail's pace. For not until January 18 of the following year, apparently after Dr. Tenenbaum took personal charge of the project, does JBC correspondence indicate that it was being actively pursued.[1]

An initiatory meeting appears to have taken place on March 30, 1939. A JBC communication bearing this date—the next available document on the subject—describes a "Luncheon Meeting of the Beads, Spangles and Jewelry Importers," at which the Boycott Council, NSANL, JWV, and "about forty importers, predominantly of the Jewelry line,"[2] were represented. This long overdue type of gathering was prompted, more than likely, by Hitler's recent takeover of the rest of Czechoslavakia.

The meeting was chaired by Marcus, who, in addition to declaring that "the unions have promised their full cooperation in the Boycott," also said that "the importers have sufficient stock to give them at least six months leeway to seek other sources of supply."[3] The League's George Harriman (p. 164) stated that his organization would "support the Joint Boycott Council completely in this work"; and Gene Matathias of the JWV placed his group's 45,000 members at the Council's disposal for "militant action."

In an October 13, 1938, letter that Marcus had written to a friend with seemingly influential business connections, he showed what a "problem" it had become, after the Sudetenland was ceded to the Nazis, to find "substitutes for precious and semi-precious stones imported into the United States from Germany." He also listed a specific number of items that "concerned" him, namely, china, glass, textiles, cottons, gloves; and asked if he could "help contact possible sources of supply for these items in Belgium."[4]

When, therefore, at the aforesaid luncheon meeting, Marcus confronted the importers with a statement regarding their "six months leeway to seek other sources of supply," he knew very well that this was easier said than done. This is precisely what they tried to point out to him in the discussion that followed, declaring that "the problem was far bigger than the imposition of a Boycott by the importers." Germany, the importers said further, with the gobbled-up territories of Austria and Czechoslovakia, had a "fairly" complete world monopoly of the products used by the jewelry industry. Total U.S. importations, it was added, probably amounted to 15 percent of that entire industry; shutting off the raw materials from Germany threatened the jobs of thousands of workmen; German manufacturers would invade the American market directly and sell their U.S. counterparts "what the importers were trying to eliminate from the country."[5]

But Dr. Marcus was not very impressed, accusing the "stone people" of not looking for substitute sources of supply. What he wanted was a pledge that they maintain the boycott for a nine-month period. The interval would be used by the Boycott Council to help jewelers overcome the difficulty of finding substitutes for their German-made stones and gems.[6]

The results of this effort are cited in a memorandum that Dr. Tenenbaum prepared for Dr. Wise on June 6, 1939: "We have succeeded in organizing some of the industries that have been importing German and then Czechoslovakian goods in a sort of association which in cooperation with the Council will endeavor to find substitutes in France and Belgium for this kind of merchandise."[7]

Dr. Tenenbaum mentions as specific examples the precious and semiprecious stone industry "comprising Jewish and non-Jewish concerns throughout the country." He then goes on to say:

> These two industries have signed a pledge to maintain the Boycott and have furthermore obligated themselves in every individual case in which there are no substitutes, to arbitrate the matter through a committee composed of their own executives and representatives of the Joint Boycott Council.

In addition, they endeavor, under the leadership of JBC, to find new sources of supply in democratic countries and to encourage wherever possible the creation of new industries by refugee industrialists and workers. Such firms have already been established and others are in the process of establishment in France and Belgium. The cost of this work which entails having representatives in Paris is quite substantial and is being met by contributions from these industries. All the firms involved have taxed themselves to carry the burden according to plans which have been worked out by the executives of these organizations. At the present time, the musical, leather, fur, linen and other industries are being organized along the same lines.[8]

The project was barely starting to gain ground when, like all other Council activities, it, too, was voided by the liquidation of the boycott movement.

ii.

The jewelry industry was not included in the limited scale of operations assumed by the Council after its resumption of boycott activities. It was incorporated into the program again at a May 1, 1940, meeting at which a new Businessmen's Advisory Committee was formed to put a stop to the activities of U.S. smugglers who facilitated both exports and imports for Nazi Germany. Dr. Tenenbaum, who gave this reason, also added that "the tragedy of the situation is increased by the fact that Jewish refugees are known to be acting as such smugglers."[9] Tenenbaum warned, moreover, that the British knew that Jews were participating in these "practices," and declared that he needed the "practical advice and experience of businessmen in various lines" to aid him in the elimination of such subterfuges.

Mr. Simons,[10] subsequent chairman of the Businessmen's Committee, was the first to respond to Tenenbaum's presentation. Taking up the subject of exports, he differentiated between the export of metals and that of industrial diamonds. He asserted that Germany was "well stocked" on metals and that she could procure them in countries other than the United States; but, added Simons, "if Germany could be prevented from acquiring stocks of such diamonds, she would find it impossible within a short period of time to keep her plants in operation regardless of her supplies of other raw materials."[11]

Simons further asserted that 97 percent of all diamond supplies was in the hands of a British syndicate headed by Jews. Prior to the war, he continued, Germany had purchased $5 million to $6 million worth of diamonds a year; but only six weeks before the outbreak of the war, he quickly added, she had purchased as much as $1.5 million worth of industrial diamonds from the British syndicate.

Next, Simons pointed to the following problem: that whereas prior to the outbreak of war there were only ten or eleven diamond dealers here, "there are now about fifty new diamond agents in this country, most of them, Belgian Jews who arrived within the past few months."[12] The majority of them, he said, were small dealers; but it was very strongly suspected that quite a few of them engaged in smuggling diamonds to Germany from "this country." The British, he further declared, because of the Neutrality Act, admitted they were powerless to cope with the problem.

Simons therefore requested that all diamond dealers "here" submit an inventory of their current stocks and sign a pledge that they would not sell their diamonds to Germany or German interests. He also suggested getting Jewish diamond smugglers together at a meeting, asking them to cease these practices voluntarily, and if they refused, "to be ready to fight them." In the event such a confrontation was necessary, Simons said in conclusion, he could furnish a list of 95 percent of all U.S. diamond dealers.

In complete agreement with Mr. Simons, Dr. Tenenbaum stated that the diamond dealers should be brought together and appealed to. However, the Boycott Council must "be prepared with threats," he added, if they refused to cooperate in helping to root out smuggling activities.

The group also discussed the question of raising special funds for this project. One of the participants suggested "that the money should be gotten from businessmen without any fuss or notice; that it should be a secret fund not responsible to the parent organizations, but only to the Businessmen's Committee or representatives of their selection."[13] Of course, a public appeal for funds to help eliminate Jewish smuggling would bring shame upon the whole Jewish community.

This was clearly expressed at the next meeting a fortnight later. JBC representatives voiced their "wish to clean house before others do it for them"; to obtain the names of "violators" against whom they could act rather than wait until "an outside agency gets to them." However, they suggested that the task of cleaning house be done by the businessmen themselves by organizing their own vigilance committees. "It has always been JBC policy," they explained, "to have each industry supervise their line of business through their own organization."[14]

In pursuit of this policy, Tenenbaum suggested the creation of a "Protective Committee" whose first task would be to "draw up a memorandum to be distributed among all industrial diamond dealers, emphasizing the importance of not selling to Germany." It was also suggested that JBC draft a letter "hinting it has a black list of firms in the field of industrial diamonds."[15] Finally, a committee of six was selected to represent the industry, and letters were to be sent out to the 250 members of the Diamond Dealers Club inviting them to attend the next meeting.

With this the narrative is cut off. It is taken up again in some of the 1941 material, but is sparse at best, giving the impression that this area of activity simply faded away.

One document, dated March 18, 1941, tells of a futile attempt to prevent the importation of stolen German goods into the United States. It was made by Moses D. Heyman, a Council staff member, who, among other things, had been appointed on July 18, 1938, by the Actions Committee to organize a Businessmen's Advisory Council.[16] He knew that it was "perfectly legal to import stolen goods in the United States provided duty is paid."[17] To surmount this obstacle, Heyman prepared "An Amendment to the Tariff Act of 1930," which was:

> a bill designed to prevent the importation of merchandise, moneys, securities or any other form of property that has been forcibly taken by foreign individuals or governments from their rightful owners.
>
> Section I.
>
> When a foreign government, or its agents, forcibly seize private or public property, in any form whatsoever, such as, merchandise, moneys, jewels, works of art, patents or materials of any nature, or any other products or properties of any nature whatsoever from a country which has been invaded or with which it is at war, such property may not be imported into the United States without a special authorization from the President of this country.
>
> Section II.
>
> If such articles are imported, then all those connected with such importation shall be considered as trading in stolen goods. The penalty for the violation of this amendment shall be as follows:
>
> A. Confiscation of the goods which it is intended to import.
> B. A jail sentence not exceeding 10 years in prison; and a fine equivalent to twice the value of the goods being imported.[18]

Tenenbaum had appointed Heyman to chair an Investigating Committee for "eradicating the traffic in German diamonds."[19] But on April 15, Heyman wrote his chieftain that he was "too busy, and besides, Marcus couldn't make the necessary contacts."[20] Heyman then added that he would not be able to remain with the Boycott Council, as he would probably be needed by the "Navy Department." This marked the collapse of any attempt to put through legislation to eliminate the smuggling of German diamonds.

Nevertheless, about three weeks later, "Dr. Tenenbaum brought up the subject of industrial diamonds," claiming that they were "being sold to South American countries and from there shipped to Russia, Japan and Germany."[21] Thereupon, "all agreed" to organize the New York diamond dealers to put a stop to this "smuggling." Three weeks later, the Diamond Industry Protective Committee, whose creation Dr. Tenenbaum had suggested the year before, came into being. Its first major act was to initiate a drive to organize the "nearly 400 dealers of the industry in a special diamond trade association who would be under obligation to sign the pledge not to sell or buy from Germany."[22] Furthermore, it was decided "to give out a press release announcing the formation of that Committee and to the Jeweler's Magazine warning against buying from and selling to the German industry any diamonds and to expose those who have any dealings with Germany."[23] Additional significant details are lacking, however.

The minutes of September 30, 1941, report that "the Businessmen's Committee was preparing to set itself up on a more or less stable basis for the purpose of preventing business dealings with Germany until Hitler's final defeat"; but an appended statement adds that "following Italy's entrance into the war, the Businessmen's Committee became quiescent."[24] Thus, Western Europe's utter prostration beneath Hitler's heels had, for all intents and purposes, put an end to another Council activity.

35

The Food Packages Issue: Racket And Controversy

i.

Despite a November, 1939, ban by the State Department against the shipment of strategic materials to the Reich, the Council learned that thousands of alleged food packages destined for Germany were leaving American shores every month. The Nazis, the Council suspected, were doing millions of dollars' worth of business via food packages solicited for Germany "by firms pretending to be independent but intimately connected with the German Consulate in New York and other official German agencies." Naturally, the Council had reason to believe that such packages contained items "other than food."

The aforesaid is cited in a May 25, 1940, JBC document,[1] which is based on a report that Bluestein submitted on January 17 of that year. Bluestein's account said that investigation of the food package business showed that the two major companies in the "racket"—Fortura and Mitropa—had "intimate connections with the German Consulate"; to which he added: "Although the companies claimed that their orders were filled out in neutral European countries on cabled instructions from them, a strong suspicion existed that the food was actually sent out of this country through the Italian Lines as the personal property of Italian seamen."[2]

In further reference to Fortura and Mitropa, the Council secretary said that:

> These were soliciting the sending of food packages to unfortunates in Germany. Whereas money was supposed to be sent to neutral countries from where the food was to be sent into Germany, it was

determined by the Council that the money actually remained in this country for the use of the German Government and its spies and that in many instances no deliveries of any food were made to the consignee.

The Council, in order to make sure that Jewish organizations which were sending food to unfortunates in Poland would not become victims of the Nazi swindle, insisted that these organizations set up agencies in neutral countries to receive the American dollars and in turn to send food from these countries to Poland. Through this means, the Nazis could not gain control of the value of foreign exchange.[3]

Bluestein gave an analogous report at a June 5 meeting, adding, though, that Fortura and Mitropa claimed that they "cable their package orders across to some neutral European countries for shipment into Germany."[4] But, asked Bluestein, "what is in the packages shipped from this country via Italian Lines allegedly as the personal property of Italian seamen?" In reply, from someone whom the Council had assigned this case, it was learned that "the F.B.I. knew about this situation, but so far has been unable to examine the contents of these packages."

Shortly afterward, however, when Rome "plunged its outstretched dagger" into France's back, German agents were prevented from using Italian neutrality to their advantage.[5]

ii.

Of the various occupied territories, Poland, which was a poor and backward country to begin with, was probably least capable of providing for its population after near total devastation from the Nazi blitzkrieg. Nor was the International Red Cross, which was permitted to bring it a measure of succor, in a position to reduce the misery on an appreciable scale.

To help ease somewhat the frightful plight of this war-ravaged land, sympathetic people began dispatching food and clothing parcels to the hapless victims. In the main, such dispatchers consisted of individual American Jews and American Jewish organizations seeking desperately, in a phase antecedent to genocidal slaughter, to allay the agony of their more than three million Polish coreligionists relegated to a life of destitution and degradation.

Dr. Tenenbaum rightly feared that the foodstuffs and supplies sent to Poland were being confiscated by the Nazis. But when he conveyed this concern to the American Red Cross, it assured him in a mid-April 1940 reply that "American shipments are being forwarded to the civilian population of the Governor General exclusively."[6] Tenenbaum was not satisfied, however, and decided to have the matter investigated.

A Council document, dated September 29, 1940, indicates that the investigation lasted "several months." This explains, of course, why, in the interim, the subject—including investigatory details—was absent from the record. It reappears in a September 10, 1940, communication that Bluestein sent R. H. Amory, the Secretary of the British Embassy in Washington, D.C. Bluestein had sent the missive in response to Amory's complaint that HIAS was forwarding "standard" kosher food parcels to Germany and German-occupied Poland. The reply stated that the matter would be "investigated and stopped." It was, and without delay, as a mere two days later Dr. Tenenbaum notified Amory that HIAS had "ceased" sending kosher food parcels to the aforesaid territories.

The Agudas Israel, the world organization of Othodox Jewry, established in Poland in 1912, also became involved in the foregoing clash. As late as 1939, it had not secured a firm position in American Jewish life. Be that as it may, the fact is that it was engaged in the dispatch of food parcels to Poland. So on September 30, 1940, Tenenbaum contacted the Agudah secretary, Oscar Z. Rand, informing him that the "sending of food packages via Yugoslavia to Poland is in violation of British wishes that no packages be sent to any of the Nazi-occupied countries."[7] This, explained the JBC chairman,"breaks" the British blockade and violates the "principles" of the boycott. Tenenbaum concluded his communication by asking Rand's "intentions in the future."

There is no record of Rand's reply; nor does the record show that Tenenbaum pursued the matter, as he was wont to do in such cases. This is probably explained by the following incident.

On November 22, Dr. Henry Szoszkes, national field director of the American Federation of Polish Jews,[8] addressed a communication to Dr. Tenenbaum, in which he expressed his desire to arrange for the dispatch of food packages to Poland from Yugoslavia. Such an operation, said Szoszkes, "would in no way interfere with the British Blockade because Yugoslavia is a neutral country."[9] In further justification of his proposal, Szoszkes explained that "up to the present we know of no instance to the effect that Germans have confiscated any food packages," or "that Jews are deprived of their food cards if they receive a food package." Poland's Jewish population, he said distressfully, "asks and writes for food."

Szoszkes added that, prior to making arrangements for the dispatch of food packages, he had discussed the matter with, and had obtained the consent of, the World Jewish Congress; namely, to secure the food in a neutral country and to make sure that the monies involved did not fall into German hands.

More letters followed; but it was not until January 6, 1941, apparently after due deliberation and consultation, that Dr. Tenenbaum informed Dr. Szoszkes that the "proper authorities" had concluded that there would be no objection to his transmitting food packages to Poland, provided the following conditions were met:

> The food is to be bought and paid for in one of the contiguous countries, such as Yugoslavia, Bulgaria, Greece, or Turkey with the proviso that absolute assurance be given that none of the cash or the equivalent will ultimately find its way to Germany.
> To safeguard against such a possibility, the proper authorities here would like to have the name and address of the agency or agencies in the aforementioned countries which receive payment for and dispatch food parcels to Poland.[10]

By "proper authorities," Tenenbaum presumably meant the British; for as we have already seen, he was being guided by their wishes and advice. If so, then the foregoing stipulations, as we shall presently see, were based either on a misunderstanding or on misinformation.

For on February 18, Tenenbaum was sent what turned out to be a definitive policy statement by A. K. Helm, another British embassy official. It advised him to inform all the organizations with which he was affiliated "that no scheme for the dispatch of food parcels at present exists which has the approval of the British Government."[11] Helm explained that the fact that food was paid for in countries such as Yugoslavia or Bulgaria, "does not by any means preclude dollar exchange becoming available to Germany." In fact, Helm continued, he had "evidence" that in the case of Yugoslavia, "the whole of the dollar sum very probably reached German hands." Helm also said that the British government felt that the "responsibility" for feeding Occupied Europe rightfully rested with Germany.

Within about a week, Tenenbaum had gotten in touch with the American Federation of Polish Jews, the HIAS, the World Jewish Congress, and the Agudas Israel, all of which were engaging in the dispatch of food parcels to Poland. Each was met with and apprized of Britain's view with regard to this activity. On March 7, Tenenbaum replied to Helm that, after meeting with the aforesaid organizations, agreement was reached not to ship parcels through Yugoslavia, but via Portugal, "which they deemed was under the strict control of the representatives of the British Blockade."[12] It was further agreed, though, that should Britain oppose this plan, too, then the sending of packages would be stopped "completely."

On March 12, Helm wrote back that "London takes the view that the whole of this parcel business is objectionable in their eyes, since they had not yet put before them any scheme which would not directly or indirectly involve advantage to Germany."[13] On June 14, apparently because the organizations concerned were still not satisfied, Helm communicated a more specific statement, saying that London "viewed with particular objection" a scheme for the dispatch of food parcels from Portugal to Jews in Poland. It claimed to have "conclusive evidence" that parcels so far sent either were not received by the addressees or if received, the latter suffered a corresponding reduction in their rationed food allowances. Besides, added the statement, London did not regard Portugal as being self-supporting in the matter of food.

About a fortnight earlier, Helm had written Tenenbaum that there was "no reply yet from London," and that "in the meantime," he left the question of the Jewish organizations' food or clothing shipments "to their own appreciation."[14] Of the various organizations involved in this practice, only the World Jewish Congress made a relatively early decision to terminate it. This determination was conveyed to Tenenbaum on April 4 by Dr. Arieh Tartakower, noted Jewish sociologist and a pioneer in the World Jewish Congress movement. On May 9, Tartakower informed Wise that he would order the World Jewish Congress office in Geneva to stop the money transfer to Poland "just as the food transfer was stopped." Actually, Tartakower replied for Maurice L. Perlzweig, World Jewish Congress leader and former London rabbi, to whom Wise had written on the aforesaid date that help to Poland in the form of food packages and money transfer was "madness." The idea infuriated Wise, who stated: "I shall not for one hour longer remain President of the American Jewish Congress, if it is to continue to run the risk of alienating the already too dubious good will of the British Government to our people. As President of the American Jewish Congress, I lay down the order of immediate discontinuance."[15]

In his reply, Tartakower said he did not think anything had been done against British interests. He may have been taken aback, though, to respond the same day Wise dispatched his message.

According to a June–September 1941 Confidential Report on JBC Activities, the HIAS followed suit "after the Council's determination to use its full power was made clear." Just when HIAS revealed its intention to discontinue its food package activities is not stated, however.

It proved more difficult, though, to obtain the cooperation of the American Federation of Polish Jews. So states the aforementioned report, citing a June 19 letter that Dr. Tenenbaum had sent the Federation. Tenenbaum stated in the letter that he had transacted with the Federation a "weary correspondence regarding their sending of parcels."[16] The nature of the strained relationship is described as follows: "Not satisfied with breaching one of the principal aims of the Boycott, you have taken the right to yourselves to advertise this fact despite the gentlemen's agreement not to do so pending the clarification of certain demands you have made upon the Embassy."[17] Citing the embassy's reply regarding Portugal, Dr. Tenenbaum concludes: "In view of this, JBC feels justified in making a demand on the Federation that it stop sending parcels to Europe. It will take the severest measures in case of recalcitrance."[18]

The letter, which was sent shortly before the Federation's annual convention, had the desired effect. The Confidential Report, which mentions this, too, also adds: "The Federation's Convention instructed the organization to end its participation in the food package business."[19]

A resolute statement to this effect was entered into the *Jewish Daily Forward* by the Federation on July 17. The British Embassy was apprized of this by Tenenbaum four days later.

iii.

Only the Agudah (p. 316) still remained out of line, its defiant resistance proving "long and acrimonious." The Confidential Report describes this controversy as well, revealing that Tenenbaum had also written the Agudah on June 19, and that his correspondence with this organization was even more wearying than his communications to the Federation.

In his June communication, Tenenbaum reminded the Agudah that he had written it "several times without even getting a reply." And whereas Tenenbaum had stopped short of a threat of picketing in his June 19 letter to the Federation, such a warning was included in that communication to the Agudah. But the Agudah was not discomposed as a result.

In a June 27, 1941, letter to Dr. Sylvester Gruszka, consul general of the Republic of Poland and personal friend, Dr. Tenenbaum specified what, in addition to the British blockade, had spurred his anti-food package crusade:

> In view of the attitude of the British Government and of the information in our possession, we have decided to take action against those firms continuing to send food parcels to Poland. While we have the deepest sympathy for the Polish people, we feel that even if the parcels sent did reach their destination, they would be insignificant in alleviating the misery of your countrymen and mine.[20]

It was in line with this outlook that around mid-July, Dr. Tenenbaum made good his threat to picket the Agudah. The event, which was given full coverage in the Yiddish press, dramatized the Council accusation that an ultrareligious organization was furnishing the bloodthirsty enemy with the provisions intended for his blood-soaked victims. The Agudah, which had up to now reacted to Council admonition with defiant silence, was compelled at last to make public statements in defense of its action.

At first, the Agudah claimed that the British government had not notified it of its attitude toward the practice of food package distribution. Technically, this was true, but it was just a deceitful way of justifying Agudah policy before an aroused Jewish public. Intercepting this distortion of the truth, M. E. Bathurst of the British Press Service wrote Tenenbaum on July 21, requesting that he publicize in the "Jewish press" that:

> Agudas were fully informed of the attitude of the British Government long before the present controversy reached its peak, and
> Conference and negotiations have been tried and failed through the uncompromising attitude adopted by Agudas.[21]

The following statement, dated August 5, 1941, could be the one that Dr. Tenenbaum had released as a result of Bathurst's bidding:

> After three weeks of continuous picketing, the Agudas Israel of America still continues in the sorry role of being the only organization breaking the British Blockade and Jewish solidarity.
> Recent investigations undertaken by the Council show that, in addition to non-delivery of food packages in Nazi Poland, the German fiscal system has developed a new means of exploiting the sympathies of those sending food packages, by charging the full amount of the American price of the package as duty, before allowing the package to go to the unfortunate to whom it is addressed. It is to be deplored that the Agudas Israel of America, a sickly weed transplanted from foreign soil to the liberal American environment, should continue to poison the atmosphere without regard for the consequences to the entire Jewish people.[22]

The statement added that the matter of food delivery should be taken up by the "large Jewish organizations" with the "proper authorities" if it was felt that it was necessary to start a large-scale project to feed the Jewish population in Poland. The Agudah's method, it said, was "haphazard, irresponsible and unsupervised." In conclusion, it was stated that "bad effects" were noted in replies received from "private companies" which felt justified in starting to send packages to the Nazi-occupied territories on account of "the Agudah example." This problem was also dealt with in JBC's June–September Confidential

Report and was stated as follows: "The 'Freezing Order' forced the purely German firms to close down when first it was promulgated. However, there was great danger that they too would reopen if the mainly Jewish firms continued to send food packages to Poland." Tenenbaum, who in matters of this kind left no stone unturned, asked the State Department, in a July 31 inquiry, if the Agudah had registered in accordance with the Neutrality Act of 1939. It had not, he was informed in an August 1 reply. This, of course, led the determined JBC chairman to explore the question of legal action against the Agudah and other violators. To his disappointment, the Department of State informed him in an August 9 communication that "inasmuch as the Act and regulations thereunder are not specific with regard to commercial food package companies, there is some question as to the requirement of their registration." Thus, it was clear that if Agudah was to be subdued, it would have to be effected through the two principal weapons of picketing and Jewish public opinion.

iv.

The Agudah has no archival material which might be scrutinized for the specific motivations and calculations that underlay its policy and attitude. An article entitled "Blockade vs. Humanitarianism,"[23] published on July 25, 1941, undoubtedly hit the mark, however, in saying that it was the "highly controversial question of whether the starving Polish Jews should be abandoned for the sake of a complete blockade." For its part, claimed the Agudah in defense of its action, it was not convinced that its means of relief meant a violation of the British blockade; and it questioned, moreover, the Council's right to act "dictatorially."

The Agudah yielded finally on August 27. As released by the *Daily News Bulletin* of the Jewish Telegraphic Agency, the Agudah World Executive announced that its organization would be guided by Britain's wishes with respect to the dispatch of parcels to Poland. In its announcement, the Agudah regretted the fact that JBC had "made a national issue of a problem which was on the verge of amicable settlement." It did not express regret, though, for having hitherto engaged in food package operations, claiming that it had been proved that such items reached the individuals for whom they were intended. Thus, maintained the Agudah, it had helped alleviate the distress of starving Jews in Poland.

What, if this is the case, prompted the Agudah to terminate this aspect of its humane and charitable activities? For want of direct documentary evidence, one can only assume that the Agudah finally concluded that its supplies were reaching too few "individuals" to make it advisable to continue remaining an object of scorn and controversy in the sight of the American Jewish community.

The Agudah did not reveal, however, with whom it "was on the verge of amicable settlement" apropos of the raging food package war. It was certainly not the Joint Boycott Council. This is learned from a September 2, 1941, communication from Dr. Tenenbaum to an inquirer, informing him that "all our efforts to get the Agudas Israel to a conference table with other organizations proved futile."[24] Britain's equally futile efforts were also mentioned. Just the same, it was Tenenbaum whom Bathurst credited three days later when he wrote him that "the sending of food packages to Poland seems to have ceased completely."[25] Dr. Tenenbaum confirmed this development on September 8, by noting that the "sending of packages to Poland had been stopped by all organizations."[26]

36

Latin American Activities

First Phase

On a number of occasions reference was made to Germany's trade with Latin America. Whereas in the early and middle thirties this did not reach distressing proportions, by 1939, it had expanded, indeed, into a very flourishing enterprise for the Reich. Alarmed by this development, the Council's eyes turned to Latin America with a view to intensifying its anti-Nazi boycott activities in that part of the world. As a result, next to its overall effort to act as an auxiliary of the British blockade, this turned out to be the most ambitious project assumed by JBC in the war years.

To be sure, an early attempt had been made to extend the boycott movement into Central and South America. This occurred in April of 1934, when Dr. Tenenbaum formed a Committee on International Coordination of the Boycott. It was an act which was in keeping with his idea of "a global boycott movement in the periphery, with the United States as its centre."[1] Thus, the worldwide boycott that Dr. Tenenbaum had called for at the first session of the World Jewish Congress of 1936 was but a variation of "International Coordination."

The International Coordination Committee consisted of a trio headed by Zelig Tygel, executive director of the American Federation of Polish Jews, William Spiegelman (p. 130), and Israel Posnansky (p. 141). To obviate the possible overdrawing of their action or conduct, Dr. Tenenbaum informed them that the purpose of the Committee was the "coordination of the boycott in the various countries where such organizations exist."[2] However, with respect to Latin American countries, "immediate steps" were to be taken "to establish contact with Central and South American Boycott Committees for the purpose of implementing the boycott there where German imports are of a considerable nature, particularly the articles of the German heavy industries, such as tools, appliances and various sorts of machinery."[3]

To this end, Dr. Tenenbaum began corresponding with some of Latin America's Jewish leaders. One of these was the Chilean president of the Comité de Protection a Los Immigrantes Israelitas, a Dr. M. Weinstein, whom he strongly urged in a July 18, 1934, letter to organize an anti-Nazi boycott in his country. Responding finally on September 12, Dr. Weinstein explained that an "organized" boycott in Chile was out of the question because of the insignificant number of Jews there. More importantly, Chilean Jews, Weinstein noted, did not exercise an influential role in their country's foreign commerce; nor did he think that an anti-Nazi boycott would gain the sympathy of either the Chilean people or their government.

A copy of the July 18 letter was also sent to an Argentinian Jewish leader. However, the absence in the record of a reply may indicate that there was even less hope for the introduction of an organized boycott in that country.

The examples of Chile and Argentina must have given Dr. Tenenbaum an inkling of what to expect if he attempted to extend boycott operations into Latin America. Consequently, for about the next five years, there were only intermittent references to this subject. One of them is cited in an undated Confidential Report by Dr. Tenenbaum, and reads:

> The boycott, to be effective in halting the progress of Nazism, would have to be universal. It devolved on the Joint Boycott Council to attempt the creation of a moral blockade throughout the Western Hemisphere. Connections were therefore established as early as 1935 with liberal, labor and Jewish organizations in South America. Efforts were hampered, however, by the lack of resources, by laws of certain Latin American countries, and by the failure of the democratic exporting countries to offer trade concessions meeting the enticing inducements of the German controlled economy.[4]

In another document, a March 26, 1936, communication to Leon Kubowitzki (see chap. 36, n. 4), Dr. Tenenbaum wrote: "JBC is now prepared, through the AF of L, to induce labor organizations in South America not to permit the conclusion of reciprocal treaties with Germany which would make it possible for Germany to flood the markets in Brazil, Uruguay, Chile, etc., with her products."[5] A similar, but somewhat less explicit, reference was made by Tenenbaum that summer to the delegates attending the first World Jewish Congress.

Aside from these, however, the thin thread of this subject disappears from JBC documents. When the matter was taken up once again, the Boycott Council, for reasons other than mere internal expansion, was in a position to cope with it on a much broader scale.

Second Phase

i.

The boycott feelers that Dr. Tenenbaum sent out to a number of Latin American leaders in 1934 may have been due to the fact that a German commercial delegation had visited South America that year and ultimately concluded trade agreements with most of the countries on that continent. Germany would deliver products, finished goods, and semi-manufactured articles. In exchange, the South American countries were to supply Germany with raw materials and staple commodities. All such agreements were based on the barter and clearing system, which enabled Germany to make great profits in most of these countries.

By 1939, Germany had become a fierce commercial rival of the United States in Latin America. Moreover, in a number of Latin American countries, principally Argentina and Brazil, the Reich succeeded in making considerable political capital from its commercial gains. And by artfully manipulating the two, it hoped to offset U.S. trade and influence in most of Latin America.

This scheme played into Germany's hands despite—or better, because of—its great distance from this region. Thus, Germany was too distant to be viewed as a competitive rival, and unlike the contiguous United States, had not, in the way of border disputes and internal intrusions, aroused the resentment or enmity of the Latin American peoples. Keenly aware of this, the U.S. government faithfully adhered to its Good Neighbor policy, committing it to the principle of noninterference in the internal affairs of Latin America. But this was ipso facto a negative policy, since its very purpose was to carefully nurture the friendship of a people indignant over a long history of "Yankee meddling." And such bitterness was not easy to allay, making it that much easier for the Nazis, as well as their Axis partners, to consolidate themselves politically and economically on the South American continent.

ii.

The Boycott Council's first apparent step in view of this challenge was to inform the public about it in a series of radio talks which it sponsored on January 24, 1939.[6] Participants, in addition to Dr. Tenenbaum, included Judge Jeremiah T. Mahoney, former AAU president, and Oswald Garrison Villard, editor of a liberal weekly, the *Nation*.

Mahoney discussed the "Nazi Designs on the Americas." Describing Hitler's ruthlessness, Mahoney warned that the German dictator would not be satisfied with Europe alone. He pointed out that "the Nazis have already stolen in South American countries much business, which rightfully belongs to America and other democracies."[7] Villard spoke on "How Can We Meet Nazi Propaganda in South America," suggesting reciprocal trade and the democratic process—slow as these might be—as the best alternatives.

Dr. Tenenbaum warned against "The Nazi Menace to the Americas," which he characterized as having taken the shape of a "trade war against the United States." According to his estimates, Nazi export trade with Latin American countries had risen from 4.4 percent in 1931 to 11.2 percent in 1937. He asserted that Germany's share in the imports of Brazil alone had jumped from 9 percent in 1932 to 23 percent in 1937. Tenenbaum further asserted that "in Argentina, Germany buys double of what we buy and Nazi influence has correspondingly expanded, fostered by propaganda and a German colony of nearly half a million."[8] The JBC chairman contrasted these gains with the "weakened trade position" of the United States and the loss of its "political prestige" in much of Latin America. This, he warned, had made the United States more vulnerable to a Nazi invasion from that region.

To ward off this threat, Dr. Tenenbaum suggested the organization of America's export industries on a cooperative basis through a special Board of Trade. He also recommended an expansion in the function of the Export-Import Bank. And in line with a "British device," Tenenbaum suggested the formation of a "fighting fund" for Latin American export trade to help counterbalance Nazi subsidization.

In his concluding remarks, the Council chieftain expressed the belief that the "conscience" of Latin American labor organizations could "be aroused and enlisted in a Pan-American anti-Nazi Boycott." He therefore urged the boycott and labor organizations "in this country" do their utmost "to forster such a drive."

JBC sources dating to the next several months, while discussing the initiation of or involvement in such a drive, are sparse and rather vague on this subject. Thus, a February 28, 1939, communication, which mentions that "the Joint Boycott Council is undertaking a campaign to fight the penetration of the Nazis into Latin America," merely adds that "several well known American organizations who are interested in our trade relations with these countries are working with the Council."[9] An address delivered by Dr. Tenenbaum on April 24, 1939, cited "the Boycott in South America" as having "been greatly strengthened the last few months," and said that "there are boycott committees in the principal cities of Latin American countries."[10] And finally, as stated in an April 27, 1939, document, JBC planned to intensify its anti-Nazi boycott, summoning "for this purpose" all organizations affiliated with the American Jewish Congress and the Jewish Labor Committee to a May 7, 1939, national conference at New York's Manhattan Center.

It would appear from the general and Yiddish press that the conference proved quite a spectacle, having been attended by some 3,500 delegates representing around 2,700 organizations. This included about 350 local labor unions and representatives of boycott organizations from France, Belgium, and Argentina. However, there are no minutes describing the conference proceedings, only speeches by Dr. Tenenbaum and some of the invited speakers.

Tenenbaum spoke on "Six Years Anti-Nazi Boycott," which contained a subtitled section called "Pan-American Boycott." It made clear the need for such a boycott by pointing to the Nazi methods of trade invasion and doctrinal penetration as preceding territorial conquest. This came after the following warning: "Hitler's dream of a colonial empire lies not in Africa, but in South America. Unless we are prepared to contest Nazi hegemony, we shall face the Nazi menace not somewhere in Europe, but here in our own backyard."[11] "The recently awakened liberal and labor elements in Latin America," added Tenenbaum, "could prevent the growing menace of Hitlerism in this hemisphere."[12]

One of the invited guest speakers was Dr. David Effron, a New York professor of Latin American culture and executive secretary of the Council for Pan-American Democracy, a JBC auxiliary and the apparent child of its national conferences. Effron spoke on "The Dangers of Fascist Penetration in Latin America," asserting that "the Nazis back home teach their recruits to train South Americans of German industry to pave the way for Greater Germany to build an empire there."[13] He denied, therefore, a statement by Hitler that Germany had no intention of launching an attack on the Americas and that this was also a military impossibility. "War, as such, can be waged from within these days,"[14] Effron said, citing the example of Czechoslovakia, as well as abortive putsches in Brazil and Chile. He also cited a December 4, 1938, statement by Spain's Generalissimo Francisco Franco, who, in discussing the fruits of his military victories, said: "Henceforth, no one will be indifferent to the sorrows of their brothers, however far away they may be."[15] In his speeches, Effron added in conclusion, Franco boasts of an "Imperio Espanol"—"under the patronage of Hitler and Mussolini, of course."[16] Effron explained that Berlin had a government institution known as the School for High Political Studies for Nazi Youth in Foreign Countries. The instruction and lectures, given on a "private" basis, were, on occasion, made public. Dr. Effron then quoted from a lecture delivered by a Dr. Emil Ehrlich, on January 17, 1938: "There are in the New World great territories peopled almost in their totality by Germans, whose task should be that of taking under their own government the lands tilled and worked by them, to bring under the direct protection of our marvellous and once more powerful fatherland." Effron also displayed published maps of Argentina from the 1938 yearbook of the Deutsche Volksband fuer Argentinien—a Nazi organization. These did not show Argentina divided into provinces, "but as inhabited by primitive Indians and German colonists." A second group of maps of the "region" showed parts of Brazil, Argentina, and Uruguay with no boundaries. In the caption, this area was referred to as "Antarktica Germanica."

On June 6, 1939, Dr. Tenenbaum drew up a memorandum for Dr. Wise, containing the following progress report on the Council's recent furtherance of its projected Latin American boycott:

> The Coordinated Boycott Committee had a few meetings with experts regarding the Latin American Boycott and we are at present engaged in forming an organization of bankers and industrialists who will conduct and finance an anti-Nazi Boycott throughout Latin America. While we are the initiators of this movement, we intend to so organize it, that it will appear as a spontaneous and autonomous movement to promote American and non-German substitutes for Nazi goods. According to confidential information, the State Department has already been approached and looks with favor on such a project in this country.[17]

Effron, who, through oral discussions, may have influenced Tenenbaum's decision to make the Latin American boycott "appear as a spontaneous and autonomous movement," prepared, a week later, a similar plan regarding the recently launched Pan-American Boycott Council. It was addressed to Executive Secretary Robert Marcus, averring the "unquestionable need for setting up such an agency" and suggesting "two fundamental considerations":

> The initiative must be left to the Latin American organizations and not come openly from those of the United States. Otherwise, the latter

will be open to prejudiced attacks of "Monroeism" on the part of reactionary as well as ultra leftist groups in Latin America. This does not mean that the American organizations cannot activize indirectly the Latin American ones. The Council for Pan-American Democracy is in a position to do that.

The Latin American organizations know either little or nothing of the activities of the American Boycott Committees. As a preliminary step in the setting up of a Pan-American Boycott Council, it is imperative that the Latin American organizations be fully informed of the activities of the Volunteer Christian Committee, the Joint Boycott Council and the American Boycott Against Aggressor Nations. This will require a special preparation of a mimeographed report in Spanish, as well as the transmission of news in the Associated Press, the United Press and the Havas (Latin American) wires on boycott committees in the United States.[18]

Yet, the following month, as is learned from the CBC minutes of July 21, 1939, "Dr. Tenenbaum advanced the idea that it might be unwise to press the boycott as the approach to combatting the Nazis in Latin America."[19] Instead, he recommended the dissemination of general anti-Nazi propaganda as "the most effective method" for presenting "the other side of the picture." This basic change in position had the support of a Cuban expert on Latin American affairs, A. Rojas Villalba, whom Dr. Tenenbaum, apparently, met in the interim and who, perhaps, influenced him to adopt this new course.

The shift from boycott to propaganda also necessitated a decision as to the most effective method of the latter's dissemination. Villalba suggested a radio campaign. He maintained that "propaganda" could best be conducted at "a reasonable cost through local stations," and "that any station, if given properly edited news periods, would be willing to allot free time to such programs."

The idea appealed to the CBC constituency, and, thereupon, "Dr. Tenenbaum suggested the formation of a committee of the prominent Latin Americans living here, who would be helpful in obtaining pertinent information." However, before the evolving project could be put on an efficacious basis, it was disrupted by the outbreak of the Second World War. The Private File folder, under a section entitled "Report of the Joint Boycott Council for 1939," contains the following information:

> In an international Congress of American Democracies, which convened at Montevideo, Uruguay, the offer to cooperate in a Pan-American Boycott Movement was warmly accepted principally by Argentina, as well as other delegation. The final resolution contained the following provisions: (1)a. Creation of boycott organizations in all

countries of the Western Hemisphere, as a defense measure against political and economic penetration by the totalitarian powers; b. Adoption of the slogan, "Buy national products, and if the country does not produce them, buy only those imported from democratic countries"; c. Coordination of all the national boycott organizations into a Pan-American federation. (2) Urge the application of anti-dumping laws in each American country. (3) Urge the application of laws requiring imported goods to be plainly marked with the country of origin. (4) Urge the cancellation of barter agreements between the American republics and the totalitarian states. (5) The resolution was passed by the Congress unanimously.

The report does not give the exact date or any other information regarding this seemingly important conference. One would expect, in view of the new approach Tenenbaum had advanced, that it was held sometime during the first half of 1939. If so, then Tenenbaum's assertion "that it might be unwise to press the boycott as the approach to combatting the Nazis in Latin America" must have been more dramatic and far-reaching than would otherwise be assumed. In his January 24, 1939 speech (p. 325), Dr. Tenenbaum claimed there were nearly one million German residents and citizens of German extraction in Latin America. Accordingly, Argentina alone boasted a German "colony" of almost 500,000. Brazil, from which the United States could be reached via the Atlantic, contained hundreds of thousands of residents of Japanese, Italian, as well as of German descent. Hence, Germany had more than enough native sons in Latin America from which to cull its Henleins and Quislings to "soften up" some key countries as a prelude to their conversion into Nazi satrapies. Tenenbaum was in receipt of such information. Furthermore, the friendly trade relations that the Nazis had fostered in this region plus their conduct of a vigorous anti-U.S. propaganda campaign made Germany correspondingly more popular with many Latin Americans. It might also be added that, living as the Latins did, in countries with totalitarian regimes, Nazism, as such, was not at all alien to their political experience.

Third Phase

i.

Latin American activities were not included in the general boycott program that the JBC reestablished after again taking "the field" in late 1939. The Council's "organizational insecurity," which set in as a result of having to function on an extension basis and a reduced office staff, precluded their immediate revival. But there was also another reason.

Tenenbaum was convinced that the outbreak of war in Europe had virtually united all opinion in the United States on the necessity of combating Nazi propaganda in Latin America as part of any program for the assurance of the safety of that region. He based himself on the fear that, in countries where the Nazis had already achieved commercial and political advantages, they were but a step from their next objective, the acquisition of military bases.[19] Accordingly, President Roosevelt met this "threat" by the inauguration of a rearmament program and the pursuit of improved relations with the Latin American countries. The governing principle of this objective was the establishment of hemispheric solidarity in fact as well as in theory. Increased trade and, subsequently, the encouragement of cultural exchanges, therefore, became the cornerstones of his administration's policy.

The task of carrying out this policy was entrusted to Nelson A. Rockefeller, who was appointed the Coordinator of Commercial and Cultural Relations Between the American Republics. His mission was both the attainment of a rapprochement with Latin America and a weakening of Nazi influence there.

In the trade war that ensued, the United States, because of its vastly greater purchasing power, began winning soon and easily enough. The European war was a more decisive factor, however, since it inadvertently led to the disruption of normal shipping schedules. This was further compounded by the British blockade with its extensive suppression of regular shipping services between German and South American seaports. Hence, despite her promises, Germany proved unable to make good on her deliveries and commitments. It devolved, therefore, upon the United States to replace not only the normally-bound German goods to South America, but also those of the Allies. Consequently, the U.S. share in the foreign trade of South America saw a tremendous increase.

This situation was short-lived, however, as with the fall of Holland and France in 1940, the acquisition of military bases by the Nazis in parts of Latin America was no longer as farfetched or academic a thing as before. The Boycott Council—particularly through Tenenbaum—had given prominence to such a possibility, but now there was genuine foreboding in the United States lest Hitler compel his prostrate foes to cede him their Caribbean possessions or seize them by attack or subversion. This threat was barely six weeks old when it was further compounded by the military clique which gained control of the Japanese cabinet.

The threatened security of the United States immediately raised the question of a sound hemispheric defense. Roosevelt acted boldly and swiftly. He warned, after a brilliant diplomatic accord secured by his

Secretary of State at a Pan-American conference held in Havana, late in July of 1940, that any transfer to Hitler of Europe's colonies in the New World would be resisted. In August, the American President met with the Canadian Prime Minister, William Lyon Mackenzie King, and it was agreed to set up a Permanent Joint Board on Defense to lay the groundwork for the security of North America. That very month, Roosevelt also came out for "a selective service training bill," which became the first peacetime conscription act in U.S. history when a wrangling Congress passed it in mid-September. Thus, as the Battle of Britain was nearing its bloody climax, America was still in the incipient stages of preparing for a continental defense.

ii.

Only with the increased threat to America's security did the Council's resumption of Latin American activities assume intensified forms.[20] The Council's cue in this instance appears to have been England's obvious rejection of Hitler's "peace" offer made from the Reichstag on July 19, 1940. For the week after, JBC held a preliminary meeting which had been scheduled in order to discuss the expansion of its Latin American program. The meeting was attended by representatives of the AFL and the White Committee (see p. 295), who assured the Council "of full moral support in any work against Nazi influence in Latin America."[21] They took the first step to honor this pledge by assisting in the formation of a Temporary Committee for Pan-American Cooperation. This newest of committees was created in August and was "expected to act as the coordinating agency for all organizations and individuals interested in drawing Latin America and the United States closer together by extirpating the Nazi influences at present poisoning Pan-American relations."[22] Like a number of other committees, the Temporary Committee was under the auspices and guidance of the Joint Boycott Council. The strategem that would presently be employed vis-à-vis Latin America was stated by Dr. Tenenbaum as follows:

> Our objective must be an appeal from the people of the United States to the peoples of the Latin American countries, rather than an attempt through official means. We believe that propaganda and information exchange through private sources will carry greater weight than the always suspected and misunderstood intervention of the most powerful government influences. We shall attempt to convince the people of Latin America rather than repeat the mistake of concentrating on the ruling groups of each country. This is precisely what the Nazis did. They presented their arguments to the large majority of the population.[23]

As its first project, the Temporary Committee took up Villalba's radio broadcasting scheme. Villalba, who had again agreed to offer his services in behalf of Latin America, presented his plan and some recommendations and arguments to support it at a meeting held on August 13, 1940. Basically, it was the same plan as the one presented the year before. However, the minutes of this meeting and a later memorandum offer a more detailed delineation based on the latest world developments. This may be summarized as follows:

For the last several years, the Latin American public had been subjected to a barrage of Nazi propaganda through the radio, press, and local resident agents. However, the most important vehicle for this propaganda had been the powerful short-wave radio stations.

After their acquisition of practically all of Western Europe, the Nazis "redoubled" their short-wave propaganda efforts "with the evident purpose of interfering with the commercial and political rapprochement between the various countries of this hemisphere."[24] The conduct of this kind of agitation was facilitated by the advantages of having a host of both conquered and friendly countries from which to broadcast. Germany also enjoyed an advantage in short-wave-station power over U.S. stations. But Germany's greatest advantage lay in its overwhelming numerical superiority in short-wave radio stations; seventy-nine to America's six or seven. To add to this extreme disparity, the FCC was reaching a limited audience.

To successfully combat this "highly developed Nazi radio propaganda," Villalba recommended the following measures:

> Use should be made of local broadcasting stations in the various Latin American countries which operate on long-wave lengths. Station time should be contracted for at prevailing rates, for two ten-minute periods daily. The local station is to supply the services of a competent announcer.
>
> News should be gathered in New York, edited, and translated into Spanish and Portuguese (for Brazil).
>
> News should be transmitted to the local Latin American stations in the form of a complete script for a ten-minute broadcasting period, prepared for reading on the air.[25]

In elucidating his approach, Villalba claimed that "the use of local broadcasting facilities on long-wave length" would enable the United States to gain an advantage over Germany by permitting her "to reach the Latin American countries without interference."[26] He then added:

> This method of operation is more efficient and has a greater power of penetration than any short-wave broadcast because local radio

stations have an established audience. Furthermore, the reception of the news or comments of the news emanating from a local station with the voice of a local commentator of established reputation, naturally, has a greater power of penetration and adds a convincing tone and a ring of sincerity to the message.[27]

Villalba estimated that a year's cost of such an operation, based on 730 broadcasts totaling 29,000 news programs over 40 stations, would run slightly more than $250,000. He not only considered this a reasonable sum, but also added that, once such broadcasts had acquired an audience of their own, local radio stations would be amenable to selling these programs for local sponsorship and in this way defray the cost of gathering, editing, and transmitting the news.

iii.

It was in the overall interest of U.S. security to encourage citizens groups seeking to help their country to improve relations with Latin America. The September 18, 1940, JBC minutes tell that Dr. Tenenbaum, who was aware of this, contacted the State Department, "informing them of our plans." In its reply, add the minutes, the Department of State "welcomed" the Council's efforts as a civilian organization to promote a "rapprochement" with Latin America. In furtherance of this interest, it referred JBC to another organization "working along similar lines"; namely, Raymond Rich Associates, Public Relations Counsel for the Twentieth Century Fund. JBC minutes describe it as a private agency in unofficial collaboration with the State Department, and "working since June to coordinate the work of private organizations for a better understanding between Latin America and the United States."[28]

A communication written by a Rich representative on August 9 (1940) reveals that Dr. Tenenbaum had informed this agency of the Council's "plans for launching here a movement with the aim of promoting a cultural and economic rapprochement with the various Latin American Republics."[29] The Rich agency expressed its interest in this project, explaining, though, that it was in the midst of conducting "preliminary negotiations" with Mr. Rockefeller (p. 330); and that as soon as these were completed, "an organization embracing the Raymond Rich Associates and all other interested parties, including the Joint Boycott Council, will be placed on an operating basis and the entire program will be put into effect."[30]

A little over a fortnight later, by official invitation, a Raymond Rich representative attended a meeting of the Temporary Committee. Basically, he described the work and aims of his organization, the essential nature of which has already been depicted. He added, however, that

Raymond Rich Associates "contemplated organizing a private group, with large financial resources and prestige, interested in promoting a cultural rapprochement with Latin America, with the cooperation of existing wire services or through other channels."[31]

Also attending was VCC's Christopher Emmet, who viewed this plan as too mild, saying that the aims of the Temporary Committee were of a "specific character"; namely, to meet the "present emergency." Emmet maintained that "ordinary news services would not suffice against the scientifically conceived Nazi propaganda in South America." Such news, Emmet felt, had to be edited "with a specific purpose in mind; that is, aimed at counteracting Nazi propaganda."[32]

Dr. Tenenbaum felt that the question of "what the organization would do" needed further discussion. He pointed to the need for the creation of a "responsible organization." And to prevent the group from degenerating into a "debating society," Tenenbaum suggested the election of a Temporary Executive Committee. He was confident, he told the group, that "means" would be found to start "practical work." In turn, the group expressed its confidence in him by electing him its executive chairman.

But despite his apparent prodding, not until January 18, 1941, was Tenenbaum able to announce officially that the Temporary Committee was being replaced by a Committee for Inter-American Cooperation (CIAC). Dr. Wise was informed about the advent of the new Committee a month before. It included notification about its first activity:

> The Committee for Inter-American Cooperation is a consultative body consisting of existing public agencies and committees for the betterment of Inter-American relations including boycotting and weeding out Nazi goods and influences. This Committee has, after long discussion, decided to explore the possibilities of dramatizing its program by organizing a so-called Week for Inter-American Cooperation. This is not a JBC venture, but a common undertaking of all the organizations interested in this field, among which, JBC happens to be the only Jewish organization.[33]

The CIAC included over one hundred "outstanding" educators, clergymen, writers, and civic leaders. In mid-November, several weeks before he wrote the foregoing communication, Dr. Tenenbaum also prepared a detailed program for sponsoring an Inter-American Cooperation Week. It had probably undergone some revision before being announced that Inter-American Cooperation Week—after a delay—would open on March 23. The character and work of the Committee for Inter-American Cooperation was outlined as follows:

The Committee for Inter-American Cooperation is a non-profit sharing, educational, philanthrophic organization.

Because the peril of war to this Western Hemisphere had made us increasingly aware of the necessity of carrying out the "Good Neighbor" policy as outlined by President Roosevelt, and

Because we know that if we are to have a Good Neighbor we must be a Good Neighbor and foster mutual understanding and respect as a foundation not only for friendship, but as an avenue to security for this country.

We wish to supplement the efforts of the government and other groups now active in meeting the menace of powerfully entrenched Nazis in Latin American countries, as well as to contribute a defense program of our own activities.

The purpose: to create and foster a popular Pan-American movement by building up a strong membership group where our common problems may be discussed and worked out, and an inter-change of cultural activities created which will be mutually helpful.

Fiesta Americana: Usually spoken in connection with religious festivals in celebration of some holy cause, it is ideally descriptive of the way we feel in launching the active Women's Division of the Committee for Inter-American Cooperation.[34]

The program of the Inter-American Cooperation Week and its aims were described as:

1. Fostering of mutual understanding and friendship between the peoples of this hemisphere.

   A. The Committee for Inter-American Cooperation will be developed on a national scale with branches in every state and larger cities of the country.
   B. Similar Committees will be organized in every Latin American country. Nuclei of such Committees exist already in Chile, Argentina, Cuba and Mexico.
   C. The Central Committee here consists of representatives of this country and outstanding personalities, representatives of the Latin American countries.
   D. Through a network of such Committees and branches, the peoples of this hemisphere will be linked together in an attempt to understand each other's problems, needs and aspirations.

2. A weekly or bi-weekly bulletin in two languages (English and Spanish) will be published by the Committee for an interchange of cultural, economic and social information.
3. A research department for inter-American problems with a

publication of special studies will be one of the major departments of the Central Committee.

4. Meetings, public discussions, round table conferences will be another feature of the work of the Committee.

5. Lending encouragement and guidance to clubs, study groups and seminars in high schools and colleges. The Committee maintains, at present, close contact with many such groups.

6. Exhibits and lectures on Latin American art, literature, music, folk songs, dances, etc., in the United States, and U.S. art, music, etc., in Latin America.

7. Publication of popular books and pamphlets on the history of Latin American countries, their geographic, economic and cultural characteristics, etc.

8. A permanent feature of economic help to Latin American countries will be a scientifically-conducted BUY LATIN AMERICAN CAMPAIGN with the close cooperation and under the supervision of the subcommittee of businessmen and experts here and in Latin America, as well as the Chamber of Commerce of those countries.

- A. A special division of economic information equipped with an up-to-date and detailed prospectus of Latin American products available for export will be maintained.
- B. Through encouraging periodic exhibits by the Chambers of Commerce, cooperation in arranging window displays and shows, radio talks and printed circulars, the public will be made conscious of the advantages of buying Latin American products.
- C. The "Buy Latin American" campaign will be supplemented by "Visit Latin America" campaigns with travelogues and illustrated magazines, especially designed for this purpose.

9. A large scale membership campaign throughout this country and in Latin America for the Latin American branches, will create the basis for a popular movement which will remain a strong force in support of a permanent good neighbor policy, irrespective of political fluctuations.

10. Periodic visits of delegates and members of this Committee in Latin America and vice versa, to cement the bonds of mutual understanding and friendship will help to solve some of the difficult problems of such cooperation.[35]

"Buy Latin American" leaflets were also prepared as a part of the Inter-American Cooperation Week campaign. They explained that, with normal markets cut off by the war, Latin America must export more to the United States. In no other way, was it said, could Latin America pay for the goods she needed or maintain a decent standard of living. This was followed by a warning and exhortation that "Nazi agents seize every opportunity offered by economic difficulties to create unrest and weaken independence. Thus, all that is possible must be done to avoid internal collapse there. To this end, the United States *must* buy more Latin American goods and strategic raw materials."[36]

Finances were derived from "the membership, contributions, and various types of entertainment."[37] In accordance with a suggestion by Dr. Tenenbaum, the Week's activities was arranged by a "special committee designated for this purpose." This included invitations to outstanding groups and individuals "to lend their names to the project."[38] Nelson Rockefeller was among the immediately sought sponsors. He expressed interest in this "undertaking," but explained that "this office is not in a position to assign any of its members to assist in promoting your proposed Inter-American Cooperation Week."[39]

As Tenenbaum's former right-hand man, Robert Marcus (p. 270) also played an important role in the planning of this project. He had agreed to act as committee secretary, and a number of features, or variants thereof, that ultimately made their way into the IACW program had been proposed by him. These included a "Buy South America Campaign," a wide distribution of travelogues, art exhibits on Central and South America, and the publication of a journal containing articles on all phases of the Latin American "question."

Also, as one of the means of gaining the public's attention, Tenenbaum instructed Marcus to send out letters to the various department stores "setting forth the purpose and time of the Inter-American Cooperation Week, and asking them to have a display of Latin American merchandise during this Week; mention in their advertisements what they have for sale in Latin American goods; utilize their radio programs to proclaim Latin American sales during this Week."[40]

An April 4 form letter, circulated, apparently, by Dr. Tenenbaum, tells that the IACW proved a "big success." Perhaps so; but neither Dr. Tenenbaum nor, undoubtedly, his co-workers entertained the illusory belief that the alleged success of their Latin American program was close at hand. Cognizance of this was taken in an address entitled "Pan-American Defense," which Dr. Tenenbaum delivered on March 23, the opening date of the Inter-American Cooperation Week. In this address, of which only an excerpted version is preserved in the JBC archives, the boycott chieftain declared:

> The problems facing Inter-American cooperation are such that it will take at least a generation of mutual education and genuine rapprochement to create a real basis for mutual understanding and cooperation.... No government is strong enough to fill the gap of such diversity as exists between the two continents. The only feasible bridge over this gap is from the people to the people.[41]

To build this Pan-American bridge, Dr. Tenenbaum urged the industrialization and intensification of noncompetitive production. He recommended the building of highways, railroads, canals, and the interchange of produce; in short, to cultivate the regional economy in Latin America. Warning that "a Hilter controlling Europe will control the world," Dr. Tenenbaum stressed the importance of "economic bases" over "mere defense bases" as a hemispheric safeguard; for he was convinced that "with an enslaved Europe and impoverished hemisphere, a free American economy would break down in competition with Hitler slave-labor wages. This, he felt, would in all likelihood happen even in the event "that U.S. forces could repulse a military invasion of this hemisphere."[42]

Additional information pertaining to the Council's Latin American activities is contained in the following source found in its Confidential Report covering the months of June–September 1941:

> One channel through which German goods came openly was Latin America. Especially since the war, the Pan-American boycott was linked intimately with the U.S. boycott. For a time, these countries were the center of shipments and transshipments between the Axis and the United States. Later, when the blockade in the Atlantic became stricter (the blockade in the Pacific was not enforced till about two months ago), German firms in Latin America set up dummy commission houses where U.S. merchandise was bought up for resale through German affiliates and agents, in order to maintain the position of the Nazi traders in the Latin American countries. JBC has for the last two years done all in its power to stop the tremendous leak in the blockade of Nazism, and has used its valuable connections in Latin America to counteract these schemes. It continued to urge and warn American firms not to do business with German firms and their dummy corporations. Through the Committee for Inter-American Cooperation, a separate, independent organization, the Council gained valuable support and connections with official and private representatives of Latin American countries, which greatly helped the boycott activities against Nazism here and in Latin America.[43]

iv.

The IACW proved the Committee's first and last major activity. Its functions just seem to have died out after that. A June 12, 1941, memorandum, which Dr. Tenenbaum sent Dr. Schieffelin, states that the basic problem was a lack of financial support and lack of sufficient interest on the part of the IAC committee to raise the necessary funds. The memorandum referred the Christian Committee leader to an April

15 meeting of the IAC Committee, in which Tenenbaum had declared that he "thought it urgent to decide whether or not the Committee should continue on the basis of a popular movement to supplement government action or whether prompt dissolution of the Committee was advisable."[44] Tenenbaum explained that he had put this question "squarely before the participants," and their reply was "a unanimous decision to continue." He had emphasized, moreover, that he did not want the Committee to be "a one-man organization," asking, therefore, for its "full cooperation." But Tenenbaum was very bitter about the results, as is indicated by the following passage from the aforesaid memorandum:

> I personally have no ambition or special axe to grind. I have taken over the work at a time when the whole thing seemed to have bogged down in interminable discussions and luncheon meetings and I have since spent more time, energy and effort than I can afford, to bring what was a vague idea into the concrete form of an organization with a purpose. This thing too costs money ($2,000 this week alone) and not one in the Executive Committee has contributed one broken cent nor has anybody ever worried how the rent is paid at present.[45]

The next available document concerning the IAC Committee definitely attests to the utter demise of this organization. It is an August 22, 1941, communication to Dr. Tenenbaum by Mrs. Mabel Hazlett Keep, organizational director of the Women's Division of the Committee for Inter-American Cooperation (see p. 334). Her opening remark that she must have an "assurance of some sum" attests to the Committee's wanting financial situation. After stating that the Fiesta did not prove "profitable," Mrs. Keep goes on to say:

> I have gone very carefully through the minutes of all meetings that are on file here in the office, and I find that this group is still a temporary committee for Inter-American Cooperation. The minutes are filled with good suggestions and good thoughts but beyond that and our last effort to raise money, there is nothing agreed upon in the way of forming a permanent organization. There is no constitution setting forth legally our names, our object, our officers and their duties, finances—how derived, etc., or any by-laws and there's really no authority vested in anyone with the exception of myself.[46]

On September 25, Mrs. Keep tendered her resignation, thereby officially terminating the Boycott Council's deep involvement in Latin American affairs.

It was now about three weeks before the Joint Boycott Council would be liquidated. For in the September 11, 1941, report, mentioned at the outset of this section (p. 295), Dr. Tenenbaum stated that in April of that year, he had asked to be "relieved" from his duties as JBC chairman "unless more appropriate means were provided for the boycott." Thereto, the report adds: "It was decided at that time by the Jewish Labor Committee that, rather than close up its offices in the midst of the war, the Joint Boycott Council should continue with its limited means to help the British Blockade and represent the sentiment of the Jewish people during the war."[47]

Dr. Tenenbaum thought this a "sound position." However, he repeated his oft-stated viewpoint that the Council's "activities, money and personnel now required much more coverage than the appropriation offered." And so, lacking both "proper finances and the necessary conviction and cooperation of the parent organizations," Dr. Tenenbaum felt it would be best to relinquish his office as chairman of the Joint Boycott Council.

Subject to Congress approval, concludes the aforesaid report, preparations were to be made to close the office of the Joint Boycott Council by October 15, 1941. It was two years to the day from the time when the JBC office had first been scheduled for liquidation.[48,49]

Summary and Conclusions

i.

Basically, the resistance movement to Nazism was spontaneous in its origin, both in Europe and the United States. As long as it retained this character, organizations opposed to an anti-Nazi boycott, like the AJC-BB, saw no particular reason for waging an open campaign against the movement. In fact, they did not oppose the boycott per se. On the contrary, in private communications and public statements, they sanctioned the so-called silent boycott, namely, a boycott conducted by private citizens on their own initiative without the accompaniment of public agitation which manifested itself in ostentatious parades and mass meetings. Subsequently, however (1937), the B'nai B'rith reversed its position and joined the boycott movement.

JWV was the first among America's defense organizations to establish an "organized" boycott. The Jewish Veterans' example was soon followed by the American League for the Defense of Jewish Rights, a new organization founded by the Yiddish journalist Abraham Coralnik as a response to the relentless Nazi threat. The ALDJR was barely six months old, however, when the renowned attorney Sanuel Untermyer, who was drawn into the organization by his outspoken pro-boycott sentiment, and who supplanted Coralnik in its leadership, altered its name to the Non-Sectarian Anti-Nazi League to Champion Human Rights. He also altered the entire character of the organization, eliminating thereby its Jewish reference and even allusion.

On August 20, 1933, the American Jewish Congress also declared a boycott against the Nazi regime. Up to that time, the Congress had taken an intermediate position, conducting giant demonstration marches and mass rallies at which Hitler Germany was bitterly denounced for its persecution of the Jews. The Congress hoped that such tactics would compel Hitler to abolish or at least reduce his intense antisemitic program. Unlike the AJC-BB, the Jewish Congress had not opposed an organized boycott on principle. But it embraced this method only as a last resort.

At the Eighteenth Zionist Congress, convened in Prague on August 21, 1933, Vladimir Jabotinsky proposed the adoption of the boycott on a worldwide scale. For a variety of reasons, such as the belief that it was not the main task of the World Zionist Congress to deal with questions relating to Diaspora defense and a strong disinclination on the part of Labor Zionists to vote for a Revisionist proposal, Jabotinsky's boycott resolution was defeated. The Transfer Agreement, in which an accord was reached with the Hitler government to permit Jewish emigration to Palestine, was also a key factor in determining this vote; for a boycott resolution by a world Zionist body, most delegates felt, could provoke Germany and cause it to ban further Jewish emigration. Notwithstanding this, the Transfer Agreement greatly angered boycott leaders, remaining a point of contention up to the outbreak of World War II.

Soon after the close of the Eighteenth Zionist Congress, the Second World Jewish Conference got under way in Geneva. And in line with Dr. Wise's conviction "that a world Jewish boycott could only be declared by a world assembly of Jews" (*Challenging Years*, p. 256), the World Jewish Conference declared a global boycott against Nazi Germany. A boycott resolution was readopted when a World Jewish Congress was convened in 1936.

Coralnik and Untermyer also took steps to give the boycott an international character. The idea was suggested by Poland's United Boycott Committee, proposing that an all-Jewish Conference be convened. After some delay, a World Jewish Economic Conference was held in Amsterdam in July of 1933. The Conference's main problem was finding substitute products for boycotting businessmen. It also sought to coordinate the growing boycott movement on a worldwide scale. To this end, a World Jewish Economic Federation was created with Samuel Untermyer as president. In his acceptance speech, Untermyer urged the League of Nations to investigate and expose Germany's persecution of the Jews and use this as a basis for invoking its rescue clause. But his demands, and similar ones by the Jewish Congress, proved vain gestures. Besides that, in November of the following year, Untermyer, in keeping with his view that the boycott was a nonsectarian movement, changed the name of the World Jewish Economic Federation to the World Non-Sectarian Anti-Nazi Council to Champion Human Rights.

ii.

Attempts to form a united American boycott front, made almost from the very inception of the movement, fell short of fruition. One reason was Untermyer's insistence that the Congress' Boycott Committee come under the League's authority, since the latter had been first in the "field." But the main stumbling-block proved to be the issue of "sectarianism" vs. "nonsectarianism." Yet, all boycott leaders (Wise, Tenenbaum, Vladeck, and Untermyer) were troubled by the idea of participating in a "Jewish" boycott movement, trying to give it a "nonsectarian" look. They did this by citing statistical figures and public statements by top and lesser Nazis who claimed that the boycott was hurting the German economy. By thus referring to boycott "effectiveness," the boycott leaders asserted that it could not possibly have been achieved by Jews alone; that the boycott obviously had the support of the non-Jewish world.

Such support manifested itself at various stages in the history of the American boycott movement. Thus, in the early phase, the AFL joined the boycott movement and extended its cooperation to both the latter, however, undoubtedly because the JLC, whose many unions belonged to the AFL, had teamed up with the Congress' Boycott Committee to form a Joint Boycott Council (1936). A later phase (1938-39) saw the creation of some Chrisitan organizations dedicated to the boycott of Nazi Germany and its Axis partners. They, too, worked almost exclusively with the JBC.

Although the American Jewish Community failed to form a united boycott front, it did succeed in bringing mass pressure against boycott offenders—especially other Jews. In a number of cases the results were quite impressive. Thus, department store colossi like Macy's, Gimbel's, Sears & Roebuck, and Woolworth sooner or later succumbed to the sales and consumer resistance to German goods.

The ominous clouds of war which appeared in Europe in 1938-39 increased boycott sentiment in the United States. But by then, the growing plight of Germany's Jewish refugees was overshadowing the boycott question. Plans to ransom them were viewed by most boycott leaders—especially Dr. Joseph Tenenbaum—as a means to break the back of the movement without bringing real relief to the refugees.

In 1938, the ANL shifted from a policy that concentrated on the boycott of Nazi goods to one of investigating and exposing Nazi activities. The outbreak of the Second World War had a similar effect on JBC, which, in addition to boycott activities, began assuming functions related to the general war effort. This was the predominant situation up to the eve of America's entry into the global conflict, when the Joint Boycott Council was dissolved.

iii.

How effective a movement was the boycott is one of the more common questions asked by people, and an occasional reference to this subject has been made in this work. The trained economist may, upon a detailed investigation of the problem, prove to be in a position to gauge the answer to this question to a reasonable extent. On the other hand, he may find that there are too many imponderables in his path. But if the world's past experience with boycotts is to act as a guide, then it must be said that, in the long run, media of this kind are ineffective; that is to say, they are incapable of bringing about the economic collapse of the country against which they are directed. An impressive array of examples bear out this assertion: the American colonial merchants' boycott of England, Napoleon's continental blockade of England; more recently, India's boycott of England, China's boycott of Japan, and thus far, the Rhodesian boycott and the Arab boycott of Israel.

There can be no denying, however, that the boycott hurt Germany, mention of which has also been made in this work. However, to those Jews and non-Jews who speak slightingly of the efficacy of the "Jewish boycott," it must be said that not they but the Nazis serve as barometers of such judgments. And as such, official Nazi documents abound in statements and reports showing the effects of the boycott in almost every branch of German industry, especially exports.

Moreover, in their uniquely twisted manner, the Nazis magnified the "Jewish boycott" by claiming that Jews were merely the avant-garde of a general conspiracy by the democratic world; that if the boycott were nothing but a Jewish affair, it would scarcely have had an injurious effect and would hardly have received any attention. Thus, what really worried the Nazis was the suspicion that the boycott movement was being backed by governments interested in capturing for themselves Germany's markets. Such backing, feared the Nazi government, could really deal Germany's economy a crippling blow. Furthermore, according to this interpretation, Germany was powerless to retaliate, as none of the governments had actually declared a boycott against her. The resultant apprehensiveness about the boycott probably explains, therefore, why Hitler, on some occasions, put a temporary halt to the public manifestations of his virulent antisemitic campaign. At least on one such occasion, his club-footed mouthpiece, Dr. Goebbels, admitted this. Speaking at a February 28, 1935, meeting devoted to a discussion of the Reich's economic problems, Goebbels, who made sure to revile Jews as "exploiters" and "vampires" found it necessary to explain: "It may be asked of you why the Administration undertakes nothing more against the Jews. It cannot for foreign political reasons, since further boycotts, foreign exchange difficulties and other troubles are thereby threatened."[1]

The situation had sufficiently deteriorated to warrant some weeks later an appeal by Dr. Julius Lippert, State Commissar for Berlin, to "America's sober business sense" to put a stop to the "Jewish boycott" in the United States against German goods. Lippert also stated that Germany's Jewish economic interests were not harmed and that, in business, Jews possessed equal rights. Addressing a meeting of the American Chamber of Commerce in Berlin, he pointed out that American trade, as well as German, had suffered as a result of the boycott. Lippert went on by citing dwindling trade figures for the respective countries. The speech was unique, however, in that it did not contain the usual derogatory expressions and vile practices that Nazis imputed to Jews. So mild, in fact, was Lippert's speech that many of his listeners wondered whether it was intended to herald a reversal in Hitler's anti-Jewish policy.

But not the boycott leadership in the United States, as cabled protests regarding Lippert's speech were sent by the AFL, the ANL, and the A.J.C. Dr. Wise dramatized his organization's protest at a reception sponsored by its Women's Division in honor of Dr. Albert Einstein, the great German-born Jewish physicist who emigrated to the United States not long after Hitler came to power. He rebutted Lippert's remarks by saying:

> Nothing could be falser than to allege that there is a "Jewish boycott" in the United States against Nazi goods and services and this Dr. Lippert knows right well. If three percent of the population of the United States, which is the percentage of the Jewish population, were alone in boycotting German goods and services, Nazi Germany would not find it worthwhile appealing for the cessation of the so-called "Jewish boycott."
>
> Dr. Lippert's appeal purports to address itself to the "Americans" sober business sense. What could be more brazenly and cynically insulting than to assume in the presence of a mighty moral problem which involves every ideal of civilization and democracy, that America had no interest at stake other than the "business interest." This is the gravest insult of all—to assume that in the last analysis every moral consideration is ignored by America in the interest of business and commercial gain.[2]

On a number of occasions, Hitler himself freely conceded that the boycott was greatly harming Germany's economic interests. He uttered his most dramatic grievance against this movement in an address delivered to the Reichstag on April 28, 1939. Replying to Roosevelt's avowed readiness to participate in discussions to seek the most practical means of improving international trade relations for all nations, the Nazi despot declared:

> It is likewise an unbearable burden for world economic relations that it should be possible in some countries for some ideological reason or other to let loose a wild boycott of agitation against other countries and their goods and so practically to eliminate them from the market.
> It is my belief, Mr. Roosevelt, that it would be a great service if you, with your great influence, would remove these barriers genuinely to free world trade beginning with the United States. For it is my conviction that if the leaders of nations are not even capable of regulating production in their own countries or of removing boycotts pursued for ideological reasons which can damage trade relations between countries to so great an extent, there is much less prospect of achieving by means of international agreements any really fruitful step toward improvement of economic relations.[3]

Hitler's reference to "boycotts pursued for ideological reasons" depicts, as this work has illustrated, the real character of the movement that sought to wring concessions out of the monstrous tyrant, and if that were not possible, to destroy him; but, in any event, to resist him, come what may. Further elucidation of this point is necessary if we are to better appreciate the purpose behind the boycott movement.

iv.

In February of 1935, the *New York World-Telegram* published a series of interviews held with some of the leading Jewish spokesmen, pro and contra boycott. One of these was Stephen Wise, who, at a time when Germany's unfavorable trade figures for 1934 were just becoming known, expounded his views on the limited strength of the boycott, but why it had to be wielded, nevertheless.

> I have never for a moment held that the boycott is the solution of the problem of Hitlerism. Too many complicated and profound issues are involved in the Hitler revolt against civilization to permit any sane man to imagine that a simple device such as an economic boycott can solve that vast complex of problems. . . . I must say that my faith in the common people, if it could be deepened, has been deepened by the rightness of the mass reaction to Hitlerism primarily among the Jews, secondarily among all people. . . . We would not if we could, and we could not if we would, wield any weapon against Germany, but we

cannot with self-respect continue to have dealings with that country which has decided we are outside the pale of decency ...

As a pacifist, I was hesitant about the boycott because it is an economic weapon, although from the beginning I believed and I still believe that its moral value is larger than its economic value. It was only after I heard from fellow Jews in other lands, in July and August, 1933, how deadly was the hurt inflicted upon Jews by Nazi Germany and that all the Jewish masses could do to express their disapproval was to boycott German goods and services that I felt it was our duty to join in the boycott.[4]

Vladeck spoke of the boycott "problem" in relation to antisemitism, economics, labor and democracy, saying: "So long as the world is economically sick, the Jews will be under attack. So will liberalism and the American tradition of liberty. The basis of the present anti-Jewish propaganda and for the wide acceptance it has received is the depression."[5]

The Jewish labor leader also explained that he did not see the boycott as a Jewish question at all, but as a defensive measure forced upon labor and freedom, adding:

Persecution of the Jews is the inevitable step toward persecution of labor and suppression of democracy.... Labor knows that the first blast against the Jews is only the forerunner of a dark storm against itself, and that permitting a government to foster anti-Semitism is to strengthen a power that will crush labor. This is why in all countries today intelligent Jews march with labor, and why labor is the staunchest defender of Jewish and human rights.[6]

Vladeck's next point gives us an insight into his conception of the boycott prior to his teaming up with the Congress Boycott Committee.

The American Federation of Labor, for example, is one of the most powerful elements in the American boycott against German goods. The non-Sectarian Anti-Nazi League to Champion Human Rights, in the front rank of the boycott movement, sedulously avoids identification as a Jewish movement.... The boycott sentiment in my heart was not Jewish, I assure you. All my life, I have been a labor man. So I joined this movement of labor.[7]

Vladeck was convinced that so long as the world continued in the grip of its economic "malady," antisemitism would persevere as a convenient tool of hate in the hands of Nazism. He saw no possibility of curing that ailment, regardless of the course of action adopted by Jews. He did not despair entirely, however, believing that by remaining loyal to the principles of labor and democracy, the cause of Jewish rights could be preserved.

Untermyer was also interviewed, setting forth his idea against the contra boycott position of Judge Joseph M. Proskauer, the first to participate in this series:

> The rescue of Christianity and the rehabilitation of organized labor and not the fate of the German Jews is the dominating issue, though the latter is an important one. It has always been the fate of American Jewry to have this handful of holier than thou highbrows separate themselves from the great majority of their brethren on every important question.
>
> What I want now to emphasize is that the importance of this small minority must not be exaggerated, that it does not even represent Jewish sentiment and that our organizations here and abroad are distinctly non-sectarian, representing men and women of all classes, creeds and positions in life, and that the public must not be mislead by a few discordant Jewish voices which have no constructive program to offer against this crime of the century.[8]

One of Dr. Tenenbaum's ideological formulations of the boycott was also made that year in a pamphlet entitled *Two Years Anti-Nazi Boycott:*

> Even if the Boycott should ultimately prove a failure, we have, nevertheless, a moral duty to strain every ounce of our energy, and if we are to fail, then at least let us leave to posterity the unimpeachable proof that we have made the most of our opportunities, fought to the last man and though downed with defeat, we have shown neither indifference nor a lack of zeal.[9]

In the initial stages, Dr. Tenenbaum, like other leaders, made the prosecution of the boycott contingent upon Hitler's persecution of German Jewry. But as seen from the following statement, this was no longer his approach after the Kristallnacht (see p. 249).

> This is not and has never been a Jewish fight only, but a fight of democracy, of which we are a part. We as Jews must do all in our power to rescue our German brethren from the Hell of Nazi Germany. But our fight and our responsibility will not lessen one iota even when there will not be one Jew left in Germany. The boycott started with Hitler and will end with Hitler. It is a fight to the finish between democracy and Nazi gangsterism.[10]

It need hardly be emphasized or elaborated that Dr. Tenenbaum (and the boycott leadership) had undertaken a herculean task. An appreciation of his role was written on September 17, 1941, by Moses Heyman (p. 311) in response to Tenenbaum's expressed wish to relinquish the JBC chairmanship:

> For the most part, you were the entire Boycott Committee.... And if you should insist upon this [i.e., resigning], I could only say that you are only human, because very few people know the handicaps under which you conducted this movement and the lack of support that you received from the parent organizations, particularly the American Jewish Congress.[11]

But it was Dr. Tenenbaum who wrote the postscript to the boycott movement:

> We Jews can be proud of having given the initiative to such a great, common human struggle for freedom and democracy. And someday when the history of the present, difficult and bloody times will be written, this movement and this initiative will be considered one of the greatest accomplishments of our generation in its struggle for human rights and the freedom of nations.[12]

Notes

Books and their page numbers, as well as other references in the Notes, are based on the editions mentioned in the Bibliography.

CHAPTER 1

1. The information in this opening paragraph is based on Dr. Tenenbaum's "Twenty-Five Years American Jewish Life," which is located among the private and unpublished notes contained in the Dr. Joseph Tenenbaum Archives, YIVO, New York.
2. *New York Times* (NYT), January 31, 1933.
3. Ibid., February 11, 1933.
4. Ibid., February 3, 1933.
5. Central Verein deutscher Staatsbuerger Juedischen Glaubens (Central Union of German Citizens of the Jewish Faith), which was founded on March 26, 1893. The Verein's purpose was to unite all German Jews, irrespective of their religious leanings or political beliefs, into an organization that would defend their civic rights and foster among them German ideas. In 1935, its name was changed to Juedischen Central Verein (Jewish Central Union). The organization was dissolved by the Nazis in 1938, following the horrors of the Kristallmacht (p. 255) in November of that year.
6. *Jewish Daily Bulletin* (JDB), January 30, 1933.
7. NYT, March 5, 1933.
8. Ibid., March 6, 1933, quoting the German journal, *Der Angriff.*
9. Ibid., March 9, 1933.
10. *The Jews in Nazi Germany,* compiled and published by the American Jewish Committee (New York, 1935), p. 39.
11. JDB, March 23, 1933.

CHAPTER 2

1. This was said despite the fact that the noted Jewish National Liberal, Eduard Lasker, warned that winter and spring, that various Conservative Party members were involved in highly speculative business deals.
2. See Document No. VI, item 12. This lament is contained in an article which Heinrich von Treitschke, noted nineteenth-century German historian, wrote in 1879 for a publication entitled *Preussische Jahrbuecher*. The context in which it was cited reads as follows: "Year after year there pours over our Eastern frontier ... from the inexhaustible Polish cradle, a host of ambitious, trouser-selling youths, whose children and children's children are one day to dominate Germany's stock exchanges and newspapers.... Right into the most educated circles, among men who would reject with disgust any thought of ecclesiastical intolerance or national pride, we can hear, as if from one mouth, "The Jews are our misfortune" (quoted from G. J. Pulzer's *The Rise of Political Anti-Semitism in Germany and Austria*, p. 249).
3. See Document No. I, p. 378.
4. From Marvin Lowenthal's *The Jews of Germany* (Philadelphia, 1936), p. 344.
5. Schoenerer was more interested in the spread of his ideas in influential circles, and thus bypassed the need for their dissemination among the masses through intense party propaganda. For the fulfillment of his goal, he counted on the various branches of the Pan-German League in Germany, and, especially, Bismarck, whom he did not cease to pester with his monomaniacal striving.
6. Loc. cit. 4, p. 353.
7. Loc. cit. 4, pp. 379–380.

CHAPTER 3

1. NYT, March 26, 1933.
2. Goebbels gave these "atrocity tales" the following twisted interpretation in his diary: "The horrors propaganda abroad gives us much trouble. The many Jews who have left Germany have set all foreign countries against us. Now we have to suffer from the omission of the former government to make propaganda abroad. We are defenselessly exposed to the attacks of our adversaries" (from his *Vom Kaiserhof zur Reichskanzlei*). Goebbels' statement is reproduced from the English translation by Kurt Fiedler, entitled *My Part in Germany's Fight*.
3. NYT, March 28.
4. Ibid.
5. Ibid.
6. Ibid.
7. Ibid., March 29.
8. For the texts of these points and their supplements, see Documents III and IV.
9. *Voelkischer Beobachter*, March 29, which is reproduced from *The Jews in Nazi Germany*, p. 40.
10. NYT, April 1.
11. Loc. cit. 2.
12. NYT, April 1.
13. *Voelkischer Beobachter*, April 1, 1933. From *The Jews in Nazi Germany*, pp. 45–46.
14. Suffice it to say that a new and violent boycott was renewed on June 14 of that year (1933). It was resumed every now and then until the outbreak of World War II. Thus, in 1938, when Hitler incorporated Austria and the Sudetenland as

part of the Greater German Reich, the boycott was one of the first items on his Nazification list.

15. See Document No. V.
16. JDB, April 3, 1933.
17. Of course, today we know that the Nazis need not have feared direct military intervention. Europe was then in one of the most pacifistic moods of its history. In this respect, the Nazis overrated the world's conscience. Thus, they may have felt that the world's "love" for Jews corresponded to their insane hatred of them. Certainly, many Nazis believed that Jews had a controlling influence over world governments, and might incite some of them to declare war against Germany. What may have been behind this scheme was the notion that, just as Nazism was using the "Jewish question" to further Germany's growth and progress, so the world was determined to use the Jews as a pretext for arresting this advancement. Goebbels depicted such thinking in his diary. On March 31, 1933, he wrote: "Many are downhearted and apprehensive. They believe that the boycott might lead to a war. We can gain nothing, however, but universal esteem by defending ourselves" (loc. cit., 2).
18. *Leipziger Tageszeitung,* March 21. Loc. cit. 13, p. 32.
19. NYT, March 29, 1933.
20. JDB, April 1.
21. NYT, April 1.
22. Ibid., April 7.
23. Ibid.
24. Ibid.
25. It is ascribed to Constantin P. Pobedonostsev, the mentor of Alexander III and Procurator of the Holy Synod, who, about half a century before the birth of the Third Reich, formulated a Final Solution of sorts. This was that one-third of Russian Jewry should emigrate, one-third would have to convert, and the remaining third would be starved to death. But at least the Tsarist government denied the existence of an official anti-Jewish policy, even apologizing in the face of world protest.
26. NYT, April 4.

CHAPTER 4

1. Stephen S. Wise Papers, Nazi Period folder, Brandeis University Library, Waltham, Mass.
2. Minutes of the Administrative Committee of the American Jewish Congress, New York, N.Y.
3. NYT, March 20, 1933.
4. Ibid., March 21.
5. Ibid.
6. Ibid. Dr. Wise's reference to "Christian friends" was an allusion to the non-Jewish speakers who were invited to speak at Madison Square Garden.
7. Ibid. March 27.
8. Ibid. As we shall presently see, the list of speakers contained some very renowned names. To these, Wallach sent copies of the telegram under discussion.
9. Ibid., March 26.
10. Ibid.
11. See item 6 on p. 7.
12. The reference is to Goering (p. 6).

13. NYT, March 27.
14. Poland, for example. Polish Jewry also proclaimed March 27 (1933) as a day of protest.
15. For some rabbinic bodies declared this date as a day of fasting and prayer for all Jews.
16. NYT, March 28.
17. Ibid.
18. Ibid.

CHAPTER 5

1. Annual Report of the Executive Committee, 27th Annual Report, New York, 1934, p. 37.
2. Ibid.
3. Archives of the American Jewish Committee, Boycott Germany Mass Meetings folder, New York, N.Y.
4. Ibid.
5. NYT, March 22, 1933.
6. Ibid.
7. The president of the American Jewish Committee was Dr. Cyrus Adler. The B'nai B'rith president was Alfred M. Cohen. The president of the American Jewish Congress was Rabbi Stephen S. Wise.
8. Archives of the American Jewish Congress, New York, N.Y.
9. NYT, March 27.
10. Loc. cit. 3.
11. Ibid.
12. Ibid.
13. Ibid.
14. Ibid.
15. NYT, April 1, 1933.
16. Records of the Joint Boycott Council, NYPL.
17. JDB, April 7, 1933.

CHAPTER 6

1. Some of the information relating to Col. Mendelsohn is based on a taped interview that this writer arranged at the Brooklyn, N.Y., home of the erstwhile JWV commander on July 20, 1965. The background information he was able to supply was necessary, since the March 18 meeting was, apparently, not reported in the press. However, according to Mendelsohn, the press had been present, but decided to leave when, in the late hours of the night, no boycott decision had, as yet, been reached by the group. Mendelsohn also claimed that it was Sperling who had proposed the boycott at this meeting. This is confirmed by the September 2, 1935, edition of the *New York Times,* in which it is said: "The convention [i.e., JWV], conferring decorations of merit tonight, bestowed one upon Benjamin Sperling, Commander of the East Post of Brooklyn, for conceiving the idea of a boycott against German-made goods being sold in this country." This, incidentally, discredits a claim that Fredman made later that year with regard to the boycott; namely, that "it was fired by myself at a meeting of the American Jewish Congress, Sunday evening March 12, 1933" (minutes of the National Boycott Conference of September 10, 1933; see the first subsection of chap. XIII). Indirectly, however, Fredman supports the contention that at least the general press—until March 21—did not report the budding reactions of the

JWV to the growing Hitler menace. In the March 1936 edition of the *Jewish Veteran* (Hoboken, N.J.), he wrote as follows: "January 30, 1933, Hitler ascended to virtual power. His numerous atrocities, including the Black Friday Decree, April 1, 1933, stimulated the JWV of the U.S. to act. Innumerable conferences and committee meetings were held followed by a mass meeting the latter part of February in Carnegie Hall . . ." This indicates that weeks before their adoption of the boycott, the Jewish War Veterans, like the American Jewish Congress, the AJC-BB, and other groups, were preoccupied with the German Jewish question. But none of this information—certainly no mention of a boycott—is reported in the general press. All in all, therefore, it would appear that Mendelsohn's information concerning the March 18–19 meeting of JWV is reliable. It might also be pointed out that JWV action was in keeping with "Object Two" of its constitution, which reads: "To combat the sources of bigotry and darkness; wherever originating and whatever their target; to uphold the fair name of the Jew and fight his battle wherever unjustly assailed."

2. NYT, March 21, 1933.
3. *Jewish War Veteran*, August, 1933.
4. Ibid.
5. As far as we know, Louis Mayer bowed out of the boycott movement right after its preliminary setup. His participation in it, as far as the record shows, is limited to the data cited herein.
6. *Jewish Chronicle* (Newark, N.J.), May 16, 1933. The paper does not state the exact date on which this statement was made. It does report, however, that Coralnik announced it before the conference was held.
7. *Der Tog*, May 13, 1933: "Foon Vort zu Taat; Vegen der Konferentz faar Boikot" (From Word to Deed; Regarding the Boycott Conference).
8. Coralnik did not, however, solve the problem of how to make the boycott an effective instrument in the face of Jewish disunity. In this regard, his was an intuitive approach, one of faith. He felt that this unprecedented crisis would unite Jews as never before; that this time they must not give battle in words, but in deeds.
9. It was also referred to as the United Boycott Committee of Poland.
10. NYT, April 14, 1933.
11. Untermyer was referring to the criticisms made by such men as Winston Churchill, Herbert Samuel, and Foreign Secretary Sir John Simon. Former Foreign Secretary Sir Joseph Austen Chamberlain also joined in the criticism, charging that the worst of the Prussian spirit had returned.
12. This is confirmed by the *London Jewish Chronicle* of April 7, 1933, under the subtitle "The English Press"; by the April 14 edition under the subtitle "The Press."
13. NYT, April 17, 1933.
14. Ibid. May 8.
15. *New York American*, May 13.
16. NYT, May 15.
17. Ibid.
18. *New York American*, May 15.
19. *New York Evening Post*, May 15.
20. *New York Herald Tribune*, May 15.
21. Ibid.
22. NYT, May 15.
23. For the text of this resolution, see Document No. VI.

24. NYT, May 16.
25. *New York Post.*
26. Ibid., May 16, 1933.

CHAPTER 7
1. Archives of the American Jewish Committee, Boycott Germany folder, New York, N.Y. This letter was a duplicate of one addressed principally to Deutsch regarding the big Garden rally of March 27, 1933. But neither the Congress archives nor the records of the Joint Boycott Council contain either the original Friedman communication or a reply by Deutsch.
2. Ibid.
3. Ibid.
4. Archives of the American Jewish Committee, Boycott Germany Public Opinion folder, New York, N.Y. Waldman's communication is undated. However, Untermyer was, apparently, on the Committee's mailing list. This should not be surprising, as he had once been the law partner of Louis Marshall, the Committee's second president.
5. Ibid. Dated May 4. In the Public Opinion folder cited in the previous note, Waldman's communication is attached to this response.
6. Ibid.
7. Ibid.
8. The reference is to Hendrik Willem van Loon (1882–1944), who was a Dutch-born American author and journalist. He was for many years a newspaper correspondent in Russia and Belgium. We do not know, however, what sort of meeting van Loon addressed.
9. Archives of the American Jewish Committee, Boycott Germany Public Opinion folder, New York, N.Y.
10. Ibid.

CHAPTER 8
1. Records of the Joint Boycott Council, NYPL.
2. Minutes of the Administrative Committee of the American Jewish Congress, April 12, 1933, New York, N.Y.
3. American Jewish Committee, 26th Annual Report.
4. Archives of the American Jewish Committee, New York, N.Y.
5. Loc. cit. 1.
6. Many such allusions are contained in the Records of the Joint Boycott Council, Boycott Correspondence: 1933 folder, NYPL.
7. JDB, April 21.
8. *New York Evening Post,* May 14.
9. *Jewish Daily Forward,* May 11.
10. Protest gatherings were held in other cities as well. In Cleveland, where more than 10,000 people appeared, the assembled heard Dr. Wise's message urging that they write immediately to President Roosevelt, their representatives in Congress, and the State Department demanding that the U.S. government express its sympathy for German Jewry and its abhorrence of conditions under Nazi rule. Statements revealing solidarity with German Jews were also heard in Philadelphia, where about 20,000 people appeared, and in Chicago, where an estimated crowd of 50,000 showed up in protest.
11. Records of the Joint Boycott Council, Minutes—May 15 folder, NYPL.
12. *New York Herald Tribune,* May 20, 1933.

13. NYT, May 21.
14. Loc. cit. 11.
15. The Hebrew name for the Union of Orthodox Rabbis of the United States and Canada, a rabbinic body formed in 1902.

CHAPTER 9

1. Cited, Preparatory Committee of the Jewish World Economic Conference, June 28, 1933, Archives of the NSANL, New York, N.Y.
2. JDB, June 12, 1933.
3. Loc. cit. 1.
4. Ibid.
5. NYT, July 15.
6. See Document No. XI, pp. 396–97.
7. Untermyer traveled in the company of Coralnik and Fredman. The latter was elected one of the Federation's vice-presidents.
8. Passports that were issued by the League of Nations to political refugees. They were named after Fridtjof Nansen, who directed its refugee work in the critical years of the post-1919 era.
9. The second subsection of Article 427 of the Versailles Treaty contains labor clauses providing the "right of association for all lawful purposes of employed as well as by employers."
10. NYT, July 21.

CHAPTER 10

1. NYT, August 7, 1933.
2. Ibid.
3. *St. Louis Post Dispatch,* June 14, 1933.
4. NYT, August 15, 1933. There can be no doubt that Dr. Wise was referring to an organized boycott (see pp. 92–96). Wise's main concern at this time was with the timing of a boycott declaration. As a letter written his daughter, Justine, indicates, Wise feared during this period that such a declaration might have portentous repercussions for German Jews. A Hitler Parteitag had been scheduled for early September, making the Congress's honorary president fearful of anti-Jewish reprisals, if some weeks beforehand, the American Jewish Congress were to pass a boycott resolution. Wise wrote his letter from Prague. The following excerpted line describes the kind of boycott he had in mind and his fears concerning its implementation: "I have the feeling that the Boycott must be declared aloud, but it is darned dangerous in the light of the pogrom threat" (*The Personal Letters of Stephen Wise,* pt. 5, 1933–1949, p. 226).
5. NYT, August 16, 1933.
6. Ibid.
7. Ibid.
8. Ibid.
9. See chapter 9.
10. Records of the Joint Boycott Council, Boycott Resolutions and Statements folder, NYPL.
11. His boycott program and two others are cited in Document No. VIII.
12. *Morgen Journal,* August 21, 1933.
13. See Document No. IX, pp. 391–92, for the complete text.
14. NYT, August 21, 1933.

15. A news item in the *New York Times* of May 22 tells that the JWV suggested this idea to him.

16. This marks the first of many abortive attempts at boycott union between the Congress and the League. Just why these attempts ended in failure will be explained later in this work.

17. This, too, was printed in the August 21, 1933, issue of *Der Morgen Journal*. It and the open letter were translated into English by this writer.

CHAPTER 11

1. NYT, August 7, 1933.
2. Archives of the American Jewish Committee, Statements folder, New York, N.Y.
3. Ibid.
4. Also referred to as the Joint Consultative Council.
5. This statement was prepared by Bernard Deutsch. The Conjoint Council, due to sharp differences concerning the use of anti-Nazi tactics, was dissolved in 1937. It was succeeded by the General Jewish Council in 1938, in the wake of the alarming events of that year.
6. Loc. cit. 2.
7. For the complete text of the AJC statement, see Document No. X, p. 393.

CHAPTER 12

1. NYT, August 22, 1933.
2. *Jewish Chronicle* (Milwaukee, Wisconsin), September 1, 1933.
3. Ibid.
4. Ibid.
5. Older brother of Lord Melchett. The latter was threatened with retaliatory steps against his business if he continued chairing the Anglo-Jewish Council. It appears that, since people other than himself would suffer the consequences of his action, he thought it best to resign.
6. *Morgen Journal*, August 21, 1933. The cablegram appeared in a Yiddish translation, and this writer, for want of an original English source, retranslated it.
7. See *Encyclopaedia Judaica*, vol. III, "Arlosoroff, Chaim" cols. 470–471.
8. JDB, August 30, 1933.
9. Ibid.
10. Ibid.
11. Cited on p. 33 of A. Leon Kubowitzki's *Unity in Dispersion* (see p. 416).
12. Quoted from p. 256 of Stephen Wise's *Challenging Years* (New York, 1949).
13. Protocole de la IIe Conference Juive Mondiale, Geneve, Septembre 5–8, 1933.
14. Ibid.
15. Ibid.
16. Ibid.
17. Ibid.
18. NYT, September 9, 1933.

CHAPTER 13

1. From the Minutes of the National Boycott Conference, Archives of the NSANL, New York, N.Y.

2. Ibid.
3. Ibid.
4. Ibid.
5. Ibid.
6. Ibid.
7. Ibid.
8. Ibid.
9. They are reproduced in Document No. XII, pp. 397–99.
10. In the minutes of the National Boycott Conference, Col. Mendelson is not referred to by name. The reference "A Voice" is used instead. But having actually mentioned his position, Col. Mendelson therewith provided us with the clue that makes it possible to identify him.
11. Ibid.
12. Ibid.
13. His first name is not mentioned in the minutes. This hardly matters, however, since the surname does not bring to mind a familiar figure.
14. Loc. cit. 1.
15. Ibid.
16. His first name is not mentioned either. However, the title "Judge" makes it quite certain that it was Judge Gustave Hartman, who was pretty active during the thirties in some of the Congress' anti-Nazi functions.
17. Loc. cit. 1.
18. Ibid.
19. The League's Women's Division was founded on June 27, 1933, at a conference held at the Hotel Astor, where ALDJR's pending conference had taken place about a fortnight earlier. The conference was attended by about 1,000 delegates of 236 women's groups, who formed the nucleus of the League's women's branch. Samuel Untermyer was featured as the principal speaker.
20. Loc. cit. 1.
21. As far as can be ascertained, ALDJR was not even represented. Certainly none of its leading members were there. Apparently, Untermyer and his associates felt that enough of the groundwork had been laid at the Amsterdam Conference. The dispatch of a congratulatory letter was the extent of Untermyer's participation.
22. Archives of the NSANL, New York, N.Y.
23. Ibid.
24. Ibid.
25. Ibid.
26. The reference is to Percy S. Straus, president of R. H. Macy & Co.
27. Loc. cit. 22
28. Note therein the "dodge" mentioned by Silver.
29. Loc. cit. 22.
30. NYT, October 2, 1933.
31. Ibid.
32. Ibid.
33. Ibid.
34. Special German currency which could be bought by non-Germans at a reduced rate.
35. Loc. cit. 1, M file.
36. Loc cit. 1
37. Ibid.
38. Ibid.

39. Ibid.
40. NYT, August 1, 1933.
41. *New York American*, September 16, 1933.
42. As will be noted in Part III, in 1934, Untermyer convened a special conference to—among other things—alter the name of WJEF.
43. Loc. cit. 22.
44. In a taped interview on July 23, 1964, Mrs. Sarah Coralnik, widow of ALDJR's late founder and leader, claimed that her husband resented the fact that Untermyer had encroached upon and eventually took over the control of the organization. It was an understandable feeling. However, Dr. Coralnik equally resented the fact that Untermyer then converted his League into a nonsectarian organization. By December 1934, Coralnik had had enough of the NSANL, venting himself in the Yiddish daily, *Der Tog*, in an article entitled "Der Sterilizirter Boikot" (The Sterile Boycott). Germany, it said, had isolated the Jews; hence it was up to the Jews to isolate Germany through the boycott. ALDJR's change in name would fool no one, since Jews still ran the organization. Its nonsectarianism only caused the Jews to lose their self-respect in the sight of the very gentiles they wished to attract. This, concluded that article, could only produce a "sterile" boycott.

In another article, written in the "Jewish Voice" of January 1935, Dr. Coralnik announced his resignation from the NSANL. It was foreign to Judaism, he wrote, and estranged itself from the Jewish people. However, the following year, after an apparent change of heart, Coralnik requested to be readmitted to the League. He was readmitted, but died in 1937.

CHAPTER 14

1. The house of worship whose founding was inspired by Stephen Wise, and wherein he served as rabbi. For more details, see *"Challenging Years,"* chap. V, "Founding the Free Synagogue."
2. Private Papers of Stephen S. Wise, American Jewish Congress, 1931–1934 folder, Brandeis University Library, Waltham, Mass.
3. Ibid.
4. Ibid. Nazi Period folder. The letter is undated. It is attached, though, to a November 24, 1933, memorandum which Miss Shultz addressed to Dr. Wise.
5. The information furnished in this paragraph is based on statements supplied this writer by Lily Shultz and Dr. Samuel Margoshes. They claimed, respectively, that Dr. Tenenbaum was "badgering for the job" and that "he wanted it very badly." Both also claimed that Dr. Wise made the assignment though exactly when is not known. However, inasmuch as a January 15, 1934, issue of the *Morgen Journal* appears to be the last date on which Dr. Winkler is described as the director of the Congress' Boycott Department, it may be assumed that Dr. Tenenbaum replaced him shortly thereafter.
6. September 20, 1933. From a news clipping in one of several ANL scrapbooks containing such clippings. The name of the newspaper does not appear on this clipping.
7. Ibid., October 14, 1933.
8. NYT, December 29, 1933.
9. Records of the Joint Boycott Council, Minutes of the Actions Committee folder, April 8, 1934 Minutes, NYPL.
10. NYT, March 17, 1934.
11. Records of the Joint Boycott Council, NYPL.

12. Ibid.
13. Loc. cit. 2.
14. Ibid.
15. March 20, 1934.
16. Archives of the NSANL, New York, N.Y.
17. Loc. cit. 11.
18. The Czechoslovak consul, to cite government agency, furnished the Boycott Committee with a partial list of importers.
19. Undated, Records of the Joint Boycott Council, 1934 Correspondence folder, NYPL.
20. NYT, March 8, 1934.
21. Loc. cit. 9, Boycott Correspondence 1934 folder.
22. The Confidential Report of June 12, 1934, says it consisted of the following men and women: Stephen S. Wise (chairman), William Green, Hon. Clifford Pinchot (governor of Pennsylvania), Hon. Hill McAllister (governor of Tennessee), Hon. Clyde Herring (governor of Iowa), Hon. Wilbur L. Cross (governor of Connecticut), Roger Baldwin, George Gordon Battle, Miriam Beard, Edwin De Rechtel, Hon. Bernard S. Deutsch, Rufus M. Hartill, Stanley High, Rev. John Haynes Holmes, Julius Klausner, Prof. Jerome Michael, Hon. Nathan D. Perlman, Simon E. Sobeloff, Dr. Joseph Tenenbaum.
23. An undated and unsigned memorandum contained in the International Trade folder of the Records of the JBC states that merchandise of Russian, Italian, and Japanese origin was also prohibited at the Fair.
24. Records of the Joint Boycott Council, International Boycott folder, NYPL.
25. They were two of the firm's vice-presidents, Edwin Marks and Delos Walker, as well as a Mr. Lauterstein. The latter's name is not mentioned in the records of the Boycott Committee. Macy's Public Relations Department informed this writer that it has no record of this man.
26. During the discussions, Mr. Walker revealed that his firm had imported $7,000 worth of German merchandise "in the past two months."

CHAPTER 15

1. Protocole de la IIIme Conference Juive Mondiale, 1934. Dr. Goldmann delivered his talk in German. The excerpted passage was translated into English by this writer.
2. Hitler's. Hindenburg died on August 2, 1934.
3. Loc. cit. 1.
4. Ibid.
5. Jewish population in Palestine.
6. Protocole de la IIIme Conference Juive Mondiale, 1934.
7. Ibid.
8. Ibid.
9. Ibid.
10. American Jewish Committee, Annual Reports, Annual Report of the Executive Committee, 27th Annual Report, 1934.
11. Ibid.
12. Ibid. 26th Annual Report, 1933.
13. Quoted in the *Jewish Post* of August 23, 1934.
14. Ibid.
15. Ibid.
16. Ibid.
17. Ibid.

18. American Jewish Committee, Annual Reports; Annual Report of the Executive Committee, 28th annual meeting, 1935.
19. Ibid.
20. *American Hebrew,* November 9, 1934.
21. Ibid.

CHAPTER 16

1. Chaitkin was an ALDJR officer at this time. He was, apparently, one of a growing number of Congress members who, dissatisfied with mere mass rallies and demonstration marches, joined the recently created and promising American Jewish Defense League. At any rate, in response to Rabinowitz's queries, Chaitkin mailed him on June 7, 1933, the texts of Sections 132, 133, and 134 of Title 19, U.S. Code Annotated. These deal with the marking and labeling of imported goods and are reproduced in Document No. XIV.
2. Archives of the NSANL, New York, N.Y.
3. Minutes of the Conference of the American League for the Defense of Jewish Rights, September 10, 1933.
4. Loc. cit. 2.
5. Ibid.
6. Quoted from the *Economic Bulletin* of February, 1934.
7. See Document No. XVI, p. 403. The Wald Bill was signed into law by Governor Lehman on May 7, 1934. Before implementation, the bill was granted a ninety-day period of grace. Untermyer contended that this was too long a period, one which would enable the Germans to dump quantities of merchandise that would take years to dispose of. He requested that the period be reduced to thirty days. The request was denied.

CHAPTER 17

1. Parentheses were inserted by this writer to indicate obvious typographical errors.
2. *Nazis against the World,* Archives of the NSANL. An anthology of anti-Nazi speeches, essays, articles, and letters by world leaders of public opinion.
3. Based on the November 21, 1934, edition of the erstwhile Chicago Yiddish paper, the *Jewish Daily Courier,* and the November, 1934, edition of the ANL organ, *Economic Bulletin.*
4. *Jewish Daily Courier,* November 21, 1934.
5. Ibid.
6. *Atlantic Monthly,* November 1934.
7. *Economic Bulletin,* November 1934.
8. Ibid.
9. NYT, November 26, 1934.
10. Ibid.
11. For the other resolution, see Document No. XVIII, pp. 405–406.
12. Five vice-presidents, each representing a different country, and seven directors, representing the rest of the national memberships, were also elected. For the constitution of the World Non-Sectarian Anti-Nazi Council, see Document No. XVIII, page 405.

CHAPTER 18

1. *Jewish Daily Courier,* February 12, 1935.

2. Archives of the NSANL Untermyer file, New York, N.Y.
3. Ibid.
4. *Morgen Journal,* December 21, 1933.
5. Ibid., B. Shellwin.
6. Archives of the NSANL, New York, N.Y.
7. Loc. cit. 2.
8. Ibid.
9. Ibid.
10. "The Waning Anti-Nazi Boycott in Europe"; a letter from London by William Zuckerman, *Morgen Journal* reporter. The letter is located in the archives of the NSANL.
11. The exact date was June 19, 1935, and the official reason was "mismanagement."

CHAPTER 19
1. NYT, March 18, 1935.
2. Ibid.
3. Archives of the NSANL, New York, N.Y.
4. *B'nai B'rith Messenger,* May 17, 1935.
5. Ibid.
6. The original letter is not available. The two quoted paragraphs stem from two separate sources. The first is cited in NSANL archives in a document entitled "The Jewish Congress Calls for a United Boycott Movement Against the Nazis." The second is cited in the July 15, 1935, issue of the *Jewish Daily Bulletin.*
7. Archives of the NSANL, July 3, Untermyer file, New York, N.Y.
8. Ibid. (undated).
9. Ibid.
10. Ibid.
11. Ibid.
12. Ibid.
13. We do learn, though, from a "File C" folder contained in the Records of the Joint Boycott Council, that a conference "for the purpose of effecting a united boycott front against the products and services of Nazi Germany" was held in New York's Hotel Commodore on August 7.
14. Independent Order B'rith Abraham. See chap. XX, n. 23.
15. Loc. cit. 7.

CHAPTER 20
1. Committee of Industrial Organization. Three years later, its name was changed to Congress of Industrial Organizations.
2. Archives of the Jewish Labor Committee, New York, N.Y.
3. Ibid. Glove Makers Union folder.
4. They made up the United Hebrew Trades, the Workmen's Circle, the Jewish Socialist Federation of America, the Socialist Territorialists, the Bundists, the Labor Zionists, and the Jewish National Workers' Alliance (Farband).
5. Archives of the Jewish Labor Committee, New York, N.Y.
6. Private Papers of Stephen S. Wise, World Jewish Congress folder, 1935–45, Brandeis University Library, Waltham, Mass.
7. *New York Journal,* July 22, 1935.
8. *Utah Tribune,* July 25, 1935.
9. Ibid.

10. *Reform Advocate*, August 2, 1935.
11. Loc. cit. 8.
12. Quoted by Dr. Samuel Margoshes in his English column in *Der Tog*, July 22, 1935.
13. For the text of these resolutions, see Document No. XIX, p. 406.
14. *Der Tog*, July 22, 1935.
15. One of these was Abe Cahan, editor of the *Jewish Daily Forward*.
16. Loc. cit. 14.
17. Archives of the Jewish Labor Committee, Labor Chest folder, 1934–1936, New York, N.Y.
18. Ibid., 1935.
19. Archives of the Jewish Labor Committee, Joint Boycott Council (1936) folder, New York, N.Y.
20. This Declaration was translated from the Yiddish and sent to Dr. Tenenbaum on December 24, 1935, by Benjamin Gebiner, executive secretary of the Jewish Labor Committee. It is located in the Private File folder of the records of the Joint Boycott Council.
21. Represented, in the main, by the Labor Zionists (Poale Zion) and smaller groups like the Hapoel Hamizrachi.
22. Records of the Joint Boycott Council, "G" folder, NYPL.
23. The IOBA was one of a number of the national affiliates of the American Jewish Congress. So were the various organizations comprising the Congress' Labor Bloc. One of these, the Poale Zion, because of its refusal to quit the Congress, was constrained to withdraw its membership from the Jewish Labor Committee. This step was followed by the introduction of a motion that no group affiliated with the JLC could simultaneously be affiliated with an analogous organization. One can readily understand, therefore, why Vladeck did not feel disposed to bestow upon a former JLC affiliate the privilege of separate representation in any new, jointly sponsored setup; for only less than a year before, he could have requested like representation for this very group. In any event, when serious discussions for boycott union got under way between the A.J.C.-JLC, the IOBA and the Congress Labor Bloc started badgering for separate representation.
24. Loc. cit. 22.
25. Ibid.
26. Agreement was entered upon in writing on February 5, 1936. A statement relating to the financial obligation of each organization reads as follows: "Each party hereto shall contribute $500 each month towards the expenses of maintaining offices, employment of personnel, and conducting such general boycott activities throughout the United States as may be determined by the Joint Boycott Council" (Records of the Joint Boycott Council, Misc. File A-J). Further, the agreement entitled the two organizations represented in the Council to ten representatives each. On August 10, the A.J.C.-JLC also signed an agreement to establish Joint Boycott offices, to take effect on August 17.
27. Records of the Joint Boycott Council, Dr. Wise—Correspondence and Memoranda folder, January 8, 1936, NYPL.

CHAPTER 21

1. Records of the Joint Boycott Council, NYPL.
2. Ibid., NSANL folder.
3. Ibid.

4. *Der Tog,* February 7, 1937.
5. This communication contains a penciled notation reading: "This letter was not sent."
6. Archives of the NSANL, New York, N.Y.
7. Ibid.
8. Records of the Joint Boycott Council, V folder, NYPL. Vladeck may have had prior contact with the League on boycott matters. For according to the January 3, 1935, minutes of the League's Executive Committee meetings, Mr. Untermyer proposed that "a Committee from the Executive be formed to confer with Mr. Vladeck for the purpose of securing the cooperation of his labor organization in support of the League as to boycott and fund-raising activities." Untermyer further proposed that Vladeck "be invited to sit in at Executive meetings as a guest so that the League may benefit by his counsel and advice . . ." The proposals passed, but it is not known whether Vladeck actually gave them his endorsement.
9. Ibid.
10. Ibid.
11. Ibid., Folder T.
12. Ibid.
13. Ibid.
14. Ibid.

CHAPTER 22
1. Records of the Joint Boycott Council, Legislation (a) folder, NYPL.
2. Ibid.
3. Ibid.
4. Ibid.
5. Ibid.
6. Ibid.
7. Ibid.
8. Ibid.

CHAPTER 23
1. Records of the Joint Boycott Council, P folder, NYPL.
2. Ibid.
3. Ibid.
4. Ibid., Steamship Lines folder.
5. Ibid.
6. Ibid.
7. Ibid.
8. Ibid.
9. Ibid.
10. Ibid. Signed by J. W. Cole, Second Assistant Postmaster General.
11. Ibid.
12. Ibid.
13. Loc. cit. 4.
14. Ibid.
15. Father of the late President John F. Kennedy.
16. Loc. cit. 4.

CHAPTER 24

1. By 1935, Dr. Wise had become disenchanted with Jabotinsky, moving closer to the Labor Zionists. These, according to unconfirmed reports, promised Wise support in his efforts to convene the World Jewish Congress, provided he did not make a fuss over the Transfer deal.
2. Protocole du Premier Congres Juif Mondial, Geneve, Aout 8–15, 1936.
3. Ibid.
4. NYT, May 16, 1934.

CHAPTER 25

1. Archives of the NSANL, Picketing folder, New York, N.Y.
2. *The Anti-Nazi Boycott Movement in the United States,* Yad Vashem Studies (Jerusalem, 1959), p. 144.
3. Protocole du Premier Congres Juif Mondial, Geneve, Aout 8–15, 1936.
4. Records of the Joint Boycott Council, Boycott Correspondence folder, 1934, NYPL.
5. Ibid.
6. Ibid. Still, as a tactical weapon, picketing was not as uncomplicated as this or other passages might lead one to believe. In the words of Tenenbaum: "My associates and myself spent many a night in night-courts trying to bail out groups of frightened pickets, arrested on the charge of 'disorderly conduct,' 'disturbing the peace' and what not, and we also had to contend with several court actions" (loc. cit. 2, p. 145).
7. Loc. cit. 4, Forms folder.
8. Ibid.
9. Ibid. Beads and Spangles folder.
10. Ibid. Boycott Correspondence folder.
11. Note, in this connection [p. 64, No. 2].
12. Loc. cit. 4, Folder I.
13. Ibid.
14. Ibid. File BM-BZ.
15. Ibid.
16. Ibid.
17. Ibid.
18. So said Posnansky to this writer. The record is silent on this point, however.
19. Loc. cit. 4, File D, NYPL.
20. Archives of the NSANL, New York, N.Y.
21. Ibid.
22. Loc. cit. 4, National Boycott Conference, NYPL.
23. Ibid.
24. Loc. cit. 4, International Boycott folder, NYPl.
25. It was formed in December of 1933, and was also called the Levinson Committee, after its chairman, the noted Chicago lawyer, Salmon O. Levinson. The Committee's president was Dr. Paul Hutchinson, author and Managing Editor of Chicago's *Christian Century.* In the boycott unity talks that followed Wise's reelection as president of the American Jewish Congress (see p. 169), both he and Untermyer vainly sought to include the Chicago Committee in the contemplated united American boycott front. The Chicago Committee lasted around two years.

26. Loc. cit. 20.

27. Ibid. On January 3, 1936, Levinson wrote Untermyer, explaining this aspect of his activities: "While I was in Maine late in the summer your organization had me write a letter to Lessing Rosenwald. I enclose copy of his reply and of my recent letter to him, which you may find of interest . . ." That the League was getting nowhere with Sears is learned from an October 17, 1935, communication by Harriman to Silver. In the missive, Harriman complains that "the Rosenwalds hadn't even replied to our communications," and that "the thing to do is exert more pressure." In desperation, Harriman must have contacted Levinson, thinking that as a Chicagoan and "friend" of the Rosenwalds, he would have better luck.

28. Ibid.

29. Cited, *Jewish Veteran,* October–November 1937.

30. Such a claim was made on May 22, 1936, by a Brooklyn store manager of Sears & Roebuck. It apparently had a basis in fact, as on May 28 of the following year, this Sears branch was removed from the list of Boycott Violators published by the *Brooklyn Jewish Examiner,* the outspokenly pro-boycott Anglo-Jewish journal. Such gestures, plus corroborative surveillance results, may have swayed the League to drop Sears from its own list of Boycott Violators; the underlying thought behind such a move undoubtedly being that the dropping of all Sears stores from the Boycott Violators list would, in due time, win over many of the non-boycotting branches.

31. Archives of the NSANL, New York, N.Y.

32. Ibid.

33. In a mid-June 1934 statement, the manager of one of Berlin's Woolworth stores declared as "nonsense" that American Woolworth stores had either joined a boycott or advertised that they carried no German goods. If he was not speaking with his tongue in his cheek, then the Woolworth statement that March, that "we have discontinued importation" (p. 136) of German goods, was a deliberate lie.

34. Records of the Joint Boycott Council, NYPL.

35. Dr. Grossman file, YIVO, The file is named after the chairman of the United Non-Sectarian Boycott Council, a local Bronx affiliate of the Joint Boycott Council.

36. Ibid.

37. See, for example, the *New York Times* and *Time* magazine, November 10 and 22, 1937, respectively.

38. Loc. cit. 35, Undated.

39. Ibid.

40. Ibid.

41. Ibid.

42. Ibid.

43. Cited in a January 6, 1935, news item in one of several ANL news clippings books. Harriman mentions the resolution in a January 15, 1935, communication.

44. Loc. cit. 20.

45. This is much less surprising than the fact that Kirby allied himself with Brundage.

46. Contained in an AOC pamphlet entitled *Fair Play for American Athletes.* The pamphlet is located in the ANL Archives. From the newspaper editorials cited in this pamphlet, one may safely conclude that it was issued in the late fall of 1935.

47. After Gustavus T. Kirby, a leading American Olympics official during this period.
48. From an AOC pamphlet entitled *Fair Play for American Athletes*. The pamphlet is located in the NSANL archives. From the newspaper editorials cited in this pamphlet, one may safely conclude that it was issued in the late fall of 1935.
49. Ibid.
50. Ibid.
51. Ibid.
52. Loc. cit. 20.
53. Ibid.
54. Ibid.
55. Ibid.
56. Ibid.

CHAPTER 26

1. The 1934 attempt occurred on July 25, when, after subversive action, Engelbert Dollfuss, Austria's diminutive Chancellor, was mortally wounded by his country's Nazi followers. But Schuschnigg, then Minister of Justice, foiled the putsch by quickly dispatching government forces which regained control of the situation. He became Chancellor about six hours after the Dollfuss assassination. Hitler, because Germany was still militarily weak, and because Britain, France, and even Italy had declared their support of continued Austrian independence, was compelled to postpone his plan for Anschluss. Anschluss was forbidden by the Versailles Treaty.
2. A plebiscite in which both Germans and Austrians voted on the Anschluss issue was held on April 10 (1938). The official results were: 99.75 percent and 99.08 percent in Austria and Germany, respectively, cast *Ja* ballots. It need hardly be emphasized that fear and intimidation accounted for the unusually high pro-Anschluss vote.
3. England made it quite plain to the Prague government that she approved the granting of concessions to the Sudeten Germans. Under separate treaties, both France and Russia were committed to the protection of Czechoslovakia's territorial integrity. However, the thought of having to depend on Russian help placed France in a predicament; for even if Russia could be trusted, it could not possibly render effective help unless Poland and Rumania permitted Soviet troops to cross their territories. Neither country was prepared to do this, for they feared the Soviet Union no less than they did Nazi Germany. Poland even had an interest in Czechoslovakia's collapse, which could conceivably bring it territorial gains. Hence, relations between the two countries were far from amicable.

CHAPTER 27

1. Ismar Elbogen's *A Century of Jewish Life*, p. 658.
2. They turned out to be the first so-called Displaced Persons, or DP's.
3. William L. Shirer's *The Rise and Fall of the Third Reich*, pp. 430–431.
4. Ibid., p. 431. These figures, according to Heydrich's revised report, were grossly underestimated.
5. In 1938, November 9 fell on a Thursday, which German Jews came to call *Der Schwarzer Donnerstag* (i.e., Black Thursday). The general German population, due to the great deal of glass (i.e., *Kristall*) that was strewn about as a result of the window-smashing of Jewish shops, named the event *Die Kristallnacht*.

6. *Contemporary Jewish Record,* November 1938.

7. If we are to believe the testimony of Dr. Helmut Krausnick, who testified at the Frankfurt Trial on February 17, 1964, Hitler informed Czech officials in the fall of 1938 that he planned to exterminate European Jewry. Hence, a genocidal plan may very well have been running through the Fuehrer's demonic mind when, on November 12 of that year, he informed Goering that the Jewish question must be "coordinated and solved, now, once, and for all, in one way or another." It is conceivable, therefore, that the "Fuehrer Order on the Final Solution," which, apparently, reached Goering in oral transmission, and which he, in turn, communicated to Heydrich in a July 31, 1941, directive, was given its tentative formulation at this time. That Goering, when on trial for his life at Nuremberg, should deny everything pertaining to "these terrible exterminations" means nothing whatever. His warning of "a reckoning with the Jews" (chap. 27, p. 249) must have been a tongue-in-cheek statement, as he was at least as well informed about Hitler's intentions as some "Czech officials." Today it can be seen as a veiled preview to Hitler's open threat in a January 30, 1939, address to the Reichstag (see p. 257); an address that Jew and non-Jew alike viewed as another one of the Fuehrer's long and rambling diatribes.

CHAPTER 28

1. Madagascar, known nowadays as the Malagasy Republic, was a French island off the southeast coast of Africa, to which Hitler felt the democracies ought to consign "his" Jews if they were "oozing sympathy" for them. The Madagascar Plan was contrived at a November 12, 1938, meeting in the aftermath of the Kristallnacht. Out of that session grew the plot to "evacuate," first, the Jews of Greater Germany, and then make the rest of Europe *Judenrein* (Free of Jews).

2. To plead the cause of mass Jewish entry into the various countries meant, admittedly, courting the resentment of the indigenous populations and the severe criticism of the opposing political parties. The delegates lacked the moral fiber to swim against this unpopular current, even though hundreds of thousands of human lives were at stake. It was easier, apparently, to gather around international conference tables and content oneself by denouncing the inhumanity of Hitler.

3. His full, official title was "High Commissioner for Refugees (Jewish and other) Coming from Germany."

4. A. Leon Kubowitzki, in his *Unity and Dispersion,* p. 115.

5. Mark Wischnitzer, *To Dwell in Safety,* p. 204.

6. Ibid.

7. Gerald Reitlinger, *The Final Solution,* (New York, 1961), p. 19.

8. This was not the first such emigration scheme. A very short-lived plan was proposed some two and a half years earlier. A full account of this plan is contained in the January 6, 1936, edition of the *New York Times.*

9. Despite the fact that both Schacht and Rublee personally ceased to participate in future negotiations, the proposed program changes continued bearing their respective names.

10. In his January 30, 1939, speech, Hitler derided the democracies by saying: "It is a shameful spectacle to see how the whole democratic world is oozing sympathy for the poor tormented Jewish people, but remains hard-hearted and obdurate when it comes to helping them, which is surely, in view of its attitude, an obvious duty" (*My New Order,* p. 582).

11. Ibid., p. 485.

CHAPTER 29

1. An account of this survey is given in the September 1, 1936, issue of the *Jewish Daily Courier*.
2. NYT, April 12, 1939.
3. *Economic Bulletin,* April, 1939.
4. Details are wanting, but there is some evidence that the League and the Council wooed the VCC for its incorporation into their respective organizations. Thus, a January 9, 1939, JBC communication credits Dr. Wise for the "promotion of the Boycott by Christians." It was written by Dr. Tenenbaum, who also expressed fear that "Untermyer may capitalize on the situation and try to get the Christian group"—an obvious reference to the Volunteer Christian Committee—"to join the NSANL." On April 25, four days after the founding of the Coordinated Boycott Committee, Tenenbaum wrote Wise again, mentioning the prevention of "various schemes of trying to detach the Christian Committee from being tied down to the NSANL."
5. From the *Declaration of Principles of the Volunteer Christian Committee to Boycott Nazi Germany.* A copy of this pamphlet is contained in the JLC archives, VCC folder, File 1937–40 (A-I).
6. Ibid.
7. Dr. Grossman file, YIVO, New York, N.Y. A proviso permitted waiver of this pledge in case of an emergency.
8. Loc. cit. 5.
9. Ibid.
10. Ibid.
11. Ibid.
12. Ibid.
13. Ibid. The organization was headed by Dr. Mary Emma Woolley, educator and past president of Mount Holyoke College. The chairman was William Loeb.
14. Loc. cit. 5.
15. Records of the Joint Boycott Council, Coordinating Committee for Boycott folder, NYPL.
16. Ibid., NSANL folder.
17. *The Anti-Nazi Boycott Movement in the United States,* Yad Vashem Studies III (Jerusalem, 1959), p. 148.
18. Archives of the NSANL, New York, N.Y.
19. Ibid.
20. Ibid.
21. In a July 15, 1964, taped interview, Bernard G. Richards (p. 166) charged before the writer of these pages that Untermyer, who, of course, usually held League meetings in New York City, often opened them in the knowledge that Rabbi Silver was in the meantime flying in from Cleveland to attend them. Thus, eventually, Silver, like a number of other League co-workers, became disillusioned with the "old man" (as some of the League's staff members referred to him).
22. Loc. cit. 18.
23. Ibid.

CHAPTER 30

1. Dr. Ernest Knopfmacher, one of the Congress' important liaison men on the European continent. He was extremely helpful to Tenenbaum, sending him regular reports on Germany's economic posture and subterfuge export activities. At this time, Dr. Knopfmacher lived in Paris.

2. Private Papers of Stephen S. Wise, Nazi period folder, 1931–48, Brandeis University Library, Waltham, Massachusetts.

3. Ibid. Brandeis is addressed here as "Dear LDB." On p. 220 of *The Personal Letters of Stephen Wise*, a note reads as follows: "Stephen Wise often referred to Louis D. Brandeis, as 'L.D.B.' " In any event, there is no record of a reply from Brandeis in Wise's papers.

4. Cited in Tenenbaum's "Twenty-Five Years American Jewish Life," YIVO, Dr. Joseph Tenenbaum file.

5. Ibid.

6. *American Jewish Congress Bulletin*, December 16, 1938.

7. Ibid.

8. Records of the Joint Boycott Council, Dr. Tenenbaum's Speeches folder (1). The conference was also presented with a "Program of Boycott Activity for Local Organizations." The complete text is reproduced in Document No. XXI, p. 409.

9. Ibid. Private File folder.

10. Loc. cit. 8.

11. Ibid.

12. Ibid., W-Z folder.

13. Neither the JBC records nor the private papers of Stephen S. Wise contain any documents pertaining to this point. The A.J.C. minutes of the Governing Council, for so important a period as 1938–39, are, for some inexplicable reason, missing from the archival record.

14. Loc. cit. 12.

15. Ibid.

16. Ibid.

17. Ibid.

18. Ibid., Refugees folder, June 28, 1939.

19. Ibid.

20. Ibid.

21. Ibid.

22. Ibid.

23. Ibid.

24. Ibid.

25. Ibid.

26. Ibid.

CHAPTER 31

1. Records of the Joint Boycott Council, Legislation (a) 1936 folder, NYPL. Representative Doughton is best remembered, perhaps, for his introduction in the House, in 1936, of the Social Security Bill, which he and Senator Robert F. Wagner of New York jointly introduced in the Congress.

2. Ibid.

3. Ibid.

4. Such as sand, coal, or ores; for it is impossible to mark with the country of origin grains of sand, pieces of coal, or specks of ore. But if such goods came in bags, the containers had to be marked with the name of the country of origin.

5. Loc. cit. 1.

6. Ibid. Walsh also had the backing of the noted Senator Arthur H. Vandenberg of Michigan. He, too, recommended some changes in HR 8099, and also claimed that Walsh's amendment strengthened the marking provisions.

7. Records of the Joint Boycott Council, Private file folder: Report of the Joint Boycott Council for 1939, NYPL.

8. Ibid., 1939 Minutes of the Joint Committee on Cases.
9. Ibid., Miss Lilie Shultz 1938 folder.
10. Archives of the NSANL, Minutes folder of the Joint Committee on Cases, New York, N.Y.
11. The JWV opposed this decision, describing it as "unjustified." The JBC (J folder) source which mentions this also states that JWV had not, "as yet," decided to participate in deliberations involving the "Committee on Cases." The reason for this is not known. Also, the August 31, 1939, minutes of the League's Executive Committee meetings state that "Woolworth was put back on the boycott list because it continues to sell German merchandise in many of its stores throughout the country."
12. Loc. cit. 7.
13. Ibid.
14. Ibid., Dr. Tenenbaum's Speeches 1936–38 (2) folder.
15. Loc. cit. 7.

CHAPTER 32
1. Records of the Joint Boycott Council, 1, W-Z folder, NYPL.
2. Archives of Dr. A. Grossman, YIVO, New York, N.Y.
3. Ibid.
4. Loc. cit. 1.
5. Archives of the Jewish Labor Committee, New York, N.Y.
6. Loc. cit. 1, Meeting Notices Minutes—Actions Committee folder.
7. Ibid. We recall (p. 363) that in 1936, the Jewish Labor Committee agreed to contribute $500 per month for office expenses. The reduction was tremendous if it was from this sum that the Council was ultimately left with the payment of $150 per month. It also explains, of course, why the minutes of the war period often mention that the Council ran its own fund-raising campaigns. A detailed rundown on the Council's operating expenses from the year of its inception up to the outbreak of World War II is contained in Document No. XXIII.
8. Loc. cit. 1, June 5, 1940, minutes, Food Package Racket folder.
9. Ibid. William Allen White was an editor, liberal Republican, and author of politico-historical studies. The "Objectives" of his organization were described in a July 1940 pamphlet and are reproduced in Document No. XXIII, p. 411).
10. Loc. cit. 1, Misc. file, Agreements Setting Up and Dissolving the Joint Boycott Council. It would appear, however, in view of the fact that the JBC office was temporarily liquidated on October 15, 1939, that Dr. Tenenbaum himself was guilty of "the erroneous opinion that the British Blockade makes Boycott obsolete."
11. Ibid. Meeting Notices Minutes—September 8, 1940.
12. Ibid., September 1940.

CHAPTER 33
1. Passed by the U.S. Congress in August 1935. It was designed to keep America out of a possible European war by placing a ban on shipments of war materials to the belligerent nations.
2. Records of the Joint Boycott, Council, Unsorted, Miscellaneous Material folder, NYPL.
3. Ibid.
4. Ibid.
5. Ibid., the *Forward* folder.

6. Ibid. The fact that Tenenbaum might not have called for an embargo prior to the mentioned date does not mean, of course, that the restrictive measure was not discussed in Council or Congress circles. A July 22, 1937, JBC document relating to the Youth Division of the American Jewish Congress cites a resolution demanding "a complete embargo on all trade and commercial relations with the Nazi Government and severance of diplomatic ties" (Letter Y, Youth Division Folder).

7. Ibid.

8. Ibid. Anti-Nazi Week folder, 1938.

9. Loc. cit. 2, Coordinating Committee for Boycott folder, March 19, 1940, minutes, NYPL.

10. Archives of Dr. Grossman, YIVO, New York, N.Y.

11. Ibid. The January 17, 1940, CBC minutes supplied the background to this decision, stating that Dr. Tenenbaum was in receipt of a communication from Dr. Knopfmacher, to whom the Secretary of the British Blockade suggested that "JBC ought not to much watch the exports from Germany," but "should see to it not to sell American raw-materials to Germany sent through neutral countries."

12. Loc. cit. 2, Anti-Nazi Week, Publicity folder, 1940, NYPL.

13. Ibid.

14. Ibid. Moral Embargo, 1940 folder.

15. An April 18, 1940, communication that Tenenbaum addressed to the various ethnic groups whose native countries had been attacked by Germany mentions that "Hitler's latest invasion of Scandinavia has helped to unite public opinion against Nazism." It may have been the event that led him to believe that the time had come to request the U.S. government to proclaim a moral embargo against the Hitler government.

16. Loc. cit. 1, K folder, Dr. Knopfmacher, Paris, France, NYPL.

17. Ibid.

18. Ibid.

19. Loc. cit. 1, Coordinating Committee for Boycott folder, NYPL. The CBC hoped that the war in Europe would induce the AFL to terminate its independent, albeit cooperative conduct of the anti-Nazi boycott, and close ranks in a common undertaking. Woll was confronted with this question at this meeting, but his answer was not exactly the one that CBC affiliates wished to draw from him. What he said was "that the AF of L will cooperate in every way possible, but is unable for a number of reasons"—which, apparently, he did not care to reveal—"to affiliate directly with the Boycott Organizations in their work." Otherwise, "he believed the AFL would be able to participate directly with the CBC in a campaign for a 'Moral Embargo against the Aggressor Nations.'" Mr. Woll agreed, though, upon Dr. Tenenbaum's suggestion, to serve on the Moral Embargo Committee.

20. One of those small, little-known organizations that mushroomed in the prewar and war periods. Council archives contain no information regarding the relationship of this group with the various boycott organizations with which it participated in this undertaking.

21. Loc. cit. 2, Minutes Actions Committee folder, NYPL.

22. Ibid.

23. Ibid., File Drawer 3:1935–1941, A-M folder.

24. Ibid.

25. Archives of Dr. Joseph Tenenbaum, Speeches, 1939–1961, YIVO, New York, N.Y.

26. Ibid.

27. Other countries also showed increased U.S. purchases which, the Boycott Council charged, were made for the benefit of Nazi Germany. Thus, in its Preliminary Draft of the Moral Embargo Campaign (prepared sometime in early 1940) JBC included "a study of American export trends since the outbreak of the war," which indicated that also Belgium, Hungary, Switzerland, Rumania, Yugoslavia, and Denmark had increased "tremendously" their purchases in the United States. Moreover, these increased purchases, this study revealed, "were concentrated mainly in war materials and raw materials for war industries." Therefore, "it was suspected that these excessive acquisitions of war materials were reaching Nazi Germany."
28. Moral Embargo, 1940 folder, NYPL.
29. Ibid.

CHAPTER 34
1. Records of the Joint Boycott Council, NYPL.
2. Ibid., Semi Precious Stones folder.
3. Ibid. The same holds for the rest of the quotations in this paragraph.
4. Loc. cit. 1, VEVA folder.
5. Loc. cit. 2.
6. According to the executive secretary of the New England Manufacturing Jewelers' and Silversmiths' Association, who expressed his "sympathy with the basic principles underlying the motives of the boycott movement," to "fully develop sources of supply for the industry's goods outside" Austria and Czechoslovakia, "would require a period of years." He wrote his communication on April 22, 1939, to dissuade the Council from introducing a boycott of the products of manufacturers dealing with these areas. Such a boycott, claimed the Association's secretary, "would jeopardize the jobs of nearly 23,000 workers in the production of this industry and 50,000 in the distribution end of this industry" (Records of the Joint Boycott Council, Semi Precious Stones folder, NYPL).
7. Ibid., W-Z folder.
8. Ibid.
9. Ibid., Businessmen's Advisory Committee folder.
10. His first name is not mentioned in the record.
11. Loc. cit. 9.
12. Ibid.
13. Ibid.
14. Ibid.
15. Ibid.
16. Actually, JBC archives contain conflicting statements regarding this. They center around two documents bearing the identical date of July 18, 1938; one, contained in the R folder, says that it was a William Rosenblatt that the Actions Committee appointed to organize the Businessmen's Advisory Council. This document also says that Rosenblatt informed Marcus that "it would be best to wait until the Fall" before the Businessmen's Advisory Council was established. The "JBC correspondence" cited on p. 307, also forms part of the aforesaid folder. It is a communication from Marcus to Rosenblatt, in which Tenenbaum is quoted as having told the Council secretary that he expected Rosenblatt to arrange a luncheon at which the Businessmen's Advisory Council would be initiated. The missive closes with Marcus "still" wondering if Rosenblatt took the steps "in this direction." The record does not make it clear whether Rosenblatt was a representative of the business world, or, possibly, one of the Council's twenty permanent representatives with an ad hoc assignment. Heyman, on the

other hand, was definitely a regular Council worker. However, we do not know the exact position he held therein.

17. Loc. cit. 1, H folder, NYPL.
18. Ibid.
19. Ibid.
20. Ibid.
21. Loc. cit. 2, Meeting Notices Minutes Actions Committee folder, May 2, 1941 minutes, NYPL.
22. Ibid., June 16, 1941 minutes.
23. Ibid., Diamond Dealers—Meetings folder.
24. See loc. cit. 21. Why Italy's entrance into the war in 1940 should have had this effect is not clear. It did, as has been mentioned earlier, make indirect trade with the Nazis obsolescent, since, by then, "there were no more neutrals to buy for Germany's account"; but diamond smuggling into Germany could and did originate from the United States. This is why Dr. Tenenbaum reintroduced the subject of industrial diamonds the following year (i.e., 1941).

CHAPTER 35

1. Records of the Joint Boycott Council, E folder, Mr. Emmet's Material, NYPL.
2. Ibid., Minutes—Actions Committee folder.
3. Ibid. Reports folder.
4. The remainder of the quotations in this paragraph are likewise taken from this source.
5. On June 14, 1941, President Roosevelt issued a proclamation freezing the funds and assets of Germany and almost every European country. It was part of a series of freezing control orders, the first of which was announced in April 1940, after the invasions of Denmark and Norway. The proclamation of June 14, 1941, put Fortura and Mitropa out of commission in the United States. According to JBC's June-September, 1941, Confidential Report, Fortura and Mitropa (between them) sent $1,213,426 to Europe and spent $203,491 in the United States for "administrative expenses."
6. Loc. cit. 1, Reports folder, NYPL.
7. Ibid. Private File folder.
8. It was founded in 1908 under the name of Federation of Polish Jews in America. In 1930, its name was changed to American Federation of Polish Jews. Tenenbaum, himself from Sassow, Poland, was sympathetic toward the organization and eventually became its president.
9. Loc. cit. 1, Food Packages A-L folder, NYPL. The rest of the quotations in this paragraph stem from this source, too.
10. Ibid., German Emigres folder.
11. Loc. cit. 7. The rest of the quotations in this paragraph also derive from this source.
12. Ibid.
13. Ibid.
14. Loc. cit. 7.
15. Loc. cit. 1, Private File folder, NYPL.
16. Loc. cit. 7.
17. Ibid.
18. Ibid.
19. Ibid.

20. Ibid. Aliens folder.
21. Loc. cit. 7.
22. Ibid.
23. It appeared in a privately circulated publication called "Trend of Events." The July 25, 1941, issue is contained in the Records of the Joint Boycott Council.
24. Loc. cit. 9.
25. Loc. cit. 7.
26. Loc. cit. 2.

CHAPTER 36

1. Joseph Tenenbaum, *The Anti-Nazi Boycott Movement in the United States* Yad Vashem Studies (Jerusalem, 1959), p. 149.
2. Records of the Joint Boycott Council, International Boycott folder, NYPL.
3. Ibid.
4. March 26, 1936 communication to Leon Kubowitzki by Dr. Tenenbaum.
5. Loc. cit. 2, *The Forward* folder, NYPL.
6. Tenenbaum, did, from time to time, discuss in both the written and spoken word, Germany's encroachment on Latin America at U.S. expense. Thus, on January 13, 1938, he expressed alarm at this development in an address entitled "Five Years of Hitlerism." However, unlike the series of addresses referred to in the present discussion, this one was not devoted exclusively to the subject of Latin America; nor did it purport to launch an anti-Nazi boycott movement in that region.
7. Archives of Dr. Joseph Tenenbaum, Speeches, 1939–1961, YIVO.
8. Loc. cit. 2, Tenenbaum Speeches folder, NYPL.
9. Robert Marcus to Flora J. Cahan, president of the A.J.C. Women's Division, Records of the Joint Boycott Council, Memos (2) 1935–1940 folder.
10. Ibid.
11. Ibid., May 7, 1939 Conference folder.
12. Ibid.
13. Ibid.
14. Effron explained that Berlin had a government institution known as the School for High Political Studies for Nazi Youth in Foreign Countries. The instruction and lectures, given on a "private" basis, were, on occasion, made public. Dr. Effron then quoted from a lecture delivered by a Dr. Emil Ehrlich on January 17, 1938: "There are in the New World great territories peopled almost in their totality by Germans, whose task should be that of taking under their own government the lands tilled and worked by them, to bring under the direct protection of our marvellous and once more powerful fatherland." Effron also displayed published maps of Argentina from the 1938 yearbook of the Deutsche Volksband fuer Argentinien—a Nazi organization. These did not show Argentina divided into provinces, "but as inhabited by primitive Indians and German colonists." A second group of maps of the "region" showed parts of Brazil, Argentina, and Uruguay with no boundaries. In the caption, this area was referred to as "Antarktica Germanica."
15. Ibid.
16. Ibid.
17. Ibid., W-2 folder.
18. Ibid., Confidential Reports and Memoranda folder.
19. Loc. cit. 2.
20. Ibid.
21. Prior to this time, with the exception of the January 17, 1940, CBC

minutes, there is no discussion of the Latin American program. These minutes, which cite the Knopfmacher letter mentioned earlier (chapter 33, n. 11), quote Tenenbaum as saying that the "gist" of it was that JBC "adjust" its activities to prevent the sale of raw materials "from here and South America." In response to this, Dr. Effron pointed out that if one wanted the Latin American people to cooperate in the effort to halt their trade with Germany, one had first "to help them solve their economic problems created by the Blockade." This, in effect, constituted the "gist" of the discussion on Latin America.

22. Loc. cit. 2, Confidential Reports (and Memos) folder. The representatives mentioned are Matthew Woll of the AFL and Christopher T. Emmet and a Clark M. Eichelberger for the White Committee.

23. Ibid.
24. Ibid.
25. Ibid.
26. Ibid.
27. Ibid.
28. Ibid. Minutes of the Committee folder, August 13, 1940.
29. Ibid., Inter-American Cooperation folder.
30. Ibid.
31. Loc. cit. 21.
32. Loc. cit. 27.
33. Ibid.
34. Ibid., Dr. Tenenbaum—Personal 1940 folder.
35. Ibid., Program of the Committee folder.
36. Ibid., March 23, 1941 folder.
37. Ibid., Buy Latin American folder.
38. Loc. cit. 34.
39. Loc. cit. 27.
40. Records of the Joint Boycott Council, Nelson A. Rockefeller folder, NYPL.
41. Loc. cit. 21.
42. Ibid., Releases-Inter-American Cooperation folder.
43. Ibid. The role the United States should play in Latin America, Dr. Tenenbaum described in far greater detail in a pamphlet entitled *The Road to Pan-Americanism*. It was released a day prior to the opening of Inter-American Cooperation Week. He highlighted the pamphlet in a memorandum dated March 28, 1941.
44. Records of the Joint Boycott Council, Confidential Report, June–September 1941 folder, NYPL.
45. Ibid., Memorandum Committee folder.
46. Ibid.
47. Ibid.
48. Ibid., Misc. File A-J Agreements Setting Up and Dissolving the Joint Boycott Council folder.
49. The NSANL was never liquidated. Today it serves as a documentation center, with a library and files, for the activities of Nazis, Neo-Nazis, and anti-democratic peoples of either the right or the left. Over the years, the League has compiled a rich collection of the propaganda literature of such groups. The League is run by Prof. James H. Sheldon, who, on May 4, 1939, became the chairman of its National Board. Prior to this, Sheldon was a member of the Board of Directors of the League's Boston branch. From July 17, 1941, he has been the League's administrative chairman.

SUMMARY AND CONCLUSIONS
1. *New York Sun,* February 28, 1935.
2. *Detroit Jewish Chronicle,* March 18, 1935.
3. Adolph Hitler, *My New Order,* p. 673.
4. *New York World-Telegram,* February 6, 1935.
5. Ibid., February 7, 1935.
6. Ibid.
7. Ibid.
8. Ibid., February 12, 1935.
9. Records of the Joint Boycott Council, Unsorted, Miscellaneous Material, NYPL.
10. Ibid., Dr. Tenenbaum's Speeches 1936–38 (2) folder. The speech does not carry a specific date. However, an attached note states that it was delivered sometime after November 10, 1938.
11. Ibid. Minutes folder.
12. Archives of Dr. Joseph Tenenbaum "Speeches" 1939–1961, YIVO. Dr. Tenenbaum made this statement in a radio address delivered on Station WHOM on August 13, 1939. The YIVO contains a Yiddish version of this address. The quoted paragraph was translated into English by this writer.

Documents

DOCUMENT NO. I: THE RACISTS' DECALOGUE

"TEN GERMAN COMMANDMENTS OF LAWFUL SELF-DEFENSE"†*

1. Be proud of being a German and strive earnestly and steadily to practice the inherited virtues of our people, courage, faithfulness and veracity, and to inspire and develop these virtues in thy children.
2. Thou shalt know that thou, together with all thy fellow Germans, regardless of faith or creed, hast a common implacable foe. His name is Jew.
3. Thou shalt keep thy blood pure. Consider it a crime to soil the noble Aryan breed of thy people by mingling it with the Jewish breed. For thou must know that Jewish blood is everlasting, putting the Jewish stamp on body and soul unto the farthest generations.
4. Thou shalt be helpful to thy fellow German and further him in all matters not counter to the German conscience, the more so if he be pressed by the Jew. Thou shalt at once take into court any offense or crime committed by the Jew in deed, word of letter, that comes to thy knowledge, lest the Jew abuse the laws of our country with impunity.
5. Thou shalt have no social intercourse with the Jew. Avoid all contact and community with the Jew and keep him away from thyself and thy family, especially thy daughters, lest they suffer injury in body and soul.

*Theodor, Fritsch, *Antisemiten-Katechismus* (Leipzig, 1893), pp. 358 ff. (from Paul Messing's *Rehearsal for Destruction*, p. 306).

6. Thou shalt have no business relations with the Jew. Never choose a Jew as a business partner, nor borrow nor buy from him, and keep your wife, too, from doing so. Thou shalt sell nothing to him, nor use him as an agent in thy transactions, that thou mayest remain free and not become a slave unto the Jew nor help to increase his money, which is the power by which he enslaves our people.
7. Thou shalt drive the Jew from thy own breast and take no example from Jewish tricks and Jewish wiles, for thou shalt never match the Jew in trickery, but punishment of the courts.
8. Thou shalt not entrust thy rights to a Jewish lawyer, nor thy body to a Jewish physician, nor thy children to a Jewish teacher lest thy honor, body and soul suffer harm.
9. Thou shalt not lend ear nor give credence to the Jew. Keep away all Jewish writings from thy German home and thy family.
10. Thou shalt use no violence against the Jews because it is unworthy of thee and against the law. But if a Jew attacks thee, ward off his Semitic insolence with German wrath.

DOCUMENT NO. II: THE NAZI PARTY PLATFORM—JEWISH REFERENCES*

4. None but members of the nation may be citizens of the State. None but those of German blood, whatever their creed, may be members of the nation. No Jew, therefore, may be a member of the nation.
5. Anyone who is not a citizen of the State may live in Germany only as a guest and must be regarded as being subject to foreign laws.
6. The right of voting on the State's government and legislation is to be enjoyed by the citizen of the State alone. We demand therefore that all official appointments, of whatever kind, whether in the Reich, in the country (i.e. "states"), or in the smaller localities, shall be granted to citizens of the State alone.
7. We demand that the State shall make it its first duty to promote the industry and livelihood of citizens of the State. If it is not possible to nourish the entire population of the State, foreign nationals (non-citizens of the State) must be excluded from the Reich.
8. All non-German immigration must be prevented. We demand that all non-Germans, who entered Germany subsequent to August 2nd, 1914, shall be required forthwith to depart from the Reich.
23. We demand legal warfare against conscious political lying and its dissemination in the press. In order to facilitate the creation of a German national press we demand:

   a. that all editors of newspapers and their assistants, employing the German language, must be members of the nation;

*Reprinted from *The Jews in Nazi Germany* (New York: American Jewish Committee, 1935), pp. 16–17.

b. that special permission from the State shall be necessary before non-German newspapers may appear. These are not necessarily printed in the German language;
c. That non-Germans shall be prohibited by law from participating financially in or influencing German newspapers, and that the penalty for contravention of the law shall be suppression of any such newspaper, and immediate deportation of the non-German concerned in it.

24. We demand liberty for all religious denominations in the State, so far as they are not a danger to it and do not militate against the moral feelings of the German race.

    The Party, as such, stands for positive Christianity, but does not bind itself in the matter of creed to any particular confession. It combats the Jewish materialist spirit within us and without us, and is convinced that our nation can only achieve permanent health from within on that principle.

MUNICH, 24 February 1920.

DOCUMENT NO. III: THE BOYCOTT MANIFESTO—INSTRUCTIONS*

1. In every local branch and unit of the N.S.D.A.P., Committees of Action must be appointed immediately to carry out a systematically planned boycott of Jewish business, Jewish doctors and Jewish lawyers. The Committees of Action are responsible that the boycott does not affect any innocent persons, but hits so much harder the guilty ones.
2. The Committees of Action are responsible for the most careful protection of all foreigners without regard to confession, origin or race. The boycott is a purely defensive measure which is directed solely against German Jewry.
3. The Committees of Action must immediately popularize the boycott by propaganda and enlightenment. Its keynote is that no good German will now buy from a Jew, nor will he accept offers of goods from a Jew or his puppets.
4. In doubtful cases, boycotting of the concerns in question may be dispensed with until the Central Committee in Munich can take a definite decision. Party Comrade Streicher is appointed chairman of the boycott committee.
5. The Committees of Action must watch the newspapers closely and observe how strongly they participate in the campaign of enlightenment of the German people against Jewish atrocity agitation

*Reprinted from *The Jews in Nazi Germany* (New York, American Jewish Committee, 1935), pp. 40–42.

abroad. Papers which do not participate or do so only to a limited extent are to be immediately removed from every home in which Germans live. No German and no German business shall give advertising to such papers. They must fall into public contempt.
6. The Committee of Action, in cooperation with the Work Cells organization of the party, must carry enlightenment into the factories as to the effects of the Jewish atrocity agitation to German work and therefore to German workers. In particular, the workers must be enlightened as to the necessity for a national boycott as a defensive measure to protect German labor.
7. The Committees of Action must penetrate into the smallest villages in order particularly to strike at Jewish traders in the country. It must always be explained that this action has been forced upon us as a defensive measure.
8. The boycott is not to start in a scattered fashion but must begin at one stroke, and all preparations are now to be toward this end. Orders will be issued to the Storm Troopers to warn the people, through pickets, from entering Jewish shops from the moment the boycott begins. The start of the boycott will be announced by placards, by the press, by handbills, etc. The boycott will begin on the stroke of 10 A.M. on Saturday, April 1. It will continue until an order of the party executive decrees its end.
9. The Committees of Action shall immediately organize tens of thousands of mass meetings which shall reach into the tiniest hamlets and which shall demand the introduction of a quota system for Jews in all professions. In order to intensify the effect of this action, these demands shall be confined for the present to the following three categories:

   a. Attendance at German middle and higher schools (colleges);
   b. Doctors; and
   c. Lawyers.

10. The Committees of Action have the further task of seeing to it that every German who has any connections whatsoever in foreign countries shall make use of them to spread the truth in letters, telegrams and telephone messages: that peace and order prevail in Germany, that the German people has no more ardent wish than to pursue its work in peace and to live in peace with the rest of the world and that it is conducting its struggle against Jewish atrocity agitation as a purely defensive battle.
11. The Committees of Action are responsible that the entire struggle be conducted in complete peace and strictest discipline. As before, not a hair on any Jewish head shall be touched. We will cope with this agitation only by means of the decisive pressure of these measures.

Voelkischer Beobachter, 29 March 1933

DOCUMENT NO. IV: THE BOYCOTT MANIFESTO—SUPPLEMENTS*

1. The leaders of the local committees for the defense against the Jewish agitation and atrocity propaganda are to be appointed immediately by the respective authorities of the Political Organization. It is advisable to appoint the district leaders of the Fighting League of the professional middle-class as leaders of the district committees, since that N.S. organization, owing to its character, commands the material and experience required for the organization of the defense action. Of course, considerations of personal suitability of the appointee remain untouched.
2. The committees of action (whose members must have no ties whatever with Jews) shall ascertain immediately which shops, department stores, offices, etc., are in Jewish hands.
3. This of course concerns enterprises which are in the hands of members of the Jewish race. Note that the religion is immaterial. Business men who were converted to Catholicism or Protestantism, or dissenters, of Jewish race, are also Jews in the sense of this decree.
4. Firms in which Jews are interested only financially will be subject to regulations yet to be enacted.
5. If the husband of a non-Jewish proprietress is Jewish, then the enterprise is considered Jewish. The same applies when the proprietress is a Jewess and the husband a non-Jew.
6. Shops with uniform prices, department stores, chain-stores which are in German hands do not fall under this boycott action. The "Woolworth" uniform-price stores are also exempt. This firm is American and non-Jewish besides. The so-called "Wohlwert" uniform-price stores, however, are Jewish and therefore to be boycotted.
7. The committees of action shall hand the lists of the enterprises ascertained to be Jewish to the SA and SS so that these can post the pickets on Saturday morning, April 1st, at 10 o'clock sharp.
8. The guards are to inform the public that the picketed enterprise is Jewish. They have to warn them against buying in the particular shop. Forcible measures are prohibited. It is also forbidden to close the shops, break shop-windows, or cause other material damages.
9. To make Jewish shops recognizable, posters or placards are to be fixed to the front doors showing a yellow spot on black ground.
10. Dismissals of non-Jewish employees and workers by the boycotted Jewish shops are not permitted; notice may not be given. Where this has already happened, the NSBO, in cooperation with the SA, has to arrange for reinstatement.
11. On Friday evening, March 31st, 1933, the committees of action, in

*Reprinted from *The Jews in Nazi Germany* (New York: American Jewish Committee, 1935), pp. 42–44.

cooperation with the political leaders, will hold great mass-demonstrations and parades in all places. On this occasion banners are to be carried, bearing the following inscriptions:

   a. "For the Defense Against the Jewish atrocity and boycott agitation!"
   b. "Boycott all Jewish Shops, beginning tomorrow morning at 10 o'clock!"

   In the larger cities meetings are to be held in as many public places as possible.
12. On Saturday morning, at 10 o'clock at the latest, the posters with the boycott proclamation must be fixed to all hoardings in cities and villages. At the same time, posters with the following inscriptions, in the order given, have to be carried through the streets on motortrucks or, still better, moving vans:

   "For the defense against the Jewish atrocity and boycott agitation!"
   "Boycott all Jewish shops!"
   "Don't buy in Jewish department stores!"
   "Don't consult Jewish lawyers!"
   "Avoid Jewish physicians!"
   "The Jews are our misfortune!"

13. For the financing of this defensive action the committees shall organize a fund-raising campaign among the German businessmen.
14. In addition, the committees for the defense against the Jewish atrocity and boycott agitation are subjected to the decrees of the Reichsadministration of the NSDAP.

Voelkischer Beobachter, 30 March 1933

DOCUMENT NO. V: OUSTERS OF JEWISH OFFICIALS AND JEWISH PROFESSIONALS*

A. THE COURTS OF KOENIGSBERG OCCUPIED BY STORM-TROOPERS

As a counter-measure to the atrocity propaganda against the German people for the purpose of restoring clean, incorruptible administration of justice, and last but not least, for the purpose of protecting Jewish citizens against possible outbreaks on the part of the population which is greatly aroused on account of the atrocity propaganda, S.A. divisions

*Reprinted from *The Jews in Nazi Germany* (New York: American Jewish Committee, 1935), pp. 35–37.

have occupied today the Superior Court at Koenigsberg, Prussia, as well as the district and county court.

Members of the Jewish race are forbidden to enter these buildings. In order to avoid a discontinuity of the administration of justice, some lawyers of the Jewish race as to whom it can be proved that they fought in the first ranks of the front lines during the War, will be permitted by the S.A., on the basis of special proofs of identity, to enter the court buildings, and at the same time to settle the case of the members of their race.

Voelkischer Beobachter, 1 April 1933

B. GERMAN TEACHERS FOR GERMAN CHILDREN

The State-Commissioner for the Berlin Board of Education decreed that, until further notice, all teachers who have Jewish blood in their veins be immediately dismissed from all schools of Berlin.

Voelkischer Beobachter, 3 April 1933

C. NONE BUT GERMAN PHYSICIANS FOR THE PATIENTS OF BERLIN SOCIAL SERVICE

At the beginning of the boycott movement against the atrocity propaganda on the 1st of April, the State Commissioner Dr. Klein, caused all Jewish physicians of the Social Service of the city of Berlin to be removed from service and be replaced by physicians of German stock. Seventy-two National Socialist physicians have taken upon themselves this extremely difficult service as a matter of honor. National Socialist physicians are also gratuitously at the disposal of the dispensaries of the National Health Service and especially at the disposal of the hospitals.

Voelkischer Beobachter, 3 April 1933

D. REMOVAL OF THE JEWS FROM THE FIELDS OF JUSTICE AND ADMINISTRATION

A conference with State-Ministers of Justice will be held on Friday in the Reich-Ministry of Justice for the purpose of preparing a uniform regulation concerning the appearance and admission of Jewish lawyers to the courts.

The Reich Commissioner for Baden, in order to appease the population and in the best interests of the Jews of Baden, has ordered that all members of the Jewish race be removed at once until further notice, from the Civil Service, from state plants, communes and enterprises of communes and from all bodies of a public nature, as well as from private schools.

Voelkischer Beobachter, 7 April 1933

DOCUMENT NO. VI: ALDJR'S BOYCOTT RESOLUTION*

Since the advent of Adolph Hitler and his party, the National Socialists, to power in Germany, the civilized world has been shocked by the inhuman persecution of the Jews in that country. The atrocious anti-Jewish propaganda carried on by the Hitler party for the preceding thirteen years, now became the official governmental policy of Germany. This policy served as a convenient blind for the utter inability of the Nazis to cope constructively with the serious problems confronting Germany today.

In pursuance of this policy, the Hitler government expelled all Jews from public office, which they earned by sheer merit; drove them from all professions which they graced by their learning and ability; took over Jewish business establishments and placed its Nazi henchmen in charge of them; drove tens of thousands of Jews to economic ruin and hundreds of them to suicide. Jews were beaten, robbed and tortured, and when they dared complain, they were incarcerated and many of them were "Spurloss versaenkt" (without a trace).

When the cries of pain and suffering of our brethren reached us across the ocean and we protested, the Nazis, with their characteristic impudence and utter disregard of the truth, not only denied that any atrocities have been committed, but, in order to scare us into silence, proclaimed a boycott against the Jews for a limited period. Since that time, they have persistently waged a war of extermination upon the Jews of Germany. They have prohibited Germans from consulting Jewish physicians and advocates, ousted from colleges and universities every professor and teacher whose forefathers were Jews, forced Germans to divorce their Jewish wives or husbands, in order to retain some government jobs, limited the number of Jewish students in schools and universities to less than 1 per cent, expelled from hospital service every one having 25 per cent of Jewish blood in his veins, and generally, sought to degrade the Jews to a state of pariahs.

The protesting and appealing voice of humanity proved futile. It is amply clear that the present rulers of Germany cannot be affected by moral suasion, and that the only means of combatting the policies and acts of the present regime in Germany is an economic boycott of goods, products and services emanating from Germany.

Now, therefore, we the delegates representing trade, social, fraternal and religious organizations, in conference assembled at Hotel Astor, New York City, this 14th day of May, 1933, conscious of our grave responsibility, in taking this action, and deploring its necessity.

Do hereby solemnly proclaim that it is the duty of every Jew and Jewess in the United States of America to boycott all goods, materials or products manufactured, raised or improved in Germany, or any part

*NYT, 15 May 1933

thereof, all German shipping, freight and traffic services, as well as all German health, pleasure and other resorts, and generally to abstain from any act which would in any manner lend material support to the present regime in Germany.

It is especially understood that the foregoing measures are directed exclusively against the goods, products and services of the German Reich proper, and shall continue until all the anti-Jewish laws, edicts and policies have been wholly repealed and renounced.

Be it further resolved that this conference directs that the American League for the Defense of Jewish rights and its affiliated bodies take such further action as may be necessary to carry the foregoing resolutions into effect.

DOCUMENT NO. VII: THE BOYCOTT RESOLUTION OF THE WORLD JEWISH ECONOMIC CONFERENCE*

Whereas the Jews of Germany have for centuries been imbedded in its soil and are loyal, useful and law-abiding citizens who have fully sacrificed their lives for their fatherland in times of war and have contributed to its prosperity and won world-wide distinction in all the arts and sciences and in literature and the professions, manifestly out of proportion to population; and

Whereas world opinion and the unanimous outcry, protests and demonstrations of Jews and non-Jews throughout the civilized world against the incredibly inhuman policy of the Hitler government toward the Jews of Germany have been unavailing; and

Whereas the Hitler Government has repeatedly expressed its determination to persist in its policy of persecution and to drive the Jews of Germany from every branch of activity in public and private life, to annihilate them economically, to deprive them of their citizenship, to reduce them to the state of pariahs and eventually to exterminate them; and

Whereas Germany under the leadership of the Nazi Government has established and is continuing and enlarging a relentless persecution of the Jews in every walk of life; now, therefore, be it

Resolved, That boycotting of German goods, products and shipping throughout the civilized world is the only effective weapon for world Jewry and humanity by way of defense and protection of Jewish rights, property and dignity in Germany.

And that we reaffirm the decision heretofore reached and now actively on the way in the form of independent action by Jews or non-Jews, to continue and internationally organize and prosecute throughout the world the boycott heretofore instituted and now in existence in the

*NYT, 21 July 1934

various countries represented by the delegates here assembled and in other countries not so represented.

We earnestly urge all the men and women of the civilized world, irrespective of race or creed, to support and join in this movement against brutal fanaticism and bigotry and to help to lead it to a victorious conclusion and until the last trace of barbarous persecutions has been eliminated from the political program and actions of the German Government.

DOCUMENT NO. VIII: BOYCOTT PROGRAMS PRESENTED TO THE AMERICAN JEWISH CONGRESS

A. Proposal for the Organization of the Boycott.*

Now that the boycott against Hitler's regime has been officially declared, the time has come for intensive work and speedy action in order to attain the desired results and aims within the shortest period of time.

In view of the fact that the heaviest imports from Germany occur from June to October inclusive, efforts should be exerted to regain as much as possible of the time that has been lost so far.

The proposal is ready to undertake this fight for years. Realizing the enemy's might and Jewish (i.e. sympathizing people) commercial inferiority, an active militant buildup must be secured.

The following rough outlines are proposed:

1. The establishment of branches of the American Jewish Congress in every Jewish community in the U.S.A., or work through organizations already existing in each locality.
2. Arousing public opinion and enlistment by written pledges of as many individuals as possible throughout the country, irrespective of creed.
3. Enlistment of all Jewish organizations and such of other religions whose sincere co-operation can be depended upon (political, scientific, foreign, national, sport, singing and other associations; also schools, colleges and universities).
4. Creation and training of active calls within each group for propaganda purposes and enrollment of new members; for this activity, young men and women should preferably be chosen—students or suitable unemployed individuals.
5. Solicitation of public expressions from prominent men in favor of our movement.
6. Enlistment of department stores, wholesale importers, custom brokers, agencies for shipping and traveling. If the wholehearted co-

*Submitted by Eugine Borovitz, August 23, 1933. Records of the Joint Boycott Council, Program on Boycott folder, 1933–1934, NYPL.

operation of such retail firms could be obtained as Macy's, Gimbel's, Wanamaker's, Hahn's chain stores, Filene's in Boston, Marshall Field in Chicago, Hudson in Detroit, etc. etc., the battle would be half won.

7. Supervision of every incoming and outgoing German steamer, examination of passenger lists and freight manifests.
8. There are throughout the country thousands of German singing, bowling and other "Vereine" who have considerable numbers of Jewish members. These should be encouraged to maintain their membership and to act as our co-operators and also to counteract against Hitler propaganda.
9. Some form and way of reminder should be found to be exercised at every Jewish gathering, be it in Temples, homes or public halls (weddings, birth ceremonies, dances, picnics, etc.).
10. Active co-operation of teachers and students in high schools, colleges and universities should be particularly encouraged.
11. Co-operation from members of Labor Unions and Socialistic organizations should be solicited. If it is within the principles and policies of the American Jewish Congress, I would suggest a conference with the leaders of the Socialistic Party and also of unions for the purpose of obtaining their official co-operation, if possible.
12. Correspondence and co-operation with the central organizations for the boycott in all foreign countries; also contact with all prominent personages who felt compelled to flee from Germany-waiters, scientists, politicians, etc.
13. Enlistment of shipping agents (spediteure) in Czechoslovakia, Austria, Hungary, Poland and Switzerland, who are in most cases Jews, for the purpose of directing their shipments for USA via Trieste, or as to avoid even rail-transportation through Germany and which cannot be done for shipments via Belgium or Holland. If necessary, it should be endeavored to obtain from the respective governments adjustment of freight rates.
14. Periodical issue of propaganda literature is essential. There should be a publication showing that anti-Semitism was the cardinal's point of Hitler's party since its inception, thereby proving that the murders, assaults and crimes were premeditated and not a consequence or necessity for so-called "atrocity lies." A list of all decrees issued aiming at persecution and extermination of Jews, liberals and Marxists. Those publications should be supplemented from time to time by additions as they occur and by suitable exhortations and encouragements.
15. All Jewish dailies and periodicals should be induced to show in every issue at a conspicuous place some slogan as a daily reminder, like, for instance, "Remember Our Brethren."
16. It should be endeavored to have German scientific and other essential books reproduced in other countries, as far as this would be legally possible.

17. Wholesale importers usually know the sources where they can get equipment or similar replacements of their particular line of German goods. Nevertheless, this angle could also be cultivated.
18. Charges should be in writing. That is, printed forms in the shape of index cards to be signed by pledger, who shall be given a copy showing also instructions how to recognize goods produced in Germany, and emphasizing avoidance of the use of German steamers and of traveling to and in Germany. Pledge cards should be provided with serial numbers and should indicate age, occupation, creed and other dates concerning the pledger (for ulterior index and classification purposes).

To cover the tremendous costs of printing, postage and correspondence, each pledge should be accompanied by a contribution towards a boycott fund. Surplus funds could be used from time to time to transport emigrants from Germany. Buttons, pins, appropriate emblems or slogans could also be used on suitable occasions.

B. Suggestions for the Boycott Campaign*
Any plan should be divided into two major functioning divisions:

a. Industrial
b. Public

A Joint Steering Committee should be appointed at once with three representatives each from the cooperating organizations. This Committee should organize (a) a so-called "Public Committee," which, in my opinion, should consist mainly of Gentiles with recognized names, and several Jewish representatives.

The boycott movement should attempt to draft or pay for an Executive Director who would be given full power to carry out the program with relentless intensity on the basis of the stated policy. What I seek is a Col. Johnson and should like to submit the following list of names:

1. Nicholas Kelly
2. Raymond Fosdick
3. Arthur Woods
4. Amos Pinchot
5. Charles Burlingham
6. Ralph Hayes

I can help to go after a number of these.
The alleged voluntary acceptance of the leadership by such an individual, backed by a committee of notable figures, would gain first page

*Records of the Joint Boycott Council, File Case C, 1933 folder, NYPL.

stories throughout the country and achieve priceless acceptance and conviction on the part of the public.

Program:

A. Industrial: An immediate investigation should be made of all businesses which are—

1. Presently buying from Germany
2. Selling German goods

A score of investigators should be on the job to collate this information through solicitations by:

1. Mail
2. Personal purchases
3. Personal questioning

Simultaneously, these companies should be informed of an organized plan underway to crystalize public opinion on the subject, on the basis of every argument but the reprisal, which I believe, would be a blunder.

The re-enforcement of the work of the investigators by a coordinated program of publicity—newspaper, radio, mail, public speaking and word of mouth—drives on the public would have its eventual results.

Aside from the initial announcement of the appointment of the major committee and the Executive Director, it is my opinion that it would be unwise to promote much further publicity on the subject. A quiet boycott, well organized, well-knit, reflecting the wholehearted cooperation of all organizations, Jewish and Gentile, would have far more results than a constant repetition of the boycott story from which the edge will be worn very soon.

I. A. Hirschman

August 28, 1933.

C. Program for the Boycott Department.*

1. Create through an extensive research an Information Bureau to compile vital material with reference to:

   a. a complete list of items exported from Germany to the United States.
   b. a complete list of similar items and countries where items may be secured.
   c. a preparation of list of manufacturers and firms in the U.S. and

Submitted by Julius Schwartz (undated)
*Records of the Joint Boycott Council, General correspondence file, 1933–1935, Program on the Boycott folder, NYPL.

foreign countries producing articles to substitute for German products.
    d. a periodical study showing comparative figures of German products affected by the boycott.
2. Establishing contact with and securing pledges of co-operation from Jewish importers, wholesalers, jobbers, etc.
3. Organize in every Jewish community throughout the country local boycott committees. These committees (are) to secure volunteers to make thorough canvases of all Jewish retail shops with a view of securing complete co-ordination.
4. An educational campaign to be carried on through lectures, communications and notices on bulletin boards in: Synagogues, Temples, Centers, clubs, women's organizations, societies, fraternal orders, Hebrew schools, etc.
5. Offer of cooperation to an American Federation of Labor executing the boycott by making available information secured through research and recommendation of methods to make the campaign more effective. (This offer is to be made unofficially.)
6. Cooperate with existing authoritative bodies and organizations, Jewish and non-Jewish, in foreign countries where boycott measures have been adopted.
    Staff: a. Research Director;
           b. Two assistants.
    Organization of activities is to be carried out in co-operation with the Organization Department.

DOCUMENT NO. IX: BOYCOTT DECLARATION OF THE AMERICAN JEWISH CONGRESS

During the six months that have elapsed since Hitler's appointment the Congress scrupulously refrained from taking drastic action in the hope that the voice of outraged public opinion and diplomatic representations by the American Government might yet succeed in paving the way for a more humane settlement of the Jewish question in Germany ... after wholesale dismissal of Jews from professions and civil employment, barring them from teaching and enrollment in the schools, after a savage boycott agitation against Jewish trade and industry, now Jewish labor too has been made ineligible for work by making the application for membership in the labor organization contingent on Aryan descent for three generations. All Jewish citizens naturalized since 1918, have been disenfranchised, and a law is being promulgated to deprive native Jews of their inviolable rights of citizenship.

*Records of the Joint Boycott Council, Boycott Resolutions and Statements folder, NYPL.

In view of such horrible crimes, and in view of a recent pronouncement by the German Chancellor that there will be no let-up in the anti-Jewish drive, the Executive Committee of the American Jewish Congress has come to the conclusion that no mercy can be expected from the savage tyrants now in the seat of the German Government, and that it is the duty of the American Jewish Congress, which stands for the defense of Jewish rights, to use all its available resources for the promotion of a vigorous and relentless nationwide Boycott movement for the self-defense of outraged humanity against the orgy of brutal persecution by the present masters of Germany.

Therefore, be it resolved that the American Jewish Congress is called upon:

1. To promote a nation-wide Boycott movement in this country.
2. To coordinate and integrate all existing agencies and sporadic endeavors under a unified leadership charged with the sole authority of representing the common will of the people and equipped with all the necessary means for an efficient organization of the Boycott movement.
3. To appeal in the name of common humanity to all the citizens of this great country of liberty and equality, and to enlist the cooperation of organizations, groups and individuals, irrespective of race, creed and partisanship, with a view of making the boycott of German goods and shipping air-tight and national in scope.
4. To enlist the cooperation and good-will of the representatives of the A.F. of L., Trade Unions, and other labor groups, for the declaration of a boycott along the lines of the announcement of the National Council of Labor in Great Britain on July 19.
5. To start a campaign of publicity and enlightenment as to the aims and scope of the Boycott movement, especially with regard to our co-citizens of German extraction with a view of clarifying the aims of the Boycott as by no means directed against the German people, but against the perfidious and barbaric methods of the Nazi Government; and that it is as much, if not more, in the interests of the German people as it is of the entire human race to combat the Nazi menace under whose yoke and shame the good name, the sanity and prosperity of Germany, as well as the most sacred interests of humanity, have been so grievously wronged and jeopardized.

Confirmed in the belief that the Hitlerite war upon the Jews constitutes a violation of the fundamental principles of justice, humanity and progress dear to the heart of civilized mankind irrespective of race, creed, partisanship or class distinction, we appeal to every right-thinking American to join in with the American Jewish Congress in its effort to conquer reaction and barbarism and restore liberty and justice in the German Reich.

DOCUMENT NO. X: THE ANTI-GERMAN BOYCOTT*—A STATEMENT OF THE POSITION OF THE AMERICAN JEWISH COMMITTEE (For the confidential information of Sustaining Members of the Committee).

IN THE immediate crisis presented by the situation in Germany, the object of the American Jewish Committee is:

1. To relieve the pressure upon the Jews and to have their human and civil rights restored to them. Our paramount motive is that of helping the German Jews.
2. With equal constancy and concern, the Committee seeks to guard the civil and religious rights of the Jews all over the world.

How will an official boycott, that is, a boycott against Germany, endorsed and promoted by responsible Jewish organizations, affect the carrying out of these aims? The movement in favor of the boycott is a natural expression of indignation at the persecutions in Germany. The impulse to strike back is understandable. But the Committee, conscious of the need for unassailable and most effective steps, has taken a position against an official Jewish boycott, guided by the following considerations:

(1) *An official boycott against Germany will immediately provide the pretext for further excesses against the Jews in Germany.*

It will lead to retaliatory measures. The statement is frequently made that the Jews in Germany can not be injured more than they have been. This is far from true. If it is the opinion of the responsible Jewish leaders that nothing can help the Jews in Germany, then they have in fact been deceiving the Jewish and the general community by participating in all the work of counter propaganda, public enlightenment, and appeals to the German conscience, of the past six months. *It is not true* that the Jews in Germany can meet with no severer treatment. Those who make that statement shut off the nightmares of pogroming, the possibilities of wholesale concentration in prison camps, deprivation of the citizenship of native Jews, the denial of the right to employment of those Jews who are still employed, etc. Reinhold Niebuhr, a distinguished and influential Christian leader, in an article in the "Christian Century" has said:

"The total situation is such a dismal one that one wonders whether anything can be done to prevent one of the darkest pages in modern history from becoming even more tragic. The Jewish boycott will probably do more harm than good, at least from the perspective of the Jews who are still in Germany and who must suffer from the increased ferocity which the boycott instills in the Nazis. *This boycott is like waging*

*Archives of the American Jewish Committee, New York, N.Y.

a war against a nation which holds over a million of your own hostages and which may be sufficiently angered by hostilities practically to exterminate the hostages. The fact is that all Jewish actions, whether boycotts or protests, are insignificant in their effect compared to what Christian pressure might be able to accomplish."

(2) *By entering on a boycott we may forfeit the friendship of Christians in many countries, including our own, and their help in our efforts to restore to the Jews in Germany their status as an integral part of the country.*
These Christians whose friendship for the Jews cannot be questioned, among them a number of leading world figures, have urged against violent demonstrations and "punitive measures" of all kinds. There is even the possibility that some Christian groups, for practical or ethical reasons, will publicly disavow the boycott and thus further confuse the public mind.

(3) *An official Jewish boycott of Germany would immediately crystallize a cleavage between German Christians abroad who number many millions, and Jews outside of Germany.*
The numbers, the wealth, the influence, and the importance of these German Christians, cannot be underestimated. Out of a sense of injured patriotism, these Germans, many of whom are opposed to Hitler, will be drawn into an alignment with the Hitler regime, and against their Jewish fellow citizens in the various countries. Whatever we do, we must convince our non-Jewish German neighbors and friends that the Jews are not hostile to Germany and the German people, that we sincerely believe that the present situation is only a tragic interlude, and that it is to the interest of Germany herself and to people of German origin everywhere to work together for a restoration of the fundamental rights of the Jews in Germany and a return to a rational and friendly relations between them and the population at large.

(4) *The boycott will lead to a general retaliation against Jewish business.*
Here it must not be overlooked, despite specious appeals to chauvinism and inflamed (although justified) Jewish resentment, that this means a battle of approximately 15,000,000 Jews all over the world against at least 100,000,000 Germans all over the world. The world is too well integrated economically not to have the boycott affect the wielders of it at least as much as those against whom it is being employed. We have already had instances of this link. Jews in Mexico who joined in a boycott on German goods are now being boycotted largely through the instrumentality of Germans and pro-Germans. The Jews in Mexico have appealed to the Jewish organizations in the United States to protect them against this counter boycott and the anti-Jewish agitation which has resulted from it. The Latvian Jews joined the boycott of Germany; Germany retaliated by an embargo on Latvian butter. Latvian Jews, desperate at the loss of an important market, then turned to the Joint Foreign Committee of England for aid in finding a substitute market. In

passing, we cannot forego pointing out that the groups now sponsoring a boycott will be utterly unable to meet the subsequent Jewish problems that will arise as a result of their actions.

(5) *There are special unfortunate consequences of this boycott likely to develop in individual countries.*

Countries which are political and economic rivals of Germany may, for purposes of their own economy, have a benevolent attitude toward this boycott, but in the United States, for example, an effective boycott of German goods is likely to have an unfavorable reaction. The United States has for a number of years been exporting very much more than it has been importing from Germany. Should trade from Germany be curtailed as a result of retaliatory measure to such a degree that it will affect American merchants, they may point to the Jew as the cause of the already complicated economic situation. Furthermore, the United States has at least a billion dollars worth of investments in Germany. The collapse of German economic life would mean that these investments would, for a time at least, be valueless. Among the investors there are Jews who may be willing to make the sacrifice; but the non-Jews cannot be expected to accept their loss without complaint. The hard-hit American investor may look for a scapegoat in the Jew.

(6) *As a method of practical politics, the boycott is unwise.*

So long as responsible organizations like the American Jewish Committee, the Joint Foreign Committee, and the Alliance Israelite have publicly confirmed their disapproval of a boycott and other warlike measures, the door will not have been closed to an understanding between the Nazi authorities and the Jewish population of Germany.

The efforts we are making to enlist the intercession of governments and the League of Nations can be made only more difficult by punitive measures on the part of Jews.

(7) *The boycott is likely to stimulate anti-Semitic activity.*

(a) Whether successful or not it will strengthen the hands of the anti-Semites, who make use of the myth that the Jews exert a so-called "world economic influence."

(b) Even if it should be successful, and that is highly doubtful, it will mean that concessions from the present regime will have been obtained for the Jews under the great pressure of a boycott (which means a war). But the world's experience with Germany as a result of the World War has shown that such a forced victory will result in a vicious counter-reaction. German Jews have asked that no organized boycott be put into effect for fear that the hostilities between Jew and non-Jew will become more deep-seated and that it would only be a matter of time before a more violent outbreak would occur. In the face of limited immigration possibilities the majority of Jews must continue to live in Germany, which they still love as their Fatherland.

(c) Should the boycott bring about a collapse, in any way leading to communism or strengthening communism in Germany, the Jews will have to bear the charge of encouragement to communism in addition to the present widespread, although baseless charge of Jewish activity in Russian communism.

(8) *The boycott is open to an ethical objection.*

We must keep our fight for the restoration of the rights of the German Jews on the plane of moral rectitude. The theory of the Jews has been that the group must not be punished for the misbehavior of individual members within it. They should carry that theory to the point, hard as it is today, of applying it to all of Germany as against its present Nazi rulers.

(9) *The Jews must be concerned for the likely effects of the boycott in the future.*

Heretofore, when Jews have been attacked by the boycott method, they have had a legitimate right to appeal to public authority and to the conscience of the world at large. They will endanger that right if they themselves engage this weapon at the present time.

CONCLUDING REMARKS

Despite the frenzied chauvinism in Germany and elsewhere throughout the world, we will not, indeed, we dare not, admit that the elemental rights to life and liberty have been permanently laid low. The civilized world, which is overwhelmed at this time by an unprecedented depression, which has produced political issues of the gravest kind, may not be in the position to defend or even assert these principles in a formal way. But we Jews must not accept the situation in Germany as a permanent disaster, or believe that the civilized world will be willing to accept that situation as normal and unchangeable. Just as the American union could not exist half-slave, half-free, so Europe cannot exist with so large and important a country as Germany, in its very centre, conducting itself as a nation of the dark ages. To accept the defeat as permanent would be a repudiation of the ideals of peace and justice proclaimed by our prophets, for which the Jews have suffered for twenty or more centuries. Because these ideals are the foundation of Christian civilization we must believe that Christendom will itself before long protect them from destruction.

*DOCUMENT NO. XI: THE BOYCOTT RESOLUTION OF THE SECOND WORLD JEWISH CONFERENCE**

The World Jewish Conference notes with deepest satisfaction that from the beginning of the Hitler regime and its anti-Jewish laws and acts the Jewish people instinctively and spontaneously resorted to the one

*This resolution was introduced by Dr. Wise.
Reprinted from Protocoles de la IIe Conference Juive Mondiale, Geneva, Switzerland.

immediately accessible weapon of self-defense: a moral and economic boycott. In the spirit of individual and collective self-respect, the Jewish people through the boycott affirms that Jews cannot hold any economic or other relation with the Nazi Government of the Third Reich and believes that its boycott must continue to be shared by millions of non-Jews in all lands, who understand and sympathize with the Jewish people's abhorrence of the Nazi anti-Jewish precept and practice.

When the Jewish boycott of German goods and wards is to be ended depends not upon the Jewish people but upon the Nazi Government. This instrumentality of moral and economic pressure Jews have been compelled reluctantly to adopt and utilize. But they will not lay this down until such time as the great wrong inflicted upon German Jews is undone and the German Jews once again be placed in the status and position which were rightly their own before the accession of the Hitler Government. The Conference solemnly calls upon the Jewish people loyally to continue in their legitimate, honorable and peaceable resistance against the war waged by Hitlerism upon the German Jews and upon the whole Jewish people.

DOCUMENT NO. XII: RESOLUTIONS OF THE NATIONAL BOYCOTT CONFERENCE*

Resolution No. 1: Whereas, the Nazi Government of Germany has violated every principle of humanity in depriving the Jewish citizens of Germany of their elementary rights of citizenship, in outlawing them from public office, in restricting them in the liberal professions, in denying their children opportunities of education, in depriving them of the means of livelihood, and by their cruel persecutions it has driven thousands of them to ruin, to exile, and to suicide, and,

Whereas, the Nazi regime has destroyed all the democratic institutions of Germany, outlawed all opposition parties, suppressed all freedom, destroyed woman's liberties and her civic usefulness and business activity, regardless of race or creed, muzzled the press, sent the best liberal minds of the country to prison camps and to exile, and has menaced the peace of the world, and,

Whereas, our protests and appeals up to now have been of no avail and the ruthless hand of tyranny is still relentlessly persecuting our defenseless people in Germany and all other freedom loving and peace loving men and women in the country,

Therefore be it resolved by the National Conference convened by the American League for the Defense of Jewish Rights, which League is the American branch of the World Jewish Economic Federation, that the boycott of all products made in Germany, and all shipping and services of that country of all agencies dealing in German goods be prosecuted with the utmost rigor until the present regime guilty of these incredible

*Reprinted from Minutes of the National Boycott Conference, September 10, 1933. Archives of the NSANL, New York, N.Y.

outrages against civilization and human decency is destroyed or until its policies are changed.

The National Conference appeals to all men and women of whatsoever race or creed to join with it in this effort and to use the boycott weapon against Germany as it is the only effective weapon left in the hands of all those who are menaced by Hitlerism.

The National Conference in urging this boycott wishes to emphasize as strongly as possible that the boycott is directed solely against the Nazi regime of Germany. It is not a declaration of hostility against the German people as such for whose present unhappy plight the Jews of the world have the profoundest sympathies. The Conference goes on record that the Jewish people is at peace with their German neighbors in this country and in every country. The Conference has been heartened by the expressions of sympathy and the offers of cooperation which have come to it from German friends in the United States.

Resolution No. 2: The National Conference calls upon the Jewish communities throughout the country to proceed at once with the organization of the boycott movement. The National Conference furthermore calls upon the Jews of America and other friends of the cause to contribute to a defense fund of $500,000 for the purpose of extending and co-ordinating the boycott activities. To this end the members of this conference representing many communities in the country, pledge themselves to raise their assigned quotas in their respective communities at their earliest opportunity.

Resolution No. 3: The National Conference invites all organizations, Jewish and non-Jewish, who are in favor of the anti-Nazi boycott to cooperate with the work of the American League for the Defense of Jewish Rights to the end that a united front may be established and maintained and a single plan of strategy made possible.

Resolution No. 4: The American League for the Defense of Jewish Rights declares that its sole activity for the present and until the boycott effort is officially ended to be the boycott against Nazi Germany. This National Conference convoked by the American League for the Defense of Jewish Rights therefore calls for the extension of the membership of the National Executive Committee of fifteen shall be elected. The National Executive Committee and the National Administrative Committee may from time to time enlarge their respective memberships by adding thereto individuals and representatives. These committees shall be charged with the prosecution of the boycott movement in all its ramifications. A nominating committee of five shall submit to this conference nominations for the National Executive Committee and the National Administrative Committee.

Resolution No. 5:† The National Conference convened by the American League for the Defense of Jewish Rights for the purpose of formulating plans for the intensification and extension of a boycott of

---

†Untermyer objected to the last resolution "because it singles out one man." The resolution was passed, however, over his objection.

German products and services throughout the U.S. hereby expresses to the Honorable Samuel Untermyer its profoundest appreciation of his peerless courage and leadership in initiating and carrying on the struggle against the German government to exterminate the Jews and to return them to the disabilities of the Middle Ages. The assembled delegates hereby pledge to Mr. Untermyer their wholehearted cooperation and unstinting loyalty to his leadership and his magnificent struggle to save from extermination 600,000 loyal and peaceable citizens and to uphold the highest ideals of humanity against the assault of the force now dominating Germany.

DOCUMENT NO. XIII: SECTIONS 132, 133, AND 134 OF TITLE 19, U.S. CODE ANNOTATED

132. MARKING IMPORTED ARTICLES AND PACKAGES TO INDICATE COUNTRY OF ORIGIN: WITHHOLDING DELIVERY.

Every article imported into the United States, which is capable of being marked, stamped, branded, or labeled, without injury, at the time of its manufacture or production, shall be marked stamped, branded, or labeled, in legible English words, in a conspicuous place that shall not be covered or obscured by any subsequent attachments or arrangements, so as to indicate the country of origin. Said marking, stamping, branding, or labeling shall be as nearly indelible and permanent as the nature of the article will permit. Any such article held in customs custody shall not be delivered until so marked, stamped, branded, or labeled, and until every such article of the importation which shall have been released from customs custody not so marked, stamped, branded or labeled, shall be marked, stamped, branded, or labeled, in accordance with such rules and regulations as the Secretary of the Treasury may prescribe. Unless the article is exported under customs supervision, there shall be levied, collected, and paid upon every such article which at the time of importation is not so marked, stamped, branded, or labeled, in addition to the regular duty imposed by law on such article, a duty of 10 per centum of the appraised value thereof, or if such article is free of duty there shall be levied, collected, and paid upon such article a duty of 10 per centum of the appraised value thereof.

Every package containing any imported article, or articles, shall be marked, stamped, branded, or labeled, in legible English words, so as to indicate clearly the country of origin. Any such package held in customs custody shall not be delivered unless so marked, stamped, branded, or

*Records of the Joint Boycott Council, Boycott Resolutions and Statements folder, NYPL.

labeled, and until every package of the importation which shall have been released from customs custody not so marked, stamped, branded, or labeled, shall be marked, stamped, branded, or labeled in accordance with such rules and regulations as the Secretary of the Treasury may prescribe.

The Secretary of the Treasury shall prescribe the necessary rules and regulations to carry out the foregoing provisions. (September 21, 1922, c. 356, Title III, Par, 304(a), 42 Stat. 936).

133. VIOLATION OF LAW REQUIRING MARKING, STAMPING, etc., PENALTY.

If any person shall fraudently violate any of the provisions of this chapter relating to the marking, stamping, branding, or labeling of any imported articles or packages or shall fraudulently deface, destroy, remove, alter or obliterate any such marks, stamps, brands, or labels with intent to conceal the information given by or contained in such marks, stamps, brands, or labels, he shall upon conviction be fined in any sum not exceeding $5,000, or be imprisoned for any time not exceeding one year, or both. (September 21, 1922, c. 356, Title III, Par. 304 (B), 42 Stat. 936).

MEDICINAL PREPARATIONS

134. NAME OF PROPRIETOR AFFIXED TO MEDICINES.

All medicinal preparations, whether chemical or otherwise, usually imported with the name of the manufacturer, shall have the true name of the manufacturer and the place where they are prepared, permanently and legibly affixed to each parcel by stamp, label, or otherwise; and all medicinal preparations imported without such names so affixed shall be adjudged to be forfeited. (R.S. Par. 2934).

DOCUMENT NO. XIV: TARIFF ACT OF 1930, SECTION 304 MARKING OF IMPORTED ARTICLES*

(a) Manner of marking. —Every article imported into the United States, and its immediate container, and the package in which such article is imported, shall be marked, stamped, branded, or labeled, in legible English words, in a conspicuous place, in such manner as to indicate the country of origin of such article, in accordance with such

*Records of the Joint Boycott Council, NYPL.

regulations as the Secretary of the Treasury may prescribe. Such marking, stamping, branding, or labeling shall be as nearly indelible and permanent as the nature of the article will permit. The Secretary of the Treasury, may, be regulations prescribe hereunder, except any article from the requirement of marking, stamping, branding, or labeling if he is satisfied that such article is incapable of being marked, stamped, branded, or labeled or can not be marked, stamped, branded, or labeled without injury, or except at an expense economically prohibitive of the importation, or that the marking, stamping, branding, or labeling of the immediate container of such article will reasonably indicate the country of origin of such article.

(b) Additional duties for failure to mark. —If at the time of importation any article or its container is not marked, stamped, branded, or labeled in accordance with the requirements of this section, there shall be levied, collected and paid on such article, unless exported under customs supervision, a duty of 10 per centum of the value of such article, in addition to any other duty imposed by law, or, if such article is free of duty, there shall be levied, collected, and paid a duty of 10 per centum of the value thereof.

(c) Delivery withheld until marked. —No imported article or package held in customs custody shall be delivered until such article (and its container) or package and every other article (and its container) or package of the importation, whether or not released from customs custody, shall have been marked, stamped, branded, or labeled in accordance with the requirements of this section. Nothing in this subdivision shall be construed to relieve from the requirements of any provision of this act relating to the marking of particular articles or their containers.

(d) Penalties. —If any person shall, with intent to conceal the information given thereby or contained therein, deface, destroy, remove, alter, cover, obscure, or obliterate any mark, stamp, brand, or label required under the provisions of this Act, he shall, upon conviction, be fined not more than $5,000 or imprisoned not more than one year, or both.

(e) Effective date. —This section shall take effect sixty days after the date of enactment of this Act.

*DOCUMENT NO. XV: CUSTOMS REGULATIONS, 1931**

Art. 509. Marking of articles and packages to indicate the country of origin.—
(a) Tariff Act of 1930, section 304(a):

*Records of the Joint Boycott Council, NYPL.

Every article imported into the United States, and its immediate container, and the package in which such article is imported, shall be marked, stamped, branded, or labeled, in legible English words, in a conspicuous place, in such manner as to indicate the country of origin of such article in accordance with such regulations as the Secretary of the Treasury may prescribe. Such marking, stamping, branding, or labeling shall be as nearly indelible and permanent as the nature of the article will permit. The Secretary of the Treasury may, by regulations prescribed hereunder, except any article from the requirement of marking, stamping, branding, or labeling if he is satisfied that such article is incapable of being marked, stamped, branded, or labeled or can not be marked, stamped, branded, or labeled without injury, or except at an expense economically prohibitive of the importation, or that the marking, stamping, branding, or labeling of the immediate container of such article will reasonably indicate the country of origin of such article.

(b) The names of the following well known capital cities and provinces have been held by the department to be a sufficient indication of the country of origin: London, Rome, Budapest, Stockholm, Paris, Belfast, Athens, Brussels, Oslo, Berlin, Bavaria, The Hague, Edinburgh, Madrid, Berne, Copenhagen, Saxony, Dublin, Lisbon, Vienna, Moscow, Warsaw, Bohemia, Rhineland, Wurttemburg, and all Canadian Provinces.

(c) Tarrif Act of 1930, section 304 (b):

It at the time of importation any article or its container is not marked, stamped, branded, or labeled in accordance with the requirements of this section, there shall be levied, collected, and paid on such article, unless exported under customs supervision, a duty of 10 per centum of the value of such article, in addition to any other duty imposed by law, or, if such article is free of duty, there shall be levied, collected, and paid a duty of 10 per centum of the value thereof.

(d) The duty of 10 per centum provided for in paragraph (c) of this article shall be assessed upon the value as defined in section 503 of the tariff act of 1930.

(e) Tariff Act of 1930, section 304(c):

No imported article or package held in customs custody shall be delivered until such article (and its container) or package and every other article (and its container) or package of the importation, whether or not released from customs custody, shall have been marked, stamped, branded, or labeled in accordance with the requirements to relieve from the requirements of any provision of this act relating to the marking of particular articles of their containers.

DOCUMENT NO. XVI: THE WALD ACT*

AN ACT TO amend the penal law in relation to the obliteration of Marks of Origin.

THE PEOPLE OF THE STATE OF NEW YORK, represented in the Senate and Assembly, do enact as follows:

Section 1. Chapter 88 of the Laws of 1909, entitled "Business and Trade" and the Penal Law are hereby amended by adding a new Section to be Section 435-c to read as follows:

Section 435-c Obliteration of Marks of Origin.

(1) Definitions.

As used in this section.

- a/ "Persons" shall be deemed to include firm, partnership, association or corporation.
- b/ "Sell" shall be deemed to include offer to sell, expose for sale, and possess with intent to dispose of or to sell.
- c/ "Article of Merchandise" shall be deemed to include a case, bottle, stopper, vessel, cask, cover, wrapper, package, band, ticket, label or other thing containing or covering an article of merchandise, or with which an article of merchandise is intended to be sold, or is sold.
- d/ "Mark of Origin" shall be deemed to mean and include any name, mark, or indication of the place or country from which an article of merchandise was imported into the United States of America or its insular possessions, or the name, mark or indication of the place or country in which an article of merchandise was manufactured, packed, assembled, grown, or produced.
- e/ "Remove" shall be deemed to include deface, alter and obliterate.
- f/ "Conceal" shall be deemed to include the original placing of a mark of origin upon an article of merchandise in any manner whatsoever, or the arranging or combining of two or more articles of merchandise into a single unit, whereby the mark of origin is removed from open view, or is rendered illegible or inconspicuous.
- g/ The terms "remove" and "conceal" are not to be deemed mutually exclusive.

(2) Any person who wholly or in part removes or conceals or who shall cause to be, wholly or in part, removed or concealed from or upon an article of merchandise the mark of origin; or who sells or causes to be sold an article of merchandise from or upon which to his or its knowl-

*Records of the Joint Boycott Council, NYPL.

edge, or to the knowledge of his or its agents, servants, or employees there has been, in whole or in part, removed or concealed the mark of origin, or who sells or causes to be sold an article of merchandise from the inspection of which such knowledge could have been obtained, shall be guilty of a misdemeanor, provided that it shall not be deemed a violation of this section if at the time of sale, said article of merchandise and the immediate and outer container or containers thereof shall be marked, stamped, tagged, branded, or labelled in legible and conspicuous English words with said mark of origin or the concealment thereof shall have completely ceased.

(3) The sale of an article of merchandise from which there has been in whole or in part removed or concealed a mark of origin shall be presumptive evidence of the violation of this section.

Section 2. This act shall take effect immediately.

DOCUMENT NO. XVII: RESOLUTIONS OF THE NON-SECTARIAN WORLD CONFERENCE*

RESOLVED, that an international organization be now established known as the WORLD NON-SECTARIAN ANTI-NAZI COUNCIL to CHAMPION HUMAN RIGHTS, the purpose of which, among others shall be vigorously to prosecute and enforce economic sanctions against Germany in every country until either the Hitler regime shall have been driven from power by the force of world opinion expressed in its economic isolation or until it have;

FIRST, restored to organized labor rights which have been taken away and the property which has been confiscated.

SECOND, renounced and abandoned its attempts by state authority and interference to destroy the Catholic and Protestant churches and religions, discard and repudiate the Old and parts of the New Testament and to substitute in their place a new religion in direct conflict with the principles and beliefs of Christianity under the misleading title of "German Christian Church," and until it shall be appropriate pledges and decrees, have fully reinstated freedom of religious belief and worship to sects uncontrolled by state authority.

THIRD, repealed all its recent laws and decrees against Jewish citizens and have ceased its persecution of and discrimination against them and its attempts to exterminate them.

FOURTH, restored to Masonic lodges the status and property of which they have been deprived.

FIFTH, until womanhood in Germany has been reinstated in their full rights and privileges that have resulted from a generation of struggle

*NYT, November 27, 1934.

and which they have been so ruthlessly deprived by the Hitler regime in Germany.

RESOLVED, that the governing body of such an organization shall consist besides the usual officers, of representatives of an organized local body in each country, including, from organized labor and one woman representative, and such representatives shall be selected without regard to race, creed, color or sex.

RESOLVED, that this world body shall immediately devote itself to organizing local bodies in all countries in which they are not now organized.

RESOLVED, that a preliminary sum of $150,000 be raised as a fighting fund for establishing and maintaining a central organization as above defined, such fund to be maintained until such time as the aims set forth have been achieved . . .

DOCUMENT NO. XVIII: DRAFT CONSTITUTION (WORLD NON-SECTARIAN ANTI-NAZI LEAGUE TO CHAMPION HUMAN RIGHTS)

*PROCEEDINGS OF THE INTERNATIONAL NON-SECTARIAN BOYCOTT CONFERENCE**

1. NAME: Shall be called the World Non-Sectarian Anti-Nazi League to Champion Human Rights;

2. OBJECTS: a. The object of the Council shall be the taking of all lawful measures to boycott German goods and services until such time as complete freedom of belief and restoration of civil rights is restored to all German subjects without distinction.

   b. The coordination and strengthening of the various boycott movements throughout the world.

   c. The publication of information as to the progress of the boycott and matters related thereto.

   d. The study of alternative sources of supply and of statistics.

3. COMPOSITION: The Council shall consist of the Honorary Officers, Executive Committee and accredited representatives of constituent organizations and various countries not exceeding 100 in all.

4. OFFICERS: The Officers of the Council shall consist of a President, three Vice-Presidents (from each country affiliated to the Council), two Chairmen, two treasurers, one Honorary Secretary and such other officers as may from time to time be found desirable.

*Archives of the NSANL, New York, N.Y.

5. EXECUTIVE COMMITTEE: The Executive Committee shall consist of the Officers and of the representatives of the countries in which the boycott is organized and of representatives of the affiliated societies throughout the world.

6. FINANCE: The income of the Council shall be derived from voluntary subscriptions and donations and the expenditure shall be regulated by a budget to be presented by the Treasurer to the annual Conference.

The accounts shall be audited by an auditor or auditors appointed by the Council and the statement of accounts and balance sheet so audited shall be presented to the annual Conference.

7. MEETINGS: The Executive Committee shall meet monthly and at such other times as it may be convened by the Executive Committee. The Executive Committee may convene a conference of delegates of Anglo-Jewish institutions at such other times when they consider desirable.

8. POWER TO CO-OPT AND TO APPOINT SUB-COMMITTEES: The Council and the Executive Committee shall have power respectively to co-opt additional members. The Executive Committee may appoint sub-committees for any special purpose and may include among the members thereof persons other than members of the Council.

9. ALTERATIONS OF THE CONSTITUTION: Alterations of the constitution must receive the assent of the majority of the Council present and voting at a meeting held for this purpose. Any resolution for the alteration of the constitution must be received by the Secretary at least twenty-one days before the meeting at which such resolution is to be moved and fourteen days notice of such meeting shall be given.

November 26, 27, 1934: Westminster Hall, London, England.

DOCUMENT NO. XIX: THE BOYCOTT*

I. This Conference regards the economic boycott as the most effective weapon in combating the Hitler menace, believing as it does that the Hitler Government cannot retain its power without economic and financial support of the peoples of the world, and that the use of economic sanctions is recognized by international law as a peaceful weapon against a common enemy. Therefore we renew our support of the boycott against the products and services of Nazi Germany, and appeal to all American citizens to give their aid and cooperation to the strengthening and the extension of the boycott as an appropriate means for expressing the condemnation of the American people of the revolting practices of the Hitler Government and as a means of liberating the German people from oppression.

*Archives of the Jewish Labor Committee, New York, N.Y.

The Conference condemns any individual Jew or any Jewish group, wherever such person or group may be located, for having any dealings with Nazi Germany whether official or otherwise.

II. This Conference calls upon the League of Nations, in agreement with covenants entered into by members thereof, to apply to Germany the clauses dealing with economic sanctions, and calls upon all nations, members of the League, to express their condemnation of the Hitler policy through abstention from trade agreements with it. We also appeal to the Government of the U.S., although not a member of the League of Nations, to refrain from entering into any trade agreements with Germany, and to abrogate all commercial treaties now existing between the U.S. and Germany.

This Conference appeals to the Government of the U.S. to give its support to the proposal that the League of Nations assume responsibility for adequate provisions to be made for the care and rehabilitation of refugees and that the Government of the U.S. cooperate in that endeavor.

III. This Conference urges upon the Amateur Athletic Union and the American Olympic Committee to rescind America's conditional acceptance of Germany's invitation to participate in the 1936 Olympic Series as a solemn obligation in defense of the spirit of sportmanship and the principles upon which the Olympic games are founded.

IV. The Conference urges upon American educational institutions to refuse the exchange of professors and students from Nazi Germany on the ground that such an exchange of professors and students must be regarded as the introduction of agents of the Hitler regime within the U.S. who carry on a Nazi propaganda against democratic and civilized society.

V. This conference urges upon the covenanters of this meeting that, for the intensification of the boycott and the coordination of the work in connection therewith, it is urgently important that a consolidated front of all agencies for the boycott be organized, and recommends that immediate steps be taken to bring about such a union of forces.

COOPERATION IN ANTI-HITLER WORK

Believing, as we do, that the Hitler regime is a menace to the foundations of civilization, which affects all elements of organized society, this Conference recommends to the conveners of the meeting that it takes steps:

a. To establish cooperation between representatives of Jewish interests, of labor interests, of the Catholic Church and of all persecuted groups in Germany in all matters pertaining to the German situation.
b. To initiate the creation of a central Jewish body representative of

Jewish organized life for the purpose of better carrying out the decisions of this conference.

The Conference urges the conveners to consider the possibility of an effective public demonstration and the presentation of the resolutions of the Conference to the proper officers and departments of the U.S. Government.

DOCUMENT NO. XX: ACTIONS COMMITTEE ON BOYCOTT CASES OF THE JWV, JBC AND THE NSANL*

The NSANL, the JWV and JBC hereby organize an Actions Committee on Boycott Cases to consist of two delegates from each organization and to be known as the Action Committee on Boycott Cases.

A. Purpose: To coordinate findings and decisions regarding violators of the Anti-Nazi Boycott.

1. Each party receives the right to start an independent investigation of any concern suspected of violating the Boycott and bringing this investigation to its own conclusion.
2. The findings before they are made public by the respective organization which conducted the invesiration, should be submitted to the Actions Committee on Boycott Cases.
3. All decisions of the Action Committee on Boycott Cases are binding when arrived at by a majority vote.

B. The Present List of Violators: The present list of violators which is in the possession of the three organizations, should be reviewed by this Committee for the purpose of revising and unifying the list.

1. Any subsequent changes in the revised list which may occur, shall be made only with the approval of the Actions Committee on Boycott Cases.

Joint Boycott Council   I. Minkoff (signed)
                                     I. Posnansky (signed)
Jewish War Veterans   Edgar H. Berman (signed)
NSANL   Dr. Wm. Kalb (signed)
                                     Mrs. Harris (signed)

(UNDATED)

*Records of the Joint Boycott Council, Letter S. NSANL folder, NYPL.

DOCUMENT NO. XXI: A PROGRAM OF BOYCOTT ACTIVITY FOR LOCAL ORGANIZATIONS*

Local organizations affiliated with the American Jewish Congress and Jewish Labor Committee in the metropolitan area should set up Boycott Committees. In those localities where there is more than one such organization, all the respective boycott committees should join together into a single body to carry on the work.

a. Organized Vigilance Committees to contact local establishments to determine whether they carry Nazi-made merchandise. All cases of boycott should be reported to the main office which will determine which action to pursue.
b. Detection of frauds: Care must be taken to investigate firms suspected of erasing the Nazi legend from imported merchandise (i.e. gloves, linens, glassware, toys, rugs, handbags). Where any such subterfuge has been discovered, the facts are to be reported to the Joint Boycott Council for federal prosecution.
c. Organization: Mobilize all local organizations of a given area, belonging to the American Jewish Congress, or the Jewish Labor Committee, as well as other organizations interested in prosecuting the boycott.
d. Literature: Local Committees are asked to call upon the Joint Boycott Council for anti-Nazi literature and other propaganda material.
e. Meetings: Local meetings should be held throughout the city wherever possible, in which representatives from all groups and faiths are to be invited. Wherever possible, these meetings should be addressed by outstanding liberals and leaders.
f. Labor: A determined effort should be made to draw in local affiliates of the AF of L and CIO, in order to promote the anti-Nazi Boycott in labor's ranks, and to appeal to workers to refuse to handle any Nazi merchandise in the process of manufacture.
g. Youth Division: An important auxiliary to the work of local organizations: It should be composed of all youth groups within the locality. The Youth Division should be very helpful in the distribution of literature and in picketing.
h. Women's Division: Also the distribution of literature, holding of meetings and house-to-house campaigns in behalf of the boycott. It should organize local consumers' Leagues. These are to approach retail stores, distributing Nazi-made merchandise and informing them that the consumers' organizations will place its strength behind the movement to persuade local residents to discontinue dealing with the firm. It is advisable to have individual shoppers visit the violators

*Records of the Joint Boycott Council, Conference folder, December 18, 1938. Hotel Astor, NYPL.

at regular intervals and refuse to make purchases on the grounds that the firm is breaking the boycott.
i. Anti-Nazi Street Demonstrations: These meetings are found to be very helpful for propaganda purposes, serving as a means of distributing literature, anti-Nazi stickers, posters and buttons.

DOCUMENT NO. XXII: FINANCIAL REPORT: 1 APRIL 1936–OCTOBER 1939*

EXHIBIT 1

The Joint Boycott Council was created as the official Boycott agency of the American Jewish Congress and Jewish Labor Committee in April, 1936. Each organization appropriated $500 per month to meet monthly expenses. In January 1937, this was increased to $625.00.

Activities: Regular meetings were held with manufacturers, wholesalers and importers to seek their cooperation in controlling the importation of Nazi merchandise in a number of industries. Out of these collaborations was formed the Businessmen's Advisory Council. The statement will show the Businessmen's Advisory Council contributed in aggregate, $3,090 for the activities of the Boycott Committee. A Women's and Youth Divisions was set up which did excellent work in picketing Boycott violators and in investigating firms suspected of handling Nazi made merchandise. The Women's Division of the American Jewish Congress contributed $951.50 to the Council.

Many pamphlets, booklets and leaflets were released for general distribution. An official publication called "Boycott," edited by the Executive Secretary, was published bi-monthly.

Offices for intensifying the Boycott on a national scale were set up in leading cities of the United States. The most active branches included: Chicago, Los Angeles, Pittsburgh, Cleveland, Detroit, St. Louis, Boston.

The medium of radio and newspapers was used for publicity and frequent releases. Mass gatherings addressed by outstanding American leaders were arranged. Outstanding among these were the Madison Square Garden demonstration against Nazi atrocities in 1937, the anti-Nazi Peace Democratic Rally in 1938 and the First National Boycott Conference in New York City in 1939.

Research was constantly carried on. Economic publications of all sorts were carefully studied for information concerning the Nazi economy, as well as the effect of the Boycott Against Germany's export trade.

As early as 1937, it became apparent that the $1,250 monthly budget was insufficient to effectively conduct the activities of the Council. As a result, it became necessary from time to time to negotiate for loans (with

*Records of the Joint Boycott Council, Financial Statements and Reports folder, NYPL.

the Amalgamated Bank) by signing promissory notes. These loans average about $500 each.

At the time the budget of $1,250 was decided upon, it was, of course, impossible to foresee the diversified activities JBC would undertake, nor could the parent bodies anticipate what the actual monthly overhead expenditures would be.

DOCUMENT NO. XXIII: OBJECTIVES OF THE COMMITTEE TO DEFEND AMERICA BY AIDING THE ALLIES*

The Committee to Defend America by Aiding the Allies is enlisted and organized for the duration of this world war and for the peace that shall follow the war. Our chief objective is to foster, aid, protect and guarantee, so far as we are able within the neighborly capacity of men and nations, the rights, privileges and duties of democracy. We are organized to uphold democracy.

FIRST OBJECTIVE—All moral and material aid which may legally be given to maintain England as our first line of defense.

To that end we feel that the first and vital duty before us is to give legally what moral and material aid this country may extend to Great Britain in her fight for life. For if the British Empire, with all the weight of its democratic economic power and its military strength and naval force, should fall, the United States would be alone in a warlike world. It is inconceivable that the richest land on earth should not be the subject of any envy that would lead to attack. If war is not checked and thwarted in Great Britain, war will come inevitably to the United States. Because our first line of defense lies around the coast of Britain, in this crisis, we should turn to Great Britain in her hour of danger and agony with such neighborly help as public opinion in the United States may seem legally to justify. To make American public opinion felt in Congress and in the White House in this tragic hour will be the first objective of our Committee. For 150 years, from the days of Kossuth, Kosciusko, Garibaldi, Steuben, wherever men have fought for freedom, they have been supported in this country by every possible moral and material aid. We cannot change this policy now, when to change it will be merely to appease tyrants and bring ourselves face to face with the ruthless, warlike forces of the world's dictators who view our riches with greed and our freedom with contempt. Here then is our first objective:

A. To supply Great Britain with such planes, guns and ships as she may

*Records of the Joint Boycott Council, NYPL.

legally purchase from our armed forces as soon as possible and in the greatest possible quantities without injuring our national defense.
B. To make available to Great Britain our surplus food supplies.
C. The immediate effective expansion of our preparedness program so that we may safely aid Great Britain in every legal way possible and quickly, as the by-product of that expansion.
D. When or if it becomes necessary, to assist in bringing mothers, children and old people from the British Isles to the Western Hemisphere.
E. To crystallize public opinion which would encourage Congress to give the President whatever legal authority necessary to accomplish these ends, or to amend to whatever extent necessary existing legislation that interferes with giving such aid to the Allies.
F. To remove difficulties prohibiting Americans from volunteering in the Allied armies.
G. To establish, if necessary, with the approval of other members of the Western Hemisphere, a trusteeship over French and Dutch possessions until the full independence of those countries is restored and they are able to exercise free sovereignty over those territories.
H. To guard against war materials reaching aggressor nations either directly or through neutral powers.

SECOND OBJECTIVE—Prepare to defend the liberties that have made us the land of the free.

The increasing need revealed by the news every hour dramatizes our lack of preparedness for our own defense. This Committee feels that the industry and the economy of this nation should have one motive, the co-ordinated direction and purpose of building up such national defense as may be needed in the day when we may stand alone among the democracies with our democratic economy threatened by totalitarian invasion and our right to trade upon the oceans of the world, and with the nations of the world challenged to the point of war by any hostile and ruthless totalitarian governments. To maintain our freedom at any point, either politically or commercially, we need air, naval and military strength to ward off from this entire Western Hemisphere the attacks of the rising enemy of democratic freedom. In a world outside our borders that speaks only the language of force, we must be able to talk in terms that will convince those who challenged democracy, not only of our sincerity but of our strength. We must prepare to defend the liberties that have made us the land of the free.

THIRD OBJECTIVE—While preparing our defense, maintain the democratic process in all its forms.

In preparing to defend democracy we must also cherish democracy. We believe it is possible to turn the economy of this country during the emergency that is rising starkly before us and still hold our democratic liberties. The temptation, of course, will be to take shortcuts, to be as ruthless within our borders as our enemies are beyond our borders. We believe that the United States can prepare itself and turn its economy whole-heartedly to the business of adequately arming this country and still maintain and uphold the Bill of Rights and the Constitution. While this necessary preparedness program is proceeding, we shall put forth every earnest endeavor to make public opinion that will defend and emphasize the democratic process in all its forms. In diverting our economy from the ways of peace to the preparation for our democratic defense, fundamental democracy itself still has its survival value at all costs.

We shall denounce the Fifth Column activities in every walk of life, among those who work in factories, among those who trade in the high seats of the market place. Both are dangerous. Neither group should be permitted to thrive and operate. But in all this we should move within the law and within regard for individual rights.

FOURTH OBJECTIVE—Education of democracy for the preservation of liberty.

Our first and last and constant aim shall be the education of democracy for the preservation of liberty. In this we shall turn eagerly to the youth of this country. We Americans all—old and young—have accepted too lightly the blessings of liberty. We have forgotten the centuries of struggle, of sacrifice, of bloodshed that have established each of our precious liberties of assemblage, of speech, of conscience, of the right to information, of the writ of habeas corpus, of trial by jury, the sacredness of contract and the security of the individual in the legitimate profits of his honest endeavors, whether he be workman or capitalist. These rights, with their duties, have grown so slowly and have come upon mankind since recorded time in such a natural evolutionary process that too many of our citizens hold these gains lightly. The process of education now must begin.

We should give to youth the same reason for ardor, enthusiasm and abiding affection for these democratic safeguards of happiness that youth in the totalitarian world have found in defending race and national arrogance and the love of conquest. Indeed more than that we should organize youth, cooperating with all the existing well-established organizations to educate definitely and instill formally into their minds the love of freedom and the sense of the duties of neighborly kindness upon which all freedom rests. In this emergency while we must defend democracy and after the critical danger is past, still there is need to reawaken in all our hearts and understanding and a passion for liberty, its obligations and its blessings.

Two dangers are immediate which our organization everywhere should combat. First, defeatism. Great Britain is not conquered. The

Dominions will not submit to Hitler no matter what happens in the British Isles. They cannot be conquered in a day, in a year, in a decade. We must realize that this struggle for democracy cannot end in any one battle or any one campaign, and that the British Empire is after all with us the bulwark of democracy.

Another thing: beware of appeasement. Beware of the man, the newspaper, the organization which says, "Let us make terms with the tyrants." So spoke the Fifth Column in Czechoslovakia; so spoke Chamberlain at Munich. So spoke Baldwin before Abyssinia fell. That was the siren song which threw Scandinavia up on the rocks. Holland heard that advice. Belgium was asked to follow that course. What did it avail? What do the promises, or treaties, or economic pacts proposed by Adolf Hitler—or any other dictator—bring to those who listen except defeat and slavery, actual economic and social slavery. The solemn promises of tyrants, however reiterated, by whomsoever presented, and however plausible they seem, are deadly poison to our democracy. He who touches pitch shall be defiled. We must not hope for security in our way of life and in our commercial freedom of the oceans of the world and in other lands until the dictators fall. So long as democracy is challenged by the presence of any great champion of totalitarian economy, appeasement is treason. There in the delusion of security while totalitarianism is armed, lies the shameful path of the Fifth Column.

Bibliography

I. *Primary Sources*
Annual Reports of the American Jewish Committee, New York, N.Y.
Archives of the American Jewish Committee, New York, N.Y.
Archives of the American Jewish Congress, New York, N.Y.
Archives of Dr. A. Grossman, YIVO, New York, N.Y.
Archives of the Jewish Labor Committee, New York, N.Y.
Archives of the Non-Sectarian Anti-Nazi League, New York, N.Y.
Archives of Dr. Joseph Tenenbaum, YIVO, New York, N.Y.
Minutes of the Administrative Committee of the American Jewish Congress, New York, N.Y.
Private Papers of Stephen S. Wise, Brandeis University Library, Brandeis University, Waltham, Massachusetts.
Records of the Joint Boycott Council, NYPL, New York, N.Y.

II. *Press*
Der Forverts (The Jewish Daily Forward)
Der Morgen-Zhurnal (The Morning Journal)
Der Tog (The Day)
Jewish Chronicle (London)
Jewish Daily Bulletin
New York Times
Yiddisher Kurier (Jewish Courier)

III. *Periodical Literature*
B'nai B'rith Messenger
Boycott Bulletin
Congress Bulletin
Contemporary Jewish Record
Economic Bulletin
Jewish Veteran

IV. *Miscellaneous Sources*
American Jewish Yearbook: 1933–1945. Philadelphia, 1978.
Encyclopaedia Judaica. Jerusalem, 1975.
The Jews in Nazi Germany. Compiled and Published by the American Jewish Committee. New York, 1935.

V. Selected Secondary Sources

Adler, Cyrus. *I Have Considered the Days.* Philadelphia, 1941.

———, and A. M. Margolith. *With Firmness in the Right: American Diplomatic Action Affecting Jews, 1840–1945.* New York, 1946.

Arendt, Hannah. *Eichmann in Jerusalem.* New York, 1965.

———. *The Origins of Totalitarianism.* New York, 1951.

Bullock, Alan. *Hitler: A Study in Tyranny.* New York, 1964.

Cohen, N. W. *Not Free to Desist: A History of the American Jewish Committee: 1906–1966.* New York, 1972.

Dawidowicz, Lucy S. *The War Against the Jews: 1933–1945.* New York, 1975.

Elbogen, Ismar. *A Century of Jewish Life.* Philadelphia, 1953.

Feingold, H. L. *The Politics of Rescue.* New Jersey, 1970.

Frank, Anne. *The Diary of a Young Girl.* New York, 1953.

Fraser, Lindley. *Germany Between Two Wars.* London, 1944.

Fritsch, Theodor (ed.). *Handbuch der Judenfrage.* Leipzig, 1938.

Goebbels, Josef Paul. *Diaries.* London, 1948.

———. *My Part in Germany's Fight.* London, 1953.

Hilberg, Raul. *The Destruction of the European Jews.* Chicago, 1967.

Hitler, Adolf. *My Battle (Mein Kampf).* Boston, 1938.

———. *My New Order.* Edited by Raoul de Roussy de Sales. New York, 1941.

Katz, Benedict. "Crisis and Response: Attitudes of the American Jewish Community Toward the Inception of the Anti-Nazi Boycott." M.A. thesis, Columbia University, 1951.

Kubowitzki, A. Leon. *Unity in Dispersion: A History of the World Jewish Congress.* New York, 1948.

Levin, Nora. *The Destruction of European Jewry: 1933–1945.* New York, 1968.

Lowenthal, Marvin. *The Jews of Germany: A Story of Sixteen Centuries.* Philadelphia, 1944.

Massing, Paul. *Rehearsal for Destruction.* New York, 1949.

Poliakov, Leon. *Harvest of Hate.* Philadelphia, 1954.

Pultzer, Peter G. J. *The Rise of Political Antisemitism in Germany and Austria.* New York, 1964.

Reitlinger, Gerald. *The Final Solution.* New York, 1961.

Shirer, William L. *The Rise and Fall of the Third Reich.* New York, 1960.

Tenenbaum, Joseph. *In Search of a Lost People.* New York, 1948.

———. *Race and Reich.* New York, 1956.

———. *The Anti-Nazi Boycott Movement in the United States.* Yad Vashem Studies, III. Jerusalem, 1959.

Trevor-Roper, H. E. *The Last Days of Hitler.* London, 1947.

Wheaton, Eliot B. *The Nazi Revolution: 1933–1935, Prelude to Calamity.* New York, 1969.

Wischnitzer, Mark. *To Dwell in Safety.* Philadelphia, 1948.

Wise, Stephen S. *Challenging Years.* New York, 1949.

———. *Servant of the People,* Philadelphia, 1970.

———. *The Personal Letters of Stephen S. Wise.* Boston, 1956.

Index

I. Names, Organizations, and Places

Abraham & Straus, 112
Action Committee, 186
Actions Committee on Boycott Cases, 195, 408
Adler, Cyrus, 42–43, 59, 84–85
AFL. *See* American Federation of Labor
Africa, 241, 326
Agudas Israel of America, 315–316, 318–321
Agudath Harabonim, 70
Ahlwardt, Herman, 12
Albany, 165
ALDJR. *See* American League for the Defense of Jewish Rights
Alexander Bernstein Co., 228
Altman & Co., 112
Amalgamated Ladies' Cutters' Union, 273
Amateur Athletic Union, 231, 233–235
American Anti-Nazi Boycott League, 269
American Boycott Against Aggressor Nations, 267–268, 303
American Civil Liberties Union, 28
American Federation of Labor, 34, 128–130, 137, 140–141, 144–148, 161, 170, 176–178, 185, 188, 265–267, 300, 301, 303, 318–321, 347
American Federation of Polish Jews, 316–318, 322
American Institute of Public Opinion, 262
American Israelite, 191
American Jewish Committee, xx, 28, 30, 35–39, 42–43, 46, 51–54, 59–64, 66–67, 83–85, 87, 102, 302, 342

American Jewish Congress, xxi, 16, 27–29, 31–33, 35–48, 50–51, 59, 65–70, 76–85, 89, 91, 94, 96, 98, 100–104, 125–128, 130–132, 134, 139, 145–146, 175, 179, 181–182, 184–185, 187, 191
American League for the Defense of Jewish Rights, 47–48, 52–53, 56–57, 65, 82, 91, 96–98, 100–101, 103–104, 106–107, 115, 117–121, 125–126, 135, 141, 153–154, 157, 172, 179, 192, 341
American Olympic Association, 231–233
American Red Cross, 314
Amory, R. H., 315
Amsterdam, 136, 147, 342
Amsterdam Conference, 73–75, 89, 107
Anglo-Jewish Association, 85
Anglo-Jewish Council of Trades and Industries, 71
Anglo-Palestine Bank, 90, 91
Annaberg, 111
Antarktica Germanica, 327
Anti-Defamation League, xx
Anti-Dumping Act of 1921, 201
Anti-Dumping Act of 1936, 201
Anti-Nazi Boycott Committee, 100, 217
Anti-Nazi League, 136, 153, 156, 160, 164, 167, 195, 213, 219, 222, 225–227, 230, 236, 261, 264, 267, 269, 271, 272, 295, 345
Antisemiten Katechismus, 12
Argentina, 323–328, 335
Arlosoroff, Chaim, 88, 90
Arnold Constable & Co., 112
Assefath Hanivcharim, 148
Associated Press, 328
Association of Commercial Agents, 50

417

Association of Engineers, 50
Association of Physicians, 50
Astor Hotel, 157, 276
Athens, 231
Auschwitz, 212
Austria, 241–246, 257, 270, 308
Avenol, Joseph, 82

Baden, 156
Baldwin, Stanley, 242
Balfour Declaration, xix
Balkan Importing Corporation, 228
Baltimore, 33, 216
Banner Brothers, 118
Banner, Max S., 118
Basle, 18
Bates, Sanford, 167
Bathurst, M. E., 319, 321
Battle, George Gordon, 170
Bavaria, 115
Belgium, 51, 257, 304–305, 308–309, 310, 326
Berlin, xx, 5, 7, 11, 15, 23, 31, 39–40, 43, 73, 77, 108, 133–134, 167, 183, 231–232, 243, 249, 254, 256, 327
Berlinger, Mrs. Joseph, 107
Bertesgaden, 242
Bessarabia, xx
Best & Co., 112
Biltmore Hotel, 290
Bismarck, Otto von, 10
Bluestein, Abe, 301–302, 313, 315
B'nai B'rith, xx, 28–29, 35–39, 43, 46, 51, 66–67, 84–85, 87, 91, 98, 126, 181, 341–342
Board of Delegates of American Israelites, xix
Board of Deputies of British Jews, xix, 51
Bologna, xix, xx
Boycott Bulletin, 141
Boycott Bureau, 130–131
Boycott Committee, 45, 47, 125, 128, 130–138, 140, 165, 169, 171, 173, 179, 185–193, 213–217, 221–222, 343
Boycott Committee of Poland, 172
Boycott Council. *See* Joint Boycott Council
Brandeis, Louis D., 67, 275
Brazil, 272, 324, 325, 327, 329, 332
Breslau, 40

Britain. *See* Great Britain
British Anti-War Council, 50
British Guiana, 257
British Press Service, 319
Bronx, 106, 164, 214
Brooklyn, 163–164, 197, 221
Brooklyn Jewish Center, 218
Bruening, Heinrich, 62
Brundage, Avery, 231–234
Buchenwald, 246
Buffalo, 165
Bulgaria, 316
Bundists, 282
Businessmen's Advisory Committee, 307, 309

Cahan, Abraham, 68
California, 84, 164
Canada, 300
Cardozo, Benjamin Nathan, 155
Carnegie Hall, 31
CBC. *See* Coordinated Boycott Committee
Celler, Emanuel, 183–184, 197–199, 201, 287–288
Central America. *See* Latin America
Central American Boycott Committees, 323
Central Boycott Committee, 18, 50, 168, 302
Central Committee for Relief and Reconstruction, 14
Central Employment Bureau, 14
Central Europe, 149, 283. *See also names of countries*
Central Labor Trades Council, 188
Central Merchants Association, 50
Central Trades and Labor Council of Greater New York, 139
Central Union, 5–7, 31–33
Chamberlain, Houston Stuart, 11
Chamberlain, Neville, 142, 244
Chemnitz, 111
Chicago, 33
Chile, 323–324, 326, 335
China, 344
Christian Boycott Pledge, 265, 267
Christian Committee. *See* Volunteer Christian Committee
Christian Socialist Workers Party, 11
Cincinnati, 191
City College, 80

Cleveland, 33, 91, 99, 271
Cohen, A. H., 67
Cohen, Alfred, 43
Cohen, William W., 45, 66
Collins & Co., 112
Comité de Protection a Los Immigrantes Israelitas, 323
Commerce Department, U.S., 305
Commercial Exposition Company, 138
Committee for Inter-American Co-operation, 334–335, 338–339
Committee for the Victims of Nazism and Fascism, 177
Committee of Industrial Organizations, 177
Committee on the International Coordination of the Boycott, 322
Commodore Hotel, 29, 171
Communists, 4–5, 185
Community Church of New York, 139
Congress, U.S., 63, 331
  House of Representatives, 26, 38, 183, 187, 197–199, 201–202, 204, 207–208, 219, 285, 287–288
  Senate, 183, 199, 201, 204, 285
Conjoint Committee, 85
Conjoint Consultative Council, 84–85
Coordinated Boycott Committee, 193, 267–269, 294, 295, 302, 327–328
Coordinated Committees for Boycott, 268–269, 303
Coordinating Foundation, 257
Coralnik, Abraham, 47–49, 55, 58–59, 70, 97–98, 103, 105–106, 119–121, 341–342
Council for Pan-American Democracy, 326, 328
Customs Administrative Act of 1937, 285
Customs Regulations of 1931, 156–157
Customs Tariff Law, 197
Czechoslovakia, 51, 88, 108, 132, 242–243, 245, 246, 283, 307–308, 326

Dachau, 246
Daily News Bulletin, 320
Damascus, xix
Danzig, 168
Darmstadt, 17
Day, The, 56
De Haas, Jacob, 53–54

Denmark, 305
Deutsch, Bernard S., 5, 27, 32–33, 38, 40, 43, 67, 69, 77
Deutsch-Voelkische Freiheitspartei, 13
Deutsche Erneuerungsgemeinde, 13
Deutsche Reformpartei, 11
Deutsche Volksband fuer Argentinien, 327
Diamond Dealers Club, 311
Diamond Industry Protective Committee, 312
Dickstein, Samuel, 81
Dodd, William E., 212
Dollfuss, Engelbert, 242
Dominican Republic, 254
Doughton, Robert L., 285
Dubnow, Simon, 92
Dubovsky, Benjamin, 175, 192, 269, 273
Duehring, Eugen, 11
Duesseldorf, 155
Dunkirk, 294

East End, 50–51
Economic Relief Committee, 73
Effron, David, 326–327
Egypt, 51
Ehrlich, Emil, 327
Einstein, Albert, 345
Eitinger and Bernstein, 228–229
Eitingon Schild Fur Corporation, 228
Embargo Nazi Germany Conference, 302
Embargo Russia Movement, 304
Emmet, Christopher T., Jr., 263, 283, 334
England. *See* Great Britain
Essen, 7–8
Ethiopia, 300
Evian Conference, 251–253
Export Import Bank, 325

Fair Play for American Athletes, 232
Fair Play in Sports Committee, 234
Farley, James A., 204
Feder, Gottfried, 13
Federal Bureau of Investigation, 314
Federal Communications Act of 1934, 221–222
Federal Communications Commission, 221–222, 232
Federation of American Zionists, 54

Federation of Boycott Committees, 100
Fiesta Americana, 335
Foreign Credits Control Office, 256
Fortura and Mitropa, 313–314
France, 5–6, 50–51, 62–63, 111, 116, 241–244, 252, 256, 303, 308–309, 314, 326, 330
Franco, Francisco, 326–327
Franklin Simon & Co., 112
Fredman, J. George, 30, 45–46, 97–98, 101, 175
Free Synagogue, 126
Frick, Wilhelm, 4
Friedman, Ralph, 60
Fritsch, Theodor, 11–13, 21
Furriers Union, 229

Gallup, George, 262, 265
Gebiner, Benjamin, 178
Geneva, 3, 71, 92–93, 95, 143, 149, 317, 342
Gerard, James W., 53–54, 63
German Jews, 5–8, 10, 14–16, 18–24, 28–33, 35–45, 46, 48, 52, 55–56, 58, 60, 69, 73–74, 78, 79, 80–81, 86–87, 91, 93–97, 99, 111–115, 117, 121, 125, 129, 144, 146, 149, 161, 163, 171, 183, 245–246, 249–250, 256–257, 281–282, 309, 348
German Land Trade League, 90–91
German Olympics Committee, 231
German People's Freedom Party, 13
German Refugee Aid Societies, 276
German Renewal Party, 13
Germany, 3–4, 6, 8–9, 11–12, 14, 16–19, 21, 23–24, 28–37, 40–44, 46, 49–54, 57–58, 60, 62, 66, 73–74, 77–82, 84, 86–91, 98–99, 102, 104, 106–115, 120, 126, 128–130, 132–136, 143–144, 148, 153, 156–157, 159–161, 169–171, 181, 183–185, 187, 197–198, 204–205, 212–213, 215–216, 229–230, 232–236, 241–242, 244, 247–250, 252–256, 261–264, 267–268, 270, 272, 274–284, 288, 295, 298–299, 301, 303–305, 308–310, 312–313, 315–317, 322, 324–327, 329–330, 332, 342, 344–346, 348
Gestapo, 257
Ghandi, Mohandas Karamchand, 48

Gimbel's, 135–136, 343
Gobineau, Josef Artur, 11
Goebbels, Josef P., 16–21, 94, 212, 247, 345
Goering, Hermann Wilhelm, 4, 6–8, 32, 246, 248–249, 255–257
Goetingen, 17
Goldmann, Nahum, 92–93, 143, 147, 252
Good Will Fair, 136, 139–142
Grand Central Palace, 138
Great Britain, 6, 15–16, 48–49, 50, 51, 52, 55, 62–63, 85, 89, 92–93, 159, 167, 242–243, 244, 295, 300, 316–319, 320–321, 331, 344
Greece, 26, 74, 231, 316
Green, William, 34, 128–130, 161, 265–266, 300
Gruszka, Sylvester, 318
Grynszpan, Herschel, 247

Haavarah, 80, 92, 274, 280
Halle, 17
Halpern, George, 91
Hamburg, 42, 135, 241
Hapsburg Empire, 13, 241, 243
Harriman, George E., 164, 169, 172–174, 192, 234, 263, 271, 307
Harris, Mrs. Mark, 102, 118, 164, 270
Harter, Dow W., 201
Havana, 331
Havas, 328
Hazlett, Mrs. Mabel, 339
Hearn's, 136
Hebrew University, 51
Hechalutz, 88
Held, Adolph, 281–282
Helm, A. K., 315–317
Henlein, Konrad, 243
Henry, Patrick, 267
Herzl, Theodor, 18, 146
Hesse, 11
Heydrich, Reinhardt, 247–248, 255, 257
Heyman, Moses D., 311, 349
HIAS, 8, 315–317
Hindenburg, Paul von, 4, 19, 22, 77–79
Hirschman, Ira A., 80, 165
Hitler, Adolf, 3–9, 12–14, 16, 18–24, 27–29, 38–41, 47–49, 52–53, 55–58, 68–69, 78, 80–81, 89–91, 94, 128, 132, 134, 139, 144–145, 168, 171,

183, 187, 212, 232, 236, 241–244, 249–250, 253, 255–257, 262–265, 267–268, 270, 272, 275, 280, 282–284, 295, 297–299, 304, 307, 312, 325–327, 330–331, 338, 342, 344–346, 348
Hoess, Rudolf, 212
Holland. *See* Netherlands
Holmes, John H., 27–28, 139
House of Representatives. *See* Congress, U.S.
Hull, Cordell, 39–41, 43, 80, 184, 270, 287, 298–299
Hungary, 252, 282, 305

Independent Order Brith Abraham, 188
India, 48–49, 344, 347
Inter-American Cooperation Week, 334–335, 337–338
Inter-Governmental Committee, 253–257, 274, 275, 277, 278, 280, 283
International Boycott Commission, 163
International Committee for Refugees, 274
International Coordination Committee, 322
International Ladies' Garment Workers' Union, 176
International Merchandising Good Will Fair, 137
International Olympic Committee, 231–232
International Prison Reform Association, 167
International Trade Union, 148
Investigating Committee, 311
Israel, 246, 344
Italy, xix, 242, 303–305, 312, 313, 314

Jabotinsky, Vladimir, 86–88, 342
Jacobs, Mike, 236
Jacoby, A. D., 217–218, 236
James McGreery & Co., 112
Japan, 164, 312, 330, 344
Jefferson, Thomas, 267
Jewish Agency for Palestine, xx, 91, 93
Jewish Daily Forward, 15, 47, 56, 68, 176, 178, 182, 318
Jewish Labor Bloc, 188–189

Jewish Labor Committee, 175–179, 181–182, 185–186, 187, 188–191, 281–282, 286, 289, 293–294, 304, 326, 340
Jewish National Workers' Alliance, 176
Jewish Socialist Varband, 176
Jewish Telegraphic Agency, 320
Jewish War Veterans, 30, 45–47, 56, 59, 97–98, 100, 195, 289, 307, 341
Jewish Workmen's Circle, 176
Jewish World Economic Conference, 71–73
Joint Boycott Committee, 140–142, 169
Joint Boycott Council, 131, 176, 189, 191–195, 197–198, 203–205, 209, 216–218, 228–229, 236, 264–270, 272, 281–282, 287, 289–290, 293, 295–297, 301, 302, 303–312, 313, 314, 315, 317, 319–326, 329, 331, 333, 334, 337, 338–340, 349, 369
Joint Committee on Cases, 288
Joint Conference Committee, 29, 84
Joint Distribution Committee, 247, 257, 277, 280–282
Joint Emergency Conference, 184–186
Juedische Rundschau, 38
JWV Minute Men, 217

Kassel, 7, 11
Keep, Mrs. Mabel Hazlett, 339
Kennedy, Joseph, 209
Kimball, Samuel E., 138, 140
King, William H., 183–184
King, William Lyon Mackenzie, 331
Kishinev, xx, 92
Knights of Labor, 176
Knopfmacher, Ernest, 275, 302
Kresge department store, 214
Kubowitzki, Leon, 323
Kurfuerstendam, 183

Labor Chest Fund, 177
Labor Zionists, 90, 342
Labour Party, 148
LaGuardia, Fiorello H., 53–54, 68, 140, 182, 217
Landsberg Fortress, 14
Land Trade League, 91
LaSalle, Robert Cavelier, 178
Latin America, 10, 272, 300, 305, 312, 322–326, 327, 328–334, 336, 337,

338, 339. *See also names of countries*
League for Human Rights, Freedom and Democracy, 303
League of Brothers, xx
League of Nations, 82, 170, 251–252, 342
Lehman, Herbert H., 34, 287
Lehman, Irving, 30
Leipzig, 11, 68
Leschinsky, Jacob, 15
Liberal Party, 10
Lippert, Julius, 345
Lipsky, Louis, 89, 171
London, 21, 51–52, 71, 73, 82, 89, 145, 149, 159, 161, 163, 167, 228, 254–255, 257, 277, 280, 316–317
London Boycott Conference, 103
London Times, 144
Los Angeles, 164
Louis, Joe, 236
Ludendorf, Erich von, 13
Luther, Martin, 230

MacDonald, James G., 251
Mack, Julian W., 27
Macy's, 107–108, 112, 119, 131–136, 142, 343
Madagascar Plan, 250
Madison Square Garden, 29, 31–34, 65, 120, 128, 131, 139
Magdeburg, 7
Mahoney, Jeremiah T., 233, 325
Manhattan Center, 326
Mannheim, 17
Marcus, Robert, 270, 289, 308, 327, 337
Margolis, Max E., 101–102
Margoshes, Samuel, 29–30, 45, 53–54, 67, 70, 80, 82, 144, 188, 192
Maritime Commission, 207–208
Marking Act, 287
Marks, Edwin I., 132–133, 135
Marr, Wilhelm, 11
Martin, Joseph W., 202
May Glove Company, 177
Mayer, Louis, 47, 175
Melchett, Lord (Sir Alfred Mond), 71, 73, 145
Memel, 262
Merchandising Council, 131–136
Mexico, 235, 272
Miklas, Wilhelm, 242–243

Minkoff, Isaiah, 195
Montefiore, Moses, xx
Morgen Journal, Der, 5, 56, 82, 120, 172
Morgenthau, Henry, Jr., 157
Mortara, Edgar, xix–xx, 1b
Moyle, J. H., 157
Munich, 13, 241, 244, 262, 298
Mussolini, Benito, 88, 241–242, 244, 300, 327

Nation, The, 325
National Administrative Committee, 100, 103
National Association for the Advancement of Colored People, 28
National Boycott Conference, 97, 102, 165
National Socialist Party. *See* Nazi Party
National Workmen's Committee, 180
Nazi Party, 6, 9, 13, 16, 18, 20–23, 40–41, 43, 202, 221, 233, 250, 271, 282, 325, 330, 332, 334
Netherlands, 51, 73, 256, 299, 304, 305, 330
Neurath, Constantin von, 20, 23
Neutrality Act, 297, 300–301, 310, 320
New Refugee Transfer Plan, 281
New York City, xx, 5, 21, 32–34, 41, 47, 51, 65, 68, 80, 105–108, 111, 113, 120, 134, 136, 139, 145, 154–155, 163, 164–166, 170–172, 177–178, 182–183, 184, 207, 217–218, 221, 261, 263, 276, 290, 295, 312, 326, 332
New Yorker Staatszeitung, 23
New York Evening Post, 56
New York Hippodrome, 170
New York Post, 301
New York Times, 118, 382
New York World-Telegram, 346
Non-Sectarian Anti-Nazi League, 119, 121, 130, 135, 140, 153, 157, 159, 164–166, 170, 173, 185, 191–195, 203, 213, 228, 230, 269–271, 273, 295, 307, 341, 343, 347
Non-Sectarian World Conference, 159, 161
Norway, 303
Nuremburg, 94

O'Brien, John Patrick, 34
Ohio, 191, 201

Index

Ovington's, 112

Palestine, xxi, 43, 51–52, 87, 93, 96, 146, 148, 211, 247, 253, 280
Palm Springs, 184
Pan-American Anti-Nazi Boycott, 268, 325, 326, 327–328, 338
Pan-American Federation, 329
Papen, Franz von, 4, 20–23, 40
Paris, 35, 143, 145, 149, 247, 249, 275, 309
Peel, Lord William Robert, 254
Perlman, Nathan D., 130, 137
Perlzweig, Maurice L., 317
Permanent Joint Board on Defense, 331
Philadelphia, xx, 33, 169
Phillips, William Randolph, 38, 41
Pilsudski, Joseph, 168
Pinkert, Alexander, 11
Pius IX, xix
Poale Zion, 176, 214
Poland, xxi, 50–51, 71, 168, 211, 241, 244, 246, 247, 252, 257, 282, 297, 314–318, 319, 320, 321, 342
Portugal, 316–318
Posnanski, Israel, 141, 175, 195, 218, 270, 322
Post Office, U.S., 204–209
Potsdam, 32
Prague, 76–77, 83, 86, 88, 133, 146, 241, 243–244, 262, 342
Preliminary Conference, 3
Proskauer, Joseph M., 30, 63–64, 348
Protective Committee, 310

Queens, 106
Quislings, 329

Rabinowitz, Ezekiel, 52–53, 104–105, 107, 120–121, 136, 141, 153–155, 165, 213, 320
Rand, Oscar Z., 315
Rath, Ernst vom, 247
Raymond Rich Associates, 333–334
Reichsbank, 255, 256
Reichstag, 4–5, 7, 12, 241–242, 257, 331, 346
Reitlinger, Gerald, 249
Retail Dry Goods Association, 115–116
Retailers Association, 50
Revisionist Boycott Association, 88

Revisionists, 88, 90, 185
Rhineland, 241
Rhodesia, 257, 344
Ribbentrop, Joachim von, 254, 256
Richards, Bernard G., 166–167
Rockefeller, Nelson, 330, 333, 337
Rome, 300, 314
Roosevelt, Franklin D., 38, 46, 69, 77, 80, 126, 184, 249, 252, 263, 275, 297, 300, 330–331, 335, 346
Roosevelt, Theodore, 264
Rosenberg, Alfred, 89
Rosenthal China Co., 166
Rotarians, 267
Rublee, George, 254–256, 272, 274–275, 278, 281–284
Ruhr, 17
Rumania, 74, 180, 228–229, 230, 252, 282, 305
Russia, xx, xxi, 24, 74, 145, 178, 244, 304–305, 312

St. Louis, 77
Saks-34th Street, 112
Sand & Simon, 11, 111, 115
San Francisco, 164
Saxony, 11, 111, 155–156
Scandinavia, 133, 299
Schacht, Hjalmar, 172, 254–256, 272, 275–276, 278, 279, 281–283
Schieffelin, William J., 263, 266–267, 300, 302, 338
Schmeling, Max, 235, 236
Schoenerer, Georg von, 13
Schuschnigg, Kurt von, 242–244
Schwartz store, 166
Seabury, Samuel, 139–140
Sear's, 288–289, 343
Segal, Louis, 138
Senate. *See* Congress, U.S.
Seyss-Inquart, 243
Sharkey, Jack, 235
Sherman, Carl, 187–188
Schultz, Lily, 125, 167, 175, 195
Silesia, 17
Silver, Abba Hillel, 91–92, 99–100, 103, 107, 121, 160, 271
Silver, Eliezer, 70
Simons, Mr., 309–310
Smith, Alfred E., 34
Socialist Bund, 178
Socialist Party (U.S.), 131

South America. *See* Latin America
Spain, 56, 241, 303, 326
Sperling, Benjamin, 45
Spiegelman, William Z., 130, 137–139, 141, 216, 221, 322
Spiro, Abraham I., 125
Sponsorship Committee, 139–140
Stalin, Joseph, 304
State Department, U.S., 38–39, 41, 43, 67, 77, 184, 262, 275, 298, 300, 302, 313, 320, 327, 333
Staten Island, 106
Stern Brothers, 112
Stern, Horace, 85
Stoecker, Adolf, 11–12
Straus, Percy S., 107, 110, 112, 115, 117, 131, 135
Street, H. Nelson, 111
Stresseman, Gustav, 62
Stuermer, Der, 18
Sudeten Germans Party, 243
Sudetenland, 242–243, 244, 307
Sweden, 305
Switzerland, 3, 51, 92, 143, 305
Syracuse, 165
Syria, 90
Szoszkes, Henry, 315–316

Tariff Act of 1930, 256, 285–286
Tartakower, Arieh, 317
Taylor, Myron C., 253, 278, 283
Temporary Committee for Pan-American Cooperation, 331–334
Tenenbaum, Joseph L., 3, 79–82, 126, 128, 130–131, 135–136, 138, 140, 165, 167, 169–174, 178–179, 185, 188–195, 214, 216–217, 221–222, 228, 230, 268, 270, 274–281, 283, 286–287, 289–290, 293–299, 301–305, 307–312, 314–319, 320–331, 333–334, 337–340, 343, 348–349
Thomas, Norman, 131
Tog, Der, 29, 47, 192
Treasury Department, U.S., 155–157, 230, 287
Turkey, 51
Tygel, Zelig, 322

Union of Jewish Artisans, 50
United Boycott Committee of Poland, 71, 342
United Palestine Appeal, 289
United Press, 328
United States, 6, 15, 16, 24, 28, 33, 35, 38–40, 49, 53–54, 71, 76, 81, 85, 97, 103, 107, 112, 116, 125–126, 154, 156, 161, 165, 167, 172, 176–177, 184, 186, 198–204, 211, 228, 230, 232–234, 236, 261–263, 267–268, 270, 272–273, 281–288, 293, 297–298, 300–301, 303, 305, 308, 311, 322, 324–325, 327–330, 333, 336, 337–338, 341, 345–346
Untermyer, Samuel, 51–52, 54–55, 61–64, 71, 74–76, 81–84, 88–89, 91–93, 97–98, 100–101, 107–108, 111–112, 115, 117–121, 126, 131, 135, 145, 147, 152, 155–157, 159, 161–167, 170–174, 192–195, 213, 229–230, 236, 270–271, 273, 298, 341–343, 348
Uruguay, 324, 327
Utah, 185

Van Loon, Hendrick Wilhelm, 63
Van Zeeland, Paul, 257
Versailles Treaty, 81, 241–242
Vienna, 13, 241, 245
Vigilance Committees, 310
Villalba, A. Rojas, 328, 332–333
Villard, Oswald Garrison, 325
Vilna, 50
Virginia, 267
Vladeck, Baruch C., 178–179, 181–182, 185–186, 188–190, 192–195, 282, 347
Voelkischer Beobachter, 282
Volunteer Christian Committee, 263–268, 272, 283, 300, 303, 328, 334, 338
Vorvertz, Der. See Jewish Daily Forward

Wagner, Robert F., 34
Wald, Albert, 157
Waldman, Morris D., 42, 60, 62, 84–85, 149
Walker, James J., 139
Wallach, Ernest, 31–32
Walsh, David I., 285–287
Wanamaker's, 107
Warburg, Eric, 42–43
Warburg, Felix M., 228, 277, 281
Warburg, Frederick, 42

Index   425

War Refugee Board, 80
Washington, D.C., 55, 62, 68, 80, 84, 130, 156, 249, 302, 315
Washington, George, 267
Wasserman, Oscar, 43
Wehrmacht, 244
Weinstein, M., 323
Weizaecker, Ernst von, 254
Weizmann, Chaim, 89
Welles, Sumner, 275
West End, 50
Westphalia, 11
White, William Allen, 295, 303, 331
Wiesbaden, 17
Wilhelm II, 11
Winkler, Max, 80, 128, 130
Winterton, Lord, 253, 256, 275
Wise, Stephen S., 27–28, 30–31, 33, 38–41, 43, 54, 61, 69–70, 76–77, 80, 83–84, 93–96, 99, 120, 125, 130, 134, 138–140, 144–147, 149, 167, 179, 189–190, 194, 210, 212, 228, 271, 274–275, 278, 280, 287, 289, 308, 317, 327, 334, 342, 345–346
Wohltat, Helmuth, 256–257, 283
Woll, Matthew, 298, 302
Woolworth, F. W., 136, 213, 226–228, 288–290, 343
World Boycott Committee, 163
World Boycott Conference, 165
World Boycott Federation, 147
World Boycott Movement, 300
World Jewish Conferences, 92–93, 144, 145, 148, 149, 342
World Jewish Congress, 3, 68, 70, 76, 87, 92–93, 95–96, 143–144, 148–149, 152, 179, 182, 210–212, 214, 252, 254, 315–317, 322, 342
World Jewish Economic Conference, 92–93, 95–96, 120, 125, 143–144, 147–149, 211
World Jewish Economic Federation, 152, 162, 343
World Non-Sectarian Anti-Nazi Council, 162, 343
World Olympic Committee, 231, 411–414
World Zionist Organization, 77, 87–93, 96, 98, 143, 145, 146, 179–180, 342

Youngstown, 91
Yugoslavia, xxi, 305, 315–316

Zbonszyn, 247, 257
Zhitlowsky, Chaim, 138
Zionist Movement. *See* World Zionist Organization
Zionist Revisionist Party, 86

II. Components of Boycott Organizations

ALDJR
Administrative Committee, 103, 121
Finance Committee, 98, 101, 121
National Executive Committee, 103
Resolutions Committee, 103
Women's Division, 103

AMERICAN JEWISH CONGRESS
Administrative Committee, 28, 42, 68, 79, 84, 102
Baltimore branch, 216
Boycott Bureau, 130
Boycott Committee, 125, 130–131, 186, 192–193, 195, 213, 269
Boycott Department, 128
Governing Council, 187
National Executive Committee, 83, 186, 195
Publicity Department, 82
Steering Committee, 67
Women's Division, 188, 214–215

JEWISH LABOR COMMITTEE
Action Committee, 186
Boycott Committee, 269
Executive Committee, 186

JEWISH WAR VETERANS
Actions Committee on Boycott Cases, 195

JOINT BOYCOTT COUNCIL
Action Committee, 289, 293, 303, 311
Boycott Correspondence file of 1934, 223
Businessmen's Advisory Council, 311
Businessmen's Committee, 312
Confidential Report, 317
Economic Committee, 198
Executive Committee, 281, 339
Executive Secretary, 195
Film Division, 195

Legislative Committee, 199
Women's Division, 218
Youth Division, 218

JOINT COMMITTEE ON CASES
Actions Committee, 293
Boycott Violators, 290

MORAL EMBARGO CAMPAIGN
Action Committee Minutes, 306
Moral blockade, 323

Preliminary Draft, 305

NON-SECTARIAN ANTI-NAZI LEAGUE
Boycott Violators, 189
Executive Committee, 192, 269
Film Division, 195
Film Industry, 195
Joint Action Committee, 196
Local units, 120

WITHDRAWN FROM CLARK UNIVERSITY LIBRARY